Anonymous

The correspondence of Prince Talleyrand and King Louis XVIII during the Congress of Vienna:

From the manuscripts preserved in the archives of the Ministry of Foreign Affairs at Paris /cwith a preface, observations and notes by

Anonymous

The correspondence of Prince Talleyrand and King Louis XVIII during the Congress of Vienna:
From the manuscripts preserved in the archives of the Ministry of Foreign Affairs at Paris /cwith a preface, observations and notes by

ISBN/EAN: 9783337717162

Printed in Europe, USA, Canada, Australia, Japan

Cover: Foto ©ninafisch / pixelio.de

More available books at **www.hansebooks.com**

THE CORRESPONDENCE

OF

PRINCE TALLEYRAND

AND

KING LOUIS XVIII.

DURING THE CONGRESS OF VIENNA

(HITHERTO UNPUBLISHED)

FROM THE MANUSCRIPTS PRESERVED IN THE ARCHIVES OF THE MINISTRY OF FOREIGN AFFAIRS AT PARIS

WITH A PREFACE, OBSERVATIONS, AND NOTES
BY M. G. PALLAIN

NEW YORK
HARPER & BROTHERS, FRANKLIN SQUARE
1881

(Stereotyped and Printed by S. W. Green's Son)

PREFACE

THE publication of the Memoirs left by Prince Talleyrand, who died in 1838, cannot be much longer delayed.

Without passing premature judgment upon the interest and piquancy of the revelations which may be looked for when those Memoirs shall see the light, we may fairly surmise that the great politician who diplomatized so much with his contemporaries, has not resisted the temptation to diplomatize a little with posterity.

It would be surprising if, having always and in all things thoroughly understood and carefully studied the *mise en scène*, he had not most skilfully arranged the conditions of perspective under which he would choose to allow himself to be seen by the generations who should come after him. But although his own evidence upon himself and his times is not yet available to us, we are enabled to take him by surprise, at the present moment, by the aid of documents deposited in the archives of the Ministry of Foreign Affairs, and to examine the details of his relations with many rulers of kingdoms and chief ministers in his character of negotiator.

At the Ministry of Foreign Affairs there is a manuscript comprising one hundred documents: sixty of these are letters written by Prince Talleyrand to King Louis XVIII. during the Congress of Vienna.

This manuscript also contains letters of Louis XVIII. The minutes of the latter are in the same archives, and constitute an annexe; there are also two letters, written, by the King's command, on the 9th of November and the 4th of December, 1814, by Count de Blacas.

The manuscript also contains some diplomatic documents which are fitly included in our publication, especially the famous report with which Prince Talleyrand furnished Louis XVIII. on his departure from Ghent for Paris.

We have been allowed access to the whole of this manuscript, and are authorized to publish it.

M. Thiers, who knew Prince Talleyrand very well, frequently spoke of this correspondence, which he had consulted in the course of his historical studies of the period of the Consulate and the Empire. He regarded the letters as among the most curious and complete of the documents bearing upon the history of that period. They had been, by a special privilege, placed in his hands at an epoch when the exclusive traditions of M. d'Hauterive still prevailed at the Foreign Office—traditions which have been so courteously set aside by the Commission of Diplomatic Archives, and by the learned and liberal Keeper of the Archives, M. Girard de Rialle.

The great diplomatic authority of Prince Talleyrand, and the numerous arguments to be drawn from his correspondence in favor of the Austro-English alliance, did not prevent M. Thiers from taking, in his history, the side of the Prusso-Russian alliance which, from 1814, General Pozzo di Borgo recommended. May we not therefore suppose that M. Thiers, who had eluded the influence of Prince Talleyrand, with respect to the history of that period, had suffered himself to be convinced by General Pozzo di Borgo, whose opinions and sayings he was fond of quoting even during the closing years of his life.

General Pozzo di Borgo never relinquished his efforts to bring about that close political alliance between France and Russia, which was attempted at Tilsit and reconsidered at Vienna, where the representative of the Czar wished to set the seal to it by a marriage between the Duc de Berry and the sister of the Emperor Alexander. That alliance was his principal object during the whole period of the Restoration. We now know that when the folly of the

Polignac ministry brought about the Revolution of 1830, the ideas of General Pozzo di Borgo were on the point of realization. France had the promise of the banks of the Rhine; Russia, on her side, was free to push her way so far as Constantinople; and the expedition to Algeria, made at that very time, in spite of the displeasure of England, makes it plain that a part of this scheme of alliance and partition was that France should be permitted to take a portion of the Ottoman Empire.[1]

The regret with which the Emperor Nicholas regarded the defeat of this plan had had, no doubt, something to do with his well-known hostility to King Louis Philippe. This supposition is all the more reasonable since the Government of the Czars has never been very fond of legitimacy; and that in the correspondence which we publish, it will be seen that the Emperor Alexander was quite willing to pass over the elder branch of the Bourbons, and at once place on the throne of France, on the occasion of the second Restoration, the prince who was afterwards Louis Philippe. No doubt there was something in these glimpses of exterior aggrandizement very seductive to the patriotic sentiments of M. Thiers, and his predilection, as an historian, for the Russian alliance is explicable.

The essential point which it is proposed to elucidate in this introduction is: Was Prince Talleyrand right, eminently right, in pronouncing in favor of the Austro-English alliance, in 1814, at the risk of clashing with the national sentiment? We do not intend to enter into a disquisition upon the Congress of Vienna; and still less do we propose to draw, in this first publication, a complete picture of the long and eventful career of one whom foreigners, more equitable it may be than ourselves, rank high among our great statesmen. It will suffice for our purpose if we can place the principle of the whole of his conduct, and the results which he obtained in this memorable negotiation, in a clear light.

That principle, or rather—for it ought to be called by its true name—that supreme expedient, of which he was about to make such great use, was legitimacy. Against the ambition of old Europe, victorious, and in coalition, it was plain he could not invoke the principles of 1789, the rights of man and of citizens, the sovereignty of the people. As he did not possess material strength, he had to seek a new force wherewith to hold his victorious enemies at bay. All tha the could do was to protect, in the name of the legitimist principle, *i.e.* of historic right, the integrity of the territory which, within its necessary frontiers, would still leave the France of 1789 able to profit by the application of the political, civil, and economical conquests of the Revolution.

Vanquished France then profited in her defeat, by the principle which it was the interest of the other European monarchies to respect in her person because those monarchies themselves had no other foundation. She was placed by Prince Talleyrand under the ægis of a principle which was sufficiently accepted by the Allied Powers, to restrict their victory. Thus she escaped that application of force pure and simple which, under the Empire, she had often inflicted upon them.

At a moment when the idea of the sovereignty of the people, perverted and ruined by the Empire which had disregarded it, had lost all practical value, Prince Talleyrand cleverly exhumed from the history of the past an idea whose moral qualities were to make the future of the France of 1789 safe. It is not necessary to believe that the scepticism of Prince Talleyrand himself was relinquished unreservedly in favor of the new doctrine which he sought to inculcate. He was the utilitarian advocate of it with crowned heads. At that epoch, the force of circumstances, with which he liked to contend, was imposing legitimacy upon the world. This was the moment when Napoleon, lamenting, with Caulaincourt, that he had received France so great and left her so small, was debating whether he should not himself send for the Bourbons.

In the "Mémorial de Sainte Hélène" (tom. vii. p. 283, edition of 1823) we find the following:

"After the defeat of Brienne, the evacuation of Troyes, the forced retreat upon the Seine, and the humiliating conditions sent from Châtillon, which he bravely rejected, the Emperor, overcome at the prospect of the deluge of evils which was about to overwhelm France, remained for some time absorbed in sorrowful meditation; but at length he started up and exclaimed, 'It may be that I still possess a means of saving France! What if I myself were to recall the Bourbons! The Allies would be obliged to stop short before them, under pain of the shame of acknowledged duplicity—under pain of proving that their action is directed against our territory more than against my person. I would sacrifice everything to the country; I would become the mediator between the French people and them; I would constrain them to accede to the national laws; I would make them swear to observe the existing compact; my glory and my name would serve as a guarantee to the French. As for me, I have reigned long enough: my career is replete with great deeds and the lustre of them; this last would not be the least among them; by means of it I should rather rise to a higher place than descend from my own.' Then, after a few moments of profound silence, he resumed, in a tone of sadness: 'But does a dynasty which has once been expelled ever pardon? . . . Could it return having forgotten anything? . . . Could any one trust them? . . . Was Fox right in his famous saying about Restorations?'"

So early as 1810 he said to M. de Metternich, "Do you know why Louis XVIII. is not sitting here in front of you? It is only because I am sitting here. Nobody else would have been able to hold the place, and if ever a catastrophe occurs, and I disappear, it will be filled by a Bourbon."

Not only was the idea of legitimacy, according to Prince Talleyrand's intention, to serve as an ægis for France; it was also to be the palladium of a European balance of power of sufficient duration to enable France, exhausted by so many struggles, to secure long years of quiet and prosperity.

Prince Talleyrand had always had a private leaning towards the English alliance; before the Revolution of 1789, he made one of that small group who, after the publication of Voltaire's "Lettres Anglaises," and the homage paid by Montesquieu to the great, free, and commercial nation, were asking whether it might not be possible to get rid of traditional jealousy and prejudice, and to form between reconciled France and England an alliance which was demanded not only by the interests of the two people, but by the cause of civilization itself.

Mirabeau had similar tendencies: the following advice is taken from two unpublished letters forming part of a correspondence between himself and his friend, the Abbé de Périgord, in 1786, during his secret mission to Berlin: "I have discussed the so-called chimerical idea of an alliance between France and England with the Duke of Brunswick; he regards it as the saviour of the world, and sees no difficulty in it except the prejudices of false science and the lukewarmness of pusillanimity.

"I talked about it philosophically, at the English Legation, and I found Lord Dalrymple and even his very British Secretary of Legation infinitely more disposed to the idea than I could have ventured to hope. Lord Dalrymple told me that on hearing the news of the Germanic Confederation, he had at once said to the Marquis of Carmarthen and Mr. Pitt that there was no longer any policy but one for England—that of a coalition with France, founded on unrestricted free trade.

"The routine politicians may do their best; they may bestir themselves as much as they like in their petty ways; there is but one great plan, one luminous idea, one project wide enough to embrace, to reconcile, and to terminate everything. That plan is yours; by putting down not only the rivalries of commerce, but the absurd and sanguinary enmity to which they give rise, it would confide the peace and freedom of the two worlds to the vigilant and paternal care of France and England.

"No doubt this idea appears romantic, but is it our fault that everything which is simple has become romantic? No doubt to the short-sighted it looks like a chapter from 'Gulliver's Travels,' but is it not the more or less remote distance from the possible which distinguishes men?

"I only want to encourage you to show that it is possible, almost easy, to establish on the imperishable and immovable basis of common interest an alliance between two countries which can and ought to command the peace of the world, and which would prevent continual strife and bloodshed between the two nations." Prophetic words not forgotten by Mirabeau's friend, for, when he was sent on a mission to London in 1792, he attempted to bring about such an alliance; and no doubt often repeated to himself during the fatal contests of the Empire, whose fall recalled him to a sense of its necessity.

The imperative obligation of securing repose for France and preserving the European balance of power induced him to decide upon making approaches to the English Legation.

That the sole aim of Russia in uniting with France would be domination had been made manifest at Tilsit. The alliance between France and Russia had a distinct preponderance of advantage on the side of Russia, that empire proposing to itself unlimited aggrandizement in Asia and even in Europe. France, on the contrary, could not, even under the most favorable conditions, claim anything beyond the Rhine. Prince Talleyrand therefore acted like a statesman in declaring that the real strength of France, especially after her defeat, lay in her clearly expressed desire for the restoration and the maintenance of peace. Recurring to the ideas of Voltaire and his *République Européenne*, at that moment, he said (the words are reported by Baron de Gagern, who heard him utter them), "We must be good Europeans and moderate. France ought to demand, and does demand, nothing, absolutely nothing, beyond a just redivision among the Powers; that is to say, the balance of power."

The balance of power was thus defined: "A combination of the rights, the interests, and the relations of the Powers among themselves, by which Europe seeks to obtain—

"First. That the rights and possessions of a Power shall not be attacked by one or several other Powers.

"Secondly. That one or several other Powers shall never attain to domination over Europe.

"Thirdly. That the combination adopted shall render a rupture of the established order and of the tranquillity of Europe difficult or impossible."

In order to obtain that equilibrium, he signed the treaty of the 3rd of January, 1815.

He saw in Europe, on the one side[2] Austria, an essentially diplomatic and conservative Power, of which he gave M. de Metternich the following definition: "Austria is the House of Lords of Europe; so long as she remains undissolved, she will keep down the Commons"—and England, a parliamentary Power, who had preceded us in the path of liberty. On the other side, he saw Russia, a new and enigmatical Power, represented by a theatrical, mystical, and versatile personage, who changed his policy, his alliances, and his friendships according to the whims of his romantic imagination—a sort of Slav Napoleon, who had risen upon the ruins of the Napoleonic Empire, and who, after having astonished the coalition by his liberalism, was in the following year to become the promoter of the Holy Alliance.

While Russia and England tended to encourage the ambition of Prussia[3]—the only Power which had presented itself at the Congress of Vienna with a seriously elaborated plan, and labored for its fulfilment with the ardent tenacity inculcated by its constitution—Prince Talleyrand applied himself to check that ambition. He had discerned in the constitution of Prussia a principle of absorption and conquest which must dispel any idea of an alliance with that Power.

The following references to this point occur in the instructions which he had received—and which were probably drawn up by himself—on the 25th of September, 1814, before he left Paris for Vienna:

"In Italy, it is Austria that must be prevented from predominating; in Germany, it is Prussia. The constitution of the Prussian monarchy makes ambition a kind of necessity. Every pretext is good in its sight; no scruple arrests it. *Convenance* is the law. The Allies have, it is said, pledged themselves to replace Prussia in the same condition of power as she was before her fall, that is to say, with ten millions of subjects. If she be left alone, she will soon have twenty millions, and *all Germany* will be in subjection to her. It is, then, necessary to curb her ambition, in the first place by restricting as much as possible her status of possession in Germany, and in the second place by restricting her influence by federal organization."[4]

An agreement between France and Prussia could not do otherwise than hasten the unity of Germany; it was easy to see that Protestant Prussia would thenceforth attract Germany, which was in majority Protestant, to herself. Now the unity of Germany, at this epoch, meant war, and Prince Talleyrand knew that France and Europe desired peace.

If Saxony had been given up to Prussia, in accordance with the persistent and unwearying demands of the Prussian plenipotentiary, would not Prussia have rapidly assimilated to herself that rich and industrious country, Protestant like herself, half Slav and half Germanic, like herself, and with tendencies similar to her own?

Would not the preponderance of Prussia over Germany have been secured by the signature of the final act of that Congress whose great object was to insure peace by an equitable distribution of the forces of attack and defence among the nations?

Would not the work of German unification, already singularly accelerated by the destruction of the former Germanic Empire, have been advanced by the space of half a century?

The existence of an autonomous Saxony guaranteed the independence of a federal Germany, at the same time that from the strategic point of view it prevented an immediate extensive contact between Prussia and Austria.

Such were the reasons which combined to decide Prince Talleyrand on signing the treaty of the 3rd of January, which gave France Austria' and England as allies.

This alliance meant peace, and, under favor of peace, the development of the new forces born of the Revolution that peace alone could secure.

By the treaty of the 3rd of January, Prince Talleyrand had obtained for France the maintenance of her frontiers of 1792. Measures were taken by which the France of 1792 was safeguarded had war broken out. Of the four Great Powers she had two with her. "She had cut Europe in two for her profit."

If we would form an idea of the anger which was aroused in Prussia by the issue of this memorable negotiation, we should read the Berlin newspapers of the period. Prince Hardenberg, who had not been able to retain Saxony in the power of the Prussians, was the object of the most violent invective—that same Prince Hardenberg who, at the first meeting of the plenipotentiaries in conference at Vienna, asked what public law had to do with their deliberations, and was answered by Prince Talleyrand, "This— that you are here."

Is Prince Talleyrand to be reproached because he did not give up Saxony? Apart from questions of strategy and equilibrium, to give up Saxony would have been to abandon the principle of legitimacy itself, that principle in which Prince Talleyrand made the whole strength of the French negotiators to abide.

Instead of Protestant Saxony, which she would have assimilated too readily, Prussia received the Rhenish Provinces; that is to say, Catholic countries, divided from her by Hanover, Hesse, the duchies of Brunswick and Nassau, etc., accustomed to a French administration, and still more widely parted from her by their religious belief, habits, and legislation. It has taken Prussia half a century to assimilate countries so different from herself.

There has been this strange phenomenon in her position, that in order to collect and amalgamate those incongruous elements, she, a Protestant Power, has had to constitute herself the protector of Catholic interests in Germany. Prussia, constituted as an absolute Government, has had to bend to the liberal ideas of the Rhenish Provinces; protectionist Prussia has had to put herself at the head of the Free Trade movement, and to enable her to rejoin her own provinces she has had to create, by dint of much persistence and many sacrifices, the great Customs Union of Central Europe (Zollverein).

But while at Vienna Prince Talleyrand was entirely occupied in the consolidation of peace, at Paris the scarcely established Government of the Restoration was working at its own destruction. The opinion of its clear-sighted friends[6] upon the policy of the new Government may be ascertained from notes taken from unpublished letters of Prince Talleyrand's Parisian correspondents. On the 9th of April, 1815, Jaucourt writes: "Alas! why could you not have stayed with us? My letters will have revealed to you my alarm and despondency, and you will have easily judged, since everything is in so false and unfortunate a position, how much there was to fear from the return of *the man*. I did not deceive myself in the least as to the fatal course we are pursuing." On the 10th, Jaucourt writes again: "Good God! what road have we travelled on since that day! (the royal sitting). It must be said in one word; it led to the island of Elba."

The Treaty of Fontainebleau had not been executed. Bonaparte was threatened with deportation to the Azores. Taking advantage of the general confusion, incapacity, and unpopularity of the Restoration, he quitted the island of Elba, the army flocked around him, and he evidently had on his side not only those whom M. de Jaucourt then called " the Jacobins," but also the constitutionalists and the parliamentarians. Under this too late reverting towards liberty, Carnot was Minister of the Interior; Sismondi joined him; Benjamin Constant himself undertook to draw up the Act to be added to the Constitutions of the Empire. The hatred felt for the old *régime* was stimulated by the errors of the Bourbons; it outweighed the former aversion of the Republicans and Liberals to Bonaparte, and also their dread of the coalition and of renewed war. On the 7th of June, Napoleon opened the session by that tardy homage which, in his distress, he rendered to liberty: "I come hither to commence constitutional monarchy. Men are too powerless to make the future secure; institutions only fix the destinies of nations."

Let us pause for a moment at this point, to remark upon the influence which the transient union between the Republicans, the Liberals, and Napoleon, during that painful period of the Hundred Days, exercised upon the destinies of France through the return of the Bonapartes in the middle of our century.

The return of Napoleon led Prince Talleyrand to draw up a memorial addressed to the Powers assembled at Vienna. This document has unfortunately been lost; but, if we may judge of it by his correspondence at that period, it must have contained formulas of exorcism directed against the spectre (*revenant*) of the island of Elba, which smacked rather of the former bishop than of the discerning friend and undeceived associate of Napoleon.

The declaration of the 13th of March and that of the 25th are known; the coalition was re-formed; and at that moment Talleyrand, on the ground of diplomacy, had a right to say that he defended the cause of France by obtaining the maintenance of the treaty of the 30th of May, which secured our frontiers to us, and by signing the final act of the Congress of Vienna.

He re-entered Paris with Louis XVIII., and resumed his post as Prime Minister, but the memories of Ghent had made only a transient impression upon the King, and he who had promoted the return of Louis XVIII. was very soon forced to retreat before the triumphant reaction and the hostility of Alexander. That hostility Prince Talleyrand had nobly earned, by defending the principles of the law of nations against the Emperor of Russia at the Congress of Vienna. On the same day on which the *Gazette Officielle* announced the retirement of Talleyrand, the Holy Alliance was concluded at Paris, under the auspices of Alexander. We were far indeed from the treaty of the 3rd of January, 1815.

Evidently, Prince Talleyrand had not sufficient strength of character to make his system of parliamentary and constitutional Monarchy, which would place the Charter above royalty itself, prevail against the personal preferences of Louis XVIII., and especially against the retrograde passions of those by whom the King was surrounded. But while he yielded to the force of circumstances with which he did not care to contend, his keen discernment and his consummate experience made it plain to him that, at a future period, more or less distant, the restored Monarchy would, like Napoleon I., have to pay dearly for the liberties it had taken with his counsels.

When the Revolution of 1830 occurred, he was perfectly prepared for it; he was not in the least surprised by it; and, while he experienced the bitter satisfaction of seeing his fears realized, he doubtless hoped that he might at length behold the establishment, by the new Charter, of that *régime* which in reality he had always preferred. It was then that, recurring to the violence and the excesses which he had witnessed, and opposing the candidature of a prince of the House of Austria in Belgium, he wrote on the 27th of November, 1830, to M. Molé, in a letter which was to be shown to King Louis Philippe:[7] "I have said to Lord Palmerston and Lord Grey, "A prince of the House of Austria in Belgium would look too like a Restoration; and you ought to bear in mind a thing which I forgot, fifteen years ago—that Mr. Fox said, and put it in print, that the worst of Revolutions is a Restoration.'"

NOTES TO THE PREFACE.

1. It is hardly necessary to remind the reader that Algeria was, with the whole coast of Barbary, the vassal and tributary of the Sultan of Turkey.

2. "There are in Europe at the present day four Great Powers; for I do not place Prussia in that rank. She is held to be great because one of her monarchs did great things, and because we are accustomed to confound the State which he rendered illustrious with Frederick II. But with a parcelled-out territory, open on all sides, a soil for the most part ungrateful, a popula-

tion of ten millions only, little industry, and small capital, Prussia is in reality only the first of the second-rate Powers.

"At the head of the four Great Powers stands France; stronger than each of the other three, capable even of resisting them all; the sole perfect Power, because she alone unites in correct proportions the two elements of greatness which are unequally distributed among the others, that is to say, men and wealth."—Talleyrand's Memorial to the Emperor Napoleon, dated from Strasburg, 25 Vendémiaire, Year XIV. (1806).

3. "An alliance between France and Prussia had been regarded as a means of preserving peace on the Continent. But an alliance with Prussia is now impossible. . . . Thus, it is not to be hoped that for half a century to come Prussia can associate herself with any noble enterprise."—Memorial to the Emperor Napoleon, 25 Vendémiaire, Year XIV. (1806).

4. See D'Angeberg, "Le Congrès de Vienne," p. 23.

5. On the day after the victory of Ulm, he advised Napoleon to form that alliance with Austria. He wrote as follows:

"I assume that after winning a great battle, your Majesty would say to the House of Austria, 'I did everything to maintain peace; you would only have war. I predicted the consequences to you. I have conquered you reluctantly, but I am the conqueror. I desire that my victory should be for the common good. I want to extirpate even the very least germ of misunderstanding between us. Our dissensions can arise from a too close neighborhood only. Let you and the princes of your house relinquish Lindau and the island of Monau, from whence you disturb Switzerland, and give us the State of Venice, Trieste, and the Tyrol. I, for my part, will separate the crowns of France and Italy, as I have promised. The kingdom of Italy shall never be enlarged.

"'The republic of Venice, to which Trieste will be joined, shall be restored under the presidency of a magistrate of its own selection. While I exact sacrifices from you, I do not intend that they shall remain without compensation; on the contrary, I desire that the compensation shall exceed them in value.

"'Extend yourself along the Danube. Occupy Wallachia, Moldavia, and Bessarabia. I will intervene to procure the surrender of those possessions to you by the Ottoman Porte, and if the Russians attack you I will be your ally.' . . .

"I venture to think that after a victory such proposals will be joyfully accepted by the House of Austria, and then a fair peace will terminate a glorious war. . . .

"In past times it was held necessary to fortify Austria, which was regarded as a bulwark against the Ottomans, then formidable to Christendom. Notwithstanding the ancient rivalry between the Houses of Austria and Bourbon, and the ancient alliance of France with the Ottoman Porte, Louis XIV. perceived the danger of Europe, and gave his rival aid. At the present time the Turks are no longer to be feared; they have everything to fear.

"But they have been replaced by the Prussians; Austria is still the chief bulwark which Europe has to oppose to them, and it is against them that Austria must now be fortified.

"So that sound policy requires, not that the sacrifices which Austria must make be recompensed, but that the compensation be such as to leave her no dissatisfaction.

"Let her, in exchange for the State of Venice, the Tyrol, and her possessions in Swabia and the neighboring States, which will remain extinct ever afterwards, be given Wallachia, Moldavia, Bessarabia, and the most northern portion of Bulgaria. She will then be mistress of two fertile provinces; she will acquire, through her former States, an outlet on the Danube, nearly the whole course of that river will be subject to her laws, and a portion of the shores of the Black Sea; and she will have no cause to regret losses so richly compensated."—Memorial to the Emperor Napoleon, 25 Vendémiaire, Year XIV. (1806).

6. We have been enabled to consult the manuscript of the letters of M. de Jaucourt, and a copy of a correspondence which is attributed in the Department to M. d'Hauterive. We give some extracts in the course of these volumes.

7. It was in the same letter that he said, "France ought not to think of making what are called alliances; she ought to stand well with all, and only better with a few Powers; that is to say, to keep up such relations of friendship with them as find expression when political events present themselves. This kind of relation is formed nowadays on a different principle from that of earlier times. The progress of civilization will henceforth form our ties of kindred. We ought, then, to endeavor to attract towards us those Governments in which civilization is most advanced. There we shall find our real family alliances."

UNPUBLISHED CORRESPONDENCE

OF

PRINCE TALLEYRAND AND LOUIS XVIII.

LETTER I.

Vienna, 25th September, 1814.

SIRE,

I left Paris on the 16th, and arrived here on the evening of the 23rd. I only stopped on my journey at Strasburg and Munich.

The Princess of Wales has just left Strasburg. She went while there to a ball given by Madame Franck, the banker's widow, and danced all night. She gave Talma a supper at the inn where I put up. Her proceedings at Strasburg entirely account for the Prince Regent's being better pleased that she should be in Italy than in England.

At Munich, the King spoke to me of his attachment to your Majesty, and of the fears with which Prussian ambition inspired him. He said, with a very good grace: "I have served France twenty-one years; a thing not to be forgotten." A conversation of two hours' duration with M. de Montgelas proved to me conclusively that we have only to carry out the principles laid down by your Majesty as the basis of the political system of France to secure the adherence and win the confidence of the minor Powers.

At Vienna, the language of the plenipotentiaries is not yet that of reason and moderation.

One of the Russian ministers said to us yesterday: "They wanted to make an Asiatic Power of us; Poland will make us European."

Russia would not ask anything better than to exchange her old Polish provinces[1] for those which she covets in Germany and on the banks of the Rhine. These two Powers ought to be regarded as closely united on that point.

The Russian ministers insist, without having admitted the slightest discussion up to the present time, upon an extension of territory which would carry that Power to the banks of the Vistula, and even add Old Prussia[2] to their empire.

I hope the Emperor,[3] who, under different circumstances, allowed me to put frankly before him what I judged to be most conducive to his true interests and to his fame, will permit me to contest the policy of his ministers in his presence. La Harpe, the philanthropist, objects strongly to the former partition of Poland, and urges its subjection to Russia. He has been at Vienna these ten days.

The right of the King of Saxony to have a minister at the Congress is disputed. M. de Schulenburg,[4] whom I have known for a long time, told me yesterday that the King had declared that he would make no act of cession, abdication, or exchange whatever which could destroy the existence of Saxony and do injury to the rights of his house. This honorable resistance on the part of the King may make some impression on those who still favor the idea of uniting Saxony to Prussia.

Bavaria has offered the King of Saxony to support these claims with a considerable body of troops, if necessary. Prince de Wrede says that he is ordered to give as many as 40,000 men.

The question of Naples is not decided.[5] Austria wants to place Naples and Saxony on the same footing, and Russia wants to make them subjects for compensation.

The Queen of Naples is but little regretted.[6] Her death seems to have made things easier for M. de Metternich.

Nothing has been settled with respect to the order and conduct of the business of the Congress. Even the English, whom I believed to be more methodical than the others, have made no preparatory plan.

I am inclined to think that there will be a general assent to the idea of two Commissions: one composed of the six Great Powers,[7] to be occupied with the general affairs of Europe; the other composed of the six leading German Powers,[8] (I should have wished the number to be seven[9]), to prepare the affairs of Germany. The idea of a Commission for Italy is highly displeasing to Austria.

The line of conduct which your Majesty has laid down for your ministers is so noble that it must necessarily, if all reason have not vanished from the earth, give them some influence in the end.

I am, Sire,
With the most profound respect,
Your Majesty's most humble and
obedient servant and subject,
TALLEYRAND.

P.S.—The Emperor of Russia and the King of Prussia[10] have just arrived. Their entry was a fine sight. They were on horseback, the Emperor of Austria in the middle. Some slight disorder occasioned by the horses led to the King of Prussia's being for a considerable part of the way on the right of the Emperor Francis;[11] the proper order of things was not restored until shortly before they reached the palace.[12]

NOTES TO LETTER I.

1. Prussia had shared in the three partitions of Poland (1773, 1793, 1795). At the last partition Warsaw had fallen to the share of that kingdom.
2. By "Old Prussia," Prince Talleyrand means Royal, formerly called Ducal Prussia, whose capital is Köningsberg.
3. The Emperor of Russia.
4. The King of Saxony had sent M. de Gærz, his confidential adviser, to Vienna in September. In the declaration of the King of Saxony, dated from Friedriechsfeld, 4th November, 1814, the following passage occurs: "The preservation and the consolidation of the legitimate dynasties has been the great object of a war which has just been happily terminated: the Powers which entered into a coalition for that purpose have repeatedly proclaimed in the most solemn manner, that far from entertaining any project of conquest or aggrandizement, they have solely in view the re-establishment of law and liberty in Europe.
In December, he entrusted all his powers to M. de Schulenburg, who had just published a pamphlet entitled, "Do the People of Saxony wish for a Change of Dynasty?"
5. Joachim Murat had remained in possession of the kingdom of Naples after the fall of Napoleon I., his brother-in-law (April, 1814).
6. Marie Caroline (1752-1814). See Appendix.
7. Russia, Austria, Prussia, England, France, Spain.
8. Austria, Prussia, Bavaria, Wurtemburg, and Hanover; the sixth ought to have been Saxony, which was, in fact, excluded.
9. No doubt by the addition of the grand-duchy of Baden.
10. Frederick William III. See Appendix.
11. Francis I. of Austria. See Appendix.
12. In the *Moniteur Universel* of 9th October, an account is given of the entry of the sovereigns into Vienna, 26th September, 1814: "The procession lasted more than an hour: a salute of one thousand guns was fired from the ramparts."
A caricature of the period represents the Emperor Alexander driving a huge travelling-carriage, the King of Prussia acting as *chasseur;* the Emperor Napoleon following the vehicle on foot, and crying out to the Emperor Francis, "Father-in-law, father-in-law, they have put me out." The Emperor of Austria, who occupies the interior of the carriage, looks out of the window and answers, "And me in!"

LETTER II.

Vienna, 29th September, 1814.

SIRE,

At last we have almost finished our round of visits to the members of the numerous Royal family. It has been most pleasant to me to meet everywhere with evidence of the high consideration with which the person of your Majesty is regarded; the interest and the good wishes of all are expressed in language more or less complimentary indeed, but with sincerity that cannot be suspected. The Empress,[1] who had been obliged since our arrival to devote herself exclusively to the Empress of Russia,[2] had appointed an hour for receiving us to-day. She is unfortunately indisposed, and although she deputed the Archduchess her mother to receive several persons on her behalf, she received your Majesty's embassy in person. She questioned me respecting your Majesty's health with interest which was not dictated by mere politeness. "I remember," said she, "to have seen the King at Milan. I was very young then, and he was all kindness to me; I have never forgotten that under any circumstances." She spoke in similar terms of the Duchesse d'Angoulême, of her good qualities, of the affection with which she was regarded at Vienna, and the remembrance of her that is preserved there. She was also pleased to say very obliging things about your Majesty's minister. Twice she mentioned the name of the Archduchess Marie Louise; the second time she called her, with a sort of affection, "my daughter Louise." Notwithstanding the cough by which she is frequently interrupted, and in spite of her thinness, the Empress has the gift of pleasing, and certain graces which I should call French were they not, to a critical eye, a little affected.

M. de Metternich is very polite to me; M. de Stadion is more confidential with me. The latter, indeed, being displeased at what the former does, confines himself altogether to matters of finance,—their management has been given to him, and I greatly doubt his understanding them,—and has abandoned Cabinet business; this, perhaps, makes him more communicative. I have to congratulate myself upon the frankness with which I am treated by Lord Castlereagh.[3] A few days ago he had a conversation with the Emperor Alexander,[4] which lasted for an hour and a half, and he came to me afterwards to tell me all about it. He states that in this conversation the Emperor employed all the resources of a subtle mind, but that he (Lord Castlereagh) spoke in very positive terms, and indeed said things so hard that they would have been unbecoming had he not, in order to make them go down, mixed up with them ardent protestations of zeal for the Emperor's glory. Notwithstanding all this, however, I am afraid Lord Castlereagh has not the spirit of decision which it would be so necessary for us that he should have, and that the idea of the English Parliament of which he never shakes himself free makes him timid. I will do all that in me lies to inspire him with firmness.

Count Nesselrode had told me that the Emperor Alexander wished to see me, and it had been arranged that I should write to him to ask for a private audience. I did this several days ago, but as yet I have no answer. Are our principles, of which we make no secret, known to the Emperor Alexander, and have they made him feel a kind of awkwardness with me?

If he does me the honor to converse with me upon the affairs of Saxony and Poland—and all that reaches me leads me to expect he will do so—I shall be mild and conciliatory, but quite firm, speaking of principles only and never departing from them.

I am convinced that Russia and Prussia are making so much noise and talking so big merely to find out what is thought, and that if they see that they stand alone they will think twice of it before they carry things to extremity. The Polish enthusiasm which the Emperor Alexander took up in Paris, cooled at St. Petersburg, was warmed up again at Pulawy,[5] and may decline once more, although we have M. de la Harpe here and we are expecting the Czartoryskis. I can scarcely believe that a simple but unanimous declaration by the Great Powers would not be sufficient to quell it. Unhappily the person who is at the head of affairs in Austria, and who lays claim to the regulation of those of Europe, regards as the infallible mark of superior genius that levity which he carries on the one side to absurdity, and on the other to a point at which, in the minister of a great State, and in circumstances like the present, it becomes a calamity.

In this state of things, when so many passions are in a ferment and so many people are disturbed in various ways, it seems to me that two errors are equally to be avoided—impetuosity and indolence; and I therefore endeavor to preserve that attitude of calm dignity which I regard as the only one befitting your Majesty's ministers, who, thanks to the wise instructions they have received from your Majesty, have to defend principles only, without having any scheme of personal interest to carry through.⁶

Whatever may be the issue of the Congress, there are two points which must be established and preserved: the justice of your Majesty and the strength of your Majesty's Government; for they afford the best, or rather the only, pledges for consideration without and stability within. These two points once thoroughly established, as I hope they will be, whether the result of the Congress be or be not in accordance with our wishes and the good of Europe, we shall come out of it with honor.

I am, etc.

NOTES TO LETTER II.

1. Maria Louise Beatrix of Austria. See Appendix.
2. Elizabeth Alexievna (1779-1826). See Appendix.
3. Giving an account of an audience of the King, Jaucourt writes, 18th October, 1814:

"I had given expression to some reflections to the effect that it appeared to me Lord Castlereagh did not present a union of very frank and exact principles and views. The king defended his personal character as that of a gallant gentleman, but said he did not rate his political character so highly."

4. On the 15th of October, M. de Jaucourt writes to Prince Talleyrand:

"Lord Wellington came to see me; his visit was a friendly one. . . . We talked freely enough. He told me that Lord Castlereagh had found the Emperor Alexander, at his first visit, in such 'a state of violence' that all he could obtain from him was the following: 'I will think of what you have said to me by way of objection, and we will talk of it another time.' With this the Czar dismissed him."

5. Pulawy, on the Vistula, a Polish town, forty-two kilomètres from Lublin. Prince Adam Czartoryski had a magnificent estate there.

6. "The King's ministers strictly observe the line laid down for them by their instructions. They recur in all their conversations to the article of the treaty of 30th May, which assigns to the Congress the honorable mission of establishing a real and durable equilibrium. That impartial method leads them to enter into the principles of public law recognized by all Europe, and which imply, in an almost obligatory manner, the re-establishment of King Ferdinand II. on the throne of Naples, as well as the succession of the house of Savoy in the Carignano branch."—Talleyrand's letter to the department, 27th September. 1814.

LETTER III.

Vienna, 4th October, 1814.

SIRE,

On the 30th of September, between nine and ten o'clock in the morning, I received from M. de Metternich a letter consisting of five lines, and dated the previous evening, in which he proposed to me, in his own name only, to come and *assist* at a preliminary conference, for which I should find the Russian, English, and Prussian ministers *met* at his house. He added that he was making a similar request of the Spanish minister, M. de Labrador.

The words "assist" and "met" were evidently employed with design. I replied that it would give me great pleasure to present myself at his house with the Russian, English, *Spanish*, and Prussian ministers.

The invitation addressed to M. de Labrador was couched in the same terms as that which I had received, with this difference, that it was in the form of a note in the third person, and written in the name of M. de Metternich *and his colleagues*.

M. de Labrador having come to communicate this note to me, and to consult me upon the answer to be sent, I showed him mine, and he wrote one exactly similar, in which France was named *with* and *before* the other Powers. Thus M. de Labrador and myself purposely combined what it seemed the others wanted to divide, and separated what it appeared to be their object to unite by a special link.

I was at the house of M. de Metternich before two o'clock, and found that the ministers of the four Courts had already met and were sitting at a long table. At one end was Lord Castlereagh, who seemed to be presiding; at the other end was a man whom M. de Metternich presented to me as "holding the pen" in their conference. This was M. Gentz. A seat had been left vacant between Lord Castlereagh and M. de Metternich; this I took. I asked why I only of all your Majesty's embassy had been summoned, and my question led to the following dialogue:

"It was wished that none but the Secretaries of State should meet at the preliminary conferences." "M. de Labrador is not one, and yet he is summoned." "True, but the Spanish Secretary is not at Vienna." "But, beside Prince Hardenberg, I see M. de Humboldt, who is not a Secretary of State." "That is an exception rendered necessary by the infirmity from which, as you know, Prince Hardenberg suffers." "If only infirmities were in question, each might have his own and an equal right to make use of them."[1]

They then seemed inclined to admit that each Secretary of State might bring one of the plenipotentiaries his colleagues, and so I thought it useless to insist any further for the moment.

Count Palmella, the Portuguese Ambassador, being informed by Lord Castlereagh that there were to be preliminary conferences at which M. de Labrador and I were to be present, but that he was not to be summoned, thought fit to protest against an exclusion which he regarded as unjust and humiliating to the crown of Portugal. He had therefore written to Lord Castlereagh a letter which the latter produced at the conference. His reasons were strong and well put. He demanded that the eight Powers who signed the treaty of the 30th of May,[2] and not six of those Powers, should form the Preparatory Commission by which the Congress for whose assembling they had stipulated was to be set going. M. de Labrador and myself supported this demand, and the rest seemed disposed to accede to it, but the decision was adjourned until the next sitting. Sweden is not yet represented here by a plenipotentiary, and is therefore not in a position to make any claim.

"The object of to-day's conference," said Lord Castlereagh to me, "is to make you acquainted with what the four Courts[3] have done since we have been here." Addressing M. de Metternich he said, "You have the protocol." M. de Metternich then handed me a paper signed by him, Count Nesselrode, Lord Castlereagh, and Prince Hardenberg. In this document the word "allies" occurred in every paragraph. I pointed out the word, and said that the use of it placed me under the necessity of asking where we were, whether we were still at Chaumont[4] or at Laon,[5] whether peace had not been made, whether there was any quarrel, and with whom. I was answered by all that they did not attribute a sense contrary to the state of our actual relations to the word "allies," and that they had only employed it for brevity's sake. On which I impressed upon them that, however valuable brevity might be, it ought not to be purchased at the expense of accuracy.

The tenor of the protocol was a tissue of metaphysical arguments intended to enforce pretensions which were supported by treaties unknown to us. To discuss those reasonings and pretensions would have been to embark upon an ocean of disputes; I felt that it was necessary to repel the whole by one peremptory argument; so I read several paragraphs and said, "I do not understand." Then I read the same paragraphs through very carefully a second time, with the air of earnestly striving to penetrate the meaning of a thing, and said, "I do not understand any the more." I added: "I hold to two dates between which there is nothing: that of the 31st of May, on which the formation of the Congress was stipulated, and that of the 1st of October, on which it ought to meet. All that has been done in the interval is foreign to me, and does not exist for me." The answer of the plenipotentiaries was that they cared so little for the paper in question that they asked nothing better than to withdraw it; upon which M. de Labrador observed that nevertheless they had signed it. They took it back, M. de Metternich laid it aside, and there was no more about it.

After having abandoned this document they produced another. This was the draft of a declaration which M. de Labrador and I were to sign with them if we adopted it. After a long preamble on the necessity of simplifying and abridging the labors of the Congress, and after protestations that there was to be no infringement of the rights of anybody, the draft set forth that the subjects to be settled by the Congress were to be divided into two series; that a committee was to be formed for each, to which the States interested might address themselves; and that, these two committees having completed their task, the Congress should then be assembled for the first time and the whole submitted to its sanction.

The visible aim of this plan was to make the four Powers who called themselves allied absolute masters of all the operations of the Congress; for on the hypothesis that the six principal Powers were to constitute themselves judges of the questions relating to the composition of the Congress, to the matters which it was to regulate, to the methods to be adopted in the settlement of them, and the order in which they were to be taken; and that they should have the uncontrolled nomination of the committees which were to prepare everything, France and Spain would never be otherwise than two against four, even supposing them to be always agreed upon every question.

I said at once that a first reading was not sufficient for the formation of an opinion upon a project of this nature, which needed to be thought over; that we must especially, and in the first place, ascertain whether it was compatible with rights which we intended to respect; that we had all come here to secure the rights of each,

1*

and that it would be most unfortunate if we were to set out by violating them; that the idea of arranging everything before convening the Congress was a novel one to me; that they proposed to finish where I had thought it would be necessary to begin; that probably the power which it was proposed to confer upon the six Powers could not be given to them except by the Congress; that there were measures which ministers without responsibility might easily adopt, but that Lord Castlereagh and I were in quite a different case. Here Lord Castlereagh said that the reflections which I was making had occurred to his mind also, that he felt all their force, but, he added, what other expedient is there by which we can avoid being led into proceedings of interminable length? I asked why the Congress could not be assembled at once—what were the difficulties in the way? Then each brought forward one of his own, and a general conversation ensued. The name of the King of Naples[6] being mentioned by somebody, M. de Labrador expressed himself unreservedly about him. I contented myself with saying, "What King of Naples is referred to? We do not know the man in question." Upon which M. de Humboldt remarked that the Powers had recognized him and guaranteed his States to him. I replied in a cold, firm tone: "Those who guaranteed them ought not to have done so, and consequently could not;" and then, in order not to prolong the effect which this speech had veritably and visibly produced, I added, "But this is not just now the question." Then, returning to that of the Congress, I said that the apprehended difficulties would perhaps be less than was supposed, and that a means of obviating them surely might be found. Prince Hardenberg stated that he did not give the preference to any one expedient over any other, but that one would be needed according to which the Princes of Layen and Lichtenstein[7] should not interfere in the general arrangements of Europe. Thereupon we adjourned until two days later, after it had been promised that copies of the draft of the proposed declaration and of Count Palmella's letter should be sent to me and to M. de Labrador. (The papers mentioned in the letter which I have the honor to write to your Majesty are appended to my official letter of to-day to the department.) After having received and reflected upon these, I thought that it would not do to wait for the next conference to make known my opinion. At first I drew up an answer in the form of a verbal note, but then, having reflected that the four Courts had had conferences between them, at which they had proposed protocols which they signed, I considered it was not fitting that between them and your Majesty's minister there should be only conversations of which no trace remained, and that an official note would be the most correct method of setting negotiation going. Accordingly, on the 1st of October I addressed to the five other Powers a signed note, to the effect that the eight Powers who had signed the treaty of May seemed to me, by that circumstance alone, and in the absence of a mediator, fully qualified to form a commission to prepare those questions which it would have to decide for the decision of the Congress, and to propose to it the formation of the committees expedient to be established, and the names of those who should be considered most suitable to form them, but that its competence ought not to extend any farther: that not being the Congress, but only a portion of the Congress, to attribute to themselves a power which could only belong to the entire Congress, would be a usurpation which I should find it very difficult, in case of my co-operating with it, to reconcile with my responsibility; that the difficulty which attended the meeting of the Congress was not of a nature to diminish with time, and that since it must be overcome once for all, there was nothing to gain by delaying; that no doubt the small States ought not to meddle with the general arrangements of Europe, but that they would not even wish to do so, and consequently could not give trouble; and that I was naturally led by all these considerations to desire that the eight Powers should address themselves without delay to the preliminary questions to be decided by the Congress, so that it might be promptly called together and those questions submitted to it.

After I had despatched this note, I set out for my private audience of the Emperor Alexander. M. de Nesselrode had come on his behalf to tell me that he wished to see me alone, and he had himself reminded me of this on the preceding evening, at a Court ball, where I had the honor of seeing him. On addressing me he took my hand, but his manner was not so affable as it usually is. He spoke in short sentences; his demeanor was grave, and even solemn. I saw plainly that he was playing a part. "First of all," said he, "what is the situation in your country?" "As good as your Majesty could desire, and better than could have been hoped." "And the spirit of the public?" "It improves every day." "Liberal ideas?"[2] "They prevail nowhere more than in France." "But the liberty of the Press?" "It has been re-established, with a few restrictions demanded by circumstances.[8] In two years those restrictions will be removed, and in the mean time they will not hinder the publication of anything that is good and useful." "And the army?"* "It is all for the King. One hundred and thirty thousand men are ready to take the field, and at the first summons three hundred thousand could join them." "The Marshals?" "Which of them, Sire?" "Oudinot." "He is devoted to the King." "Soult?" "He was rather sulky at first; but he has been given the government of La Vendée, and gets on admirably there. He has made himself both liked and respected." "And Ney?" "He frets about his endowments a good deal. Your Majesty might diminish his regrets." "The two Chambers? It seems to me there is opposition."[10] "As is always the case where there are deliberative assemblies; opinions may differ, but affections are unanimous; and in the difference of opinions that of the Government always has a large majority." "But there is no agreement." "Who can have told your Majesty such things? After twenty-five years of revolution, in a few months the King is as firmly established on his throne as if he had never left France; what more certain proof can be given that everything tends to the same end?" "Your own personal position?" "The confidence and the kindness of the King surpass my hopes."[11] "Now let us talk of our affairs: we must finish them here." "That depends on your Majesty. They will be promptly and happily terminated if your Majesty brings to bear on them the same nobility and greatness of soul as in the affairs of France." "But each must find what suits it here." "And what is right." "I shall keep what I hold." "Your Majesty would only wish to keep that which is legitimately yours." "I am in accord with the Great Powers." "I do not know whether your Majesty reckons France among those Powers." "Yes, certainly; but if you will not have each have its *convenances*, what do you propose?" "I place right first, and *les convenances* after." "The *convenances* of Europe are the right."[12] "This language, Sire, is not yours; it is foreign to you, and your heart disowns it." "No, I repeat it; *les convenances* of Europe are the right."[13] I turned towards the wall near which I was standing, leaned my head against the panelling, and exclaimed, "Europe, unhappy Europe!" Then turning once more to the Emperor, "Shall it be said," I asked him, "that you have destroyed it?" He answered me, "Rather war than that I should renounce what I hold." I let my arms drop in the attitude of one grieved indeed but resolute, and with the air of saying to him, "The fault is none of ours," I kept silence, which for some moments the Emperor did not break. Presently he said, "Yes, rather war." I remained in the selfsame attitude. Then, lifting up his arms, waving his hands as I had never seen him do previously, and in a manner which reminded me of the passage at the end of the "Éloge de Marc-Aurèle," he cried rather than said, "It is time for the play; I must go. I promised the Emperor; they are waiting for me." He then withdrew, but returned from the open door, put his two hands on my sides, gave me a squeeze, and said, in a voice quite unlike his own, "Adieu, adieu; we shall meet one another again." In all this conversation, of which I can only convey the most striking part to your Majesty, Poland and Saxony were never once named; they were only indicated in roundabout ways. Thus, when the Emperor said, meaning Saxony, "Those who have betrayed the cause of Europe," I was in a position to answer, "Sire, that is a question of date;"[14] and after a pause, I added, "And the effect of difficulties into which one may have been thrown by circumstances."

Once the Emperor spoke of "the allies," but I took up the phrase, just as I had done at the conference, and he set it down to habit.

Yesterday, which was to have been the day of the second conference, M. de Mercy was deputed by M. de Metternich to inform me that it would not take place. A friend of M. de Gentz called on him in the afternoon, and found him busy with some work which he said was urgent. I thought it was an answer to my note.

That evening, at Prince Trautmansdorff's, the plenipotentiaries reproached me with having addressed that note to them, and especially with having given it an official character by signing it. I replied that as they wrote and signed amongst themselves, I thought that I too must write and sign. I concluded from this that my note had embarrassed them not a little.

To-day Count Metternich wrote to me that there would be a conference at eight o'clock, and then sent me word that it could not take place because he had been summoned to attend the Emperor. Such, Sire, is the present situation of affairs.

Your Majesty sees that our position here is difficult; it may become more so every day. The Emperor Alexander gives full play to his ambition, which is fostered by M. de la Harpe and Prince Czartoryski; Prussia hopes for large increase; pusillanimous Austria has only a shamefaced ambition, but she is complaisant that she may get help; and these are not the only difficulties. There are others, springing from engagements which the hitherto allied Courts have entered into at a time when they did not expect to defeat him whose overthrow they have witnessed and when it was their purpose to make such a peace with him as would permit them to imitate him.

Now that your Majesty, being replaced upon the throne, has seated justice there once more, the Powers for whose advantage those engagements were made do not wish to renounce them, and those who probably regret having made them do not know how to get out of them. Your Majesty's ministers may have to encounter such obstacles that they shall have to abandon all hope except that of saving honor. But we have not come to that yet.

I am, etc.

NOTES TO LETTER III.

1. Prince Hardenberg was deaf, and M. de Talleyrand was lame.
2. The treaty by which France re-entered in 1814 her frontiers of 1790.
3. England, Russia, Austria, Prussia.
4. Chaumont, the principal town of Haute Marne, on the Marne. At Chaumont the treaty of the 1st of March, between Austria, Russia, Great Britain, and Prussia, was concluded.
5. Laon, chief place of the department of the Aisne, 150 kilomètres to the north-east of Paris. Napoleon was defeated under its walls, 9th and 10th March, 1814. The declaration of the Allied Powers after the rupture of the negotiations of Châtillon, bearing a solemn confirmation of the preceding treaties which intervened, was made from Vitry and Laon, and bore date 25th March, 1814.

During the "campaign of France" diplomatic conferences took place in these two towns.

6. Murat. See Appendix.
7. The principality of Layen (its chief place is Ahrenfel-on-the-Rhine) is one of the smallest in Germany. It was incorporated with the grand-duchy of Baden in 1815. The principality of Lichtenstein, situated between the Tyrol and Switzerland (its chief place is Vadaz), contains at the present time only eight thousand inhabitants.
8. The charter had promised freedom of the Press.
9. The Minister of War wrote to M. de Talleyrand (8th October): "The army is in a state of perfect submission, in every part of the kingdom; and most satisfactory and praiseworthy manifestations have been made by all the corps on the occasion of the journey of the princes."

At the same date, M. de Jaucourt wrote to M. de Talleyrand: "Yesterday I gave a great dinner to several generals—the Duke of Placentia, General Maison and his staff, etc., etc., and I am well enough pleased with them. To say that they have no regrets, and are in a completely good humor, would be too much, but they like the King, and they are all agreed that it is to the military condition of 1792, and not to that of Bonaparte, that we must return.

The military nobility of recent date is certainly jealous of the hereditary nobility."

10. "It is difficult to form an idea of the slovenliness and makeshift character of the administration. Every day affords some fresh proof of this."—D'Hauterive to M. de Talleyrand, 18th October, 1814.

11. "The King pronounced an eulogium on you, Prince, the day before yesterday. He praised your talent and your conduct at the Congress, and seemed to me to bring all the justice and eminent sagacity of his mind to bear on this subject."—Jaucourt to Talleyrand.

Later, he writes: "He (the King) seems convinced that if you do not succeed in all that he wishes, you will succeed in all that is necessary, just, and useful for France."

12. "It is to be hoped that in Europe force will no longer be transformed into law, and that equity, not expediency, will be made the rule."—Circular to the Ambassadors by M. de Talleyrand, 3rd October, 1814.

13. For the expression used here, "les convenances," there is no entirely exact equivalent in English.—TRANSLATOR.

14. Talleyrand thus discreetly reminded the Emperor Alexander I. that he also had betrayed the cause of the Kings in 1807 (Treaty of Tilsit).

LETTER IV.

Vienna, 9th October, 1814.

SIRE,

The ministers of the four Courts, embarrassed by my note of the 1st of October, and finding no argument with which to contest it, have taken the line of being offended. That note, said M. de Humboldt, is a firebrand flung into our midst; the object of it, said M. de Nesselrode, is to disunite us; it shall not be successful. While they openly avowed what it was easy to perceive, that they had formed a league to make themselves masters of everything, and constitute themselves supreme arbiters of Europe, Lord Castlereagh, speaking with more moderation and in a milder tone, told me it had been intended that the conference to which M. de Labrador and myself had been summoned should be entirely confidential, but that I had deprived it of that character by my note, and especially as it was a signed note. I replied that the fault was theirs, not mine; they had asked my opinion, and I was bound to give it, and if I had thought proper to give it in writing and signed, it was because I had observed that in their conferences between themselves they wrote and signed, and therefore I considered that I too ought to write and sign.

Meantime, the contents of my note having transpired, these gentlemen, in order to lessen its effect, have had recourse to the habitual ways of the Cabinet of Berlin; they have spread it abroad that the principles which I set forth are merely a decoy, that we are demanding the left bank of the Rhine, that we have designs upon Belgium, and that we want war. This has reached me from all sides, but I have given orders to all connected with the Legation to explain themselves to everybody with such frankness and simplicity, and in so positive a manner, that the authors of those absurd rumors will reap nothing from them except the shame of having disseminated them.

On the 3rd of October, in the evening, M. de Metternich, whom I met at the house of the Duchesse de Sagan,[1] handed to me a new draft of declaration drawn up by Lord Castlereagh. This second scheme did not differ from the first, except as it tended to represent the proposal of the four Courts as nothing more than a consequence of the first of the secret articles of the 30th of May. But neither was the principle from which it took its departure just (for Lord Castlereagh evidently lent to one of the provisions of the article a sense which it has not, and which we could not admit), nor, if it had been just, would the consequence which is drawn from it have been legitimate; the attempt was therefore doubly unfortunate.

I wrote to Lord Castlereagh. I gave my letter a confidential form; I strove to bring together all the reasons that militate against the proposed plan. (The copy of my letter is appended to the despatch which I forward to-day to the department). Your Majesty will see that I have taken particular care to make it evident, in the politest manner possible, that the motive for proposing the plan has not escaped me. I thought it right to declare that it was impossible for me to coalesce in anything which would be contrary to principles, because it was only by remaining steadily attached to them that we could resume the rank and consideration in the eyes of the nations of Europe, which, since the return of your Majesty, are ours of right, because to depart from them would be only to revive the Revolution, which had been one long oblivion of them.

I ascertained that Lord Castlereagh, when he received my letter, handed it to the Portuguese minister, who was with him, and that he acknowledged we were right in point of fact; but that it remained to be seen whether what we proposed was practicable. This was, in other words, asking whether the four Courts could dispense with arrogating to themselves a power over Europe which Europe had not given them.

That day we had a conference, at which only two or three of us were present at first, the other ministers arriving at intervals of a quarter of an hour. Lord Castlereagh had brought my letter, on purpose to communicate it to the conference; it was passed from hand to hand. M.M. de Metternich and Nesselrode merely glanced at it with the air of men who require only to look at a paper to lay hold of all its contents. I had been forewarned that I should be requested to withdraw my note; and in fact M. de Metternich did ask me to do so. I replied that I could not. M. de Labrador said it was too late, and would serve no purpose, because he had sent a copy of it to his Court. "Then we must answer you," said M. de Metternich to me. "If you will kindly do so," I replied. "I should," he resumed, "be of opinion that we ought to settle our affairs by ourselves, meaning by *us* the four Courts." I answered unhesitatingly, "If you take the question in that way, I am altogether your man; I am quite ready, and ask nothing better." "What do you mean?" said he. "This; it is very simple," I replied: "I shall take no more part in your conferences; I shall be nothing here but a member of the Congress, and I shall wait until it is opened." Instead of renewing his proposition, M. de Metternich reverted, by degrees and in circuitous ways, to general statements concerning the inconvenience which would attend the actual opening of the Congress. M. de Nesselrode said, without much reflection, that the Emperor Alexander wanted to leave Vienna on the 25th; to which I replied, in a tone of indifference, that I was sorry to hear it, as he would not see the end of the business. "How can the Congress be assembled," said M. de Metternich, "when nothing is ready to lay before it?" "Well, then," I replied, to show that I did not want to make difficulties, and was prepared to agree to anything that did not clash with the principles from which I could not depart, "since nothing is ready as yet for the opening of the Congress, and since you wish to adjourn, let it be put off for a fortnight or three weeks. I consent to that, but on two conditions: one is that you summon it for a fixed day; the other is that in the note of convocation you lay down the rule for admission to it."

I wrote out that rule on a sheet of paper, almost exactly as it is drawn up in the instructions given to us by your Majesty. The paper was passed from hand to hand, some questions were asked, a few objections were made, but no resolution was adopted, and, the ministers who had come in one after the other going away in like manner, the conference, so to speak, evaporated rather than ended.

Lord Castlereagh, who remained to the last, and with whom I walked downstairs, endeavored to bring me over to their way of thinking by giving me to understand that certain matters which were of special interest to my Court might be arranged to my satisfaction. I told him that the present question was not one of such and such particular objects, but of the law by which they were all to be regulated. "If," I said, "the thread be once broken, how shall we reunite it? We have to respond to the desire and demand of all Europe. What shall we have done for Europe if we have not re-established the rule of the maxims whose breach has wrought so much evil? The present epoch is one of those which hardly occur once in the course of several centuries. A fairer opportunity can never be offered to us. Why should we not place ourselves in a position to profit by it?" "Ah," he said, with some embarrassment, "there are difficulties of which you are not aware." "No, I am not aware of them," I answered, in a tone implying that I had no curiosity to learn them. We parted then, and I dined with Prince Windischgratz. M. de Gentz was there. We talked for a long time over the points that had been discussed in the conference at which he had been present. He seemed to regret that I had not arrived earlier at Vienna; and was pleased to think that things with which he professed to be discontented might have assumed a different complexion. Lastly, he acknowledged that in reality they all felt I was right, but that their *amour-propre* was concerned, and even the best intentioned among them felt it difficult to retreat from the position they had taken up.

Two days elapsed without a conference: a fête on one of them, and a hunting party on the other, were the causes of this.[2]

In the interim I was presented to the Duchess of Oldenburg. I expressed my regret that she had not accompanied her brother to Paris, and she answered that she hoped the journey thither was only delayed. Then she began at once to put questions to me, such as the Emperor had not put, about your Majesty, about public opinion, the finances, the army—questions which would have surprised me much, coming from a woman of twenty-two years old, even if they had not contrasted still more strongly with her bearing, her expression, and the tone of her voice. I replied to all in a sense conformable with the things which we have to do here, and the interests which we have to defend. She questioned me further about the King of Spain,[3] his brother,[4] and his uncle,[5] speaking of them in somewhat unbecoming terms, and I answered in a tone which I thought would give weight to my opinion of the personal merits of those princes.

M. de Gentz, who called on me just as I returned from my visit to the Duchess of Oldenburg, told me that he had been charged to draw up a plan for the convocation of the Congress. On the preceding day I had made one in conformity with that which I had proposed in the conference of the day before, and I had sent it to M. de Metternich, with a request that he would communicate it to the other ministers. M. de Gentz assured me that he had no knowledge of it; he told me that in his plan there was no question of the rule of admission which I had proposed, because M. de Metternich feared that by publishing it we should drive him who reigns at Naples to some extremity, his plenipotentiary being excluded by it.[6] M. de Gentz and I discussed this point; and he declared his conviction that what M. de Metternich feared would not happen.

I expected there would be a conference on the morrow, but three-fourths of the day having passed over without my hearing anything of it, I no longer reckoned on it, when I received a note from M. de Metternich, announcing that a conference would take place at eight o'clock, and that if I would come to him a little earlier, he would find means of *conversing with me on very important subjects.* (These are the exact terms of his note.) I was at his residence at seven o'clock, and was admitted at once. He spoke to me at first about a draft of a declaration which he had had drawn up, and which differed slightly, he said, from mine, but still approached very near to it, and with which he hoped I should be satisfied. I asked him for this draft, but he had it not.

"Probably," said I, "it is in circulation amongst the allies." "Do not talk of allies," he answered; "there are no longer any." "There are people here who ought to be allies in the sense of being of the same way of thinking, and desiring the same things without any concert between them. How can you possibly contemplate placing Russia like a girdle all round your principal and most important possessions, Hungary and Bohemia? How can you endure that the patrimony of an old and good neighbor, into whose family an archduchess has married,[7] should be handed over to your natural enemy? It is strange that it should be we who want to oppose this, and not you who do not wish it to be." He said then that I had no confidence in him. I replied that he had not given me much reason for having any, and reminded him of some circumstances in which he had not kept his word. "Besides," I added, "how am I to be inspired with confidence in a man who is all mystery towards those who are most disposed to make his affairs their own? As for me, I make no mysteries; I do not need them; that is the advantage of those who deal with principles only. Here," I continued, "are pen, ink, and paper; will you write that France asks nothing, and even that she will accept nothing? I am ready to sign." "But," said he, "there is the affair of Naples, that is properly yours." "Not mine," I answered, "more than everybody else's. For me it is only a matter of principle. I ask that he who has a right to be at Naples should be at Naples; that is all. Now, that is just what every one, as well as myself, ought to wish. Let principles be acted upon, and I shall be found easy to deal with in everything. I am going to tell you frankly to what I can consent, and to what I never will consent. I feel that in the present situation the King of Saxony may be obliged to make sacrifices. I suppose that, as he is a wise man, he will be disposed to make them; but if it be proposed to despoil him of all his States, and give the kingdom of Saxony to Prussia, I will never consent to that. Moreover, I will never consent that Luxembourg and Mayence shall be given to Prussia. Nor will I consent that Russia shall pass the Vistula, and have forty-four millions of subjects in Europe, and her frontiers on the Oder. But, if Luxembourg be given to Holland and Mayence to Bavaria, if the King and the kingdom of Saxony be maintained, and if Russia does not pass the Vistula, I shall have no objection to make about that part of Europe." M. de Metternich then took my hand, saying, "We are much less divided than you think; I promise you that Prussia shall have neither Luxembourg nor Mayence; we are no more anxious that Russia should be unreasonably aggrandized than you are, and as for Saxony, we will do all that in us lies to preserve at least a portion of it." It was only in order to find out how he was disposed on these various points that I had spoken thus. Then, returning to the convocation of the Congress, he dwelt on the necessity of not publishing at this moment the rule of admission that I had proposed; "because," he said, "it startles everybody, and embarrasses myself just now, seeing that Murat, finding his plenipotentiary excluded, will think his affair decided, and no one can tell what headstrong course he may take; he is prepared in Italy and we are not."

We were informed that the ministers were assembled, and we repaired to the conference. M. de Metternich opened the proceedings by announcing that he was going to read aloud two plans, one drafted by me, the other by himself. He then read them, mine first, his own afterwards. The Prussians declared themselves for that of M. de Metternich, on the ground that it prejudged nothing, and that mine prejudged a great deal. Count Nesselrode was of the same opinion. M. de Löwenhielm, the Swedish minister, who had not been present at the previous conference, said that nothing must be prejudged. This was also the opinion of Lord Castlereagh, and I knew it was that of M. de Metternich. His plan limited itself to adjourning the opening of the Congress to the 1st of November, and contained nothing more, which drew from the Portuguese minister the remark that a second declaration to convene the Congress would be necessary, and this was admitted. All that was done was, therefore, to adjourn the difficulty without solving it; but as the former pretences were abandoned, as it was no longer a question of having everything settled by the eight Powers, and leaving the Congress nothing but the privilege of approving; as nothing was now talked of except preparing the questions upon which the Congress would have to pronounce, by free and confidential communications with the ministers of the other Powers, I thought that an act of complaisance which would not impinge upon principles, might facilitate the progress of affairs; and I stated that I consented to the adoption of the scheme, but on the condition that at the place where it was said that the formal opening of the Congress was to be adjourned to the 1st of November, there should be added: "*And shall then be conducted in conformity with the principles of public law.*" At these words, a tumult of which it is difficult to form an idea arose. Prince Hardenberg, standing up, with his clenched hands on the table in an almost threatening attitude, and shouting, as those who are afflicted with deafness so often do, said, in stuttering agitation, "No, sir, 'public law' is a useless phrase. Why say that we shall act according to public law? That is a matter of course." I replied, "If it be a matter of course, it can do no harm to specify it."[8] M. Humboldt exclaimed, "What has public law to do here?" "This," I answered: "that it sends you here."

Lord Castlereagh, taking me aside, asked me whether, if this point should be settled according to my wishes, I would afterwards be more accommodating. I asked him in my turn what, if I were accommodating, I might hope he would do in the affair of Naples. He promised to second me with all his influence. "I will speak of it," said he, "to Metternich; I have a right to have an opinion upon this matter." "You give me your word of honor to that?" said I. He answered, "I do." "And I give you mine that I shall not be difficult, except where the principles which I could not abandon are concerned."[9] Meanwhile, M. de Gentz, having drawn near to M. de Metternich, represented to him that it was impossible to avoid the mention of public law in a document of the nature of the one in question. Count Metternich had previously proposed to put the matter to the vote, thus betraying the use which they would have made of the power that they had wanted to secure to themselves if their first plan had been accepted. They ended by consenting to the admission which I demanded; but there was an equally animated discussion concerning where it should be placed. At length it was agreed that it should come in a sentence earlier than that at which I proposed to insert it.[10] M. de Gentz could not refrain from saying at the conference, "This evening, Gentlemen, belongs to the history of the Congress. It is not I who shall narrate it, because my duty prohibits me from doing so, but it will certainly be told." He has said to me since that he had never seen anything like it. For this reason, I regard it as fortunate that I have been able, without departing from principles, to do something that may be considered as a step towards the meeting of the Congress.

M. de Löwenhielm is the Swedish minister in Russia, and very Russian. It is most probably for that reason that he has been sent here, for the Crown Prince of Sweden [11] wishes everything that the Russians wish.

The princes who formerly belonged to the Confederation of the Rhine are beginning to unite in pressing for the opening of the Congress;[12] they are already forming plans among themselves for the organization of Germany. I am, etc.

NOTES TO LETTER IV.

1. **Sagan is a Silesian principality.** The Emperor Ferdinand II. sold it in 1627 to the famous Wallenstein. In 1646 Prince Lubkowitz became the purchaser of it, and from his descendants Peter Biren, Duke of Courland, bought

it. At his death (1800) it passed to his eldest daughter, the Princess Catherine Wilhelmina, whose third husband was Count Charles Rodolph von Schulenburg. When she died, in 1839, the duchy passed into the hands of her sister, Pauline, Princess of Hohenzollern-Hechingen, who sold it to the third daughter of Peter Biren, Dorothea, Duchesse de Talleyrand. The Duchess died on the 19th of September, 1862, leaving her principality to her son, Prince Napoleon Louis de Talleyrand, Duc de Sagan and Valençay, born 12th March, 1812. The chief place of the principality is Sagan, on the Bober (9940 inhabitants). The château is large and handsome; it was built by Wallenstein, Lubkowitz, and Peter Biren.

2. A commission of persons belonging to the court had been appointed to render the stay of the foreign sovereigns at Vienna as pleasant as possible.

3. See Appendix.

4. See Appendix.

5. See Appendix.

6. His name was Campo-Chiaro; he was a former servant of Ferdinand I., and had joined Joseph Bonaparte first, and Murat afterwards. Murat had a *chargé d'affaires* at Paris, who was not recognized, and had no *official* relation with the King's Government.

7. See note concerning Prince Antoine.

8. This is an idiomatic passage, of which the above is the sense, but it is more neatly put in the original: "'Cela va sans dire.' 'Je lui répondais que si cela allait bien sans le dire, cela irait encore mieux en le disant.'"—TRANSLATOR.

9. See Appendix.

10. On the 12th of October Prince Talleyrand writes to the department: "We are held to have achieved a victory because we have had the expression 'public law' introduced. This will make you understand the spirit that animates the Congress."

11. Bernadotte. See Appendix.

12. The Confederation of the Rhine, created in 1806, and of which Napoleon I. had been the protector.

LETTER V.

FROM LOUIS XVIII. TO PRINCE TALLEYRAND.

No. 1.

October 13, 1814.

MY COUSIN,

I have received your despatch of the 25th September, and in the interest both of your eyes and my own hand, I borrow a hand which is not mine, but that of a person who is far from being a stranger to my affairs

'The Kings of Naples and of Saxony are my kinsmen in the same degree; justice makes equal demands in favor of both; but my interests in those demands cannot possibly be equal in each case. The kingdom of Naples, in the possession of a descendant of Louis XIV.,[1] adds to the power of France; but, remaining to an individual of the family of the Corsican, *flagitio addit damnum*.[2] I am no less shocked at the idea of that kingdom and Saxony being used as compensation. I need not set down here my reflections upon such a breach of all public morality, but what I must hasten to tell you is, that if I cannot prevent this iniquity, at least I will not sanction it, but that I shall, on the contrary, reserve to myself or to my successors liberty to redress it, if opportunity should arise.

I say this indeed only to push the hypothesis to the utmost; for I am far from despairing of the success of the cause, if England holds firmly by the principles which Lord Castlereagh professed when here, and if Austria abides by the same resolutions as Bavaria.

What M. de Schulenburg has told you of the determination of the King of Saxony is perfectly correct; that unfortunate prince has informed me of this himself.[3]

You may readily judge with what impatience I am expecting news of the Congress; its operations ought to have begun by this time. Upon which, etc.

NOTES TO LETTER V.

1. Since the Treaty of Vienna of 1735, to 1738.
2. Here the King uses the obsolete phrase "demeurant à."
3. For the King of Saxony's letter of the 19th of September, 1814, to Louis XVIII., see Appendix.

LETTER VI.

Vienna, 13th October, 1814.

SIRE,

I have forwarded the declaration, as published this morning, in my despatch to the department. It adjourns the opening of the Congress to the 1st of November; some changes have been made in it, but they are only changes of phrase, upon which the ministers agreed without meeting, and through the medium of M. de Gentz. We have had no conference since the 8th, and consequently none of those discussions with which I am afraid I must have wearied your Majesty in my two last letters.

The Prussian minister at London, old Jacobi-Kloest,[1] is here; he has been summoned to the aid of M. de Humboldt; he is one of the lions of Prussian diplomacy, and an old acquaintance of mine. He came to see me, and our conversation promptly took a direction which led me to speak of the great difficulties that were presenting themselves, and the greatest of which, according to him, was created by the Emperor Alexander, who wants to have the duchy of Warsaw. I said that if the Emperor Alexander wanted to have the duchy, he would probably present himself with a formal deed of surrender from the King of Saxony, and then we should see. "Why from the King of Saxony?" asked he in astonishment. "Because," I answered, "the duchy of Warsaw belongs to him in virtue of the cessions which you and Austria have made to him, and of treaties which you, Austria, and Russia have signed." Then he said, with the air of a man who has just made a discovery, to whom one has revealed something totally unexpected: "It is true, the duchy *does* belong to him!" M. de Jacobi, at all events, is not one of those who holds that sovereignty is lost and acquired by the fact of conquest alone.

I have reason to believe that we shall obtain Parma, Placentia, and Guastalla for the King of Etruria;[2] but in that case we must not think any more about Tuscany, although he might have rights to it; the Emperor of Austria has already given the Archduchess Marie Louise to understand that he had but slight hopes of keeping Parma for him.

It is frequently asked by people about me whether the treaty of the 11th of April is being carried out, and Lord Castlereagh has spoken to me directly about it.[3] The silence of the budget on this head has been remarked by the Emperor of Russia. Count Metternich says that Austria cannot be held bound to discharge the assignments on the *Mont de Milan*,[4] if France does not execute the clauses of the treaty that are binding on her; in short, this affair is constantly turning up under different forms, and almost always in a disagreeable manner. However unpleasant it may be to give one's mind to this kind of business, I cannot refrain from saying to your Majesty that it is desirable it should be attended to. A letter from M. de Jaucourt,[5] apprising me, by order of your Majesty, that something had been done, would certainly produce a good effect.

A very decided intention of removing Bonaparte from the island of Elba⁶ is manifesting itself. As yet no one has any settled idea of a place in which to put him. I have proposed one of the Azores; it is five hundred leagues from any coast. Lord Castlereagh seems inclined to think that the Portuguese might be induced to agree to such an arrangement; but when it comes to be discussed, the question of money will turn up again. Bonaparte's son⁷ is no longer treated as he was for a short time after his arrival at Vienna. There is less state and more simplicity. They have taken the grand cordon of the Legion of Honor from him, and substituted that of Saint Stephen.⁸

The Emperor Alexander talks, according to his custom, of nothing but liberal ideas. I do not know whether it is those ideas that have induced him to regard an expedition to Wagram, to contemplate the scene of their defeat, as a delicate manner of making himself agreeable to his hosts. It is a fact that he sent, by M. de Czernicheff, for certain officers, who, having been present at the battle, could inform him as to the positions and movements of the two armies, which he wished to study on the ground.⁹ The day before yesterday, the Archduke John asked where the Emperor was, and was answered, "At Wagram, your Highness." It seems that he is to go from hence to Pesth in a few days; he has asked for a ball there on the 9th, and means to appear at it in Hungarian costume. Either before or after the ball he will make a visit to his sister's tomb.¹⁰ A crowd of Greeks who have been informed beforehand, and will be eager to behold the only monarch who belongs to their rite,¹¹ are to be present at the ceremony. I do not know to what extent all this is pleasing to the Court here, but I should think it is not very agreeable.

Lord Stewart, brother of Lord Castlereagh, and Ambassador to the Court of Vienna, arrived here a few days ago. He was presented to the Emperor Alexander, who said to him what follows— he related it to me himself: "We are going to do a fine thing, a grand thing. We are going to raise up Poland again by giving it one of my brothers as its king,¹² or else the husband of my sister (the Duchess of Oldenburg)." Lord Stewart said, frankly, "I do not see independence for Poland in that, and I do not think that England, although less interested than the other Powers, can agree to such an arrangement."

Either I deceive myself greatly, or the union between the four Courts is more apparent than real,¹³ and depends solely on the fact that some of them do not choose to believe that we have the means to act, while the others do not believe that we have the will.

Those who know us to be against their pretensions think that we have nothing but reasoning to oppose to them. A few days ago the Emperor Alexander said, "Talleyrand *acts* the minister of Louis XIV. here;" and Humboldt, endeavoring to coax and at the same time to intimidate the Saxon minister, said, "The minister of France presents himself here with words which do not lack nobility, but either they conceal mental reservation, or there is nothing behind to sustain them; woe be to those who put faith in them." It would silence all this foolish talk and put an end to the present state of irresolution if your Majesty would, in a manifesto addressed to your people, after having made known to them the principles which your Majesty has commanded us to adhere to, and your firm resolution never to depart from them, allow it to be seen that the just cause would not be left without support. Such a declaration, as I conceive it, and as I shall presently submit a draft of it to your majesty, would not lead to war, for which nobody wishes, but it would bring those who have pretensions to moderate them, while it would give courage to others to defend their own interests and those of Europe. But as such a manifesto would be premature at this moment, I ask your Majesty's permission to recur to it hereafter if ulterior circumstances appear to me to demand it. Our language begins to make an impression. I greatly regret that an accident [14] which has happened to Count Munster has hitherto prevented his being with Lord Castlereagh, who has great need of support. From what we are told we may hope that he will be here in two days, and able to take part in affairs.
I am, etc.

NOTES TO LETTER VI.

1. Jacobi-Kloest, designated by the *Moniteur Universel* under the title of Minister of State, came to Vienna during the Congress. He was Ambassador to London, and occupied that post until 1817, when he was replaced by Baron Humboldt.

2. Louis II. (Charles Louis de Bourbon-Parma), son of Louis I. and Marie Louise de Bourbon of Spain, King of Etruria, succeeded his father on the 27th of May, 1803, and reigned until the 10th of December, 1807.

3. The Treaty of Fontainebleau.

4. See Appendix.

5. Arnail-François, Marquis de Jaucourt, born at Paris in 1757, died in 1852,

deputy to the Legislative Assembly in 1791, President of the Tribunate in 1802, senator in 1803, member of the Provisional Government on the fall of the Emperor Napoleon I. in 1814. He directed the department of Foreign Affairs during Prince Talleyrand's stay at Vienna, accompanied Louis XVIII. to Ghent, and was for a time Minister of Marine after the Hundred Days. He was a zealous Protestant. Hardly had he been installed in temporary command of the department than he wrote to Prince Talleyrand: "It is not, my dear friend, without some pain and timidity that I take my seat before that little table at which I have so often seen you seated, and at which that business which in your absence will be done in groping and uncertainty, was conducted with such superiority."

6. On the 8th of October, 1814, the Minister of War wrote to Prince Talleyrand: "The inhabitant of the island of Elba receives frequent posts from Naples and elsewhere. He rises several times at night, writes despatches, and seems very busy, although he talks ostentatiously of his tranquillity and his forgetfulness of affairs. It is really important that he should be placed at a distance from Italy, by consent of the Powers. No doubt there will be no war, but if it did recur, it is indisputable that Napoleon could collect Italian and even French deserters and disturb certain points of the Continent."

7. The King of Rome.

8. Saint Stephen, the first Christian and Catholic King of Hungary, Apostle of Hungary (997-1038). Pope Sylvester II. sent him a crown, which is still used at the coronation of the Kings of Hungary (Emperors of Austria). The Order of Saint Stephen was instituted by the Empress Marie Theresa.

9. It was not to Wagram, but to Aspern (Essling) that Alexander went. The *Moniteur* of the 23rd of October inserts the following among "faits divers" from Vienna of the date of the 11th: "The Emperor of Russia and the King of Prussia visited yesterday morning the environs of Aspern, where his Imperial Highness the Archduke Charles had the honor of showing the Emperor the field of the battle which was fought there on May 21st and 22nd, 1809."

10. The Grand-Duchess Paulowna.

11. "He (the Emperor Alexander) returned yesterday evening from his trip into Hungary with the Emperor of Austria and the King of Prussia. This journey, which was his own doing, was also made an occasion for scheming. He wanted to cajole the Hungarian nation, and to surround himself with the heads of the Greek clergy, which is very numerous in Hungary. We have it from Lord Castlereagh himself that the Greeks are already stirring up war with Turkey. The Servians have just taken up arms again."—Letter from Talleyrand to the department, 31st October, 1814.

12. The Grand-Duke Constantine, or the Grand-Duke Nicholas. The former died in 1831, after having been Viceroy of Poland; the other became Emperor of Russia in 1825. Here Talleyrand must be mistaken. Prince Peter Frederick George, married to the sister of the Emperor Alexander, died on the 27th of December, 1812; but he left a son, Constant Frederick Peter, born on the 26th of August, 1812, and who still survives: he received the title of "Highness" in Russia.

13. "It cannot escape us that the real difficulty of the Allied Powers at the Congress arises from the delusion which they cherished, in believing that they could settle the affairs of Europe upon bases which they commend to us as fixed, and which are not so."—Talleyrand to Jaucourt, 23rd November, 1814.

14. "The carriage of Count Munster, the Hanoverian Minister, was over-

turned on his way hither. Two of the Count's ribs are broken. This accident prevents the minister from taking part in the proceedings of the Congress."—*Moniteur Universel*, 24th October, 1814.

LETTER VII.

FROM THE KING TO PRINCE TALLEYRAND.

No. 2.

14th October, 1814.

My Cousin,

I have received your despatches of the 29th September and the 4th October. (It will be well, in future, to number them, as I do this one. Consequently, those whose receipt I acknowledge hereby ought to bear the numbers 2 and 3.)

I begin by telling you, with real satisfaction, that I am perfectly content with the attitude which you have taken up, and the language which you have held, both towards the plenipotentiaries, and in your trying conference with the Emperor of Russia. You know, of course, that he has summoned General Pozzo di Borgo.[1] God grant that his wise mind may bring his sovereign to more sensible views! But it is upon the contrary hypothesis that we must reason.

The object at which we ought to aim is to prevent the success of the ambitious projects of Russia and Prussia. Pozzo di Borgo might perhaps have been able to succeed unassisted, but he had means which will never be mine, therefore I need help. The petty States could not offer me any that would be sufficient—of themselves only, I mean; I must, then, have that of at least one Great Power. We should have Austria and England if they understood their own interests aright; but I fear that they are already bound. I am especially afraid of a policy which is advocated by many of the English, and with which the Duke of Wellington himself seems to be imbued; that of entirely separating the interests of Great Britain from those of Hanover. I cannot, then, employ force to make the right triumphant, but I can always refuse to be answerable for iniquity; we shall see whether they will venture to attack me for that.

What I am now saying refers to Poland and Saxony only, for as regards Naples I shall always stand by the complete answer which you have made to M. de Humboldt.

I put things at the worst, because I think that is the true way in which to reason; but I hope much from your skill and firmness.
On which, etc.

NOTE TO LETTER VII.

1. The Minister of War wrote to M. de Talleyrand on the 8th of October: "I am charmed that General Pozzo di Borgo has been summoned to Vienna; he knows us well, and does not wish us ill."

LETTER VIII.

No. 6.

Vienna, 17th October, 1814.

Sire,

I have received the letter with which your Majesty has deigned to honor me. I am happy to find that the line of conduct which I have followed is in accord with the indications that your Majesty has been pleased to convey to me. I shall take every care never to depart from it.

I have to give an account to your Majesty of the position of things since my last letter.

Lord Castlereagh, being anxious to make a fresh attempt to induce the Emperor Alexander to abandon his ideas on Poland, which disarrange everything and tend to upset everything, asked for an audience. The Emperor wanted to make a sort of mystery of it, and did him the honor of going to his house; then, knowing well on what subject Lord Castlereagh had to speak to him, he opened the matter himself, by complaining of the opposition with which his views were met. He did not understand, he never should understand, how France and England could be adverse to the restoration of the kingdom of Poland. Its re-establishment, he said, would be a reparation made to public morality, which the partition had outraged—a sort of expiation. In reality the point was not to restore Poland in its entirety, although there was nothing to prevent that being done some day, if Europe desired it; at present the thing would be premature, and the country itself needed to be prepared for it. There could be no better means of doing this than the erection of one part of Poland into a kingdom, to which should be given institutions calculated to implant and cultivate all the principles of civilization, which, when it should be thought right to unite the whole in one, would afterwards spread themselves over the entire country. The execution of his plan would entail no sacrifices on any but himself, since the new kingdom would be formed of only those portions of Poland over which conquest gave him indisputable rights, and to which he would also add those that he had acquired before the last war and since the last partition. Nobody had therefore any right to complain of his choosing to make those sacrifices; he would make them with pleasure, on principle, for conscience' sake, for the consolation of an unhappy nation, for the advance of civilization; to do this he held essential to his honor and his glory.

Lord Castlereagh, who had his arguments prepared, brought them all forward in a very long conversation, but he neither persuaded nor convinced the Emperor Alexander, who withdrew, leaving Lord Castlereagh very ill at ease respecting his intentions; but, as he did not consider himself beaten, he put his reasons in writing and presented them to the Emperor that same evening, under the title of a Memorandum.

After having given me the preceding details in a very long conversation, Lord Castlereagh asked me to read the document. I may here observe that M. de Metternich, when he knew this, betrayed surprise which he would not have shown, had it not been agreed between the ministers of the four Courts that what was done amongst them should not be communicated to others.

The Memorandum begins by quoting the articles of the treaties concluded by the Allies in 1813, which set forth that "*Poland shall remain divided between the three Powers in proportions which shall be agreed upon by their common consent, and without the interference of France.*" (Lord Castlereagh hastened to tell me that the France here alluded to was that of 1813, and not the France of to-day.) It then textually reports speeches made, promises and assurances given, by the Emperor Alexander at different times, in various places, and especially at Paris, and which are in opposition to the plan which he is now pursuing.

This is followed by a statement of the services rendered by England to the Emperor Alexander. In order to secure to him the tranquil possession of Finland, England began by making Norway pass under the yoke of Sweden; in this she sacrificed her own inclination, and perhaps even her interests. She then obtained for him, by her mediation, certain cessions and other advantages from the Ottoman Porte, and from Persia the surrender of a considerable territory. She therefore holds herself entitled to speak to the Emperor Alexander more plainly than the other Powers, who have not been in a position to render him similar services.

Passing on to an examination of the Emperor's present plan, Lord Castlereagh declares that the re-establishment of the whole of Poland as a completely independent State would obtain a general assent, but that to make a kingdom out of the fourth part of Poland would be to create discontent in the three other parts, and just apprehensions in those who possess any portion of it whatsoever, and who, from the moment there existed a kingdom of Poland, could no longer rely upon the fidelity of their subjects for an instant. Thus, instead of a focus of civilization, a focus of insurrection and disturbance would have been established, just when repose is the universal desire, as it is the universal need. While acknowledging that conquest has given rights to the Emperor, it maintains that the boundary of his rights is that point which cannot be passed without injury to the security of the Emperor's neighbors. It conjures him by all that he holds dear, by his humanity and his glory, not to desire to go beyond that point, and it concludes by indicating that he is all the more earnestly entreated to weigh the reflections submitted to him, because, in the case of his persisting in his views, England would be under the painful necessity of refusing her consent.

The Emperor Alexander has not yet replied. In proportion as Lord Castlereagh is sound on the subject of Poland, he is unsound on that of Saxony.[1] He talks only of treason, of the necessity for an example; principles do not appear to be his strong point. Count Munster, whose health is better, has endeavored to convince him that the balance, perhaps even the existence, of Germany depends on the preservation of Saxony; but he has at most only succeeded in inspiring him with doubts. Nevertheless he has promised me, not indeed to take the same line as ours on this question (he seems to have given some pledge to the Prussians which binds him in that respect), but to make friendly representations in our sense.

The step he has taken with regard to the Emperor Alexander was made not only with the knowledge, but also at the request of M. de Metternich. I cannot doubt, although neither one nor the other has told me so, that Austria is alive to the consequences of the Russian projects;[2] but not venturing to take the initiative herself, she has contrived to make England take it. If the Emperor Alexander persists, Austria, too much interested in not yielding, will not, I think, yield, but her timidity will lead her to let things drag on slowly. There are, however, dangers in such a course which daily become greater, and might become extreme. I am the more bound to call the attention of your Majesty to them, that their cause may be prolonged far beyond the present time, and in a manner to excite your solicitude during the whole of your Majesty's reign. The revolutionary ferment has spread all over Germany; Jacobinism is reigning there, not as it did five and twenty years ago in France, in the middle and lower classes, but among the highest and wealthiest nobility—the result of this difference is that if a revolution should break out there, its progress could not be calculated on the scale of the progress of ours. Those whom the dissolution of the Germanic Empire and the charter of the Confederation of the Rhine[3] have brought down from the rank of petty rulers to the condition of subjects, bear impatiently a state of things which turns personages whose equals they were, or believed themselves, into their masters, and they aspire to the reversal of conditions which hurt their pride, and to the replacement of all the governments of this country by one only. The men of the universities, and young men imbued with their theories, conspire with these malcontents, as do all those who attribute the calamities inflicted upon Germany by the many wars of which she is continually the theatre, to her division into petty States. The unity of the German land is their cry, their dogma; it is a religion carried to the height of fanaticism, and this fanaticism has infected even the reigning princes.[4] Now, that unity, from which France might have nothing to fear if she possessed the left bank of the Rhine and Belgium, would be of grave import to her at present; besides, who can foresee the consequences of the disturbance of a vast bulk like that of Germany, when its divided elements should come to be agitated and mixed? Who can say where the impulse, once given, might stop?

The situation of Germany, which is that a great part of the country does not know who is going to be its master, military occupations, with the hardships which are their ordinary accompaniment; fresh sacrifices demanded after so many previous sacrifices, present suffering, future uncertainty—all is favorable to subversive projects. It is too evident that if the Congress adjourns, if it delays, if it decides nothing, it will aggravate this state of things, and it is much to be feared that such an aggravation would bring about an explosion. The most pressing interest of the time being is that the labors of the Congress should be accelerated, and that it should come to an end, but how is it to finish? By yielding to what the

Russians and the Prussians want? Neither the safety of Europe, nor honor, would permit that. By opposing force to force? To do that, it would be necessary that Austria, who I believe has the desire to do it, should have the firmness of will. She has immense forces on a war footing, but she is afraid of risings in Italy and dares not commit herself backed only by Russia and Prussia. Bavaria[5] may be counted on; she has pronounced very decidedly, and has offered Austria fifty thousand men to defend Saxony. Würtemberg would furnish her with ten thousand; other German States would join her. But this is not sufficient security; she would like to be able to count upon our co-operation, and does not believe that she can count upon it.

The Prussians have spread a report that your Majesty's ministers have received double instructions, one set prescribing the language which they are to hold, and the other directing them to promise nothing. M. de Metternich had Marshal Wrede informed that he believed this to be the case. A person intimately in his confidence said, a few days ago, to M. de Dalberg:[6] " Your Legation talks very cleverly, but you do not want to act, and as for us, we do not want to act alone." Your Majesty will readily believe that I do not like war, or wish for it any more than your Majesty does, but in my opinion it would suffice to hint at it, and we should not require to make it; in my opinion also the fear of war ought not to prevail over the fear of a greater evil which may be preventable only by war. I do not think that Russia and Prussia would like to run the chances of a war with Austria, France, Sardinia, Bavaria, and a good part of Germany, or if they would run that risk, so much the less would they be likely to retreat before Austria only, supposing that she were to enter upon the contest single-handed, which is inconceivable. Thus Austria, deprived of our support, would have no other resource except to prolong the Congress indefinitely, or to dissolve it, thereby opening the door to revolution; or to yield, and consent to things which your Majesty is resolved never to sanction.

In the latter case it would remain only for your Majesty's ministers to retire from the Congress, relinquishing the effort to obtain any portion of that which your Majesty most desires. Nevertheless, the state of things that would be established in Europe might, in a very few years, render inevitable the war which it was sought to avoid, and we might then find ourselves in a more disadvantageous position for making war. I believe it not only possible, but probable, that if the answer of the Emperor of Russia destroys all hope of his yielding to persuasion, Prince Metternich will ask me whether, and to what extent, Austria may count upon our co-operation. The instructions which have been given us by your Majesty point out that the domination of Russia over the whole of Poland would threaten Europe with so great a danger, that if it were to be avoided by force of arms only, there must not be a moment's hesitation in taking them up. This would seem to authorize me to make a general promise of the assistance of your Majesty in such a case, but to reply in a positive manner to a precise demand, and to promise defined support, require an authorization and special instructions. I venture to entreat your Majesty to be pleased to give me these, and to be convinced that I will not make use of them except in the event of an evident and extreme necessity; but I still believe that the case for which I am preparing will not arise. However, that I may be ready for everything, I would wish that your Majesty should deign to honor me with your commands as promptly as possible. The ministers of the eight Powers have not met since the declaration which I have had the honor of sending to your Majesty. A committee composed of the Austrian minister, the Prussian minister, and the ministers of Bavaria, Würtemberg, and Hanover are occupied with the federal constitution of Germany. They have already held a conference, but it is doubtful whether, considering the interests of those whom they represent, and their own individual characters, they will succeed in coming to an agreement.

I am, etc.

NOTES TO LETTER VIII.

1. The policy of the Powers arises from the fright in which they still are. . . . The English policy comes out very clearly here. . . . Still, alarmed by the effect which the Continental policy has produced upon England, the English ministers want to place Powers sufficiently strong in the North, and on the Baltic, to prevent France from interfering at any time with English trade with the interior of the Continent. For this reason they lend themselves to all that Prussia demands."—Letter from the French plenipotentiary to the department, 30th October, 1814.

On the 3rd of January, 1815, M. de Talleyrand wrote to Jaucourt: "The English embassy at the Congress, which in the beginning had adopted a policy by no means acceptable to us, has changed entirely, and is now proceeding in harmony with our views."

2. "Prince Metternich, although in general guided by a timid and uncertain policy, is, however, sufficiently alive to the opinion of his country and the interest of his monarchy, to feel that the Austrian States, hemmed in by Russia, Prussia, and a Poland entirely in the hands of the former, would be

constantly menaced, and that France only can aid them in this difficulty."—Letter to the department, 16th October, 1814.

3. In 1806.

4. See Appendix.

5. Count Alexis de Noailles reported the following words as spoken by the King of Bavaria in an audience granted to him on the 9th of the following November: "I have learned that the proceedings of the French envoys in every respect have been closely watched here; everything that they have done has been observed, and it has been discovered with much surprise that they avoid all secret manœuvres, have not expended any money at all, and that their conduct is stainless and free from intrigue. I have made a protest respecting the affairs of Saxony. *I am with you.* I will not separate myself from your policy" M. de Noailles adds, "Do you wish to know what is privately said? It is that his loyalty and his principles may be counted on, but it is thought that he (the King of Bavaria) will not be master of the army, and that after the negotiations he will be forced into war by the clamor of generals greedy for conquest."

6. "And this has been confirmed by a man attached to Prince Metternich, who, in explaining himself to the Duke of Dalberg, said to him, 'You appear to us to be dogs, who bark very loud, but you do not bite and we do not want to bite unassisted.' "—Letter from the French plenipotentiary to the department, 16th October, 1815.

LETTER IX.

Vienna, 19th October, 1814.

SIRE,

M. de Labrador has been reproached, by the ministers of the four Courts, for having been of the same opinion as myself in the conference to which we were both summoned, and also perhaps because he has come pretty often to my house, where Lord Castlereagh found him on one occasion. He has been called a turn-coat, a man who separates himself from those to whom Spain owed its deliverance, and it is worthy of remark that M. de Metternich has taken up this point most warmly. M. de Labrador has not changed his opinion for all that, but he has thought it necessary to visit me less frequently. We may judge by this how far ministers who are, from position or personal character, less independent, are, or believe themselves, free to have constant relations with your Majesty's Legation.[1] The five ministers who met to prepare a draft of a federal constitution, have been required to give their word of honor that they will not communicate to any one the proposals which may be made to them. This precaution, quite a useless one, is especially directed against the French Legation. The plan is now to isolate it, as it has been found impossible to make it accept the *rôle* proposed to it in the negotiations. One ray of light has, however, pierced the darkness in which it was sought to shroud the Legation, and which, as time advances, they would fain deepen. It may be that we have got hold of the clue which will enable us to penetrate into the labyrinth of intrigue in which it was hoped we should lose our way. The following facts I have learned from a man whose position affords him an opportunity of acquiring accurate information.

The four Courts have never ceased to be allied in this sense, that the feelings with which they made war have survived that war, and that they carry into the arrangements of Europe the spirit with which they fought. Their intention was to make those arrangements themselves entirely; but they felt that to ensure their being regarded as legitimate, it was necessary to invest them with an apparent sanction. That is why the Congress was convened. They would have wished to exclude France from it, but they could not do so after the happy change which had taken place in France, and for that reason this change has vexed them. Nevertheless, they flattered themselves that France, having been for so long fully occupied by her internal difficulties, would only formally intervene at the Congress. Seeing that she presented herself there with principles which they could not contest, and did not want to follow, they have adopted the course of setting her aside practically, without excluding her, and keeping everything in their own hands, so that they may proceed to carry out their plan unopposed. This plan is, at bottom, no other than that of England.[2] It is she who is the soul of it all. Her indifference to principles ought not to surprise us; her principles are her interests. Her object is simple; she wants to preserve her naval supremacy, and, with that supremacy, the commerce of the world. To do this it is necessary for her that the French navy should never become formidable, either in itself or in combination with others. She has already taken care to isolate France from the other naval Powers, by the engagements into which she has induced them to enter. The restoration of the House of Bourbon having led her to apprehend a renewal of the family compact, she hastened to conclude with Spain the treaty of the 5th of July, which provides that the compact shall never be renewed. She has now to place France, as a continental power, in a position which will permit her to devote only a small portion of her forces to the naval service, and with this in view, she wants to unite Prussia and

Austria closely, by rendering the latter so strong that it would be possible to place them both in opposition to France. It was in pursuance of this design that Lord Stewart was sent to Vienna. He is entirely Prussian; hence the selection of him as ambassador. They will endeavor to place a man allied to Austria by inclination at Berlin, and the purpose of strengthening Prussia could not be better served than by giving Saxony to her. England, therefore, would have Saxony sacrificed and given to Prussia. Lord Castlereagh and Mr. Cook are so determined on this question that they venture to assert that the sacrifice of Saxony without any abdication, without any cession on the part of the King, does not violate any principle. Naturally, Austria ought to reject such a doctrine: justice, propriety, even safety, require her to do so. How has her resistance been overcome? The explanation is very simple; she has been placed face to face with two difficulties, and assisted to surmount the one on condition that she yields to the other. The Emperor of Russia comes in, in the very nick of time, with his desire to have the whole of the duchy of Warsaw, and to erect a phantom kingdom of Poland. Lord Castlereagh opposes this.[3] He is drawing up a Memorandum which he will present to Parliament, to make believe that he has had so much trouble in arranging the affairs of Poland that no blame can be imputed to him for not having saved Saxony; and, as the reward of his efforts, he is pressing Austria to consent to the disappearance of that kingdom. Who can say whether the desire to form a phantom Poland has not been suggested to the Emperor Alexander by the very persons who are opposing it, or if that desire is sincere? Who knows but that the Emperor, in order to please the Poles, has made them promises which he would be very sorry to keep? In that case, the resistance with which he meets is precisely what he most desires, while a consent to what he appears to wish would place him in the greatest difficulty. Meanwhile M. de Metternich, who piques himself on being the motive power of the whole thing, is himself set in motion without knowing it, and, being the mere tool of the intrigues of which he believes himself the leader, allows himself to be deceived like a child.[4] Without affirming that all this information is perfectly exact, I may say that it appears to me extremely probable. A few days ago, a certain number of persons whom M. de Metternich is in the habit of consulting, met at his house; they were all of opinion that Saxony ought not to be abandoned. Nothing was settled, and the day before yesterday I learnt, in the evening, from a trustworthy source, that M. de Metternich personally relinquished Saxony, but that the Emperor of Austria still held out. A member of the Commission for the drawing up of the Federal Constitution says that the proposals which were made to them implied that Saxony was no longer to exist.

The whole of yesterday was devoted to two *fêtes :* one was military, and commemorative of the battle of Leipsic; the other was given by Prince Metternich in honor of the peace. At the former your Majesty's Legation could not be present, but at the latter I hoped to find an opportunity of saying a word to the Emperor of Austria. I was not so fortunate as to succeed in this. I had been more so at the preceding ball, where I laid before him certain reflections upon the circumstances calculated to produce some effect upon his mind. He then appeared to understand me very well. Lord Castlereagh talked to him for nearly twenty minutes, and I learned that Saxony was the subject of the conversation. An arrangement by which Saxony should be given to Prussia would be regarded in Austria, even by the members of the Cabinet, as a misfortune for the Austrian monarchy, and by Germany at large as a calamity.[5] It would be held there to be a certain indication that Germany itself is destined to be partitioned, sooner or later, as Poland has been. Yesterday the King of Bavaria commanded his minister to make fresh efforts for Saxony, and he said, " This project is grossly unjust, and it deprives me of all repose." If Austria wants to maintain Saxony it is probable that she will, at all events, wish to make sure of our co-operation, and it is that I may be ready to answer any demand of that nature that I have entreated your Majesty to honor me with your commands. Still, as I have had the honor to tell your Majesty, I hold it for certain that Russia and Prussia will not enter into the contest. If Austria yields without having asked our co-operation, it will be because she has decided that she will not save Saxony. In that case she would indeed deprive your Majesty of all hope of preserving that kingdom, but she could not deprive you of the glory of defending principles on which rests the security of every throne. After all, so long as Austria shall not have finally yielded, I will not despair, and I believe I have even found means, if not of preventing the sacrifice of Saxony, at least of embarrassing those who would sacrifice her. It is to make it known to the Emperor of Russia that we do not oppose his possession of, under whatever denomination, that portion of Poland which shall be awarded to him, provided that he does not extend his frontiers so as to disturb his neighbors, and provided also that Saxony be maintained.

If the Emperor does not really wish to make a Kingdom of Poland, and if he be only seeking for an excuse to offer to the Poles, this declaration will embarrass him. He cannot tell the Poles, and they cannot think, that it is France who opposes the accomplishment of their dearest wish. Lord Castlereagh will on his side find it difficult to explain to the English Parliament how, when France was not against it, he came to oppose a thing which many persons in England desired.⁶ If the Emperor Alexander really abides by the idea of this kingdom of Poland, the consent of France will be a reason for his persisting in it. Austria, thus thrown back into the difficulty from which she thought to extricate herself by the abandonment of Saxony, will be obliged to rescind that abandonment, and will be brought back to us. In no case can such a declaration do us harm. What concerns us is that Russia should have as little of Poland as possible, and that Saxony should be saved. It concerns us less, or does not concern us at all, that in one way or another Russia should possess that which ought to be hers; that is the affair of Austria. Now when she sacrifices needlessly what she knows is of interest to us, and which ought to be of greater interest to herself, why should we hesitate to replace her in the position from which she wanted to extricate herself, especially when it depends upon her to put an end to her own embarrassment and also to ours, and in order to do so she has only to join us? I am informed that the Emperor Alexander has, within the last few days, repeatedly expressed an intention of summoning me; if he does so I shall have recourse to the expedient which I have had the honor to explain to your Majesty. General Pozzo, who has been here for some days, speaks of France in a most becoming manner. The Elector of Hanover, being no longer able to preserve that title, since there is to be neither a Germanic Empire nor an elective Emperor, and not choosing to be of inferior rank to the sovereign of Würtemberg, having once been a much greater personage, has taken the title of King. Count Munster, who is almost recovered from his fall, has notified the fact to me. I await the authorization which your Majesty will no doubt think proper to give me, to reply to him and recognize the new titles which his Master has assumed.

         I am, etc.

NOTES TO LETTER IX.

1. "The King of Bavaria had asked M. de Labrador whether he sometimes saw Prince Talleyrand, and the Spanish ambassador had replied in the affirmative. 'I should like to see him also,' said the King, 'but I dare not.'"—Talleyrand to Jaucourt, 28th October, 1814.

2. "I found Lord Castlereagh but indifferently informed respecting the continental situation, very upright, totally free from all bias and every kind of prejudice, as just as he was kindly. I was speedily convinced that his ideas upon the subject of the reconstitution of France in a sense conformable with the general interests of Europe did not differ from my own in any point."—"Mémoires du Prince de Metternich, tom. 1. p. 181."

3. In his letter on Poland Lord Castlereagh reminded the Emperor of Russia of the assistance which he had received from England, and said to him, "I do not hesitate to impart to your Majesty my private conviction that it will exclusively depend upon the spirit in which your Majesty shall treat the question directly connected with your own Empire, whether the present Congress is to insure the welfare of the world, or merely to present a scene of disorder and intrigue, an ignoble contest for power at the expense of principles. The place which your Majesty occupies in Europe gives you the means of doing everything for the general good, if your Majesty's intervention is founded upon principles of justice to which Europe may do homage, but if your Majesty ceased to set store by public opinion . . . I should despair of the possibility of a just and stable order of things in Europe. And I should have the mortification of seeing your Majesty for the first time regarded by those whom you have delivered, as the object of their dread, after having been that of their hope and confidence."

The Emperor Alexander answers Lord Castlereagh on the 30th October, 1814:

". . . I go on to the clause in which you remind me of events the memory of which I shall never lose, that is to say, of the frank and cordial assistance that I received from England when I was contending against the whole Continent, led by Napoleon. It is always a mistake to remind an obliged person of services rendered. If I had thought that your remarks had such an intention, or were meant to convey the unjust suspicion that I did not sufficiently appreciate the lofty character of the English nation, and the friendly and enlightened policy of the British Cabinet during the course of the war, I should not have replied to them."

4. "M. de Metternich's blindness in continuing to second the designs of the three Powers is singular: he is making it easy for Russia to lay hold of the duchy of Warsaw, for Prussia to occupy Saxony, and for England to exercise the most absolute power over what was called, and may still be called, the coalition. This state of things produces a strange effect; the Austrian monarchy draws near to us in all that concerns it, while the ministry, in all that concerns them, keep aloof."—Talleyrand to the department, 20th October, 1814.

5. The reigning Duke of Saxe-Coburg-Saalfeld wrote to Lord Castlereagh:

"You have told me that in point of right the affair of the King of Saxony is settled, and that there is nothing to be hoped for, except clemency. I confess to your Excellency that I am at a loss to understand how as a matter *of right* the matter could be decided against the King of Saxony. How, in fact, can he have lost his States? By conquest? By surrender? By sentence? By conquest? You do not think so, my lord. England has never believed that the King had lost the sovereignty of Hanover because Bonaparte conquered that country. Bonaparte himself, who desired to transform conquest into sovereignty, was ready to protect such an abuse when, as an act of reprisal, you ceded Guadaloupe to Sweden. By surrender? The King has not ceded and never will cede his rights. By sentence? Is the King to be judged without being heard? And who shall judge him? His oppressors? Those who want to enrich themselves with his spoils? Shall it be the nation? The nation claims him. *Shall it be Germany? All the States of which Germany is composed, with one single exception, look upon Germany as lost if Saxony be destroyed.*

"Are the interests of Germany to be consulted? Doubtless it will not be supposed that all the States which compose it are so blind to their own interest as to mistake between what may save and what may ruin Germany, and I have alredy told you, my lord, they all regard the loss of Saxony as the sentence of their own ruin."

6. See Lord Donoughmore's motion in the House of Lords, 1st December, 1814, and the same proposal in the House of Commons during the sitting of that day.

LETTER X.

THE KING TO PRINCE TALLEYRAND.

No. 3.

Paris, 21st October, 1814.

MY COUSIN,

I have received your Nos. 4 and 5. The most certain proof that your note of the 1st of October was good is, that it has displeased the plenipotentiaries of the formerly allied Courts, and that at the same time it has forced them to retrace their steps. But we must not let ourselves sleep on this success.[1] The existence of the league, of which you tell me in No. 4, is made clear to me, and especially the design of revenging upon France *ut sic* the humiliations which the Directory, and still more Bonaparte, have inflicted upon Europe.[2] I shall never allow myself to be reduced to submitting to this; therefore I strongly adopt the idea of the declaration, and desire that you send me the draft at once. But this is not all. We must prove that *there is something behind*, and for that it seems to me necessary to make preparations for placing the army, at need, upon a more considerable footing than the present.[3] I shall get M. de Jaucourt to write the letter which you desire at once, but, between ourselves, I shall go beyond the stipulations of the 11th of April if the excellent idea of one of the Azores be carried out. I shall be very glad if Parma, Placentia, and Guastalla are restored to the young prince; they are his patrimony. Tuscany was a possession not very justly acquired. The unfortunate Gustavus IV. announces to me his intention of coming here very shortly. If this be spoken of at Vienna, you may boldly affirm that the journey conceals no political speculation, but that my door shall never be shut to him who opened his to me. I cannot conclude this letter without renewing the expression of my satisfaction with your conduct.

Upon which, etc.

NOTES TO LETTER X.

1. In the manuscript, the following passage, struck out by a line, may still be read:
"Of the four Cabinets, I find three bent on aggrandizing, or at least on maintaining themselves at the expense of their neighbors; but what I observe in all is a design of enmity and vengeance."

2. On the 12th of June, 1799, Sandoz Rollin, the Prussian ambassador to Paris, wrote to his Court: "Talleyrand appears content and settled in his place since the arrival of Siéyès; at least, so I judge from his countenance and his conversation. 'You shall be satisfied,' he said to me the day before yesterday; 'in the space of six weeks we shall have a system of foreign policy which will, I hope, procure us allies. It will no longer be a question of hitting Europe blows that afterwards recoil upon France.'"

3. "Count Dupont laid before the Council yesterday a scheme for placing the whole effective strength of the army on a peace footing, and passed in review the men who are discharged, but liable to be recalled under arms."— Jaucourt to Talleyrand, 29th October, 1814.

It was proposed to remove Napoleon I. from Elba to the Azores. On the 27th of September, 1814, Jaucourt replied to anxious inquiries from Talleyrand: "Stories of all sorts are told about the interview between Napoleon and a lady and a young child at the island of Elba. The fact is that Madame Walewska has been there, and remained a few hours. The Minister of War persists in believing that there is a garrison of from three to four thousand men in the island. I have details here, and they all agree that from six to eight hundred men, and about as many more Corsicans and others, picked up here and there, form the guard. Count Dupont is informed of this by an officer who has just come from that country." Chateaubriand, writing to Talleyrand at Vienna, gave him the same information and similar advice. On the 12th of October, 1814, Talleyrand wrote to Jaucourt: "M. Mariotti (consul at Leghorn) has done well to refuse passports to the merchants who asked him for them for the island of Elba; he always ought to be exceedingly circumspect about this kind of passport."

LETTER XI.

No. 8.

Vienna, 25th October, 1814.

SIRE,

I was very happy to receive the letter with which your Majesty deigned to honor me, bearing date the 11th of October. It has sustained and consoled me. Your Majesty may judge how much need I have of support and consolation by the account which I am about to give your Majesty of an interview which I had with the Emperor Alexander, two hours before the arrival of the post. As I have had the honor to write to your Majesty, I had been informed that the Emperor had repeatedly expressed his intention of seeing me. This information having been given me by three persons who have constant access to him, I believed that it was conveyed by his orders, while I understood that he wished me to request an audience. He had not answered Lord Castlereagh, but had instead caused it to be notified to Austria that he was about to withdraw his troops from Saxony, and to hand over the administration of that country to Prussia. The rumor was current that Austria had consented to this, although with regret; the report of this consent was accredited by the Prussians; and, lastly, the Emperor Alexander was on the point of starting for Hungary. All these reasons made me decide upon asking for an audience, and I was informed that the Emperor would receive me at six the day before yesterday. Four days ago Prince Adam Czartoryski, to whom Poland constitutes the whole world, having come to visit me, and excusing himself for not having come before, acknowledged that he had been especially prevented from doing so by hearing that I was very ill disposed on the Polish question. "I am better disposed than anybody else," said I; "we wish Poland to be complete and independent." "That would be a fine thing," he replied, "but it is a chimera; the Powers will never consent to it." "Then," said I, "Poland is no longer our principal affair in the north. The preservation of Saxony concerns us much more. We are in the first rank on this question;[1] we are only in the second on that of Poland. When it becomes a question of boundaries, it is for Austria and Prussia to secure their frontiers. We desire that they should be satisfied on that point, but only let us be easy about your neighborhood, and we shall place no obstacle to the Emperor of Russia giving any form of government he pleases to the country which shall be ceded to him: for which readiness on our part I demand the maintenance of the Kingdom of Saxony." This communication was so pleasing to Prince Adam, that he went straight from my house to the Emperor, with whom he had a conversation of three hours' length; and the result was that Count Nesselrode, whom I had never seen at my own house since just after my arrival, called upon me the next day in the evening, to obtain an explanation, which I gave him, without however making any advance on what I had said to Prince Adam. I restricted myself to impressing upon him that the preservation of the kingdom of Saxony was a point from which it was impossible your Majesty could ever depart.

The Emperor thus knowing beforehand to what extent he might and might not hope that I would bend to his views, I was placed at the advantage of being enabled to discern his disposition by his manner of accosting me, and to judge whether his object in the interview which he granted me was to propose means of conciliation or to notify his own will. He accosted me with some embarrassment. I expressed my regret at having seen him only once. "He had been pleased," I said to him, "not to accustom me to a deprivation of that nature when I formerly had the happiness of finding myself in the same places with him." His answer was that he should always be pleased to see me, and that it was my own fault if I had not seen him; why did I not come? He added this singular sentence, "I am a public man; I am always to be seen." It is to be remarked that his own ministers and those of his servants whom he likes the best are often unable for several days to approach him. Then said he, "Let us speak of affairs." I will not fatigue your Majesty with idle details of a conversation which lasted an hour and a half. I am the less afraid to limit myself to the essential, as whatever pains I may take to abridge what I have to report as proceeding from the mouth of the Emperor of Russia, your Majesty will probably still hold it to be beyond all belief.

"At Paris," said he, "you had a mind to a kingdom of Poland, how is it that you have changed?" "My mind, Sire, is still the same. At Paris the question was of the restoration of the whole of Poland; we wished then, as we wish now, for its independence. But the present is quite another matter; the question is subordinate to a settling of boundaries which places Austria and Prussia in safety." "They need not be alarmed. Besides, I have two hundred thousand men in the duchy of Warsaw; let them put me out of that. I have given Saxony to Prussia; Austria consents." "I do not know," I replied, "whether Austria does consent; I should find it difficult to believe that she does—it would be so much against her interest. But can the consent of Austria render Prussia the proprietor of that which belongs to the King of Saxony?" "If the King of Saxony does not abdicate he shall be taken to Russia. He will die there; another has already died there."[2] "Your Majesty will permit me not to believe that; the Congress has not been called together to witness such an outrage." "How, an outrage? Why did Stanislas go to Russia? why should the King of Saxony not go to Russia? The case of the one is the case of the other; I see no difference." I had only too much to say in answer; but I confess to your Majesty that I did not know how to control my indignation. The Emperor spoke rapidly; one of his sentences was the following: "I thought that France owed me something. You are always talking of principles. Your public law is nothing to me; I do not know what it is. What do you suppose I care for all your parchments and all your treaties?" (I had reminded him of the treaty by which the Allies agreed that the grand-duchy of Warsaw should be divided between the three Courts.) "There is one thing which is important above all to me; that is my word. I have given my word and I will keep it. I promised Saxony to the King of Prussia at the moment when we met again." "Your Majesty promised the King of Prussia from nine to ten millions of souls; your Majesty can give them to him without destroying Saxony." (I had a table of the districts which might be given to Prussia, and which, without ruining Saxony, would form the number of subjects stipulated by the treaties. The Emperor took and has kept it.) "The King of Saxony is a traitor." "Sire, the qualification of traitor can never be given to a king, and it is of importance that it never should be given to one." I may have laid some emphasis on the latter portion of my sentence. After a brief silence, "The King of Prussia," said he, "shall be King of Prussia and of Saxony, as I shall be Emperor of Russia and King of Poland. The compliance of France with me on these two points shall be the measure of mine on all that may interest her." During the course of this conversation, the Emperor did not give way to restlessness and gesticulation, as he had done at my first interview with him; he was imperious, and his manner plainly showed irritation. After having said that he would see me again, he went away to a private ball at the Court. I followed him, having had the honor to be invited.

I found Lord Castlereagh there, and I was beginning to talk to him, when the Emperor Alexander, observing us in the embrasure of a window, called him, and then took him into another room and spoke with him for twenty minutes. Lord Castlereagh came back to me afterwards, and told me that he was very ill satisfied with what had been said to him.

I cannot doubt that Lord Castlereagh has either prescribed to himself, or received an order from his Court, to pursue the plan of which I had the honor to inform your Majesty in my letter of the 19th of this month. That plan consists of isolating France, reducing her to her own unaided strength, by depriving her of alliances and preventing her from having a powerful navy. Thus, while your Majesty brings to the Congress no purposes but those of justice and good will, England is actuated by a spirit of jealousy and interested selfishness; but Lord Castlereagh finds unforeseen difficulties cropping up in the way of his plan. As he would like to escape the reproach of having left Europe a prey to Russia, he wants to detach from her those Powers which he desires to place in opposition to France; and his main object is that Prussia shall become, like Holland, an entirely English Power, which England may, by subsidizing, manage according to her pleasure. As it suits this view that Prussia should be strong, he desires to aggrandize her, and to have all the merit of it in her eyes. But the zeal of the Emperor Alexander in the interests of the King of Prussia will not allow of this. The object for which Lord Castlereagh is striving is, if possible, to unite Prussia and Austria, and the kind of aggrandizement which he wants to procure for Prussia is precisely an obstacle to that union. He wants to break the ties which exist between the King of Prussia and the Emperor Alexander, and he endeavors to form others, which are rejected by habit, by remembrances, by a rivalry which is suspended but not extinct, and which a number of interests will inevitably revive. Besides, before Prussia and Austria can be united, the interests of the latter monarchy must be secured, and its safety provided for; and Lord Castlereagh finds the claims of Russia an obstacle to the accomplishment of those ends. Thus the problem which he has proposed to himself, and which I hope he will not succeed in solving in a sense injurious to France, at least to the extent which he probably desires, presents such difficulties as might check a greater political genius than he. So far as he is himself concerned, he sees none but those which proceed from the Emperor Alexander, because he does not hesitate to sacrifice Saxony. I told Lord Castlereagh that the trouble he was in was created by his own conduct and that of M. de Metternich; that it was they who had made the Emperor of Russia what he is, and that if, from the beginning, instead of rejecting a proposal to convene the Congress, they had supported it, what is now going on would not have happened; that they wanted to take up a position of their own towards Russia and Prussia, and that they found themselves too weak; but that if the Emperor of Russia had been confronted by the Congress, and consequently by the common desire of all Europe, he would never have ventured to hold the language that he is holding to-day. Lord Castlereagh assented to this,[3] regretted that the Congress had not met sooner, hoped it would meet shortly, and proposed to me to arrange in concert with him a form of convocation which could not leave room for any objection, and would reserve the difficulties which might crop up until the time for the verification of the Powers had come.

M. de Zeugwitz, a Saxon officer, just come from London, and who before his departure had seen the Prince Regent, states that the prince spoke to him of the King of Saxony in terms of the strongest interest, and told him that he had given his ministers orders to defend conservative principles at the Congress, and not to depart from them. The Prince Regent had spoken in the same sense to Duke Leopold of Saxe-Coburg,[4] who told me this two days ago. I cannot but believe, therefore, that the line which the English mission is taking is opposed to the Prince Regent's views and personal wishes.

Austria has not yet consented, though the Emperor of Russia told me she had, to Saxony's being given to Prussia. She has said, on the contrary, that the question of Saxony is essentially subordinate to that of Poland, and that she could not reply on the first until after the latter had been settled; but although in her note she spoke of the design of sacrificing Saxony as odious and infinitely painful to her, she has allowed her disposition to yield on this point, if she can obtain satisfaction on the other, to become too plainly evident. It is even affirmed that the Emperor of Russia told his brother-in-law, Prince Antoine,[5] that the cause of Saxony was lost.

What is certain is that Austria consents to the occupation of Saxony by Prussian troops, and its administration on behalf of the King of Prussia. Meantime public opinion becomes day by day more favorable to the cause of the King of Saxony; it is certainly to this that I am to attribute the flattering reception with which the Archdukes and the Empress of Austria were pleased to honor me, at a ball given by Count Zichy three days ago, and at a Court ball on the day before yesterday.

Yesterday morning the Emperor of Austria set out for Ofen, preceding the Emperor of Russia, who started in the evening. He is going to visit the tomb of the Grand-Duchess his sister, who married the Archduke Palatine, after which the ball and the fêtes which have been prepared for him will occupy him entirely. He will return to Vienna on the 29th. As he has gone away without leaving either powers or directions with anybody, nothing can be discussed, and of course nothing of importance can take place during his absence. I saw M. de Metternich this evening; he is plucking up a little courage. I spoke to him as strongly as it was possible to speak. The Austrian generals, of whom I have seen a great number, declare for the maintenance of Saxony; they advance military arguments on this subject which are beginning to make an impression.

I am, etc.

NOTES TO LETTER XI.

1. The instructions given to Prince Talleyrand on the 10th of September, 1814, classed the questions in which France was interested at the Congress of Vienna in the following order of importance:

a. To prevent its ever being possible for Austria to get possession of the dominions of the King of Sardinia.

b. To secure the restitution of Naples.

c. To prevent Russia from getting possession of the whole of Poland.

d. To prevent Prussia from getting possession either of Saxony, at least in its entirety, or of Mayence.

2. Stanislas Poniatowski.

3. "Lord Castlereagh himself now admits that he thought he was stronger with regard to the Emperor of Russia; and that he has to regret that he did not confront him with the whole of Europe assembled in Congress, as it had been proposed to him at Paris."—Letter from the French plenipotentiaries to the department, 24th October, 1814.

4. Afterwards King of the Belgians as Leopold I.

5. Prince Antoine, afterwards King of Saxony, 1827-1836, was brother of King Frederic Augustus III., and married the eldest sister of the Emperor Francis II.

LETTER XII.

THE KING TO PRINCE TALLEYRAND.

No. 4.

Paris, 27th October, 1814.

MY COUSIN,

I have received your No. 6. I was very much hurried when I sent you by Wednesday's post the supplement to your instructions for which you asked me, and I hope that the proceedings you will have taken in consequence may suffice; but, as I said to you in No. 3, we must make it evident that *there is something behind*, and I am about to give orders that the army be placed in a state to take the field. God is my witness that, far from wishing for war, my desire would be to have some years of quietude, that I might heal the wounds of the State at leisure; but I desire before all things to preserve the honor of France intact, and to hinder principles and an order of things which are as contrary to all morality as they are prejudicial to repose from being established. It is no less necessary, and it is also my desire, to cause my own personal character to be respected, and not to allow it to be said, as it was in the matter of the Spanish *chargé d'affaires*,[1] that I am strong only with the weak. My life, my crown, are nothing to me in comparison with interests so much greater.

It would, however, be very painful to me to be forced to ally myself for this with Austria, and with Austria only![2] I cannot conceive how Lord Castlereagh, who has spoken so well on the subject of Poland, can be of a different opinion respecting Saxony. I would count much upon Count Munster's efforts to persuade him, if the language of the Duke of Wellington on the same subject did not lead me to fear that this policy is not that of the minister, but of the ministry. Arguments with which to meet it will be readily forthcoming, but examples often produce more effect; and I know one striking example, that of Charles XII. The punishment of Patkul is a sufficient proof of how vindictive Charles XII. was, and how unscrupulous about the rights of nations; and yet, though he may be said to have been master of all the dominions of King Augustus, he was content with taking Poland from him, and did not consider it allowable to touch Saxony. It seems to me that, on comparing the two circumstances, the analogy of the duchy of Warsaw with the kingdom of Poland, and that of Saxony with herself, is evident. On which, etc.

NOTES TO LETTER XII.

1. The Spanish *chargé d'affaires*, Count Casaflores, had given orders directly to a commissary of French police to arrest the celebrated Spanish general Mina. The commissary was guilty of the grave fault of acting on the instructions of the representative of Spain, without a previous reference to the Prefect of Police. The King's Government, offended at this, dismissed the Spanish *chargé d'affaires*. In consequence of that occurrence, the Duke de Laval-Montmorency, ambassador of France at the Court of Spain, was on the point of asking for his passports and leaving Madrid, when the landing of Napoleon took place.

"I have seen General Mina; at first sight he strikes one as being merely an active quartermaster of a hussar regiment."—Jaucourt to Talleyrand, 29th October, 1814.

2. "He (the King) feels strongly the situation of Italy, and the position in which your proceeding has placed us; for the burden of a war, if it takes place, will fall almost entirely upon us. The Austrian armies will take care of the fate of Italy, and the Bavarians and ourselves must bear the brunt of the efforts of the Prussians and the Emperor Alexander.

"The Duke of Wellington said to me here just what the English minister said to you at Vienna; principles are settled, therefore, and not sentiments only. The King of Saxony has ceased to interest: it is said that Prussia powerful is useful as a rival to Austria, and a future barrier against Russia; that the independence of Poland is necessary, and self-evident, if she is united as one corporate nation; that the war movements, however they are accomplished, will probably bring about a revolution in Germany, and set Europe on fire. On the spot, as you are, and with your experience, you will smile, dear prince, at our Parisian notions. I shall, therefore, only add that the union of our troops with the Austrian troops would be entirely opposed to the national feelings and to public opinion, and especially distasteful to our soldiers."—Jaucourt to Talleyrand, 25th October, 1814.

LETTER XIII.

THE KING TO PRINCE TALLEYRAND.

No. 5. *

My Cousin,

I have received your No. 8. I have read it with great interest, but also with great indignation. The tone and the prin-

---

* No date is given in the original.

ciples with which Bonaparte was so justly reproached were no others than those of the Emperor of Russia. I hope that the opinion of the army and that of the Imperial family will recall Prince Metternich to more wholesome views, that Lord Castlereagh will enter more than he has yet done into those of the Prince Regent, and that then you will be able to use the weapons which I have given you with advantage. But, however that may be, continue to merit the just eulogium which I have great pleasure in reiterating on the present occasion, by remaining firm in the course that you are pursuing, and rest assured that my name shall never be affixed to an act which would sanction the most disgraceful immorality. On which, etc.

LETTER XIV.

No. 9.

Vienna, 31st October, 1814.

Sire,

The state of things is still the same in appearance, but there are certain symptoms of a change, and these may be increased by the demeanor and language of the Emperor Alexander. On the morning of the day of his departure for Hungary he had an interview with M. de Metternich, in which it appears quite certain that he addressed that minister with such haughtiness and violence of language such as might have appeared extraordinary even if applied to one of his own servants. M. de Metternich having said, on the subject of Poland, that if it were a question of making a Poland they also could do that, he not only stigmatized the observation as unbecoming and indecent, but went so far as to say that M. de Metternich was the only man in Austria who could thus *take a tone of revolt.* It is said that things reached such a point that M. de Metternich informed the Emperor he would at once beg his master to nominate another minister in his place for the Congress. M. de Metternich came away from this interview in a state in which the persons who know him intimately say they never before saw him. He who a few days previously had said to Count Schulenburg that he *entrenched himself behind time* and made *a weapon of patience,* would be likely to discard that weapon if it were often put to a similar trial.

It is not likely that he will be inclined to any increase of complaisance towards the Emperor of Russia by all this, and the opinion of the Austrian officers whom I see, and that of the Archdukes, ought not to make him more ready to abandon Saxony. I have reason to think that the Emperor of Austria is now inclined to make some resistance. There is here a certain Count Sickingen, who enjoys much intimacy with the Emperor, and whom I know. After the departure for Hungary he went to the house of Marshal Wrède, and then came to mine, to request us, on the part of the Emperor, to let everything remain in abeyance until his return. It is said here that during the journey the Emperor Alexander complained of M. de Metternich, and the Emperor Francis replied that he thought it was better that affairs should be dealt with by the ministers;[1] that by this means they were handled with more freedom and greater result; that he never did his own business, but his ministers did nothing except by his orders. Afterwards, and in the course of conversation, he said, amongst other things, that when people who had never forsaken him, who had done everything for him and had given him all, were disturbed as they were at present, his duty was to do all in his power to tranquillize them. Upon that, the Emperor Alexander having asked whether his character and his loyalty ought not to prevent or remove every kind of alarm, the Emperor Francis replied that good frontiers were the best securities for peace. This conversation was repeated to me, and almost in the same terms, by M. de Sickingen and M. de Metternich. It seems that the Emperor, who is but little in the habit of putting out his strength, came back very well pleased with himself.

All the precautions that are taken to deprive me of the knowledge of what is being done at the Commission of the Political Organization of Germany have failed.

At the first sitting it was proposed by Prussia that all the princes the whole of whose States are included in the Confederation shall renounce the right to make war and peace, and also that of legation. Marshal Wrède having declined this proposal, M. de Humboldt explained that it was plain Bavaria still had at heart an alliance with France, and that the fact was a fresh reason for them to insist; but, at the second sitting, the marshal, who had taken the King's orders, peremptorily rejected the proposal, and it was withdrawn.

It was then proposed that one-half of the entire military force of the Confederation should be placed under the direction of Austria, and one-half under that of Prussia. Marshal Wrède demanded that the number of directors should be augmented, and that the direction should alternate between them. It was proposed, in addition, that a close league should be formed between all the confederate States for the defence of the possessive status of each, such as it should be defined by the arrangements about to be made. The King of Bavaria, who was well aware that Russia especially intended by this league to secure to herself the possession of Saxony against the opposition of the Powers who wanted to preserve that kingdom, who felt that he should have everything to fear if Saxony were once sacrificed, and is ready to defend her if only he be not left to his own strength, has given orders to levy 20,000 recruits in his territory. This will bring his army up to 70,000 strong. Far from wishing to enter into the proposed league, his intention, at least at present, is that so soon as the Prussians shall have got hold of Saxony his minister shall retire from the Commission, declaring that he will not be an accomplice of such a usurpation, and still less its guarantor.

The Prussians do not know that this is the King's intention, but they are aware of the state of his armament, and they very probably suspect him of being inclined to join his forces with those of the Powers who would like to defend Saxony. They also feel that, without the consent of France, Saxony would not be a secure acquisition. It is said that the Cabinet, which does not share the blind attachment of the King to the Emperor Alexander, is not at all easy about Russia; that it will probably renounce Saxony, provided it can find elsewhere the means of making up the number of subjects which Prussia, according to the treaties, ought to have. Whatever may be their sentiments and their desires, the Prussian ministers are making approaches to us; they send us invitation after invitation. Lord Castlereagh, who has conceived the idea of fortifying Prussia below the Elbe, under the pretext of making that river serve as a barrier against Russia, has this project much at heart. In a conversation with me a few days ago he reproached me with making the question of Saxony one of the first order, whereas according to him it is nothing, and that of Poland is everything. I answered him that the question of Poland would have been for me the foremost of all if he had not reduced it to a simple matter of boundaries. If he wants to restore the whole of Poland to complete independence, I should be with him in the first rank; but when it was merely a question of boundaries, it was for Austria and Prussia, who were the most interested, to put themselves forward. My part was then limited to supporting them, and I should do so. I put before him certain arguments on his project of uniting Austria and Prussia which he could not meet, and I quoted facts concerning the policy of Prussia for the last sixty years which he could not deny; but, while condemning the former acts of the Cabinet, he declared that his hopes of a better future were strong.

Nevertheless I know that various persons have made objections by which he has been impressed. He has been asked how he could consent to place one of the largest cities of Germany, Leipsic,[2] in which one of the greatest European fairs is held, under the supremacy of Prussia, with which country England cannot be certain to be always at peace, instead of leaving it in the hands of a prince with whom England cannot have any cause of quarrel. This took him by surprise, and evidently made him feel some alarm lest his project should compromise the mercantile interests of England.

He had asked me to draw up a plan for the convocation of the Congress in concert with him. I sent him one and he was pleased with it. I also drew up some plans for the first meeting of the ministers, the verification of powers, and the Commission to be formed at the first sitting of the Congress. These documents are appended to my despatch to the department, which M. de Jaucourt will submit to your Majesty.

As M. de Dalberg, as well as myself, owed a visit to Lord Castlereagh, we went together to call upon him yesterday evening. He had nothing to say, but he observed that the fear of us which the Prussians evidently entertained was a sure indication that they suspected some concealed design. The real or affected apprehensions of Prussia naturally led the conversation to the everlasting subject of Poland and Saxony. There were maps on the table, and I pointed out to him upon them how that, Saxony and Silesia being in the same hands, Bohemia might be taken in a few weeks,[3] and that if Bohemia were taken the heart of the Austrian monarchy would be laid bare and defenceless. He seemed astonished; he had talked to us as if he had allowed all his hopes to turn towards Prussia because he found it impossible to place any in Austria.[4] He was quite surprised when we told him that she only wanted money to muster her troops; that she had very large forces, and would at present require only one million sterling for that purpose. At this he became animated, and seemed inclined to support the affair of Poland to the end. He knew that an answer to his memorandum was in course of preparation at the Russian Chancellery, and he did not seem to expect that it would be satisfactory. He had been apprised that the Servians[5] had again taken up arms, and informed us that a Russian corps, commanded by one of the most distinguished of the Russian generals, was advancing to the frontiers of the Ottoman Empire. It was plain, therefore, that nothing was more necessary and more urgent than to oppose a barrier to the ambition of Russia; but he wanted this to be done without war, or, if war could not be avoided, he wanted it to be done with the help of France. From his way of estimating our forces, it is easy to see that it is France he fears most.

"You have," said he, "twenty-five millions of men; we rate them as forty millions." And once he let the following sentence escape him: "Ah! if you only had relinquished your designs on the left bank of the Rhine!" It was easy for me to prove to him, by the situation of France and Europe, all in arms, that it was impossible to impute ambitious projects to France without supposing her to be mad! "That may be," he answered; "but a French army marching through Germany for any cause whatsoever would make too much impression and awaken too many memories." I represented to him that war would not be necessary, and that it would suffice if Russia were confronted by Europe united in one purpose; and this brought us back to the opening of the Congress. But he still went on talking of difficulties without stating what those difficulties were, and advised me to see M. de Metternich. I conclude from this that something has been agreed to between them, which they would not have kept secret from me if they had not reason to believe that I should object to it. Moreover, by accusing us of having retarded everything, they have foolishly acknowledged to us that only for us everything would now be settled, because they were agreed in principle. This avowal gives us the exact measure of the influence which, in their opinion, belongs to your Majesty in the affairs of Europe.

On the whole, Lord Castlereagh's inclinations, without being exactly good, seem to me to tend that way, and it may be that the Emperor Alexander's answer, for which he is waiting, will help to improve them.[6]

Yesterday morning I received a note from M. de Metternich, inviting me to attend a conference at eight o'clock in the evening. I will not weary your Majesty with the details of this conference; it abounded in words and was barren of facts. These details will be found in my letter to the department. The result was that a Commission of verification, composed of three members named *by lot*, was formed; that the powers are to be sent to them; and that after the verification the Congress is to meet. This evening another conference took place, at which the draft of declaration relative to the verification of powers was read and agreed to. This declaration will be published to-morrow, and I send a copy of it in a despatch to the department this evening. I thought your Majesty would prefer that all documents should be added to the letter which I address to M. de Jaucourt, so that the department may have and preserve them in their sequence. The situation of France has been such for eight months that no sooner has she reached one goal than another of equal importance is set before her, and it most frequently happens that she has no choice of means for its attainment. Hardly had the oppressor been overthrown, and those desires for the restoration of your Majesty to the bosom of your kingdom which had been long and universally entertained in secret found utterance, than it became necessary to provide for your Majesty's finding France disarmed at the moment of your arrival—France, which then contained five hundred thousand foreigners. This could only be obtained by procuring the cessation of hostilities, by an armistice at any cost. And then, to rid the kingdom of the troops which were devouring its substance, we had to direct all our efforts to the conclusion of peace. Afterwards it seemed as though your Majesty had nothing more to do, and might enjoy the love of your people and the fruit of your wisdom; but a fresh demand was made upon your Majesty's firmness and energy; they had to be exerted to save Europe, if possible, from the perils with which it is menaced by the ambition and the passions of some Powers and the blindness and pusillanimity of others. All the difficulties of that enterprise have failed to make me regard its success as entirely impossible, and the letter with which your Majesty has been pleased to honor me, dated the 21st of October, raises my hopes, while the testimony it bears to the satisfaction with which your Majesty deigns to regard my zeal gives me fresh courage.   I am, etc.

NOTES TO LETTER XIV.

1. "The sovereigns meet every day an hour before dinner, and discuss familiarly among themselves the principal subjects with which the ministers plenipotentiary are occupied.

"They show the documents to each other, talk of their interests like private individuals, and definitely note the points to which they agree."— *Moniteur Universel*, 21st November, 1814.

2. This city was subjected to a strong military occupation. On the 7th of November, 1814, the Prussian Major-General von Bismarck arrived at Leipsic to take command of the city.

3. In each of their wars with Austria the tactics of the Kings of Prussia have been to fall on Bohemia in the first instance (1741, 1759, 1778, 1866).

4. "Metternich lacks confidence in the resources of his monarchy; he is not of a decided character." This estimate of Metternich is frequently repeated in the letters transmitted to the department by the French plenipotentiaries at the Congress of Vienna.

5. George Czerny was justly entitled the Liberator of Servia. He was abandoned by the Russians at the treaty of Bucharest (1812), and emigrated to Bessarabia (1813); but at this time he was preparing to return to his native country.

6. On the 3d of January Prince Talleyrand wrote to the department: "The English embassy to the Congress, whose system we at first did not like, have entirely changed it and are now taking the same course as ourselves."

LETTER XV.

No. 10.

Vienna, 6th November, 1814.

SIRE,

The Count de Noailles, who arrived here on Wednesday morning, the 2nd of November, has brought me the supplementary instructions which your Majesty has been pleased to have addressed to me.[1] The resolutions of your Majesty are now known to the Austrian Cabinet, to the Emperor of Austria himself, and to Bavaria. I have thought it best not to speak of them to Lord Castlereagh, who is always ready to take alarm at an intervention on the part of France, and I have not spoken of them to Count Munster, who, hardly out of the hands of his doctors, is making preparations for his marriage with the Countess of Lippe, sister of the reigning Prince of Buckberg. On the day of his arrival, M. de Noailles was present at a conference which terminated without any result. The matter in hand was to examine whether, when the verification of powers was completed, commissions should be nominated to prepare the papers, and how and by whom they should be named. Prince Metternich argued at great length that the name of "commission" could not be applied, because it supposes a delegation of powers, which in its turn supposes a deliberating assembly, and that the Congress could not be. He proposed various denominations, instead of that one to which he objected, but he was not himself satisfied with any; at last he said that we must fix on one at the next conference. None has as yet taken place. These scruples about the term "commission" were no doubt strange, and certainly came rather late, as no difficulty had been made about giving that name to the three ministers who are charged with the verification of powers, and to the five who are preparing the political organization of Germany. But if I could have supposed M. de Metternich to have any other intention in this than a pretext to gain time, I should have been undeceived by himself. After the conference he requested me to accompany him into his cabinet, and he told me that he and Lord Castlereagh were resolved not to suffer Russia to pass the line of the Vistula; that they were working to induce Prussia to make common cause with them on that question, and that they hoped to succeed. He conjured me to give them time to do this, and not to hurry them. I wanted to know on what conditions they expected to obtain the co-operation of Prussia. He replied that they would promise Prussia a portion of Saxony, that is to say, four or five hundred thousand souls of that country, and particularly the fortress and circle of Wittenberg, which might be considered necessary to cover Berlin, so that the King of Saxony would still preserve from fifteen to sixteen hundred thousand souls, Turgau and Köningstein, and the course of the Elbe from the circle of Wittenberg to Bohemia. I learned that in a Council of State presided over by the Emperor himself, and composed of M. de Stadion, Prince Schwartzenberg, M. de Metternich, Count Zichy, and General Daka, it was laid down as a principle that the question of Saxony was of still greater interest for Austria than even that of Poland, and that the safety of the monarchy was concerned in not allowing the passes of Thuringia and Saal to fall into the hands of Russia. (I enter more fully into details on this subject in my letter of to-day addressed to the Department.)

This circumstance has made me place more confidence than I generally do in what M. de Metternich had said to me. If four-fifths or three-fourths of its actual population, and its principal strong places and military positions, can be preserved to the kingdom, we shall have done much for justice, much for utility, and much for your Majesty's glory..

The Emperor of Russia has replied to Lord Castlereagh's memorandum. I shall see his answer, and I shall have the honor of speaking of it to your Majesty in my next despatch, more positively than by *on dit*. I only know, of a certainty, that the Emperor complains of the injustice which he asserts is done to him, by imputing to him an ambition that has no place in his heart; he represents himself as ridden over, so to speak, and then, with very slight transition, goes on to declare that he will not desist from any of his pretensions.

Lord Castlereagh, who took fire at this answer, has made a reply, which Lord Stewart was to deliver yesterday. His brother charged him with this commission because he had during the war, and still has, the *entrée* to the Emperor Alexander. M. de Gentz has translated the document for the Austrian Cabinet, to whom it has been communicated, and tells me that it is very strong and very good.[2]

The affairs of Sweden are to be set going; I have made choice of M. de Dalberg to take part in the conferences at which they are to be discussed. I do not recapitulate to your Majesty in this letter all that has passed on that matter; my despatch to the Government gives an account of it.

I went yesterday at four o'clock to see M. de Metternich, who had requested me to do so; there I found M. de Nesselrode and Lord Castlereagh. M. de Metternich began with great protestations of his wish to be confidential with me, to have a good understanding with France, and to do nothing without her. What they desire is, he said, that all feelings of irritation should be laid aside, and that I should aid them to advance matters, and to get out of the difficulty in which he frankly acknowledged they find themselves.[3] I answered that their position with regard to me was quite different from mine with regard to them; that I neither wanted, did, nor knew anything with which they were not as well acquainted as myself; but that they, on the contrary, had done, and were daily doing, many things of which I either knew nothing, or came to hear of them through the town talk; that it was in this way I had been apprised of the existence of the Emperor Alexander's answer to Lord Castlereagh. I saw that I embarrassed him, and I perceived that he did not want to appear to Count Nesselrode to have committed any indiscretion in that respect; so I hastened to add that I did not know the bearing of that reply, nor, indeed, for certain, whether there was any such thing. Then I remarked that as for the difficulties of which he complained, I could only attribute them to one single origin—that they had not convened the Congress. "It must meet one day or another," said I, "sooner or later, and the more delay there is, the more appearance of self-accusation, of purposes which will not bear daylight. So much procrastination will seem to indicate a bad conscience. Why," I continued, "should you make any difficulty about proclaiming, that, without waiting for the verification of powers, which may be tedious, all those who have delivered theirs at the State Chancellery are to meet at an appointed place? The Commission will be announced there; it will be made known that each may send in his demand, and then the meeting will break up. Afterwards the Commission will get to their work, and business will go on with some sort of regularity." Lord Castlereagh approved of this course, which had the merit in his eyes of disposing of the difficulties respecting the contested powers; but he observed that the mere word "Congress" frightened the Prussians, and that Prince Hardenberg especially had a horror of it. M. de Metternich reproduced the greater part of the arguments which he had brought before us at the last conference. He considered it preferable that the Congress should not meet until we were agreed, at least upon all the great questions. "There is one," said he, "with which we are face to face." He meant Poland, though he did not choose to name that country, and he passed at once to the affairs of Germany proper, saying that everything was in the best train among the persons who are occupied with them. "The affairs of Sweden are also to be taken up," he added, "and they ought not to be regulated without France taking part in them." I told him that I never thought there could be any other intention, and that I had consequently chosen M. de Dalberg to assist at the conferences which were to be held on the matter. Passing from thence to the affairs of Italy, the word "complications"—of which M. de Metternich is perpetually making use, so as to keep up the vagueness which his weak policy requires—was employed throughout, from the affairs of Germany and Tuscany to those of Naples and Sicily; he wanted to arrive at proving that the tranquillity of Italy, and consequently that of Europe, depended on the Naples business not being settled at the Congress, but relegated to a more distant epoch. "The force of circumstances," said he, "will necessarily bring back the House of Bourbon to the throne of Naples." "The force of circumstances," said I, "appears to me to be now at its full height; it is at the Congress that this question must end. This question is the last of the Italian questions in the geographical order, and I consent that the geographical order should be observed; my compliance can go no farther." M. de Metternich then spoke of Murat's partisans in Italy. "Organize Italy," said I, "and he will no longer have any. Put an end to a provisional situation which is detestable; fix the possessive status in Upper and Central Italy; let there not be a foot of ground in military occupation from the Alps to the frontiers of Naples; let there be legitimate sovereigns everywhere, and a regular administration to fix the succession of Sardinia.[4] Send an Archduke into the Milanese province to govern it, recognize the rights of the Queen of Etruria, restore to the Pope the territory that belongs to him and which you occupy, and Murat will have no longer any hold upon the people; for he will be no more to Italy than a brigand." This geographical method of treating the affairs of Italy seemed to take, and it was decided that M. de Saint-Marsan should be summoned to the next conference, and the affairs of Italy regulated with him in conformity with this plan. M. de Brignolé, deputy from the city of Naples, is also to be heard on matters concerning the commercial interests of that city. Lord Castlereagh insists strongly that Genoa ought to be a free port, and he spoke with both approbation and bitterness of the enfranchisement of that of Marseilles.

It looks as if our position were bettering itself a little, but I dare not trust to appearances, having only too much reason not to rely upon the sincerity of M. de Metternich; and besides this, I do not know how to regard the unexpected departure of the Grand-Duke Constantine, who leaves Vienna the day after to-morrow, and goes direct to Warsaw. It is said that the Emperor Alexander is about to make a journey to Gratz, and that he proposes to go as far as Trieste. One of the Archdukes is to do the honors of that portion of the Austrian monarchy. The journey is to commence on the 20th.

The Court of Vienna continues to entertain its noble guests with hospitality, which, considering the state of its finances, must be very onerous to it. Everywhere are to be seen emperors, kings, empresses, queens, hereditary princes, reigning princes, etc., etc.; the Court pays everybody's expenses, and the expenditure of each day is estimated at two hundred and twenty thousand paper florins. Royalty certainly loses some of the grandeur which is proper to it, at these gatherings. To meet three or four kings and a still greater number of princes at balls and teas at the houses of private individuals, as one does at Vienna, seems to me to be unbecoming. It is in France alone that royalty preserves the *éclat* and the dignity that render it at once august and precious in the eyes of nations.

I am, etc.

NOTES TO LETTER XV.

1. "The supplementary instructions of the King, brought by M. de Noailles, has rendered it possible for the plenipotentiaries to hint that 'France would take an active part to secure a real and durable equilibrium, and to prevent Russia from laying hold of the grand-duchy of Warsaw, and Prussia of Saxony.'"—Letter from the plenipotentiaries to the Department.

2. See D'Angeberg, p. 394.

3. Talleyrand writes to the Department, 23rd November, 1814: "It cannot escape us in general that the real difficulty of the Allied Powers at the Congress arises from the delusion which they cherished by thinking they could settle the affairs of Europe upon bases which they had announced to us as decided, and which are not so."

4. The reigning King, Victor Emanuel I. (1802-1821), and his brother, Charles Felix (1821-1851), had no children. The matter in hand was the appointing of the branch of Savoy-Carignan to the eventual succession. This branch descended from Thomas, fifth son of Duke Charles Emanuel I. (a contemporary of Henry IV.), and has since given to Piedmont and Italy the kings Charles Albert (1831-1849), Victor Emanuel II. (1849-1878), and Humbert I.

Talleyrand, faithful to his instructions, as much with the object of maintaining the principle of dynastic rights, which he called the principle of legitimacy, as with that of giving check to the House of Austria and preventing it from acquiring at a future day the inheritance of the House of Savoy, was working for the accession of the Savoy-Carignan branch.

LETTER XVI.

THE KING TO PRINCE TALLEYRAND.

No. 6.

Paris, 9th November, 1814.

MY COUSIN,

I have received your No. 9. I observe with satisfaction that the opening of the Congress draws near, but I still foresee many difficulties. I charge Count de Blacas to inform you, firstly, of an interview which he has had with the Duke of Wellington: you will see that the latter speaks in terms much more explicit than those of Lord Castlereagh; which of the two speaks in accordance with the real intentions of his Court, I do not know, but the Duke of Wellington will be in any case a good weapon in your hands: secondly, of a document which that ambassador asserts is authentic. Nothing can astonish me on the part of Prince Metternich, but I should be surprised if on the 3rd of October you were not yet cogni zant of a step that had been taken. However that may have been, it is necessary that you should be informed of it.

You will be glad to know that my brother arrived on Sunday in good health. On which, etc.

LETTER XVII.

FROM COUNT DE BLACAS TO PRINCE TALLEYRAND.

[MINUTE.]

Paris, 9th November, 1814.

In obedience to an order of the King, I hasten to transmit to you, prince, certain important information, and also instructions which his Majesty considers no less essential. Your recent interview with the Emperor of Russia, and still more your apprehensions of compliance on the part of Austria and England, have made the king most anxious to ascertain everything that can throw a light on the real intentions of the latter Power. The language that has been reported to you, as that held by the Prince Regent, and what his Majesty was already aware of in that quarter, made him think it necessary to sound the intentions of the British Cabinet. A conversation which I have just had with Lord Wellington has accomplished that object, or at least afforded the King an opportunity for invoking more strongly than ever the aid of England on the most intricate points of the negotiation.

Lord Wellington, after having assured me that he knew what instructions had been given to Lord Castlereagh, and that they were entirely opposed to the designs of the Emperor Alexander upon Poland, and consequently upon Saxony, since the fate of Saxony depends absolutely on the determination which shall be taken with regard to Poland, said to me that by applying ourselves solely to this great question, and laying aside all secondary interests, we might readily arrive at an understanding. According to him, Austria will not lend her hand to the scheme which France rejects, and Prussia herself, for whom Saxony is a *pis aller*, would be extremely well satisfied with being reinstated in the duchy of Warsaw. Finding him so explicit upon this point, I thought I should be carrying out the wishes of the King by making an overture which, while entirely devoid of an official character, might still more explicitly pledge him in such communications as the Court of St. James's may be willing to authorize. I pointed out to him that if the intentions of his Government were such as he represented them, and that the only difficulty in the way of a prompt and happy issue to the negotiations was that of reducing opposition of various kinds to a compact and uniform resistance, it seemed to me that a convention concluded between France, England, Spain, and Holland, for the sole purpose of setting forth the views which they conjointly hold upon this question, would speedily obtain the consent of the other Courts. This expedient, by exhibiting an imposing unanimity of purpose, would at once dispel the charm which is leading so many States in a direction that is contrary to their respective interests; and the King, whose only ambition is the restoration of the principles of public law, and of a just balance of power in Europe, might fairly hope that those who, sharing his sentiments, had been invited to ally themselves with his policy, would not be induced by any motive to swerve from it. Although Lord Wellington could not entirely refuse to recognize the advantages of this proposal, he rejected it as superfluous; but he thereupon protested all the more strongly that the purposes of his Government in the question of Poland and Saxony, and even in that of Naples,[1] are sound; and he repeated that, if exclusive attention were directed to those great interests, the plenipotentiaries would soon be brought to the goal from which the Court of St. Petersburg is wandering.

You see, prince, that England, whatever may be the reserve of its negotiator at the Congress, here acknowledges openly the nature of his instructions, and that those instructions, when the question of Poland is linked with that of Saxony (as it is by Lord Wellington), tender to the King most important support. Under these circumstances, his Majesty thinks that you may usefully avail yourself of the information which I have the honor to transmit to you.

You are now enabled, by appealing to Lord Castlereagh's instructions, to place him under the necessity of giving you an answer, which he can hardly make negative, as he will hereafter be bound to prove that he has acted in conformity with the views of his Government and the interests of his country. The independence of Poland would be very popular in England, if it were complete; but it will not be at all popular on the Russian plan. You, prince, will doubtless appreciate the importance of observing the distinction between these two hypotheses in your communications with the English minister. The King is convinced that the more strongly you express yourself in favor of the real and complete independence of the Polish nation, in case that should be practicable, the more effectually you will deprive Lord Castlereagh of the means of justifying, in the eyes of the English nation, the abandonment of the grand-duchy of Warsaw to the Emperor Alexander. The King has informed you that his Majesty has ordered the Minister of War to raise the army to its full strength on a peace footing. I am in hopes that this resolution, which has been dictated by considerations of whose gravity you are fully aware, will shortly become superfluous.

Receive, prince, the most sincere assurance of my unalterable attachment and high consideration.

NOTE TO LETTER XVII.

1. "From the 14th December, 1814, Austria decided on supporting Saxony, and England changed her tone. The Russian and Prussian intrigues were exposed. . . . Lord Castlereagh has communicated to Prince Talleyrand the whole correspondence in reference to the affair of Naples, and he appeared to wish in order rather to confirm what he had said than what he had written —that our presses should be searched for every paper that might prove to the coalition that Murat, while going along with them, had been carrying on a double intrigue with Bonaparte. . . ."—The French plenipotentiaries to the Department.

LETTER XVIII.

No. 11.

Vienna, 12th November, 1814.

SIRE,

M. de Metternich and Lord Castlereagh had persuaded the Prussian Cabinet to make common cause with them on the question of Poland. The hopes which they had built upon the co-operation of Prussia have, however, been of brief duration. The Emperor of Russia, having invited the King of Prussia to dinner a few days ago, had a conversation with him, some details of which I have learned from Prince Adam Czartoryski. The Emperor reminded the King of the amity subsisting between them, the value which he set upon it, and all that he had done to render it lasting; adding that, as they are about the same age, he had hoped to witness for a long time the happiness for which their respective peoples would be indebted to their close friendship, and that he had always connected his own glory with the re-establishment of a kingdom of Poland. Now that he was on the eve of the accomplishment of his desires, was he to have the grief of counting his dearest friend, and the only person upon whose sentiments he had reckoned, among those who opposed them? The King made a thousand protestations, and swore that he would support him on the Polish question. "It is not enough," said the Emperor, "that you should be of this mind; your ministers also should be of the same;" and he urged the King to send for Prince Hardenberg. The prince arrived, and the Emperor repeated in his presence what he had previously said, and the promise that the King had given him. Prince Hardenberg endeavored to object; but, being pressed by the Emperor Alexander, who asked him whether he would not obey the orders of the King, and those orders being absolute, there was nothing for him except to promise that he would punctually execute them. This is all that I have been able to learn respecting the scene; much must have occurred of which I know nothing, if it be true, as M. de Gentz has assured me, that Prince Hardenberg said he had never seen anything like it.

This change on the part of Prussia has greatly disconcerted M. de Metternich and Lord Castlereagh. They would have wished that Prince Hardenberg should have resigned—and such a step would certainly have embarrassed the Emperor and the King—but he does not seem to have even thought of doing so.

For my own part, suspecting as I did that M. de Metternich had obtained the co-operation of the Prussians by greater concessions than those which he acknowledged, I was inclined to regard the defection of Prussia as an advantage, and your Majesty will see that my surmises were but too well founded.

The Grand-Duke Constantine, who left Vienna two days ago, is to organize the army of the duchy of Warsaw; he is also entrusted with the civil organization of the country, and the tone of his instructions indicates, according to the report of M. d'Anstetten, who drew them up, that the Emperor Alexander will not retire from any of his pretensions. The Emperor must likewise have induced the King of Prussia to give a civil and military organization to Saxony. It is reported that he said to him, "It is not far from civil organization to ownership." A letter which I have just received from M. de Caraman, tells me that the brother of the Prussian Minister of Finance, General de Bulow, and several generals have left

Berlin for the purpose of effecting the organization of Saxony in both the civil and military departments. M. de Caraman adds that the occupation of Saxony is nevertheless represented at Berlin not as definitive, but as provisional only. I am also told that the Emperor Alexander, speaking of the opposition of Austria to his views, said, after complaining bitterly of M. de Metternich, "Austria thinks herself certain of Italy, but there is a Napoleon there, and use may be made of him." I am not sure that this saying is authentic, but it is in circulation, and if it be true it gives the exact measure of the speaker.

Lord Castlereagh has not yet received a reply to his last Note. Some persons think that the Emperor will not deign even to answer it.

While the affairs of Poland and Saxony are in suspense, the views respecting the organization of Italy which I put forward, in the conference of which I have had the honor to give an account to your Majesty, have borne fruit. The day before yesterday I called on Lord Castlereagh and found him full of them; also M. de Metternich, who dined yesterday with M. Rasoumowski, as we all did. M. de Metternich brought Lord Castlereagh, M. de Nesselrode, and myself together to-day to talk about them. On my arrival, he informed me that no other subject was to be discussed; that tomorrow, the day after to-morrow, or perhaps even an hour hence, he might be in a condition to speak to me of Poland and Saxony, but that at present he could not do so. I did not insist. The conference was solely occupied with Genoa. It was proposed, not to incorporate that country with Piedmont, but to give it to the King of Sardinia by a treaty, by which special privileges and institutions should be secured to it. Lord Castlereagh had brought certain memoranda and plans which had been addressed to him on the subject, and these he read aloud. He strongly urged the establishment of a free port, an *entrepôt*, and transit through Piedmont with very moderate duties. It was agreed that we should meet to-morrow, and that M. de Brignolé and M. de Saint-Marsan should be summoned to the conference.

After the conference, I remained alone with M. de Metternich, and as I wanted to know how he stood with regard to Poland and Saxony, and what he proposed to do, instead of putting questions to him on those points, which he would have avoided, I spoke to him about himself only, assuming the tone of an old friend, and said that while attending to affairs, he ought also to consider himself; that it seemed to me that he did not do so sufficiently; that one might be compelled by necessity to do certain things, but that necessity ought to be made evident to everybody; that although one might act upon the purest motives, unless those motives were known to the public, one was none the less certain to be calumniated, because the public in that case could only judge by results; that he was exposed to reproaches of all sorts; that he was accused, for instance, of having sacrificed Saxony; that I earnestly hoped he had not done this, but why leave any pretext for such reports? Why not give his friends the means of defending and justifying him? The unrestraint with which I spoke led him to open his mind a little way. He read me his Note to the Prussians on the question of Saxony, and my warm thanks induced him to entrust it to me. I promised him that it should be kept secret. I subjoin a copy which I have had the honor to make for your Majesty, and beg that your Majesty will be pleased to keep it and permit me to ask for it on my return.

Your Majesty will see by this document[1] that M. de Metternich had promised the Prussians, not a portion of Saxony, as he had assured me, but the whole of it. This promise he had fortunately made subject to a condition, whose non-fulfilment renders it null and void. Your Majesty will also see that M. de Metternich gives up Luxemburg to the Prussians,[2] after having repeatedly assured me that it should not be given to them. This same Note also reveals the plan which was formed long ago, for placing Germany under what is called the influence, but would be really the exclusive and absolute dominion, of Austria and Prussia.

Now, M. de Metternich protests that he will not forsake Saxony. As for Poland, he has given me to understand that he will yield much; this signifies that he will yield all, if the Emperor Alexander persists in refusing to concede anything. I was still with him when the report of the state of the Austrian army was brought to him, and he allowed me to see it. The actual strength of that army consists of three hundred and seventy-four thousand men, of which fifty-two thousand are cavalry, and eight hundred pieces of cannon. With such forces as these, he believes that the Austrian monarchy can do no better than resign itself to everything, and put up with everything! Your Majesty will be pleased to remark that the number of the troops is the *effective strength* of the army. I will not close the letter which I have the honor to write to your Majesty until after my return from a conference to be held this morning.

The conference is over. M. de Nesselrode, M. de Metternich, and Lord Castlereagh were there. M. de Saint-Marsan, who came by appointment, was admitted. No question except that of the union of Genoa with Piedmont was discussed.[3] A kind of power given by the provisional Government of Genoa, fabricated a few months ago by Lord William Bentinck, has given rise to some difficulties, but they will be removed by its being granted that Genoa is vacant territory. It has been agreed that the eight Powers shall meet to-morrow to make a declaration to that effect, and to hand to M. de Brignolé, the deputy from Genoa, a copy of the protocol containing a declaration to that effect. Nothing will then remain to be decided, except the mode of meeting. I have availed myself of to-day's conference to speak of the Sardinian succession. M. de Saint-Marsan, to whom I had previously given notice, had received instructions conformable to the rights of the House of Carignan from his Court. I proposed a form of words which recognizes them; M. de Saint-Marsan has adopted it; it has been drafted, and I have every reason to believe that it will be admitted. The conference on the affairs of Switzerland will now begin without delay.

I am, etc.

NOTES TO LETTER XVIII.

1. See Appendix.
2. Luxemburg, the capital city of the grand-duchy of Luxemburg, was a federal fortress. Prussia furnished the garrison from 1815 to 1867.
3. By a secret provision of the Treaty of Paris the departments that previously composed the State of Genoa were to form an addition to Piedmont, and the port of Genoa to remain free.

LETTER XIX.

THE KING TO PRINCE TALLEYRAND.

No. 7.

Paris, 15th November, 1814.

My Cousin,

I have received your No. 10, and I await with impatience the important further details which you notify to me. I lay hold eagerly on the hope for Saxony which you extend to me, and I think that I may rest in it with some confidence, now that Prince Metternich speaks, not his own mind, but that of a council. I should certainly be much better pleased that Saxony should remain a whole, but I think its unfortunate King ought to esteem himself happy if two-thirds or three-fourths of it be saved for him.

As for the proposed exchange, I do not in general like to cede what is mine; it is still more repugnant to me to despoil others; and, after all, the rights of the Prince-Bishop of Basle,[1] though no doubt less important to the repose of Europe, are no less sacred than those of the King of Saxony. If, however, the spoliation of the Prince-Bishop be inevitable, I will consent to the exchange, moved thereto by the double consideration of preserving a portion of his States to the King of Sardinia, and rendering a great service to the canton of Berne. I send you an authorization *ad hoc*,[2] of which you will make use on the five following conditions, the first of which is only a rule of conduct for yourself:—

1. The impossibility of saving the Prince-Bishop of Basle.
2. The securing to the King of Sardinia that part of Savoy[3] which remains to him.
3. The restoration of its portion of Aargau to the canton of Berne.
4. The free exercise of the Catholic religion in the portion of the territory of Gex ceded to the canton of Geneva.[4]

Free navigation for France on the Lake of Geneva.

On these terms you may sign the exchange.

On which, etc.

NOTES TO LETTER XIX.

1. The bishopric of Basle, an ecclesiastical principality of the Germanic Empire until 1801, had been incorporated with France. It was about to be partitioned between the cantons of Basle and Berne.
2. The treaty of the 30th of May, 1814, had left Chambéry and Annécy to France (she lost them by the treaty of the 20th of November, 1815); besides, the canton of Geneva was about to receive several communes of Savoy to the south and east of the town. The largest of those communes is Carouge.
3. Four free states—Aaran, Brugg, Leinburg, Zofingen—under the sovereignty of Berne. Aargau was constituted a canton.
4. The part of the country of Gex bounded by Lake Leman, the chief town of which is Versoix.

LETTER XX.

No. 12.

Vienna, 17th September, 1814.

Sire,

Before the Emperor Alexander brought Prussia round to his views, he was advised by persons in his confidence to turn to the side of France, to come to an understanding with her, and to see me. He answered that he would willingly see me, and that in future, when I wanted to make application for an audience, I must apply, not to Count Nesselrode, but to Prince Wollonsky, his first aide-de-camp. I said to the person by whom I was told this, that if I were to have the Emperor asked for an audience, the Austrians and the English would certainly be aware of the fact; that they would take umbrage at it, and build all sorts of conjectures upon it; and that to make the request through the unusual medium of an aide-de-camp would give an appearance of intrigue to my relations with the Emperor, which would be unbecoming to both one and the other. A few days afterwards, as he asked why he had not seen me, my motives were explained to him, and he approved of them, adding, "Then I will attack him first." At the great assemblies where I have frequently occasion to meet him, I make it a rule to put myself in his way as little as possible, to avoid him as much as I can without a breach of propriety, and I acted on this rule at Count Zichy's, where he was, on Saturday. I had remained almost all the evening in the card-room, and was about to avail myself of the announcement of supper to retire—I had indeed reached the door of the ante-chamber—when a hand was placed upon my shoulder. I turned and saw that it was that of the Emperor Alexander. He asked me why I did not go to see him, when he should see me, and what I was going to do on Monday; then he told me to go and see him on that day at eleven o'clock, and to come in plain clothes, to resume my plain clothes ways with him; and, saying this, he took my arm and gave it a friendly squeeze.

I took care to inform M. de Metternich and Lord Castlereagh of what had passed, so as to remove any idea of concealment, and prevent all suspicion on their part.

I waited on the Emperor at the appointed hour. He said, "I am very glad to see you; and you too—you did wish to see me: is it not so?" I made answer that I never concealed my regret at seeing him so seldom while in the same place with him. After this the conversation was set going.

"How do affairs stand, and what is now your position?" "Sire, it is always the same. If your Majesty wishes to restore Poland as a completely independent State, we are ready to support you." "At Paris, I desired the restoration of Poland, and you approved of it; as a man, ever faithful to liberal ideas which I never will relinquish, I desire it still. But, in my position, the man's wishes cannot be the rule of the sovereign's conduct. Perhaps the day may come when Poland can be restored, but as for the present time, it is not to be thought of." "If the partition of the duchy of Warsaw only be in question, that is much more the affair of Prussia and Austria than it is ours. Those two Powers once satisfied on that point, we shall be satisfied also; but so long as they are not, we are instructed to support them, and our duty is to do so, since Austria has allowed so many difficulties to arise, which it would have been easy for her to prevent." "In what way?" "By claiming, at the time of her alliance with us, the right to occupy by her troops that portion of the duchy of Warsaw which had belonged to her; you would certainly not have refused this, and if she had occupied that country you would not have thought of taking it from her." "Austria and I are of one accord." "That is not what the public believe." "We are agreed upon the principal points; the only dispute is about a few villages." "France is in the second rank on that question; but on the question of Saxony she is in the first rank." "True; the question of Saxony is a family matter[1] for the House of Bourbon." "Not at all, Sire. In the matter of Saxony there is no question of the interests of an individual or of a family; the interests of all kings are concerned in it; in the first place, those of your Majesty, because the foremost of your interests is the care of that personal glory which you have acquired, and whose lustre is reflected upon your Empire. Your Majesty must guard that glory, not for your own sake only, but also for the sake of your people, whose patrimony it is; and you will set the seal upon it by protecting those principles which are the foundation of public order and security, and by making them respected. I speak to you, Sire, not as the Minister of France, but as a man who is sincerely attached to you." "You talk of principles, but that one ought to keep one's word is one of them, and I have given mine." "Pledges have different degrees of gravity, and that which your Majesty gave to Europe when you passed the Niemen ought to carry more weight than any other. Allow me, Sire, to add, that the intervention of Russia in the affairs of Europe is regarded with general jealousy and uneasiness, and that it has been suffered to take place solely on account of your Majesty's personal character. That character must therefore necessarily be preserved intact." "That is a matter which concerns nobody but myself, and I am the sole judge of it." "Pardon me, Sire, when one is a man of history all mankind is one's judge." "The King of Saxony is a man little worthy of interest; he has violated his engagements." "He had not entered into any with your Majesty, but only with Austria;² therefore she alone would have a right to be resentful towards him; and so far is she from being so, that I know the designs that are formed upon Saxony cause the greatest pain to the Emperor of Austria. Your Majesty must most certainly be unaware of this; for otherwise, living, as your Majesty and your family have been living, with him and as his guests for two months past, your Majesty never could have made up your mind to inflict such pain upon him. These same designs also afflict and alarm the people of Vienna; of that every day brings me proofs." "But Austria has abandoned Saxony." "M. de Metternich, whom I saw yesterday, manifested a very different disposition from that of which your Majesty does me the honor to tell me." "And yourself? It is said that you consent to abandon a portion." "We shall only do so with extreme regret. But if it be necessary to give Prussia from three to four hundred thousand Saxons, so that she may have a population equal to that which she had in 1806, and which did not exceed nine million, two hundred thousand souls, we will make the sacrifice for the sake of the blessing of peace." "And that is just what the Saxons are most afraid of; they do not ask anything better than to belong to the King of Prussia; all they desire is that they shall not be divided." "We have the means of knowing all that is taking place in Saxony, and we know that the Saxons are in despair at the idea of becoming Prussians." "No; the only thing they fear is being divided; and indeed there is nothing more unfortunate for a people." "Sire, if that argument were applied to Poland?" "The partition of Poland is none of my doing; it is no business of mine to repair that evil. I have already said to you that it may perhaps be undone some day." "The cession of a portion of the two Lusatias would not be a dismemberment, properly speaking, of Saxony. They were not incorporated with her; they were until recent times a fief of the crown of Bohemia; they had nothing in common with Saxony, except the fact that they belonged to the same sovereign."

"Tell me, is it true that you are raising troops in France?" (As he put this question, the Emperor approached me so closely that his face almost touched mine.) "Yes, Sire." "What troops has the King?"[3] "One hundred and thirty thousand men under the colors, and three hundred thousand who have been sent back to their homes, but who can be recalled at any moment." "How many are being recalled at present?" "The number necessary to make up the peace footing. We felt at one and the same time that we must get rid of an army, and that we must have an army; that we must get rid of the army that was Bonaparte's, and have one which should be the King's. To do this we had to dissolve and to recompose, first to disarm and then to rearm, and we are just now completing those operations. Such is the motive of our present armament; it is not a threat to any one; but when all Europe is armed, it seemed necessary that France should be armed also, in fitting proportion." "That is well. I hope that these affairs here will lead to a good understanding between France and Russia. What are the King's inclinations in that respect?" "The King will never forget the services which your Majesty has rendered them, and will always be ready to recognize them. But he has his duties as the sovereign of a great country, and the head of one of the most powerful and ancient houses of Europe. He could not abandon the House of Saxony, he wishes us to protest in case of necessity. Spain, Bavaria,[4] and other States as well would protest together with us."[5] "Listen; let us make a bargain: be amiable to me in the matter of Saxony, and I will be the same to you in that of Naples. I am not pledged to anything on that side." "Your Majesty knows well that no bargain is practicable. There is no parity between the two questions. It is impossible that your Majesty should not be of the same mind as ourselves with respect to Naples." "Very well, then, persuade the Prussians to let me retract my word." "I see very little of the Prussians, and should certainly not succeed in persuading them. But your Majesty has facilities for doing so. You have complete power over the mind of the King. Besides, your Majesty can requite them." "In what manner?" "By leaving them something more in Poland." "You propose a singular expedient to me. You want me to take upon myself to give to them."

The conversation was interrupted at this point by the Empress of Russia's coming into the room. She was pleased to say some obliging things to me; but she remained only a few minutes. The Emperor resumed: "Let us sum up the case." I briefly recapitulated the points upon which I could, and those upon which I could not come to terms, and I concluded by saying that I must insist upon the maintenance of the kingdom of Saxony with sixteen hundred thousand inhabitants. "Yes," said the Emperor, "you insist strongly upon a thing that is *decided;*" but he did not utter that word in the tone which conveys an unchangeable resolution.

His object in summoning me to him was to learn—

1. To what extent the arming that was talked about was going on in France, and what was its purpose. I think I answered him in such a manner as neither to let him believe himself threatened, nor yet to leave him too much at his ease.

2. Whether your Majesty would be inclined to make an alliance with him at some future day. Unless he should lay aside his spirit of conquest, which is by no means likely, I do not see that it would be possible for your Majesty, whose spirit is so entirely conservative, to ally yourself with him, if indeed it were not in an exceptional case, and for a temporary object. But it was not advisable, if he wished for such an alliance, to deprive him of all hope of it, and I avoided doing so.

3. What determination we had really come to with regard to Saxony. On that point I left him so little in doubt that he said to Count Nesselrode, from whom I heard it, "The French are decided on the question of Saxony, but let them settle it with Prussia. They want to take from me to give to her, but I do not consent to that." I have related this conversation in so much detail so that your Majesty may be enabled to judge how much the Emperor's tone has changed since I had my last audience of him. During the whole course of our conversation, he never exhibited a single symptom of irritation or temper. All was calm and pleasant. He is certainly less moved by the interests of Prussia, and less withheld by his friendship for the King, than he is embarrassed by the promises which he has made him; and I am inclined to believe that, notwithstanding the chivalrous disposition which he affects, and his desire to pass for being strictly bound by his word, in his own secret heart he would be enchanted to have a fair pretext for releasing himself from it. I base this opinion especially upon a conversation which he has had with Prince Schwartzenberg, and which I think contributed in no small degree to making him wish to see me. He asked the Prince how matters stood, and whether they would succeed in coming to an understanding, and then pressed him to give his opinion, not as the Austrian minister, but as a

friend. After having parried the question for some time, Prince Schwartzenberg told him plainly that his conduct towards Austria had been hardly frank, and even hardly loyal; that his pretensions tended to place the Austrian monarchy in actual danger, and things in general in a position which would render war inevitable; that if war were not made now (either out of respect for the incipient alliance, or to prevent their figuring in the eyes of Europe as blunderers, utterly devoid of foresight, whose blind confidence had placed them at the mercy of events), it would inevitably break out in eighteen months or two years. Then the Emperor said, incautiously, "Oh, if I had only not gone so far!" but he added, "How am I to get out of it now? You must feel that it is impossible for me to withdraw from the point where I now stand."

At the very time when M. de Schwartzenberg was representing war as inevitable sooner or later, the movements of a body of Austrian troops in Galicia seemed to indicate that it might be near at hand. The Cabinet of Vienna appears to be waking up from its lethargy. M. de Metternich talked to Prince de Wrède of an alliance, asking him whether Bavaria would not now add twenty-five thousand men to the Austrian forces; to which Prince de Wrède replied that Bavaria would be willing to furnish as many as seventy-five thousand men, under the following conditions:

1. That an alliance should be concluded with France.

2. That Bavaria should furnish twenty-five thousand men, and no more, for each hundred thousand men furnished by Austria.

3. That if England gave subsidies to Austria, Bavaria should receive her portion of them in proportion to their respective strength.

I am convinced that up to the present time these are words only, mere demonstrations, but it is no slight thing that Austria should have resolved upon making them; and, in consequence, the Emperor Alexander was naturally anxious to know what he had to fear or to expect from us.

Knowing that his habit, when he is speaking to any one of those who are opposed to his wishes, is to affirm that he is in agreement with the others, and being desirous that the results of my interview with him should not be presented in a false light, I took advantage of a visit made to me by M. de Sickingen, to make them known to the Emperor of Austria through him. The Emperor repeated them to M. de Metternich, by whose recapitulation I have ascertained that M. de Sickingen has reported them faithfully.

This disclosure has produced the best effect; the universal feeling of distrust with which we were regarded at the beginning of our sojourn here is lessening day by day, and the opposite feeling is gaining ground.

On my return from my audience of the Emperor Alexander, I found the Saxon minister here. He had come to communicate to me—firstly, a protest by the King of Saxony, which the King had sent to him, with orders to lay it before the Congress, after having communicated it to M. de Metternich, upon whose advice he is directed to act; secondly, a circular of Prince Repnin, who was Governor-General for the Russians in Saxony.[6] This document (a copy of which I subjoin to my despatch to the Department for publication in the *Moniteur*) has given rise to the protest of the King, which cannot be printed until after it has been officially laid before the Congress; until then I shall not have a copy of it. This circular—by which Prince Repnin announces to the Saxon authorities that, in consequence of a convention concluded on the 27th of September, the Emperor Alexander, with the consent of *Austria and of England*, has ordered the administration of Saxony to be handed over to the delegates of the King of Prussia, who is in future to possess that country, not as a province of his kingdom, but as a separate kingdom, whose integrity he has promised to maintain—has thrown M. de Metternich and Lord Castlereagh into the greatest perplexity, and is bitterly complained of by them.

It is very true that their consent has been shamefully perverted by being represented as absolute, whereas it was purely conditional, and that this justifies their complaints, but it is no less true that they have given a consent which they now bitterly regret.

Your Majesty is already in possession of the Note of M. de Metternich.

I have the honor this day to forward to your Majesty that of Lord Castlereagh.[7] I received it only two days ago; it was procured for me under a promise of profound secrecy, therefore I address it directly to your Majesty. I am told that Lord Castlereagh tried hard to induce the Prussians to return it to him. The Note confirms all that I have had the honor to convey to your Majesty during the last six weeks, and even reveals things which I should not have believed, did it not afford so undeniable a proof of them.

However strange M. de Metternich's Note may be, on comparing it with that of Lord Castlereagh, differences entirely to the advantage of the former become apparent.

M. de Metternich endeavors to persuade Prussia that she ought to renounce her views upon Saxony; he sets forth the moral and political reasons which lead him to object to giving his consent, and, while giving it, acknowledges that it is wrung from him by a sort of necessity.

Lord Castlereagh, on the contrary, after some expressions of vain and sterile pity for the royal family of Saxony, declares that he has no sort of *moral or political repugnance* to abandon Saxony to Prussia.

M. de Metternich's consent is given on the ground that Prussia will have sustained losses, for which it will be impossible to compensate her in any other manner. Lord Castlereagh's consent, on the contrary, is given on the grounds that Prussia shall preserve that for which M. de Metternich talks of making compensation to her; he means her to have Saxony as an increase of power, and not an equivalent.

Thus they both make the question of Saxony subordinate to that of Poland, but in essentially opposite senses, which shows how little real agreement there is between these much-united allies, who cried out so loudly that France wanted to divide them.

They are, however, agreed upon getting Prince Repnin's circular withdrawn, and I think it will be repudiated by the Prussians themselves.

For the rest, it appears to me that neglect, if not contempt for the principles and even the commonest notions of sound policy, could hardly be carried farther than in that Note of Lord Castlereagh's.

He came yesterday to ask me to dinner, and proposed an interview for to-day. I had expected some disclosure or some important overture, but he came to talk to me solely of his troubles. Deceived in the hopes that he had built upon Prussia, and finding the ground cut completely from under his feet in consequence, he is greatly depressed. He came to consult me as to how an impulse might be given to affairs so as to set them going. I told him that the Emperor Alexander asserts that he is in agreement with Austria on the question of Poland, and that only a few details remain to be settled; that if this were really the case, the best thing he could do would be to induce Austria to terminate that arrangement promptly; that they had subordinated the question of Poland and Saxony one to the other, and this not having succeeded, they must be separated, and that of Poland terminated first; that Austria, quiet on that side, and no longer obliged to divide herself between the two questions, might give her entire attention to that of Saxony, which all the Austrian officers regarded as much more important of the two; that Russia, being satisfied on the point which directly interests her, will probably give little trouble upon the other; and that when Prussia finds herself standing alone relatively to Austria, England, France, and Spain, the affair will be easily and promptly settled.

Prince Repnin's circular was the signal for which Bavaria was waiting, to declare that she would not subscribe to any arrangement, and would not enter into any German league, until the maintenance of the King of Saxony had been previously secured; this Prince de Wrède declared positively to M. de Hardenberg, who, while saying that he could not take anything upon himself, and would refer it to the King, hinted, nevertheless, that the King of Saxony might be maintained with a million of subjects. Thus all is still in abeyance, but the chances of saving a great part of Saxony are increased.

I had written so much of my letter when I received that with which your Majesty has honored me, of the 9th of November, and also that of the Count de Blacas, written by your Majesty's orders.

Your Majesty will judge by Lord Castlereagh's Note, which I have the honor to forward, either that the minister has instructions of which the Duke of Wellington knows nothing, or that he does not consider himself bound by those which have been given to him; and that if he has made the question of Saxony depend upon that of Poland, he has done so in a sense precisely inverse to that which the Duke of Wellington supposed.

As for what concerns Naples, I have given an account to your Majesty of the proposal made by M. de Metternich in one of those conferences, at which only he, M. de Nesselrode, Lord Castlereagh, and myself were present, that we should not enter upon this affair until after the Congress, and of my answer. (In No. 10 of my correspondence this detail is given.) The threats contained in the letter from which the Count de Blacas has sent me an extract, are contained, I am told, in a pamphlet published by an aide-de-camp of Murat's, named Filangieri, who was at Vienna quite recently.[8] (This pamphlet has been seized by the police.) But I hope that if Italy be once organized, from the Alps to the frontiers of Naples, as I have proposed, such threats will be no longer formidable.

I waited to close my letter until I had returned from a conference to which we were summoned for this evening at eight o'clock. Nothing was done there but the reading and signing of the protocol of the last conference.

The Emperor of Russia is indisposed, sufficiently so to keep his bed, but it is only an indisposition.

I am, etc.

NOTES TO LETTER XX.

1. Louis XVIII. and Frederick Augustus III. were cousins-german.

2. On the 26th of April, Prince Metternich had denounced the treaty, or Franco-Austrian alliance, of the 14th of March, 1812. He had withdrawn the auxiliary aid stipulated by that alliance. Austria, who became neutral in the interval before declaring war against us, had obtained a promise of neutrality from the King of Saxony which Napoleon's victories at Lutzen and Bautzen made it impossible for him to keep.

3. See Appendix.

4. His Majesty the King of Bavaria used the following words to Count Alexis de Noailles on the 9th of November, 1814:

"I learn that a close watch has been kept on the French envoys; their proceedings have been minutely observed; and it has been discovered with much surprise that they keep aloof from all secret manœuvring, that they have not distributed the smallest sum of money, and that their conduct is stainless and free from intrigue. I have made a protest on the affairs of Saxony. I am with you. I will not separate myself from your policy. Would you like to know what is privately said? The word of the King, his loyalty, and his principles are relied upon; but it is believed that he will not be master of the army, and that after the negotiations he will be forced into war by the clamor of generals greedy for conquest."

5. On the 8th of November, 1814, the Archduke Charles used the following words to Count Alexis de Noailles:

"I have no doubt that France will play a fine part in the Congress, and that the talents and experience of M. de Talleyrand will be as useful to Europe as to your own country. You have set a valuable example by your manner of not demanding increase of territory. That example will be useful in Europe in the restoration of the former relations between nations. France is a sufficiently fine country, by reason of its situation, to regain its former preponderance without any extraneous aid. We soldiers have drawn the sword: now let the politicians finish the work, and build up the welfare of Europe upon solid foundations, so as to prevent fresh devastation. I have read your scheme of finance; it appears to me to be a good one, but I do not pretend to understand the subject thoroughly. The chief thing in politics and in finance is to do what you will do, no doubt—that is, to hold to what has been promised; mark out a certain course, as I am sure you have done, and follow it inexorably; to perseverance of that quality success is certain."

6. See D'Angeberg, "Congrès de Vienne," p. 413.

7. In this Note of the 11th of October, 1814, Lord Castlereagh wrote confidentially to Prince Hardenberg:

4*

"As for the question of Saxony, I declare to you that if the incorporation of the whole of that country in the Prussian monarchy is necessary to secure so great a boon to Europe, however deeply I should personally regret to see so ancient a family so profoundly afflicted, I could not feel any moral or political repugnance to the measure itself. If ever a sovereign has placed himself in a position in which he ought to be sacrificed to the future tranquillity of Europe, I think the King of Saxony has done so; both by his perpetual tergiversation, and because he has been not only the most devoted, but the most favored of the vassals of Bonaparte, contributing zealously, and with all his might, in his double capacity of head of a German State and of a Polish State, to extend the general thraldom even to the heart of Russia."

8. "A pamphlet of a revolutionary and threatening character, by one Filangieri, an aide-de-camp of Murat's, is in circulation here. The police have had it bought up. Prince Metternich makes use of scares of this kind to mislead public opinion with respect to the maintenance of Murat on the throne of Naples; but he is the only one, even of the ministers of the Emperor of Austria, who supports this cause, of which Europe will dispose."—Letter of the French plenipotentiary to the Department.

LETTER XXI.

THE KING TO PRINCE TALLEYRAND.

No. 8.

22nd November, 1814.

MY COUSIN,

I have received your No. 11. It would afford me ample matter for observations, if I had not forbidden myself to make any, when they can serve no purpose beyond that of personal satisfaction. Count Alexis de Noailles' report of what he heard from the lips of the princes with whom he has conversed, has afforded me pleasure. I am especially struck with what the King of Bavaria says. But what will any good intentions avail, if they be not sustained by Austria and England? Now, I very much fear that, notwithstanding the infinitely adroit manner in which you have spoken to Prince Metternich, notwithstanding the unfulfilled conditions of the Note of the 22d of October, Poland and Saxony will be abandoned. If this misfortune does befall, there will still remain to my unfortunate cousin his firmness and patience in adversity, and to me the consolation (for I am more resolute in this than ever) that I shall not have shared, by any consent, in these iniquitous spoliations. I believe in the utterances attributed to the Emperor Alexander, on the subject of Italy; it is of the utmost importance, in this case, that Austria and England should be imbued with the adage—a trivial one it may be, but full of good sense, and eminently applicable to the circumstances—*Sublata causa, tollitur effectus.*

I am better satisfied with the turn which the affairs of Italy are taking. The union of Genoa, the male succession in the House of Savoy, are two important points, but one of much greater importance is that, notwithstanding all the boasting of Murat in his gazettes (perhaps too well founded in reality), the kingdom of Naples is turning back to its legitimate sovereign.

On which, etc.

LETTER XXII.

No. 13.

Vienna, 25th November, 1814.

SIRE,

No sooner had we uttered the word *principles* here, and demanded the immediate meeting of the Congress, than a rumor was industriously spread on all sides, that France was still hankering after the left bank of the Rhine and Belgium,[1] and would never rest until she had recovered them; that your Majesty's Government might well share the desire of the nation and of the army on these points, seeing that if it did not share, it would not be strong enough to resist it; that under either supposition the danger was the same; that therefore the utmost precaution should be taken against France; that barriers through which she could not break must be opposed to her; that the arrangements of Europe must be co-ordinated to that end; and that all should hold themselves vigilantly on their guard against her negotiators, who would not fail to do everything to defeat it. We at once found ourselves exposed to prejudices against which we had to contend for two months. We have succeeded in conquering the most painful of these; it is no longer said that we have been given double instructions (as M. de Metternich assured Prince de Wrède), that we have been ordered to speak in one sense and to act in another, and are sent here to sow discord. The public does justice to your Majesty, to whom they no longer impute a hidden purpose; they praise your Majesty's disinterestedness, and applaud your defence of principles. They acknowledge that no other Power plays so honorable a part as that of your Majesty. But those whose object it is that France should still be regarded with distrust and fear, being unable to excite those sentiments under one pretext, are rousing them under another. They represent the internal condition of the kingdom in an alarming light, and, unfortunately, they found their statements upon news from Paris given by men whose names, reputation, and official position inspire respect.[2] The Duke of Wellington, who keeps up a very active correspondence with Lord Castlereagh, talks to him of nothing but conspiracies, secret discontent, and murmuring, the precursors of a storm about to burst.

The Emperor Alexander says that his letters from Paris foretell coming trouble. Mr. Vincent informs his Court that a change of ministry is to take place, that he is sure of it, and they affect to regard a change of ministry as a certain indication of a change in foreign and domestic policy.[3] From this they conclude that they cannot reckon upon France, and ought not to enter into any agreement with her. In vain do we refute these statements, quote dates and facts which contradict them, meet them with the counter information of which we are in receipt, indicate the source from which we have reason to believe the Duke of Wellington has derived his, and show how little trustworthy is that source; they still persist in asserting that, at our present distance from Paris, we do not know what is taking place there, or that it is our interest to conceal it, and that the Duke of Wellington and Baron Vincent, being on the spot, are better informed or more sincere.

I will not accuse Lord Castlereagh of having disseminated the prejudices with which we have had to contend,[4] but he has either conceived them himself, or they have been suggested to him, for he is certainly more deeply imbued with those prejudices than anybody. The long war that England has had to wage almost single-handed, and the danger in which it placed her, have made an impression upon him so strong, that it deprives him, so to speak, of the power of recognizing the total change of the times. The least reasonable of all fears, at present, is certainly that of the restoration of the continental policy. Those persons, however, who have the closest relations with him, assert that he is always full of that particular apprehension, and that he thinks it impossible to pile up too many precautions against this imaginary danger. He fancies himself still at Chatillon, treating with Bonaparte, and wanting to treat for peace. It is easy to imagine the effect which the Duke of Wellington's reports produce upon a mind thus disposed, and to perceive that the Duke himself forms an obstacle to that good understanding which he seemed to think it would be easy to establish between Lord Castlereagh and us.

I have done everything I can to bring about such an understanding, not only since we have been at Vienna, but before Lord Castlereagh left London, when he was on his way through Paris. That it has not been established is due not only to Lord Castlereagh's prejudices, but also to the real and complete opposition that exists between his views and ours. Your Majesty has directed us to defend principles; the Note of the 11th of October, which I have had the honor to send to your Majesty, shows what respect Lord Castlereagh has for them. We are to employ every means to maintain the King and the kingdom of Saxony. Lord Castlereagh absolutely wants to treat the one as a condemned criminal, of whom he, Castlereagh, has constituted himself the judge, and to sacrifice the other. We wish that Prussia should acquire or preserve a great part of the duchy of Warsaw, and Lord Castlereagh wishes this as well, but from motives so different, that he takes the same means for the destruction of Saxony which we employ for its salvation. He wants to turn the assistance which we shall have given him in the question of Poland against us. It is impossible to reconcile such opposite purposes.

I have often spoken, and to the Emperor Alexander himself, of the restoration of Poland as a thing which France desires, and which she would be ready to support. I have not demanded that restoration without an alternative, because, as Lord Castlereagh has not demanded it himself, I should have stood alone in making the demand, and should thereby have irritated the Emperor Alexander without acquiring any merit in the eyes of the others; and I should also have offended Austria, who, up to the present at all events, is against the restoration. Only two days ago Lord Castlereagh, with whom I was remonstrating upon the way in which he had conducted affairs for the past two months, answered me, "I have always thought that when one was in a league, one must not separate one's self from it." He regards himself then as in a league; that league is certainly no other than a sequel to their treaties prior to the peace. Now, how can we hope that he will come to an understanding with those against whom he acknowledges he is leagued?

The other members of the league, or coalition, against France are in a similar case. Russia and Prussia expect nothing but opposition on our part; Austria may desire our support in the question of Po land and in that of Saxony, but her minister dreads our interference in other matters, much more than he desires it on behalf of those two objects. He knows how much we have the Neapolitan question at heart, and he has it no less at heart himself, but in a very different sense from ours. Last Sunday, on coming away from a dinner at Prince Trautmannsdorf's, I went to see him. On the previous evening I had received a letter from Italy, informing me that Murat had seventy thousand men; mostly armed, thanks to the Austrians, who had sold him twenty-five thousand muskets. I wished to have an explanation about this with M. de Metternich, or at all events to let him see that I knew it. I led him to talk on the Neapolitan question; and as we were among a great many people in the salon, I offered to withdraw into his cabinet in order to show him the letter. He said there was no hurry, and that the question would come up again afterwards. I asked him whether it was not already decided. He replied that it was, but that he did not want to set things in a blaze all at once; and, as he alleged his customary fear that Murat would raise Italy, "Why, then," said I, "do you furnish him with arms? If you are afraid of that, why have you sold him twenty-five thousand muskets?" He denied the fact, which was just what I expected, but I did not allow him to have the satisfaction of thinking that his denial had convinced me. After I left him he went to the Ridotto,[5] for he spends three-fourths of his time at balls and *fêtes;*[6] and his head was so full of the Neapolitan question, that having met a lady whom he knew, he told her he was harassed about this matter, but that he could not consent; that he had some consideration for the position of a man who had made himself beloved in the country which he governs; and that he passionately loved the Queen, and was in constant communication with her.[7] He was masked while saying all this, and perhaps a little more on the latter point. It is to be expected that, in accordance with the hint which he gave some time ago in a conference, of which I have had the honor to send your Majesty an account, he will resort to every imaginable device to hinder the Neapolitan question from being treated at the Congress.

The four Allied Courts, having each some reason to dread the influence that France might exert in the Congress, have naturally united, and they are afraid to approach us when there is any division between themselves, because an approach would involve concessions which they do not want to make. *Amour propre* is also, as might be expected, concerned in this. Lord Castlereagh believed that he would be able to make the Emperor of Russia give way, and he has only irritated him.

Lastly, jealousy of France is added to these motives. The Allies believed that they had weakened her to a greater degree; they were not prepared to find that she has the best army and the soundest finances of all Europe; now they believe this, and say so; and they even go so far as to regret that the Peace of Paris was made. They reproach each other with it, wonder how they were ever induced to make it, and admit this, even at the conferences and in our presence.

It cannot, therefore, reasonably be expected that England and Austria should make real and sincere approaches to us, except in a case of extreme necessity, such as would arise should their disputes with Russia end in an open rupture.

Still, notwithstanding this position of affairs, the difficulties in which it involves us, and those which the letters from Paris create, the Powers here are now in an attitude of consideration and complaisance towards us, such as we could hardly have hoped for six weeks ago—an attitude which, I may even say, is surprising to themselves.

Up to the present the Emperor Alexander has not wavered.

Lord Castlereagh, personally piqued, although he has recently received a blandly worded note from Russia, says, but not to us, that if the Emperor will not stop at the Vistula, he must be forced to do so by war; that England can only furnish a small body of troops on account of the American war, but that she would furnish subsidies, and that the Hanoverian and Dutch troops might be employed on the Lower Rhine.

Prince Schwartzenberg inclines to war, saying that it can be made now with more advantage than some years hence.

A plan of campaign has been already drawn up at the Chancellery of War; and Prince de Wrède has also made one.

Austria, Bavaria, and the other German States would put three hundred and twenty thousand men in the field; two hundred thousand, under the orders of Prince Schwartzenberg, would advance upon the Vistula, by Galicia and Moldavia; a hundred and twenty thousand, commanded by Prince de Wrède, would advance from Bohemia, upon Saxony, where they would produce a rising, and from thence between the Oder and the Elbe. At the same time Glatz and Neiss would be besieged. The campaign would not commence before the end of March.

But this plan necessitates the co-operation of a hundred thousand French troops; one half to be directed upon Franconia to prevent the Prussians from turning the army of Bohemia, the other half to occupy them on the Lower Rhine.

We must therefore expect that this co-operation, upon the absolute necessity of which the military authorities are agreed, will be demanded of us if the war is to take place.

Up to the present time, however, neither M. de Metternich nor Lord Castlereagh talks to us of war, and I am even assured that there has been no question of it between them. It is only with Bavaria that they have severally exchanged confidences on the subject.

Either they continue to build some hope upon the negotiations they are still carrying on, or they want to gain time. Lord Castlereagh having failed, they wished to put Prince Hardenberg forward again, but he could not see the Emperor Alexander either yesterday or the day before. The Emperor is much better, but he still keeps his room, and I do not think that Prince Hardenberg has seen him to-day.

The arrangements relative to Genoa are agreed to in the Italian Commission. They are now being drawn up; the commissaries requested M. de Noailles to undertake that task. The rights of the House of Carignan being recognized, M. de Noailles has instructions from me not to accept the arrangements made for Piedmont, except as an integral portion of a settlement to be made for the whole of Italy, with the concurrence of France. This is a sort of reservation which I have thought it well to make on account of Naples.

The affairs of Switzerland are to be treated in a Commission of which M. de Dalberg is, as I have had the honor to inform your Majesty, a member.

The affairs of Germany are brought to a stand by the refusal of Bavaria and Würtemberg to take part in the deliberations until the fate of Saxony shall have been fixed.

A thousand reasons make me desire to be with your Majesty. I am, however, retained here by the belief that I may be more useful to your Majesty's service in this place, and by the hope that, in spite of every obstacle, we shall succeed in carrying out a good part at least of your Majesty's desires.

I am, etc.

NOTES TO LETTER XXII.

1. "No doubt all the soldiers, and even the recruits, would rush to retake Belgium, and to advance once more upon the Rhine; but if you should have to go to Naples, you could not put France in motion except by submitting to that."—Jaucourt to Talleyrand, 29th October, 1814.

2. For a letter from Fouché to Talleyrand, bearing on the state of things in France at that date, see Appendix.

3. On the 3rd of the following December, Marshal Soult succeeded General Dupont at the Ministry of War, Beugnot was made Minister of Marine, and D'André Prefect of Police. Jaucourt wrote to Talleyrand at the same date:

"You will see by the newspapers that Marshal Soult has been appointed to War, Beugnot to the Navy, and D'André to Police. . . . The latter appointment astounds me. About Marshal Soult I had a sort of notion, because M. de Blacas asked me a number of questions concerning him, but the idea had gone out of my head. This morning the Marshal made a positive declaration of love for you, to me; and I received it so as to let him think that in your opinion nobody could be better fitted to enter a conjointly responsible (*solidaire*) ministry than himself. D'André will please you; so will Beugnot."

4. "I assure you that during the course of the Congress, and in your absence, a less considerable personage (than the Duke of Wellington) would be more convenient for us; small affairs seem to take the place of great ones in his head, and to occupy him quite as much."—Jaucourt to Talleyrand, 2nd October, 1814.

"The Duke of Wellington is not popular, and the English become daily less so. He went to a hunt and ran two wretched wolves to earth across the newly-sown corn-fields. He did not think fit to indemnify the farmers; this has caused great annoyance. He is going to renounce that sort of amusement."—Jaucourt to Talleyrand, 19th November, 1814.

"The Duke of Wellington gets on well with us. I endeavor to remove his *prejudices*. I have no reason to be anything but satisfied with him. Just at this moment there is a slight cause of annoyance which I wished to do away with, but M. de Blacas would not assist me. His hunting over the fields with dogs has given rise to complaints; he gives up doing so, and even wants to give his dogs to the Duc de Berry. At first I had an idea of offering him one of the King's forests; I do not know why I could not obtain it. The result would have been the same, only we should have been polite. You know so well what politeness can do, prevent, or excuse, that I shall not be so foolish as to add a word."—Jaucourt to Talleyrand, 27th November, 1814.

5. For a description of a Ridotto, taken from the Vienna correspondence of the *Moniteur Universel*, see Appendix.

6. On the 7th of December, 1814, M. de la Tour du Pin wrote to the Department:

"The public is generally discontented with the position of affairs; they lay the blame especially on the Emperor of Russia, who loses ground with them day by day. It is not that he is not gracious, and it may even be said affable, in society, in which he likes to mix without being noticed; he dines with a party of twenty guests chosen without restriction, and at a small dance where there were only forty persons, he danced with almost all the women:

but these pleasant ways do not compensate, in the minds of clear-sighted Austrians, for the faults of his ambition, and they are held to be aggravated by the fact that in the very palace of his host he is contriving means to injure him. Any other minister than M. de Metternich would turn this mood of the public mind to great account; but what is to be expected of one who, in the most solemn position in which a man can be placed, passes the greater part of his time in mere follies, who did not hesitate to have the *Bacha de Surène* performed at his house, and many of whose days, since the Congress, have been wasted in equally futile amusements? After that, Count, you need not be surprised that our affairs make but little progress.

In the *Moniteur Universel* of the 10th November, we find the following: "Prince Hardenberg is so busy that he can hardly spare a moment to fêtes and public ceremonies. He is less often seen than any of the ministers."

7. "In the course of that summer, there arrived in Paris M. de Metternich, the Austrian ambassador, who has played a considerable *rôle* in Europe, taken part in most important events, and made an immense fortune, without possessing talents to raise him above the intrigue of a second-rate politician. At this period he was young, agreeable, and successful with women. A little later he seemed to attach himself to Madame Murat, and continued to entertain feelings towards her which for a long time maintained her husband on the throne of Naples."—"Mémoires de Mme. de Rémusat," tom. iii. p. 48.

LETTER XXIII.

THE KING TO PRINCE TALLEYRAND.

No. 9.

Paris, 26th November [1814].

MY COUSIN,

I have received your No. 12, and I can say with truth that it is the first with which I have been satisfied; not but that I have always been so with your conduct, and your manner of rendering me an account of the state of affairs, but because I perceive that, for the first time, ideas of justice are rising to the surface. The Emperor of Russia has made a retrograde step; and in politics, as in everything else, one such step leads to another. The Emperor will, however, deceive himself if he thinks to pledge me to an alliance (political, be it understood) with him. You know that my system is a general alliance, but no particular alliances. The latter are a source of war, the former is the guarantee of peace; and although I do not fear war, peace is what I most ardently desire. That I may secure peace I have augmented my army, and I have authorized you to promise my co-operation to Austria and Bavaria. These measures are beginning to succeed; I may hope for *otium cum dignitate*, and that is enough to inspire me with satisfaction. You have said all that I could have said concerning Lord Castlereagh's Note. I account for the difference between his language and that of the Duke of Wellington by their respective positions— the one follows instructions, the other gives them.[1] I wish I could see the affairs of Italy settled from the Alps to the Terracina, for I ardently desire the important result which must ensue from the arrangement.

On which, etc.

NOTE TO LETTER XXIII.

1. "We exult in our chief! You have won the battle of talent and principles, in the King's name and your own. No matter what turn things may take, you have obtained a great personal success, and France fresh honor. That is much.

"We expect more. We think here that they will draw back in the affair of Saxony; the Duke of Wellington expresses himself plainly about it, and urges forward the proceedings of Lord Castlereagh."—Jaucourt to Talleyrand, 3rd December, 1814.

LETTER XXIV.

No. 14.

Vienna, 30th November, 1814.

SIRE,

I have received the letter with which your Majesty deigned to honor me on the 15th of this month, and by the same post the authorization to consent to the exchange of a small portion of the country of Gex for a part of Porentruy, which your Majesty has been pleased to give me. The former Prince-Bishop of Basle has already resumed, as bishop, the spiritual administration of Porentruy, but he will not be able, as prince, to recover the possession of it, which he has lost, not merely by the fact of conquest, but by the general consolidation of the ecclesiastical States of Germany in 1803. He enjoys, as prince, a pension of sixty thousand florins, and he does not claim anything more; he cannot therefore be an obstacle to the exchange which we have had the honor to lay before your Majesty, but that exchange might be rendered difficult by one of the conditions upon which your Majesty makes it depend, viz. the restitution of Bernese Aargau to the canton of Berne; for, according to all appearance, that restitution will encounter great, and perhaps even insurmountable opposition. I suppose, however, that if a few bailiwicks of Aargau only were restored to Berne; that those portions of the bishopric of Basle comprised within the former boundaries of Switzerland were given as compensation for the surplus; and that Berne were content with this arrangement, your Majesty would also be content.

The Commission charged with the affairs of Switzerland has done nothing up to the present, except ascertain that the multiplicity and the divergence of claims will make its task very onerous. They who at first were all for regulating those claims without any intervention on our part, and even contested our right to a voice in the matter, have been the first to ask for our assistance and our advice. It is true that the Swiss envoys here, who have been friendly with us from the beginning of our stay at Vienna, assured them that if they believed they could establish a stable order of things in Switzerland, without the intervention and even without the assent of France, they were entertaining an entirely groundless hope.

When the Allies treated for, and wanted to make peace with Bonaparte, they addressed themselves to the cantons which had suffered most from Swiss revolutions, appealing to the memory of their losses, and to their regrets, and holding out a prospect of repairing those losses. Their object was to detach Switzerland from France, and this expedient appeared to them to be infallible. But it so happened that those were precisely the cantons that were most attached to the House of Bourbon; then the Allies cared no longer to employ means which did not lead to their end, but rather led away from it, and nothing came of their attempts, except the difficulty of retracing their steps and quieting things down again. A scheme was then formed for uniting Switzerland and Germany in the same coalition. That idea is now given up, and there seems to be a sincere desire to terminate matters by satisfying the most considerable and the most just claims, and beyond that, making as little change as possible. We may therefore hope that an arrangement for Switzerland will be come to, which, if not the best in itself, is at least the best that can be made under the circumstances; that the independence of the country will be proclaimed, and, which is no less important for us, its neutrality.

The Commission on the affairs of Italy has made a report on the question of Genoa, and prepared a draft of articles, which will be signed to-morrow, and addressed to the eight Powers. I shall have the honor of sending a copy of this draft to your Majesty by the next post.

After the affairs of Genoa will come those of Parma. These will be more difficult, if it be true, as it is reported, that the emperor of Austria and M. de Metternich have recently given positive assurances to the Archduchess Marie Louise that she shall retain Parma. It is a certainty that the Archduchess, who up to the present carried only her husband's arms on her carriages, has had the arms of the duchy of Parma painted on one of them. I hope, nevertheless, that we shall succeed in having the duchy restored to the Queen of Etruria.

It is at Venice that the twenty-five thousand muskets sold to Murat were taken. It seems that, notwithstanding the patronage of M. de Metternich, he does not feel very safe; for he has just written a long letter to the Archduchess Marie Louise, in which he announces, among other things, that if Austria will assist him to remain at Naples, he will raise her once more to the rank from which she ought never to have descended. These are his own words. Such an extravagant utterance, even from a man of his country and his character, can only be explained as an effect of self-betraying fear.

The conferences of the German Commission are still suspended. Würtemberg has declared that it can give no opinion whatever upon portions of a whole which it is only allowed to see one by one, and that it will not deliberate upon any until it is acquainted with all. This has been met, on the part of Austria and Prussia, by a Note in which those two Powers plainly manifest the kind of predominance they want to exercise over Germany.[2] All the States of the Rhenish Confederation, with the exception of Bavaria and Würtemberg, being convinced that influence thus divided between two Powers would soon be converted into predominance and sovereignty, have united to express their desire for the restoration of the former Germanic Empire in the person of him who was its head.

These same States are on the point of forming a league, with the object of resisting, by non-consent and inertia, the system which Austria and Prussia are endeavoring to establish. The Grand-Duke of Baden held aloof at first, but he has joined the others by the advice of the Empress of Russia, his sister, who in this matter has been simply the mouth-piece of the Emperor Alexander.

The affairs of Poland and Saxony are still in the same position. The step which Prince Hardenberg took, at the instigation of M. de Metternich, and which was not approved by Lord Castlereagh, has produced no result, neither has the discussion of Lord Castlereagh with the Emperor Alexander.

I have the honor to forward to your Majesty the papers respecting that discussion, six in number. A letter which I shall get, and which I have read, is still wanting; it is the Emperor Alexander's last, and in it he says to Lord Castlereagh that there has been enough of all this, and directs him henceforward to take the official course. Those who have read these documents do not see how Lord Castlerergh, having put himself so much forward as he has done, can recede, but he himself does not see how and in what direction he can take another step.

For the rest, your Majesty will see that Lord Castlereagh has concerned himself about Poland only, being resolved to sacrifice Saxony, in pursuance of that policy which regards masses only, but takes no account of the elements of which they are formed. This is the policy of schoolboys and coalitions.

I have to make the same request of your Majesty, with respect to these papers, as I have made concerning those I have already had the honor to forward; for I obtained them in the same manner and under the same conditions.

The Emperor Alexander seems inclined to make approaches to us. He complains of those who, since we have been here, and especially in the early days, intervened between him and us, and he designates M. de Metternich and M. de Nesselrode. It is Prince Adam Czartoryski whom he employs to communicate with me. The Prince is now high in his confidence, and has been taken into his Council, to which M. de Nesselrode is no longer summoned. The Council is composed of Prince Adam, Count Capo d'Istria, and Baron Stein.[3]

The Emperor is convalescent, and goes out. M. de Metternich is ill, and has not left his room either yesterday or to-day, so that there could be no meeting of the ministers of the eight Powers. Lord Castlereagh came to me this morning to propose that we should profit by this idle time to enter upon the affair of the negroes. I spoke jestingly about his proposal, and the personal motives which led him to make it, but said to him so positively that this matter must come last of all, the affairs of Europe having to be attended to before we entered upon those of Africa, that I hope he will not give me occasion to repeat it.

I am, etc.

NOTES TO LETTER XXIV.

1. At the commencement of the Revolution, the Bishop of Basle, a prince of the Holy Roman Empire and an ally of the Swiss Cantons, was Joseph Sigismund von Roggenbach. The French invasion put him to flight on the 27th of April, 1792; on the 22d of November of the same year the Republic of Raurasia, which only lasted until the 23rd of March, 1793, was constituted. Roggenbach died on the 9th of March, 1794. He was succeeded by a prelate named Neveu, who figures in the "Almanach de Gotha" until the fall of the Empire, notwithstanding the secularization of 1803.

2. On the 29th of September, Talleyrand wrote to the Department: "The agents of the small Courts are trying to make approaches to France, and we are encouraging them."

3. "After the retreat of Napoleon in 1812, the Emperor Alexander selected Baron Stein to make of him the future arbiter of the destinies of Germany. Stein played a considerable part in the conferences of Kalisch, and his influence made itself felt until the second peace of Paris in 1815."—Mémoires de Metternich," tom. i. p. 169.

LETTER XXV.

THE KING TO PRINCE TALLEYRAND.

No. 10.

4th December, 1814.

MY COUSIN,

I have received your No. 13, and while I am still equally satisfied with your conduct, I am, as you will not be surprised to hear, very ill-pleased with the position of affairs,[1] which seems to me to be very different from that which they had attained when you dispatched your No. 12. God only can rule the minds of men; man can do nothing in that; but, whatever may happen, if I hold firmly by my principles, and perhaps deserve that the phrase *justum et tenacem propositi virum* should be applied to me, honor at least will remain, and that is what I most desire.

I am not surprised at the reports that are current, the news that is sent, and the confirmation which ill-will lends to them. As for myself, if I heeded all that is said, I should never have an instant's peace, but nevertheless my sleep is as tranquil as in my youth. The simple reason is that I have never had any other expectation than that the mixture of so many heterogeneous elements would produce a state of ferment when the first days of the Restoration were past. I know that it exists, but I do not let it disturb me.

Resolved as I am never to depart, outside my kingdom, from the dictates of equity, or, inside it, from the constitution which I have given to my people, and never to relax in the exercise of my legitimate authority, I fear nothing; and a little sooner or later the clouds, whose gathering I have foreseen, will be dispersed.

They talk to you of changes in the ministry, and I now announce them to you. I do all justice to the zeal and good qualities of Count Dupont, but I cannot equally commend his administration, and therefore I have removed him from his department, and confided it to Marshal Soult.² I give the Navy to Count Beugnot,³ and the general direction of Police to M. d'André; but these removals, of which I wished you to be the first informed, make no change in the system of policy which is *mine*, and this you will be careful to say plainly to whomsoever may speak to you of these occurrences.

I shall be very glad to see you again when the time comes, but the reasons which have determined me to deprive myself of your services here have gathered additional force from the very difficulties which you experience. It is necessary that you should continue to represent me at the Congress until its dissolution, as ably as you are now doing. On which, etc.

NOTES TO LETTER XXV.

1. "The King seemed to me to be much pleased with the order, perseverance, and success of our negotiation, but not with our progress in general. He had the extreme goodness to impart to me the conversation of the two Emperors, and although he said with satisfaction, 'Here, you see, is a little firmness on the part of the Emperor Francis,' I thought I could perceive that he did not as yet put any confidence in the reconciliation with the Emperor Alexander, of which you have hopes."—Jaucourt to Talleyrand, 18th December, 1814.

2. "The last point in my last letter will be the first in this—the dismissal of General Dupont. Everybody declares that the nomination of Marshal Soult was unexpected. *Monsieur* (the Count d'Artois) talked, on his arrival, about the complaints; the subject of those complaints was the ill-provided condition of the regiments."—Jaucourt to Talleyrand, 7th December, 1814.

3. See Appendix.

LETTER XXVI.

COUNT DE BLACAS TO PRINCE TALLEYRAND.

Paris, 4th December, 1814.

The letter, Prince, which the King has received from you, by a post which could not have brought me your answer to that which

I had the honor to write on the 9th of last month, had already furnished me with important information on the principal subjects treated of in the letter which you were so good as to address to me on the 23rd. His Majesty was pleased to communicate to me your dispatch, as well as Lord Castlereagh's Note, and while it is, as you observe, impossible to avoid observing the difference that exists between the style of that Note and the language of the Duke of Wellington, yet I confess that I am unable to make up my mind as to the real causes of that difference. The King recoils from the idea of attributing it only to a cunning policy whose object would be the discrediting of France. The Duke of Wellington, both by semi-official communications such as I have already mentioned to you on the subject of the relations of Naples with Paris, and by his recent conduct on the occasion of a correspondence found in Lord Oxford's possession, and seized,[1] has manifested a disposition, which is quite opposed to the notion of his spreading abroad unfounded apprehensions. It may, indeed, be possible that he has done an ill office to the King's policy, without meaning to do so, by taking an exaggerated view of the dangers with which timid minds are constantly alarmed by too readily credited rumors. It is certain that several circumstances have, independently of the views of England, furnished pretexts for the vexatious notions from which you apprehend ill effects. You know, Prince, and you have often deplored with me the insecurity from which the Government of his Majesty suffers, for want of vigor and unity in the ministerial operations.[2] This defect, which was for some time known to the Cabinet only, cannot fail to acquire an unfortunate publicity in the long run. If there be added to this the discontent of the army[3]—its complaints have been incessantly dinned into the ears of the Princes throughout the entire duration of their journeys in the departments—the disturbance kept up by constant protests against the incompetency of the police; lastly, the constant accusations against men whose known views and manner of talking point them out, perhaps without justice, but certainly not without probability, as instigators of dangerous plots; it is clear that all these things, including measures of safety, which have been taken too openly, owing to the zeal of the military commandants, has produced an impression by which foreigners may profit without having helped to create it.

This state of things will explain to you, Prince, the imperative motives by which the King has been actuated in making a partial change in his ministry. His Majesty made known his resolution on this subject yesterday. While doing justice to the zeal and the good intentions of Count Dupont, his Majesty was aware that the army, probably imputing to that minister evils which were rendered inevitable by the difficulties of the moment, ardently desired the institution of a new system, and the King selected the Duke of Dalmatia for the portfolio of War. That choice, in which his Majesty has been guided by a desire to restore to his troops the obedience, confidence, and ardor that are necessary to the maintenance of the national strength, will no doubt appear to you to be in accordance with the principles on which the King has invariably acted.

The Ministry of Marine confided to Count Beugnot, and the general direction of Police entrusted to M. d'André, are other alterations by which the King hopes to be enabled to realize the public expectation.

You will no doubt think, Prince, that this change, although not very considerable when considered in its relation to the composition of the Council, will nevertheless bring about important results. In fact, a good spirit in the army and the efficiency of the police are so imperatively demanded by public opinion, that, from this point of view, the King's resolution is of the greatest interest. His Majesty relies upon you to present this event in its true light at Vienna, and to cause it to be regarded, not as a ministerial revolution, but rather as a gain of additional strength and intelligence to the Government. The King deeply regrets that, instead of having to entrust this task to your care, he cannot have you with himself, to strengthen the favorable impression which he hopes his ministry will inspire.[4] Nevertheless, his Majesty feels the truth of your observations upon the advantageous effect which has been produced by your continuous efforts. It may be that affairs, taking a more rapid course, will detain you for a shorter period than you lead us to fear, and, for myself, I greatly wish that you may be able to return sooner than you seem to hope.

NOTES TO LETTER XXVI.

1. The *Moniteur Universel* of the 16th of September, 1814, contains the following:

"The Earl of Oxford arrived recently from Naples, where he has left the Countess and their children. It is known that the chief object of his journey is to communicate the exact state of affairs at the Court of Naples at present to the Government of the Prince Regent."

The following is the incident referred to, as explained in the private correspondence of M. de Jaucourt with M. de. Talleyrand: "The Earl of Oxford was arrested yesterday at a short distance from Paris. I only know this from the Marquis de Saint-Elie, *chargé d'affaires*, but not recognized by King Murat; he insisted upon seeing me this morning, and told me that the police agent, on arresting Lord Oxford, had said that he must examine his papers, knowing him to be especially in communication with the Marquis de Saint-Elie. I did not enter into any explanation with him; I merely said, 'You have nothing to do with me in all this, no relations existing between us; but you can see the Minister of Police, and you had better do so.'

"Lord Oxford was on such intimate terms, and so openly, with the Bonapartist brawlers and the zealous Muratists here, that the police were obliged to take action. They alleged that he had broken the rules of the Post Office, which forbid travellers to carry letters, as a pretext for seizing those which he had in his possession. At Villejuif a police agent presented himself at the carriage-door, and Lord Oxford was brought back to Paris. His papers were handed over in a packet sealed with his arms; the packet was opened in the presence of M. de Beugnot, and not only his papers but his letters were returned to him, with the exception of three addressed to King Joachim."— 20th November, 1814.

"I have, I think, sent you some details of the affair of the Earl of Oxford, through which letters that prove the agitation and alarm of the King of Naples' people have fallen into Beugnot's hands. Madame de Staël figures in those letters, but as a high priestess of the temple of peace and liberty. She loves Joachim because of his love for those two benefactresses of the world."— 3rd December, 1814.

2. On the 20th of September, M. de Jaucourt wrote to M. de Talleyrand: "Yesterday we met at the Chancellor's . . . the customary persons and the new-comer. If the Minister of War had not told me that this dinner was not so unmeaning as others at which the same persons had met, I should have thought they were all waiting to talk until I should have gone away. M. de Montesquiou slept and snored, or listened derisively; poor Ferrand contemptuously put his head on his knees; the Chancellor talked. . . .

"I made some observation on the want of forethought, ability, and, above all, sincerity, that was shown in the way in which the Chambers were treated, and said that public opinion was not grasped in any way; that there was no useful writing, no sincere communication. Believe, my dear friend, that I have the same feelings which animated us on the 30th of April, but a time of crisis and danger gives much advantage. It is easier to place a hundred senators at the foot of the scaffold than to construct a united and responsible ministry now and here."

1st October.

"The departure of the deputies, the time of their return, the disposition of the Assembly, which, as well as a great part of that of the peers, will not form its opinion except on the presumption that what is proposed is more or less constituent—all this annoyed him (Baron Louis) and rendered him less tractable.

"It has been proposed, with the good faith of alarm, and the confidence of fear, to put the ministers into the Assembly, to increase the number of deputies, to declare the Assembly formed for a period of five years, and then to renew it wholly. . . . Madame de Staël is starting from Clichy to make a constitutional disturbance."

4th October.

"M. de Vitrolles came here to scent out something that he might put in the *Moniteur*.

"I should not be too much disposed to use the *Moniteur;* its official character gives it an embarrassing importance, and its *Vitrolique* supervision is very disagreeable.

"The purchasers of national property are uniting, preparing to canvass the electors and get themselves nominated. Their fortune is at stake; it is designed to despoil them of their goods, if possible, if not, of their honor."

On the 1st of November, 1814, D'Hauterive writes: "A fresh quarrel has just broken out between the Abbé de Montesquiou and Beugnot. The former has authorized the prefects to have agents, who have been sent by the latter into the departments, unknown to the minister, to study what is called public opinion, but as the prefect, sub-prefects, mayors, etc., write, to spy upon them and misrepresent their conduct by lying reports. There is still great enmity between the two magistrates. The Abbé de Montesquiou expresses his sentiments very openly."

3. "It is reported as certain, and this comes from the principal personages at the War Office, that a certain regiment of infantry of the Guard has burnt its eagles, collected the ashes, and each soldier swallowed a portion of them while drinking a cup of wine to the health of Bonaparte."—D'Hauterive to Talleyrand, 14th November, 1814.

4. M. de Jaucourt writes on the 10th of December: "We are not confirming ourselves in the principles of a representative government, of the collective responsibility (*solidarité*) of the ministers, and of the kind of ministerial authority and independence, without which responsibility is nothing but an obstacle and a hindrance to all public service."

LETTER XXVII.

No. 15.

Vienna, 7th December, 1814.

SIRE,

The letter I now have the honor to write to your Majesty will be short. I have only just learned the facts which I am about to narrate; substituting them for others of a more vague and less interesting character which I had collected.

I am informed, as I have every reason to believe correctly, that a post which arrived last night brought Lord Castlereagh and Count Münster orders to support Saxony (I do not yet know to what extent, and whether under any hypothesis, or only within given conditions). It is added that Lord Castlereagh has, this morning, addressed a Note to M. de Metternich announcing this to him, and that Count Münster, who has always, though rather timidly, taken our side of the question of Saxony, means to declare himself on the matter very strongly indeed. Prince de Wrède must have read Lord Castlereagh's Note when he was with M. de Metternich.

The day before yesterday M. de Metternich had an interview with the Emperor Alexander, in which each of them displayed all the tricks and subtleties of which he is capable; but it came to nothing. As, however, M. de Metternich had declared that his master would never consent to give up Saxony to Prussia, the Emperor Alexander accosted the Emperor Francis in the evening, after the *carrousel*, and said, "At the present day, we sovereigns are obliged to conform to the wishes of the people, and to observe them. The wish of the Saxon people is not to be divided. They would rather belong to Prussia as a whole, than that Saxony should be divided or parcelled out." The Emperor Francis replied to this: "I know nothing about that doctrine; but this is mine: a prince may, if he likes, give up a portion of his country and the whole of his people; but if he abdicates, his rights pass to his legitimate heirs. He cannot deprive those heirs of them, and Europe has no right to do so." "That is not according to the intelligence of the age," said the Emperor Alexander. "It is my opinion," replied the Emperor of Austria; "it ought to be that of all sovereigns, and consequently yours. As for me, I shall never depart from it."

This conversation (which was reported to me by two different persons in precisely the same way) is a certain fact. It was, then, quite right to say that the Emperor of Austria held an opinion on the Saxon affair which did not leave M. de Metternich free to choose between defending and abandoning it, and it was not without reason that the Saxon minister flattered himself Saxony would not be forsaken.

It is reported that the Emperor Alexander has said, "One conversation with the Emperor Francis is worth more than ten conversations with M. de Metternich, because the former always expresses himself clearly, and with him one knows what one is about."

The princes of Germany, who have met to consult upon the means to be taken for the defence of their rights against the designs which they know or suppose to be entertained by the Commission charged with German affairs, are about, I hear, to issue a statement of their desire for the maintenance of Saxony, with reasons assigned. Prince de Wrède, to whom most of them have addressed themselves, has told them to make haste, for this is a favorable moment. He has promised that Bavaria will join them; but Würtemberg, on the contrary, ranges itself, at present, on the side of Prussia. The Prince Royal, who is in love with the Grand-Duchess Catherine, has induced the Cabinet to take this new turn: a mean act on the part of the Court of Stuttgard, and one that will neither profit that Court nor hurt any other. It seems to me that conduct so far from noble and loyal, to say no worse of it, on the part of the King of Würtemberg, is not calculated to make it very desirable to become his nephew.[1] On another occasion I shall beg your Majesty to permit me to speak more at length on the subject to which I allude here.

The Emperor of Russia wished to see me; then he wished before doing so to clear up the confusion with which, as he desired Prince Czartoryski to tell me, his head was "encumbered." I could not make use of General Pozzo in this, for he is on indifferent terms with him. His servants find it difficult to see him. The Duc de Richelieu had to wait a whole month for an audience.[2] Prince Adam, although he is an interested party in our discussions, is my most serviceable go-between. I have not seen the Emperor as yet, and I am told he is shaken, but still undecided; I do not know when or to what he will ultimately make up his mind.

I have the honor to forward to your Majesty copies of the two documents by which he closed his correspondence with Lord Castlereagh. He has been generally blamed for having engaged in a hand-to-hand contest (so to speak), which might have been considered derogatory to his rank even if he had had the best of it, and the opposite was the case. Thus, instead of the triumph which he no doubt anticipated, the result was wounded *amour propre.*

Your Majesty will see that in the whole of this discussion Lord Castlereagh regarded the question of Poland from one point of view only, and that he kept it apart from every other question. Not only has he not demanded the restoration of independent Poland, but he has not expressed any desire for such a restoration; and he has even spoken of the Polish people in terms which are calculated rather to hinder than to conduce to it. He has been especially careful to abstain from uniting the Polish question with that of Saxony, which he had completely given up, but is going henceforward to sustain.

I have also the honor to forward to your Majesty a letter from your Majesty's consul at Leghorn.[3] I have made efficient use here of the information which it contains, and which I have had conveyed to the Emperor of Russia. M. de Saint-Marsan has received similar information, and M. de Metternich has acknowledged that the same particulars have reached him from Paris. The conclusion which I draw from all this is that it would be well to get rid without delay of the man of the island of Elba, and of Murat. My opinion is spreading. Count Münster shares it, and with ardor: he has written about it to his Court, and talked of it with Lord Castlereagh, whom he has excited to the point of going to M. de Metternich, to stir him up in his turn; but M. de Metternich does all in his power to support an opposite view.

His favorite artifice is to make us lose time, thinking to gain by that device. The Commission on the affairs of Italy have settled the Genoa business a week ago. I have already had the honor to inform your Majesty that they had been regulated according to your Majesty's wishes. I forward the report of the Commission together with my letter of to-day to the Department. Your Majesty will find that it contains the clauses, and even the express terms prescribed by our instructions. To-morrow, the Commission of the eight Powers will take cognizance of the report, and will pronounce upon it. Afterwards Tuscany and Parma will be dealt with. This section of the task, which ought to have been finished already, has been retarded by the slight illness of M. de Metternich, who, that nothing may be ended, calls his present condition "convalescence."

The time which is lost to our business is consumed in fêtes; the Emperor Alexander asks for, and indeed commands them, as if he were at home. We are invited to these fêtes, attention is paid to us, we are treated with great distinction, as a mark of the feelings entertained towards your Majesty, whose praises are sounded everywhere; but all this does not make me forget that it is nearly three months since I left your Majesty.

I have spoken to Lord Castlereagh about the arrest of Lord Oxford, of which M. de Jaucourt had informed me. Far from showing any displeasure, he told me he was "charmed" at it, and described Lord Oxford as a man who deserved no kind of esteem. I should be very glad if among his papers some were found which would compromise Murat[4] with this Court.

The two last mails from Paris have brought me the letters with which your Majesty has honored me, bearing date the 22nd and 26th of November. I am, etc.

NOTES TO LETTER XXVII.

1. If the Duc de Berry had married the Grand-Duchess Anne, he would have become the nephew of King Frederick of Würtemberg.

2. On the 24th of December, 1814, M. de Jaucourt writes from Paris to Prince Talleyrand: "If you have been told that the Duc de Richelieu was ill-disposed towards you here, do not believe it; I am certain of the contrary. I do not know the exact measure of his regard, but that of his praise was unmistakable. He speaks highly of the character, the intentions, and the sentiments of the Emperor Alexander, and yet he condemns his policy."

On the 4th of January, 1815, he writes: "I assure you that, let his motive be what it may, calculation, belief, personal liking, or any other, nothing can possibly be more friendly than the tone of the Duc de Richelieu with respect to you, everywhere and always. There is no doubt that he wants to be sent to Vienna."

M. de Talleyrand was replaced at the Ministry of Foreign Affairs by the Duc de Richelieu on the 26th of September, 1815.

3.

"To Prince Talleyrand.   "Leghorn, 15th November, 1814.

"MONSEIGNEUR,

" I think it my duty to inform your Most Serene Highness, directly, that for some days past the number of travellers who arrive at and depart from the island of Elba is considerable, and that they all speak in the same way to persons who are in my confidence. They are Italians, Swiss, or Piedmontese. They all say that Bonaparte will not remain in banishment at Elba; that he will get out of the island; and that so soon as he appears at the head of his Guards in Italy, more than fifty thousand men, who are ready, will rise and rally round his standard, and thousands of French soldiers will join them. Two persons, among others, have been more particularly pointed out to me; they are men named Eltovi and Louis Cavani, from Milan. At a supper which they gave yesterday in the outskirts of the town, they named more than one hundred and fifty superior officers of the former Army of Italy, who are scattered about in the different cantons of the former kingdom, and who keep up correspondence among themselves. These two individuals had come on the day before from Porto Ferrajo Eltovi left the town this morning, stating that he was going to Lucca; the other says he is shortly going to Parma. I have sent a description of them to the Governor of Leghorn, but as Italian and Austrian subjects, these bearers of correspondence and agents of secret intrigue cannot be proceeded against in any vigorous way. The Austrian consul at this port is an estimable man, but he is over seventy years of age. He has probably no instructions to watch the subjects of the Emperor his master who come and go, and he has neither the means nor the activity that would be requisite for doing so. If severe measures be not taken to prevent and stop this correspondence, the tranquillity of Italy will not last long. Recruiting has ceased in Italy and Tuscany, since the recruiters have been arrested and put in prison.

"King Joachim received Bonaparte's officers well. He questioned them concerning the health and the occupations of the Prince of Elba, and particularly inquired into the quality and number of his troops. Captain Jaillade having answered that there were only fifteen hundred men on the island, Joachim replied, 'Well, that is the nucleus of five hundred thousand.'

"If soldiers are not recruited, officers are. The latter are content with a very small sum, and they are afterwards placed in the Guard.

"The Tunisians have been well received at Porto Ferrajo, and one of them has availed himself of that fact to maintain a cruiser in these waters, and strike terror into the coast. The Tuscan Government has ordered a levy of National Guards, to defend it against these pirates.

"I beg you to accept, etc.,
"CHEVALIER MARIOTTI,
"His Majesty's Consul at Leghorn."

4. The Duke of Campo-Chiaro then stated that Murat had an army of fifty thousand men; that he had it in his power to raise the whole of Italy, and to have himself declared head of the Confederation; and that certainly he would die a king.

In December, 1814, he sent the following note to Prince Talleyrand:

"Vienna, 7th December, 1814.

"The King of Naples was included in the coalition by whose successful efforts Louis XVIII. was raised to the throne of France; his accession to that coalition was not without utility to the common cause.

"The King of Naples is therefore entitled to expect friendly relations with the House of Bourbon, on whose side he had found himself on the battle-field.

"In the treaty of peace, concluded 30th May, 1814, Austria stipulates as much in her own name as in that of her allies, and the King of Naples had a solemn treaty of alliance with Austria, which was known to all Europe."

LETTER XXVIII.

THE KING TO PRINCE TALLEYRAND.

No. 11.

10th December, 1814.

MY COUSIN,

I have received your No. 14. You have quite correctly interpreted my meaning on the subject of the canton of Aargau. I should certainly prefer that Switzerland should become what she formerly was;[1] but I do not want the impossible, and provided that the canton of Berne be satisfied, so far as it can be under the circumstances, I shall be satisfied also. As for the Prince-Bishop of Basle, I had not remembered the last decrees of the Empire; but I see that he has settled the question with respect to himself, and I have no objections to make to the arrangements concerning Portentruy.

I have read with interest, and I shall carefully preserve the papers you have sent me. Lord Castlereagh speaks very fairly with regard to Poland, but his Note of the 11th of October contradicts his language. If, however, he should succeed in persuading the Emperor of Russia, that would be a great advantage for Saxony; but I do not see any appearance of this, and we must continue to pursue our own course.

You know Prince Czartoryski; I know him also. The fact that the Emperor Alexander has selected him as an intermediary leads me to believe that his Imperial Majesty wishes rather to draw me towards him than to approach me himself. Go on, nevertheless, with these conferences, but at the same time pursue my designs. No evil can result from them, and perhaps they may do some good.

I am inclined to think that it is from fear that Murat is playing the braggart.² Never lose sight of the fact that if there exists a resource for Bonaparte, it is in Italy, and by means of Murat, and that thus *Delenda est Carthago.*

On which, etc.

NOTES TO LETTER XXVIII.

1. Before 1789, the Republic of Switzerland was formed of Sixteen Cantons: it now consists of twenty-two.
2. Murat had made an offer of his services to Louis XVIII. through the Marquis de Saint-Elie, who said to Jaucourt in November, 1814: "I can assure you once again that only the devoted services of the King of Naples, which are at the disposal of the King of France, can secure the execution of Prince Talleyrand's designs."—Jaucourt to Talleyrand, 27th November, 1814.

LETTER XXIX.

No. 16.

Vienna, 15th December, 1814.

Sire,

The Note by which the German princes of the second and third order intended to record their unanimous desire for the maintenance of Saxony was on the point of being signed; it has not been, and it will not be signed.¹

The Duke of Coburg was at the head of those princes. His conduct cannot be too highly praised. One of his sisters is married to the Grand-Duke Constantine. His younger brother is aide-de-camp to the Grand-Duke and a major-general in the Russian service. In the last campaign the Duke himself wore the Russian uniform. He stands high in the good graces of the Emperor Alexander, and is on very intimate terms with the King of Prussia. If he opposed the designs of those sovereigns he might very reasonably have dreaded their resentment; and, on the other hand, he had every reason to hope that if Saxony came to be sacrificed, he might obtain a share of the fragments. All these motives have not availed to silence the voice of gratitude and justice in the Duke's heart, or to make him oblivious of what he owes to his House and to his country. When, after the death of the Duke, his father, in 1807, his possessions were sequestrated because he was in the Russian camp, and Bonaparte wanted to proscribe him, he was protected by the intercession of the King of Saxony. Since then the King might have extended his sovereignty over all the duchies of Saxony, had he chosen to do so, but he refused. The Duke, in his turn, zealously defended the cause of the King. He made his brother Leopold plead that cause in London, and the Prince Regent heard him with attention and favor. He had pleaded it here himself with the Sovereigns and their ministers. He even went so far as to send a Memorandum in his own name to Lord Castlereagh refuting his arguments; this he drew up in consultation with us. The Emperor Alexander, being informed by the Duke of Weimar, of the Note that was in preparation, sent for the Duke of Coburg, and overwhelmed him with reproaches as much on account of the Memorandum which he had sent to Lord Castlereagh as of his recent proceedings; accused him of scheming; quoted the conduct of the Duke of Weimar as an example which he ought to have followed; told him that if he had representations to make, it was to Prince Hardenberg he ought to have addressed them, and declared that of what had been promised to him he should have nothing.

The Duke's demeanor was firm and noble. He spoke of his rights as a prince of the House of Saxony, and of his duties as a German prince and a man of honor. He did not hold himself free to leave them unfulfilled: if the Duke of Weimar thought otherwise, he could only compassionate him. For the rest, he had, he said, twice risked his existence for the sake of his Imperial Majesty; if he had to sacrifice it to-day for the sake of honor, he was ready to do so.

On the other hand, the Prussians, their emissaries, and particularly the Prince Royal of Würtemberg, have intimidated a certain number of German ministers by declaring that they would regard all those who should sign anything in favor of Saxony as enemies.

This is why the Note has not been signed; but that it was to have been done is known, and also what prevented its being done, and the desire which that Note was to have expressed has probably gained in intensity by the violence that has been used to suppress it.

Perhaps I have dwelt at too great a length upon this particular circumstance; but I have been led to do so by the double motive of wishing to do the justice to the Duke of Coburg that I believe to be his due, and to make the nature and the diversity of the obstacles with which we have to contend better known to your Majesty.

While these things were happening, the Prussians received a Note from M. de Metternich, in which he stated to them that the kingdom of Saxony ought to be maintained; showing by statistical calculations appended to his Note, that their population would be the same as in 1805, if only three hundred and thirty thousand Saxons were added to that of the territory which they have kept, and that of the disposable territories which are destined for them.

I hasten to inform your Majesty of Count Münster's statement that, if it be necessary to secure the maintenance of Saxony, he will renounce the aggrandizement promised to Hanover. Your Majesty will assuredly learn this with pleasure, because of the facilitation of affairs which it affords, and also because of the esteem with which your Majesty honors Count Münster.

A passage in M. de Metternich's Note, in which he backed himself up with the opposition of France to the Prussian views upon Saxony, led the Emperor Alexander to fear that an agreement was already formed, or was about to be formed between Austria and us, and he immediately sent Prince Adam Czartoryski to me.

The Prince began by renewing the proposal which the Emperor himself had made to me in the last interview with which he honored me—that we should lend ourselves to his wishes in the matter of Saxony, while he would promise us his utmost support in that of Naples. He regarded his proposal as all the more acceptable because he now no longer demanded the relinquishment of the whole of Saxony, but consented that a *nucleus* of the Kingdom should remain.

I answered that, as regarded the question of Naples, I held by what the Emperor had said to me; that I placed my confidence in his word; that, at all events, his interests in the matter were the same as our own, and he could not be of any other mind than ours; that if the question of Poland, which must be regarded as personal to the Emperor Alexander, since he set his satisfaction and his fame upon it, had been decided in accordance with his wishes (this is not yet completely, but it is very nearly, done), he owed it to the conviction of Austria and Prussia that we should be only in the second rank in that respect; that on the question of Saxony, which was really foreign to the interests of the Emperor, we had taken it upon ourselves to pledge the King of Saxony to certain sacrifices; but that the spirit of conciliation could not lead us to go so far as the Emperor seemed to desire. The Prince talked to me of alliance and of marriage: I said to him that so many grave matters could not be discussed at the same time; and that, besides, certain things must not be mixed up with others, because such a combination would assume the base character of a bargain.

He asked me whether we had entered into engagements with Austria. I said, no. Then he asked whether we would enter into any in case of our not coming to an agreement about Saxony, to which I replied, "*I should be grieved at that*" [*J'en serai fâché*]. After a moment's silence, we parted, politely, but coldly.

The Emperor, who was to have gone in the evening to a fête given by M. de Metternich, did not go there. A sudden headache was the cause of, or the pretext for, his absence. He sent the Empress and the Grand-Duchesses. Next morning M. de Metternich waited on him by his request.

At the ball, M. de Metternich came up to me, and after having thanked me for a small service I had rendered him, he complained of the difficulty in which Lord Castlereagh's Notes on Saxony placed him. I thought there had only been one Note of a compromising nature (that of the 11th of October). But he talked of another, which I have procured, and have the honor to send your Majesty a copy of it. Although it bears the title of a Verbal Note of Lord Castlereagh's, I know that it is the work of Mr. Cook, to whom it does little credit in point either of doctrine or style. This Note has been sent to the three Powers who for so long a time called themselves *Allied*.

M. de Metternich promised me that on leaving the Emperor Alexander he would come to me, if it were not too late, to tell me what had passed; this time he kept his word. The Emperor was cold, stiff, and severe. He maintained that M. de Metternich said things to him on the part of the Prussians which they disavowed, and that the Prussians said things on the part of M. de Metternich which were entirely opposed to what he wrote in his Notes, so that he (the Emperor) did not know what to believe. He reproached

M. de Metternich with having inspired Prince Hardenberg with I know not what ideas. M. de Metternich had with him a letter from Prince Hardenberg which proved the contrary, and he produced it. The Emperor took that opportunity to reproach M. de Metternich with writing unbecoming letters, and this charge is not unfounded. The Emperor had in his hands certain communications of an entirely private and confidential character, which could only have reached him through a most culpable indiscretion on the part of the Prussians. Lastly, the Emperor appeared to be in doubt whether M. de Metternich's Note contained the expression of the real sentiments of the Emperor of Austria, and added that he wished to have an explanation on the point with the Emperor himself. M. de Metternich went at once to give his master notice of this, and the Emperor of Austria, if questioned on the subject by the Emperor Alexander, will reply that the Note was drawn up by his orders, and contains nothing that he does not endorse.

In a conference between M. de Metternich and Prince Hardenberg the only difficulties that arose were concerning the statistical calculations appended to M. de Metternich's Note. They parted without having arranged anything, on M. de Metternich's proposing to nominate a Commission to verify his statistics.

This, Sire, is the state of things at present. Austria, in her calculations, lets Saxony off with a loss of four hundred thousand men only. She does not want to abandon Upper Lusatia, on account of the Gabel Pass, which lies before the entrance into Bohemia, and through which the French penetrated in 1813.

The Emperor of Russia consents to allow a kingdom of Saxony to subsist, but one which, according to Prince Czartoryski, must be only one-half of what it is at present.

Lastly, Prussia now seems to limit her claims to a numbering of population, and consequently she subordinates them to the result and the verification of her reckoning.

No doubt the question is not yet decided, but the chances are now more favorable than they have ever hitherto been.

M. de Metternich proposed that I should read his Note. I thanked him, and said I was already acquainted with it, but that I begged he would communicate it officially to me; that I considered he ought to do so, since he had quoted us in it, which I might object to his having done without informing us; that it was necessary we should sustain the Note, but that we could not do so with propriety unless a regular communication of it were made to us. He gave me his word that what I desired should be done. My particular motive for making a point of a formal participation is because that will be the real date of the rupture of the coalition.

A few days ago, I proposed that a Commission should be formed to deal with the affair of the Slave Trade. This proposal was about to be made, and I wanted to get hold of it myself in order to propitiate Lord Castlereagh, and induce him by that means to act with us in the difficult Italian questions which we were approaching. I did obtain something, for he asked me of his own accord to let him know in what way I proposed to settle the affair of Naples, and promised to send a courier for the orders which he might require. I have written the subjoined letter to him.[2] After having received it, he proposed to let me see his correspondence with Lord Bentinck. This I have read, and it is certain that the English are perfectly free in that matter. But certain promises have been made to Murat, the breach of which would place the promiser in a difficult position *as a man*, if Murat himself had observed his own promises strictly. "I believe," said Lord Castlereagh, "I am correctly informed that Murat kept up communications with Bonaparte in the months of December, 1813, and January and February, 1814,[3] but I should be very glad to have positive proofs of this; it would greatly facilitate my course of proceeding. If you have such proofs among your archives, you would do me a great favor by procuring them for me." I am writing to-day, in my letter to the Department, to have a search made for any that may be at the Ministry of Foreign Affairs. It is possible that traces of a correspondence between Murat and Bonaparte may be found in the Secretary of State's office. Lord Castlereagh made no objection to the form which I proposed to him to adopt.

Count de Jaucourt will of course lay before your Majesty the two letters which I address to the Department to-day; I entreat your Majesty to be pleased to reject the proposals with respect to Gex which will be made to your Majesty at Paris. We have much reason to be displeased with the Genevese who are here. The authority of the Chancellor is more than sufficient to justify the abandonment of this question, which has been conducted too hastily.

I am, etc.

NOTES TO LETTER XXIX.

1. This protest in favor of the King of Saxony, signed by the Ministers of the princely houses of Germany, then assembled at Vienna, was couched in the following strong terms:

"The general voice, not of Germany only, but of all Europe, is raised on behalf of the King of Saxony. His restoration ought, without doubt, to be effected simultaneously with that of peace. To doubt for a moment the keen interest taken by the monarchs in the fate of their unfortunate brother, would be to wound them deeply, and it would be doing them a still greater wrong to believe that they could, by sanctioning the deprivation of an entire family of their most sacred rights of possession, sanction an act of violence in the modern, which is unexampled in the ancient history of the Fatherland.

"Assuredly, if it be established beyond question that no prince of the Empire can be condemned except by a judgment of his peers; that hostile enterprises on the part of the legitimate sovereigns of Germany have been sternly opposed, such an attempt on the part of the other States ought to be much less to be apprehended in our day. Let the grand-duchy of Warsaw be treated as a conquered country, and as the expiatory sacrifice for a moment of error or weakness; let even the legitimacy of its creation be contested,— but can such a term ever be applied to a principality of Germany? And is not the first article of every treaty of peace, according to the practice of the law of nations, amnesty and restitution to the *status quo ante bellum?* Where is there a prince to whom the most sacred and solemn of titles could secure the inheritance of his ancestors and the cradle of his race, if it might be wrested from him by a mere agreement, or he could even be forced into some exchange, utterly reprobated by his people, who would demand their former master?

"When, in the last century, the princes of Germany—alarmed by the apprehended exchange of Bavaria, in virtue of which one of the ancient German corporations was to be subjected against its will to a foreign dynasty, and which might disturb the balance of the States of the Empire—rallied round the banner of Frederick the Great, in a close federation, with the purpose of protecting property against systems of *arrondissement* and projects of *convenances*, it was not held allowable to contest the legitimacy of that precaution, and Bavaria owed her preservation to it.

"If Germany is the keystone of the arch of the political edifice of Europe, Saxony is the corner-stone of the new federation in that portion of it. To remove it would be to shake the new building to its foundations, and we believe ourselves to be expressing the unanimous desire of all the integral portions of the German nation by declaring loudly: *Without a free and independent Saxony, there is no stable federal Germany.*"

2. See D'Angeberg, p. 525.

3. Towards the end of December, 1813, Murat had an offer of his co-operation conveyed to Napoleon, on condition that he should be allowed to put himself in possession of the whole of Italy on the right of the Po, and to proclaim Italian independence. This proposal received no reply. About the middle of January, 1814, La Besnardière sounded the ex-Emperor once more on this subject, in consequence of the receipt of letters from Naples, probably

from Queen Caroline. "What answer would you have me make to a madman?" said Napoleon. "How can this fool fail to see that only my entire preponderance in Europe could prevent the Pope's being at Rome? It is the interest and the desire of Europe that he should return thither, and I myself am the first to wish it." And when it was observed to him that it would perhaps be well to do something to attach Murat to himself, he answered, "What good would that do? He is a man with a weathercock for a head. You can see that by his continual changes."

"The Emperor Napoleon," adds La Besnardière, "did not doubt that it depended entirely on himself to keep King Joachim in alliance with him, or to recall him how and when he choose."—Memorandum from La Besnardière to Talleyrand, 5th February, 1815.

LETTER XXX.

THE KING TO PRINCE TALLEYRAND.

No. 12.

18th December, 1814.

My Cousin,

I have received your No. 15, and it has given me great satisfaction. If England declares frankly in favor of Saxony, her agreement with Austria and the greater part of Germany ought to triumph over *the lights of the age*.[1] I like the firmness of the Emperor Francis, and I care little for the defection of the King of Würtemberg. I await the explanation of what you tell me on the subject of that prince, but, from what I know of him, I should not attempt to advise any one to form a close alliance with him.

The letters found among Lord Oxford's papers have not thrown any light upon Murat's proceedings;[2] but the facts contained in the letter from Leghorn, whose truth is not to be questioned, since Prince Metternich admits his knowledge of them, speak for themselves;[3] and it is more than time that all the Powers should combine together to eradicate the evil. M. de Jaucourt will certainly have informed you of the unjust, and I must say ungrateful, reproach which has been made to Count Hector d'Agout on this subject. It would be well that you should speak to M. de Labrador about this, so that his testimony may serve to enlighten M. de Cevallos, if he be in error, or at least to shame him, if, as I very strongly suspect, he lies to himself.

I look upon the wish of the Emperor of Russia to see you again as a good sign. I have nothing to add to what I have said to you concerning the great affairs, but there is one of them which I should like to see brought to a conclusion; it is that of the marriage. I have given my *ultimatum*. I shall not look into what may take place in a foreign country, but the Duchesse de Berry, whomsoever she may be, shall not cross the frontiers of France without making open profession of the Catholic, Apostolic, and Roman religion.⁴ On that condition I am not only ready, but eager, to conclude the matter. If that condition does not suit the Emperor of Russia, let him say so; he and I will be none the less good friends, and I will arrange another marriage.

I feel your absence as deeply as you do, but in affairs of such importance we must apply to ourselves what Lucan said of Cæsar.

On which, etc.

NOTES TO LETTER XXX.

1. The Emperor Alexander and Councillors La Harpe, etc.

2. General Exelmans was the person most seriously compromised in this affair. Among the papers which were seized was a letter written by him to Murat, which M. de Jaucourt described as " altogether insensate."

3. In his letter to Talleyrand of the 18th of December, Jaucourt speaks of "this roundabout correspondence that goes from the island of Elba to Tuscany, from Florence to Chambéry, to Franche Comté, to Paris."

At this very time the French minister in Switzerland, M. Auguste de Talleyrand, had a watch kept on King Joseph, who had taken refuge at Prangins, and was demanding his expulsion.

4. "The Duc de Berry has asked me whether you said anything to me concerning his mariage; he displayed some annoyance at the papistical and Roman rigidity of the King. I replied that you said nothing to me about it. I suppose the birth of the Duc de Nemours has inspired him with this matrimonial avidity."—Jaucourt to Talleyrand, 29th October, 1814.

"The Duc de Berry is much occupied about his marriage, no matter with whom; and on this point he is right: it is necessary that he should marry and have children. It is your affair, Prince, to get him married, in the interests of France."—Jaucourt to Talleyrand, 1st November, 1814.

" I have just left Monsieur (the Count d'Artois, afterwards Charles X.). At the close of the conversation he returned to the themes of Vienna and the marriage of his son, who has quite made up his mind to that important step. If one were to search for the cause among the smaller feelings hidden in his heart, I think the birth of a prince in the family would be found to have contributed to it. Monsieur asked me whether you had written to me about the Emperor Alexander's sister. He said, 'It is this chapel business, on which it seems there is to be no concession, that is stopping everything. And, after all, I do not know why so much importance is attached to a political marriage. I don't believe in the results. Has M. de Talleyrand said anything to you about the King of Saxony's niece? You might question him concerning her, that is to say, after having taken the orders of the King.' "—Jaucourt to Talleyrand, 9th November, 1814.

LETTER XXXI.

No. 17.

Vienna, 20th December, 1814.

SIRE,

I have received the letter with which your Majesty has deigned to honor me, bearing date the 10th of December, and numbered 12.

I have the honor to forward to your Majesty copies of the Note of Prince Hardenberg to M. de Metternich, on the subject of Saxony, the tables attached to it, and the official letter written to me by Count Metternich, which accompanied them. There was also a note in his own hand,[1] in which he repeated to me, but less explicitly, what he had already said in conversation, *i.e.*, that this document should be the last to proceed from the coalition, and added that he was happy to find himself side by side with your Majesty's Cabinet in the defence of so good a cause.

I earnestly desired this communication for the reason which I have had the honor to explain to your Majesty in my previous letter; I was also anxious for it, because it would give me a perfectly natural opportunity of making such a profession of faith as would place the principles, views, and resolutions of your Majesty beyond the possibility of doubt. I had long been seeking for an opportunity, I had tried in many ways to create one, and so soon as it offered, I hastened to turn it to account by making the answer of which I have the honor to send your Majesty a copy herewith.[2]

I pointed out what the question of Poland might have been for us, and why it had lost its interest, and I added that the fault had not been ours.

In dealing with the question of Saxony, I refuted the revolutionary arguments of the Prussians, and those of Mr. Cook in his "Saxon Point," and I think I have proved what, up to the present time, Lord Castlereagh either could not or would not understand— that, as regards the balance of power, the Saxon question was more important than that of Poland in the terms to which the latter is reduced. The equilibrium of Germany would be destroyed if Saxony were sacrificed, and it is evident that she could not then contribute to the general balance of power.

While doing my best to convince, I was careful to say nothing that could offend him. I attributed the opinions which I contested to a kind of fatality, and praised the monarchs who maintain, in order to lead them to abandon, them.

I did not bestow any praises upon your Majesty; I only set forth the instructions with which we have been honored. What more could I have said? The facts speak for themselves.

I am assured that the Prussians had, on their side, prepared a Note in answer to that of M. de Metternich, and that it was very strong; but that the Emperor of Russia, to whom it was shown, would not have it sent.

Lord Castlereagh is like a traveller who has lost his way, and does not know how to find it. He is ashamed of having narrowed the Polish question, and, after having expended all his efforts on that question in vain, being duped by Prussia, in spite of our warnings, into giving up Saxony to her. He knows not what to do. He is also very uneasy about the state of public opinion in England, and intends, it is said, to return thither for the opening of Parliament, leaving Lord Clancarty here to carry on the negotiations.

The affairs of Italy are getting on pretty well. I am disposed to think that the Queen of Etruria will get the advantage over the Archduchess Marie Louise in the matter of Parma; and I am endeavoring so to dispose things that these arrangements shall be made without touching the Legations.

The Commission of Precedence,[3] for which I have nominated M. de la Tour du Pin, to whom I have given instructions on this subject in conformity with your Majesty's, will probably be in a condition to make its report in ten or twelve days from the present.

Your Majesty will perhaps consider my Note addressed to M. de Metternich rather long; but I could not make it shorter, having calculated upon its being published and read in England as well as in France. Every word that I used has a special object which your Majesty will recognize in my voluminous correspondence.

I am, etc.

NOTES TO LETTER XXXI.

1. At the beginning of December, Austria joined France on the question of Saxony, by sending to Prince Hardenberg a Memorandum from Prince Metternich, in which Austria pronounced against the incorporation of the whole kingdom of Saxony with Prussia.

M. de Metternich transmitted this Memorandum to M. de Talleyrand on the 16th December, 1814. He ended as follows:

"I congratulate myself on being on the same side as your Cabinet on a question so worthy to be defended."

2. On the 19th of December, 1814, M. de Talleyrand replied to M. de Metternich:

" I am enabled to answer for the satisfaction with which the King will learn the resolutions announced by this Note, by comparing them with the orders given by his Majesty to his ambassadors at the Congress:

"'France does not bring thither any ambitious project or personal interest; she is replaced within her former boundaries, and she no longer thinks of extending them. Her armies, crowned with glory, aspire to no fresh conquests. Delivered from that oppression of which she was rather the victim than the instrument, happy to have recovered her legitimate princes, and with them the repose that she might have feared was lost for ever, she has no claims to make, she advances no pretensions, nor will she advance any; all that remains for her to desire is that the restoration of the whole of Europe should, like her own, be accomplished.' "—D'Arenberg, p. 140.

3. This Commission was nominated to fix precedence, the rank of the Crowned heads present or represented at the Congress, and other matters of State etiquette.

LETTER XXXII.

THE KING TO PRINCE TALLEYRAND.

No. 13.

Paris, 23-24th December, 1814.

MY COUSIN,

I have received your No. 16, and have heard with much satisfaction of the firm and noble conduct of the Duke of Saxe-Coburg and Count Münster. You know how much I think of the latter, and the Duke, in addition to the ties of kindred between us, is brother to a princess for whom I entertain a great affection, the Duchess Alexander of Würtemberg; but this satisfaction does not prevent me from regretting that the Note was not signed. *Verba volant, scripta autem manent.* I am also pleased with your interview with Prince Adam. You will have seen by my last number that I am desirous of a definite answer in the matter of the marriage, but that I am far from wishing to give it the character of a bargain.

The affair of the Slave Trade seems to me to be going well. As for that of Naples, which concerns me much more nearly, a very vexatious report was spread in Vienna at the departure of the Duc de Richelieu—a report which was confirmed by private letters, but which your silence hinders me from crediting: no other than that Austria had declared openly in favor of Murat,[1] and was endeavoring to induce England to do likewise. The success of your letter to Lord Castlereagh, and that of the steps which I have ordered to be taken in consequence, will speedily apprise me of what I have to hope or to fear. Nothing can be better than what you propose in that letter, but I am not free from uneasiness respecting *certain promises* made to Murat. Even if we should find the plainest proofs —of which I feel by no means certain, for Bonaparte had many things destroyed at the last—we know too well that a crafty policy can always draw what deductions it chooses from anything. Let us, however, pursue our own course; I shall never be found making a backward step.

It was for the advantage of Berne that I consented to the exchange of a portion of Gex; but since the conditions which I required are not acceptable, I shall absolutely refuse my consent; and neither will I accord it to an arrangement by which something more would be taken away from the King my brother-in-law.[2]

On which, etc.

NOTES TO LETTER XXXII.

1. "A general who is still almost in the service of Murat, whose wife is still at Naples, and who will re-enter the King's service if the freedom with which he has answered Marshal Soult has not ended his military career—came to see me. He even told me that Murat had begged him to do so; that he reckoned on the pledges formerly given by Austria and recently renewed; that it was a mistake to have refused to come to an understanding with him. . . . You know more about that than Murat, and probably more than Prince Metternich. As for me, I speak only of *the late* (*feu*) Murat; not even of the former (*ci-devant*) General Murat."—Jaucourt to Talleyrand, 14th February, 1814.

2. Victor Emanuel, King of Sardinia.

LETTER XXXIII.

THE KING TO PRINCE TALLEYRAND.

No. 14.

27th December, 1814.

MY COUSIN,

I have just received the news that a treaty of peace and amity between England and the United States was signed on the 24th.[1] You will, no doubt, be informed of this before the present despatch reaches you, and I feel sure of the steps which you have taken in consequence. Nevertheless, I hasten to charge you, in congratulating Lord Castlereagh on this happy event, on my behalf, to call his attention to the purpose to which Great Britain may turn it. She will be henceforth free to use all her resources, and what nobler use can she make of them than to secure the repose of Europe upon the only solid basis, that of equity? And how can she do that more effectually than by uniting herself closely with me? The Prince Regent and I are the most impartial in this affair; for Saxony never was the ally of France, Naples never was in a position to assist her in any war, and the same is the case with regard to England. It is true that I am the nearest relative of the two Kings, but I am, above all, King of France and father of my people. It is for the honor of my crown, it is for the welfare of my people, that I will not consent to allow a germ of European war to be sown in Germany; that I will not tolerate in Italy a usurper, whose existence is a disgrace to all the Sovereigns and a menace to the tranquillity of all their States. The Prince Regent entertains similar sentiments; and it is with the utmost satisfaction that I find him in a better position to act upon them.

I have just spoken to you as a King, and now I cannot refrain from speaking to you as a man. There is a case, but I must not forecast it, in which I could think only of the ties of blood. If the two Kings, my cousins, were, as I was for so long, wanderers on the face of the earth, deprived of their sceptres, then I would hasten to receive them, to supply their wants, to mitigate their ill fortune by my good offices—in a word, to imitate on their behalf what several sovereigns, and especially the Prince Regent, did on mine; and, like them, I would consult at once both my feelings and my dignity. This case, however, will never arise. I have a sure guarantee for that in the generosity of some and the interests of all.

NOTE TO LETTER XXXIII.

1 Under President Madison, war was declared against England by the United States, which defended the principle of the freedom of the seas (1811-1814). Peace was concluded at Ghent on the 24th of December, 1814, on the footing of the *status quo ante bellum.* "In my opinion," Jaucourt wrote to Talleyrand, 28th of December, 1814, "the Duke of Wellington had a great deal to do with the conclusion of the peace."

LETTER XXXIV.

No. 18.

Vienna, 28th December, 1814.

SIRE,

While I was writing the letter to Prince Metternich, of which I have had the honor to send your Majesty a copy, the Prussians were replying to his Note of the 10th of December, referring to that which he had addressed to them on the 22nd of October, and showing that he was contradicting himself. They endeavor to justify their claims on Saxony by authority and example, and they especially challenge the correctness of the calculations on which M. de Metternich relies.

Lord Castlereagh came to me, bringing this answer from the Prussians, which he had obtained permission to communicate to me. (It will be given to me, and I shall have the honor of sending it to your Majesty by the next post.) He read it to me. I pointed out the sophistry of their reasoning, and showed that their authorities had no weight and their examples no force, the times and the circumstances being quite different. Then, in my turn, I made Lord Castlereagh read my Note to M. de Metternich. He read it very attentively, and quite through, and then handed it back to me without a word either of approval or dissent.

The object of his visit was to talk to me about a Commission which he wants me to have appointed for the verification of the calculations that are produced by Prussia and Austria respectively. I told him I had no objection to make to this, but that if we were to set about accomplishing the object, as we have done in so many other cases up to the present time, we should not arrive at any result; that we must begin by laying down principles; that before these calculations were verified, the rights of the King of Saxony must be recognized; and that we—M. de Metternich and I—might come to an agreement on this subject. "An agreement?" he repeated. "It is, then, an alliance that you are proposing?" "This agreement," said I, "can very well be made without an alliance; but it shall be an alliance if you wish. For my part, I have no objection." "But an alliance supposes war, or may lead to it, and we ought to do everything to avoid war." "I agree with you. We ought to do everything, except to sacrifice honour, justice, and the future of Europe." "War," he replied, "would be regarded with disfavor among us." "War would be popular with you if it had a great object—one truly European." "What would that aim be?" "The restoration of Poland."[1] He did not reject this idea, but merely answered, "Not yet." I had only given this turn to the conversation in order to sound him, and to find out how he would be inclined in a given case. "Whether it be," said I, "by a Convention, or by Notes, or by a protest signed by you, M. de Metternich, and myself, that we recognize the rights of the King of Saxony, is a matter of indifference to me. I do not care about the form; the thing only is important." "Austria," he answered, "has officially recognized the rights of the King of Saxony; you have also recognized them officially; I recognize them *vehemently*. Is the difference between us, then, so great that it requires an act such as you demand?" We parted, after having agreed that he should propose the formation of the Commission, for which each of us was to nominate a plenipotentiary.

The following morning, he sent Lord Stewart to tell me that every one consented to the formation of the Commission, and that the only objection made was to a French plenipotentiary being included in it. "Who opposes that?" said I to Lord Stewart, sharply. "It is not my brother." "Who is it, then?" He answered me hesitatingly, "Well—it is——" and then he stammered out the word "Allies." At that word my patience gave way, and, without allowing my expressions to go beyond the limit I was bound to observe, I put more than warmth, more than vehemence into my tone. I drew a picture of the course which, under circumstances like the present, Europe had a right to expect such a nation as the English to follow, and going on to speak of what Lord Castlereagh had never ceased doing since he came to Vienna, I said his conduct should not remain unknown; that it would be judged in England, and *how* it would be judged, and I hinted at the consequences to him. I dealt no less severely with Lord Stewart himself for his zeal for the Prussians, and I ended by declaring that, if they persisted in being men of Chaumont, and in promoting the coalition, France would owe it to her dignity to retire from the Congress; and that if the projected Commission was formed without a French plenipotentiary being summoned to it, your Majesty's embassy would not remain a single day at Vienna. Lord Stewart was quite confounded, and, with an air of alarm, hurried off to his brother.

In the evening I received a note from him, written by his own hand, in which he said that, having learned my wishes from his brother, he had hastened to make them known to *our* colleagues, and they all acceded with great pleasure to what they were informed would be agreeable to me.

The same evening, M. de Metternich, whom I had seen during the day, made a proposal, which I had suggested to him, to the Powers who were to co-operate in the formation of the Commission. This was that they should agree to grant the authority and force of an adjudicated matter to the estimates made by the Commission. He added two other proposals, to which I readily subscribed: one was that the valuation should comprise all territories conquered by France and her allies; the other was that it should bear only upon the population. But I requested it to be added that the population should be estimated not by numbers merely, but by its condition also; for a Polish peasant, without capital, land, or industry, ought not to be placed upon a par with an inhabitant of the left bank of the Rhine, or the richest and most fertile districts of Germany.[2]

The Commission, on which I had nominated M. de Dalberg, met on the following day. It is working unremittingly, and Lord Clancarty exhibits the same zeal, firmness, and uprightness which have distinguished him in the Commission for the affairs of Italy, of which he is also a member.

It is but just to say that Lord Castlereagh has been weak rather than ill-intentioned in this matter; but his weakness has been all the more inexcusable in that the opposition, of which he has made himself the mouthpiece, proceeded from the Prussians only.

My Note to M. de Metternich was pleasing to the Austrian Cabinet on two points: the declaration that France does not claim and does not demand anything for herself, and the conclusion. After he had read the Note, the Emperor of Austria said to M. de Sickingen, "All that is written in that I agree with."

The Emperor of Austria having asked him whether he had read the reply of the Prussians to M. de Metternich's Note of the 10th of December, he answered, "Before reading it, I had taken my own line, and I adhere to that line more strongly, after having read it." It is said that he added, "Settle the affair, if it be possible; but I beg your Majesty not to talk to me any more of these '*factums*.'"

He said to the King of Bavaria, "I am an Austrian born, but my head is Bohemian" (this answers to the French phrase, "a Breton head "). "My line is taken in the Saxon affair, and I will not deviate from it."

Prince Czartoryski, to whom I had communicated my Note to Prince Metternich, had a copy made of it, which he submitted to the Emperor Alexander. The Emperor was satisfied with the portion that related to him and his interests. He acknowledges that France is the only Power whose language has not varied, and which has not deceived him. Nevertheless, he thought he discerned that he was indirectly reproached with having departed from his principles, and he sent Prince Czartoryski to tell me that his principle was the welfare of the people; to which I replied that such was also the principle of the leaders of the French revolution, and at all its stages. The Emperor was also seized with a scruple arising from the fear that the King of Saxony, if maintained as we wish him to be, will be very unhappy. He compassionates him, not in his actual position, as a captive and despoiled, but in the future, when he shall have reascended his throne, and re-entered the palace of his ancestors. This scruple means that he is more firmly resolved than before to avert such a misfortune from the King.

The Prussians, by consenting to the formation of the Statistical Commission and sending their plenipotentiaries thither, have evidently subordinated their claims upon Saxony and their hopes to the result of the labors of the Commission, and that result will, most probably, be favorable to Saxony.

Thus, the affair of Saxony is in a better position than it has yet been.

That of Poland is not concluded, but its termination is talked of.

Counts Rasoumowski and Capo d'Istria will act for Russia; M. de Metternich will be the Austrian plenipotentiary. It has been resolved that a thoroughly official character shall be given to these conferences. M. de Wessenburg is to draft the protocol; M. de Hardenberg will be the Prussian plenipotentiary; he will be alone. As boundaries only are to form the subject of this negotiation, the matter ought to be arranged in a few days.

Although I had given Lord Castlereagh my letter to M. de Metternich to read, I have thought it well to send him a copy of it, so that it may be placed among the documents which he may be called upon to lay before Parliament, and I have sent with it, not a letter of advice, pure and simple, but one of which I have the honor to subjoin a copy.[3] The great problem which the Congress is to solve is therein stated under a new form, and reduced to its simplest terms. The premises are so incontestable, and the consequences are deduced so inevitably, that I cannot think any reply to it is possible. I was not, therefore, at all surprised when M. de Metternich told me that Lord Castlereagh, who had shown him my letter, seemed much embarrassed by it.

There exists in Italy, as in Germany, a sect of "unitarians," or people whose aspiration is to make of Germany one single State. Austria, being warned of this, had a great number of arrests made, all in one night. Among the persons arrested are three generals of division. The papers of the sect have been seized at the house of a professor named Rosari. It is not known from whence Austria got the information; some believe that Murat was the informer,[4] and that he has betrayed men with whom he was hand in hand, in order to curry favor with the Austrian Court.

Your Majesty will have perceived, by the documents which I have had the honor to forward, that I do not lose sight of the affair of Naples. Neither do I forget the *delenda Carthago;* but it is not possible to commence in that way. I am also mindful of the marriage. Circumstances have so changed, that while a year ago your Majesty might have desired that alliance, it is now for the Emperor of Russia to desire it. But the matter requires explanations which I must beg your Majesty's permission to reserve for a special letter, which I shortly shall have the honor to write.

When this letter reaches your Majesty, we shall have entered upon a new year. I shall not have the happiness of being with you, Sire, on the first day of it, and of offering your Majesty my respectful congratulations and best wishes in person; but I beg to be permitted to make them, and that your Majesty will accept my homage. I am, etc.

NOTES TO LETTER XXXIV.

1. "Of all the questions which are to be treated at the Congress, the King would have regarded that of Poland as the first, the greatest, the most eminently European—as, indeed, beyond comparison with any other—had it been possible for him to hope as reasonably as he desires ardently that its ancient and complete independence might be restored to a people, so worthy, by reason of its antiquity, its valor, and the services which it has rendered to Europe, of the interest of all other peoples. The partition which erased Poland from the number of the nations of Europe, was the prelude to, the cause of, and, up to a certain point, the excuse for, the convulsions of which Europe has been the victim. But when the force of circumstances, overriding the noblest and most generous inclinations of the Sovereigns to whom the provinces which were formerly Polish are subject, had reduced the question of Poland to a mere matter of partition and boundaries, which was dis-

cussed among themselves by the three interested Powers, and from which France was excluded by their previous treaties, it only remains for the latter, after having offered, as she had done, to support the most equitable claims, to wish that you may be satisfied, and in that case to be so herself."—Letter from Talleyrand to Metternich, 19th December, 1814.

2. In his letter to Metternich of the 19th of December, Talleyrand refers to the following passage from Montesquieu:

"Athens had the same forces within her, during her rule in pride and glory, and during her servitude in shame. She had twenty thousand citizens when she defended the Greeks against the Persians, when she contested for supremacy with Lacedemonia, and invaded Sicily; and she had twenty thousand when Demetrius of Phalaris counted them, as slaves are reckoned in a market."

3. See D'Angeberg, p. 570.

4. "A secret sympathy with revolutionary principles acts in his favor. A man like us is the king for plebeians. He inspires them with a feeling of private satisfaction, which they will regret to part with. To the nobles such a being is an object of ridicule, but the cause of the nobility is at least difficult to defend.—We raise our hands to Heaven during the fight; that is all we can do."—Jaucourt to Talleyrand, 28th February.

LETTER XXXV.

THE KING TO PRINCE TALLEYRAND.

No. 15.

30th December, 1814.

My Cousin,

I have received your No. 17. I am pleased with M. de Metternich's Note, because it positively pledges Austria; but I am still more pleased with your answer. I do not know whether it could be abridged; but I know quite well that I should not wish it to be shorter; first, because it says everything, and nothing but what ought to be said; and secondly, because I think that more of the amenity so useful and frequently so necessary in affairs, is displayed by amplifying one's ideas a little than in stating them too laconically.

What you tell me of the difficulty in which Lord Castlereagh finds himself, proves to me that I was right to send you my last despatch; it is possible that he may fail to perceive how excellent an opportunity for retracing his steps is afforded him by the peace with America.[1]

I am very glad that the affairs of the Queen of Etruria are assuming a more favorable aspect; but I regard that point as only an advance towards another, far more excellent, and to which I attach much greater value.

M. de Jaucourt is, no doubt, informing you of what M. de Butiakin has said to him; you have much better means than I have of learning the truth of what he reports on the subject of Vienna; but if it be true, as it seems likely, that the *amour propre* of the Russian nation, which counts for something in spite of the aristocracy, is excited on behalf of the marriage, let that nation remember that *he who desires the end desires the means.* As for me, I have given my *ultimatum,* and it is irrevocable.

On which, etc.

NOTE TO LETTER XXXV.

1. "The Duc de Berry said to me this morning (31st December), that he had seen the Duke of Wellington, who had spoken to him of Murat, and that he had given him to understand that it would be for England, in the position in which she was now placed, to settle the destinies of the world.

"The Duke of Wellington replied by acquiescing in these assertions, undertaking to write, and even, if the Duc de Berry is to be believed, so far pledging himself as to say *that he would bring it to pass.*"—Jaucourt to Talleyrand, 31st December, 1814.

LETTER XXXVI.

No. 19.

Vienna, 4th January, 1815.

SIRE,

I have received the letter of the 23rd of last month, with which your Majesty has deigned to honor me.

On the 21st of the present month, the anniversary of a day of horror and eternal mourning, a solemn expiatory service will be celebrated in one of the principal churches of Vienna. I am having the preparations made; and, in giving orders for them I have acted not only on the impulse of my feelings, but from a sense that it becomes the ambassadors of your Majesty, while acting as the interpreters of the sorrow of France, to proclaim that sorrow aloud in a foreign land and before the eyes of assembled Europe. All, in this sad ceremony, must bear proportion to the grandeur of its object, the splendor of the Crown of France, and the quality of those who are to witness it. All the members of the Congress will be invited, and I am assured that they will come.[1] The Emperor of Austria has had me informed that he will be present, and no doubt his example will be followed by the other Sovereigns. All that is most distinguished in Vienna, of both sexes, will feel it a duty to attend on the occasion. I do not yet know what it will cost, but the expense is a necessary one.

The news of the signature of peace between England and the United States of America was announced to me on New Year's Day by a note from Lord Castlereagh. I hastened to offer him my congratulations, and I also congratulated myself on the event, feeling that it may influence both the disposition of the minister and the resolutions of those with whose pretensions we have hitherto had to contend. Lord Castlereagh showed me the treaty. It does not affront the honor of either of the two parties concerned, and consequently it will satisfy both.

This happy intelligence was only the precursor of a still more fortunate event.

The spirit of the coalition and the coalition itself had survived the Peace of Paris. My correspondence has, up to the present time, supplied your Majesty with repeated proofs of this. If the plans which, on arriving here, I found had been formed, had been carried into execution, France might have stood alone in Europe without being in good relations with any one single Power for half a century to come. All my efforts were directed to the prevention of so great a misfortune, but my most ardent hopes did not reach the height of a complete success.

Now, Sire, the coalition is dissolved, and for ever. Not only does France no longer stand alone in Europe, but your Majesty already has a federate system such as it seemed that fifty years of negotiation could not have procured for her. France is in concert with two of the greatest Powers, and three States of the second order, and will soon be in concert with all the States which are guided by other than revolutionary principles and maxims. Your Majesty will be in reality the head and the soul of that union, formed for the defence of the principles which your Majesty has been the first to proclaim.

So great and happy a change is only to be attributed to that special favor of Providence, which was so visibly marked by the restoration of your Majesty.

Under God, the efficient causes of this change have been—

My letters to M. de Metternich and Lord Castlereagh, and the impression which they have produced;

The suggestions which I gave Lord Castlereagh, relative to a union with France, and of which I gave your Majesty an account in my last letter;

The pains I have taken to lull his distrust by exhibiting perfect disinterestedness in the name of France;

The peace with America, which, by releasing him from difficulty on that side, has left him more liberty of action, and given him greater courage;

Lastly, the pretensions of Russia and Prussia, as set forth in the Russian project, of which I have the honor to subjoin a copy, and especially the manner in which those pretensions were advanced and argued in a conference between their plenipotentiaries and those of Austria. The arrogant tone of that insolent and nonsensical document so deeply offended Lord Castlereagh, that, departing from his habitual calmness, he declared that the Russians were claiming to lay down the law, and that England was not disposed to accept it from anybody.

All this had influenced him, and I took advantage of the disposition of his mind to urge the union concerning which I had so often talked to him. He received all I said with animation, and proposed that he should write to me his ideas on the subject. The day after this interview, he called on me, and I was agreeably surprised when I saw that he had put his ideas into the form of articles. Up to the present, he has been very little accustomed to praise from me, and he was therefore all the more pleased with the compliments which I bestowed upon his draft. He requested that M. de Metternich and I would read it with attention. I made an appointment for the evening, and, after we had made a few slight alterations, we adopted it under the form of an agreement. In certain particulars it might have been more carefully drawn up, but in dealing with weak people delay is dangerous; so we have signed the document to-night. I hasten to forward it to your Majesty.

Your Majesty had authorized me by your letters in general, and by particular instructions of the 25th of October, to promise to Austria and Bavaria your Majesty's *most active co-operation*, and as a consequence to stipulate for such aid in favor of those two Powers as would probably be rendered necessary by the forces which would be opposed to them in case of war. Your Majesty had authorized me to do this, even supposing that England were to remain neutral; now, England has become an active party, and with her the United Provinces² and Hanover; thus the position of France is a superb one.

General Dupont having written to me on the 9th of November that your Majesty would have a hundred and eighty thousand men available on the 1st of January, and a hundred thousand more in the month of March, without having recourse to a fresh levy, I thought that an auxiliary corps of a hundred and fifty thousand men might with propriety be stipulated, as England engages to furnish the same number of troops, and France could not do less. The agreement³ being made for defensive purposes only, the succors should not be furnished except in case of attack, and there is every reason to believe that Russia and Prussia will not run that chance.

Still, as this case might arise, and render a military treaty necessary, I beg that your Majesty will be pleased to give orders for General Ricard's being sent here to assist me. He enjoys the confidence of Marshal Soult; and, having been for a long time in Poland, and especially at Warsaw, he has local knowledge which may be very useful in arrangements likely to occur. The report that has been made to me of his worth and ability leads me to prefer him to any other; but it is necessary that he should come *incognito*, and that the Minister of War, after having given him the requisite documents, should enjoin the profoundest secrecy upon him. According to what I have been told of him, he is a gentleman, one to whom your Majesty might, if you thought proper to do so, give your orders in person.

I entreat your Majesty to be pleased to command that the ratifications of the treaty be expedited, and sent to me as soon as possible.⁴ Your Majesty will no doubt think it well to impress upon M. de Jaucourt that none but men of well-tried discretion ought to be employed in that business.

Austria does not wish to send a courier to Paris to-day, lest suspicions should be aroused, and as it is desirable that her minister should be acquainted with the treaty, she requests that M. de Jaucourt will let M. Baron Vincent read it, and will also tell him that it is to be kept strictly secret.⁵

I hope your Majesty will add these two papers to those which I have previously had the honor to forward.

The object of the agreement which we have just made is to complete the provisions of the treaty of Paris in the manner most in conformity with its true spirit and the greatest interest of Europe;

but if war were to break out, it might be given an aim which would render its success almost infallible, and procure incalculable advantages for Europe.

France, by a war thus nobly waged, would completely reconquer the esteem and confidence of all nations; such a conquest is better worth having than that of one province, or of many; for their possession is, happily, not necessary either to her real strength or to her prosperity.[6]

I am, etc.

NOTES TO LETTER XXXVI.

1. "The day before this ceremony, the Emperor of Russia stated that it served no useful purpose, and his envoy at the Austrian Court alleged sundry pretexts for not being present at it."—Letter from the French plenipotentiaries to the Department, 24th January, 1815.

2. The former Republic of the Seven United Provinces, which was shortly to be called the kingdom of the Netherlands.

3. M. de Talleyrand's celebrated report of the 25th of November, 1792 [the report which, in the sitting of the Convention of the 5th September, 1795, Chènier invoked in support of his petition to be allowed to re-enter France], was supposed to have been lost. It has been our good fortune to recover it. In it we find the following words:

"In principle, an alliance is a reasonable and just act only when it is reduced to a treaty of mutual defence. It is then, first, on the probability of attack, and afterwards on the calculation of the chances that in such or such time may bring about a success, that a treaty of this kind depends for a nation."

4. "Augustin, the courier who brought the original instruments of the treaty of the 3rd of January to Paris, arrived here (at Vienna) on the 19th, and brought me back the ratifications."—Talleyrand's letter to the Department, 21st January, 1815.

5. "Baron Vincent notified to me yesterday, when we met at dinner at the Danish ambassador's, that he would come this morning, to read the treaty. I have a suspicion that M. de Butiakin has a suspicion of something, for he eyed me, observed me, and listened to me, and also to Baron Vincent, persistently."—Jaucourt to Talleyrand, 13th February, 1815.

6. "After having recognized that the territory of the French Republic suffices for its population, and for those vast industrial combinations which the genius of liberty will call into being; after having been convinced that the territory could not be extended without danger to the welfare of the former as well as the new citizens of France, we ought to reject without reserve all the projects of foreign union and incorporation which may be proposed by the zeal of gratitude, or attachment more ardent than intelligent. It ought to be understood that any acceptance, or even any public desire of this kind, on the part of France, would in the first place counteract, without either honor or profit, and afterwards with peril to her, those renunciations so solemnly and gloriously made, and which Europe is far from expecting to find inoperative just at the moment when she is giving her best wishes for the

success of a cause which she believes can be soiled neither by ambition nor by greed. France ought then to remain circumscribed within her own boundaries; she owes this to her glory, to her justice, to her reason, to her interest, and to that of the nations who shall be made free through her."— Talleyrand's Memoir of the 25th of November, 1792.

LETTER XXXVII.

No. 20.

Vienna, 6th January, 1815.

SIRE,

The courier by whom I had the honor to send to your Majesty the treaty signed by M. de Metternich, Lord Castlereagh, and myself on the 3rd of January, had been twenty-four hours gone when I received the letter of the 27th December, with which your Majesty has deigned to honor me. By augmenting my hopes that I had not on that occasion done anything that would not meet the views and intentions of your Majesty, it has richly rewarded my efforts to obtain so happy a result, which has hitherto been so far from probable; and it has made me feel more deeply how sweet it is to serve a master, whose sentiments, as a King and as a man, are so generous, so impressive, and so noble.

I had just received your Majesty's letter when Lord Castlereagh called on me. I thought it right to allow him to read the passages which refer to him and to the Prince Regent. He was extremely gratified, and as he wished to make the terms in which your Majesty speaks of the Prince known to his Court, he begged me to let him take a note of them; to which I consented, induced by the double consideration that the matter would be, as he assured me, an inviolable secret, and that the praises bestowed upon the Prince Regent by your Majesty might produce an excellent effect under present circumstances.

The Emperor of Russia is sending General Pozzo back to Paris,[1] after having kept him here for two months and a half, during which time he saw him only once; and some people say that he sends him away as a too plain-spoken censor, of whom he wants to get rid. The Emperor of Russia would like your Majesty to think that it is out of regard to your Majesty, and in order to do something agreeable to you, that he has started the idea of giving the King of Saxony some hundreds of thousands of souls on the left bank of the Rhine, as a substitute for his kingdom.[2] General Pozzo is no doubt charged to try and obtain your Majesty's consent to that arrangement.

But your Majesty is aware that the question of Saxony cannot be regarded merely in relation to legitimacy—that it must also be considered with respect to the balance of power; that the principle of legitimacy would be violated by the enforced translation of the King of Saxony over the Rhine; that the King of Saxony would never consent; lastly, that, legitimacy apart, Saxony could not be given to Prussia without sensibly altering the relative strength of Austria, and entirely destroying all equilibrium in the Germanic body.

The attempts of the Emperor of Russia at Paris, as well as at Vienna, will then be defeated by the wisdom of your Majesty, who has made it your glory to defend those principles without which there can be nothing stable in Europe, nor in any State, because they alone can guarantee the security of each and the tranquillity of all.

The language held by General Pozzo di Borgo at Vienna, was too favorable to France to harmonize with what the Emperor of Russia wanted to do here. The General is to leave Vienna on Sunday, the 8th, or Monday, the 9th.

I persist in believing that the case of war to which the agreement made between your Majesty, England, and Austria relates, will not arise. Nevertheless, as it is prudent to foresee the worst and be prepared for every event, I have thought it necessary to consider the means of strengthening that union, if the case does arise, and making other Powers enter into it. I have therefore proposed to Lord Castlereagh and M. de Metternich to act conjointly with us upon the Ottoman Porte, so as to induce it to make a useful diversion, at need. They have adopted my proposal, and it has been agreed that we shall draw up in concert instructions to be given to the ministers of each of the Courts at Constantinople.[3] I think it would be well that your Majesty should hasten the departure of your ambassador.

It would probably be advantageous to establish a similar concert with Sweden, but the means of arriving at it require to be well weighed, and I must reserve my exposition of them to your Majesty for another letter.[4]

The commemorative service of the 21st of January will be performed in the cathedral. The Archbishop of Vienna will officiate at it. He is an old man of eighty-four; the Emperor was brought up by him. Nothing shall be neglected that can render the ceremony imposing.

I am, etc.

NOTES TO LETTER XXXVII.

1. On the 4th of April, 1814, the Emperor Alexander, when accrediting Major-General Pozzo di Borgo to the Provisional Government in the capacity of Commissary-General, said of him—" He enjoys my entire confidence, and he will surely justify it again on this occasion, by neglecting no means of cementing the relations of peace and amity so happily established between Russia and France."

2. Count Nesselrode's Note of the 31st of December, 1814, proposed to give Saxony to Prussia, and to form a separate State with a population of seven hundred thousand souls on the left bank of the Rhine. That State would have been given to the King of Saxony with full rights of possession and sovereignty for himself and his descendants, according to the order of succession which it should have pleased him to fix. In this system the King of Saxony occupied a place in the first Council of the Germanic Diet, and the fortress of Luxemburg became a strong place of the Germanic League.

3. The Marquis de Rivière (France), Mr. Liston (Great Britain), M. Sturmer (Austria), then represented these three Powers at Constantinople.

4. " We have once more to call your attention to the French journals, and in particular to what they report concerning the Prince of Sweden. They deal with him as with Murat, and ignore the difference between the positions of the two, and their engagements with us. The present state of Europe, which has much to fear from the encroaching spirit of the Russian Cabinet, and everything to hope from a unanimous agreement between the former Cabinets, demands great consideration towards Sweden on our part, and seems to lay it upon us as a law that we should neglect no means of maintaining a good understanding with that country. . . . We think it right to report to you certain observations of an almost official character, addressed to M. de Noailles, by Count Löwenhielm, Swedish plenipotentiary to the Congress. We quote his exact words:

"'The *ci-devant* King of Sweden proposes to go to France. I have reason to believe that he wishes to do so; and the Gazettes say so. We were witnesses of what he did for the House of Bourbon; we cannot imagine that the King of France, whose generosity is known to us, will refuse him an asylum. We only ask for a communication of some kind on the subject, and we shall be satisfied.

"'The Prince Royal is completely established in Sweden since the union with Norway. He has great influence, and is extremely popular. He wishes to form bonds of friendship with France. We ask very little of you. The Prince of Sweden knows his origin; he will always have a feeling of uneasiness; he has need of some tokens of consideration. He is a *parvenu*, and he has the sensitiveness of one; we cannot prevent that. But he will be very sensible of the least attention; for instance, an act of kindness on the part of the King towards the Princess Royal, who is in Paris, would deeply affect him, and produce the best effect.

"'Your journals are constantly speaking of the Prince Royal in a most unbecoming manner, and quoting articles which may injure him, with the addition of their own stinging comments. The Department of Foreign Affairs has influence over the press in every country. Prevent those invectives, then, which do not proceed from the Cabinet. I reiterate this request; I conjure you to grant it.'"—Letter from the French plenipotentiaries to the Department, 8th February, 1815.

LETTER XXXVIII.

THE KING TO PRINCE TALLEYRAND.

No. 16.

Paris, 7th January, 1815.

My Cousin,

I have received your No. 18. I am very glad of your conversations with the two brothers. I confess I thought the time for attempting to exclude my plenipotentiaries from the most important deliberations was past. Your firmness has entirely prevented its recurrence. But we must not go to sleep on our success; the root of the evil will remain so long as the Powers, whose alliance ought to have come to an end last April, regard it as still existing. Your letter to Lord Castlereagh is perfect, and I defy any one to deny its conclusions; but I acknowledge that I tremble when I find false pity turning against the King of Saxony the sophism which Robespierre used to hasten the consummation of the greatest of crimes. I am well pleased that the Emperor of Austria's "Bohemian head" should defend the right in Saxony, provided he does not let it do the same with respect to usurpation at Naples. He does not know, perhaps, how much he is involved in the matter; and yet the discoveries recently made, and the measures recently taken, ought to have taught him that: these are cards which you may play in demonstrating to him that there will never cease to be "unitarians" in Italy while the focus of the sect is permitted to exist. They talk of pledges; they pretend to want proofs that these engagements have not been kept. But it is not that which injures the good cause,—it is another motive, more shameful than any which history has hitherto recorded; for, if Antony basely abandoned his fleet and his army, at least it was himself, and not his minister, whom Cleopatra had captivated.[1] Despicable as this obstacle is, it is none the less real, and the only remedy is to supply him whom we would restore to himself with such great motives, that they may help him to contend against his little weaknesses.

I am impatiently expecting your letter about the marriage. That object seems to be of secondary importance when compared with those for which you are treating at Vienna; but it is urgent, in the interests of France, that the Duc de Berry should marry, and to that end it is necessary that the Russian affair should be settled.

I receive with pleasure, and reciprocate, your good wishes for the new year.

On which, etc.

NOTE TO LETTER XXXVIII.

1. At Actium Antony abandoned his army and his fleet to follow Cleopatra. Madame de Rémusat says of Metternich (as we have previously quoted a few pages back): "He seems to have become attached to Madame Murat, and he entertained feelings for her which for a long time kept her husband upon the throne of Naples."

LETTER XXXIX.

No. 21.

Vienna, 10th January, 1815.

SIRE,

I should not have the honor of writing to your Majesty to-day, but that I have to reply to a question put to me in your Majesty's name by Count de Jaucourt, on the subject of the satisfaction demanded by the Court of Madrid for the dismissal of M. de Casaflores.[1] My opinion, since your Majesty deigns to desire that I should express it, is that no sort of satisfaction is due, because satisfaction implies a wrong, and the Cabinet of your Majesty has not committed one; and also that if any satisfaction is to be given, it cannot be that which the Court of Madrid has thought proper to demand.[2] I will not importune your Majesty with the repetition of the motives on which I base this opinion, having fully explained them in the letter which M. de Jaucourt will have the honor to lay before your Majesty. The theory of extradition, which M. de Cevallos[3] wants to set up, after the law of the Hebrews and the practice of some ancient nations, is altogether extravagant. M. de Labrador, to whom I showed his letter, groaned over it. I am inclined to think that the Court of Madrid has some cause of annoyance, at which I cannot guess, apart from the dismissal of M. de Casaflores, which only serves as a pretext. I judge of this by the complaints which it makes of not being supported here by France in the affairs of Naples and the Queen of Etruria. Spain is, I think, the only country not thoroughly acquainted with the fact that your Majesty's embassy began by demanding the restitution of Naples to its legitimate sovereign, and has renewed that demand at every opportunity, by speech and in writing, confidentially and officially. M. de Labrador has protested to me that he never has, in any of his despatches, given any reason for the belief that we do not second them to the utmost. The Court of Madrid is, then, making complaints which it perfectly well knows to be unfounded.

Affairs have made no sort of progress here since my last letter. We shall have a conference to-morrow, I believe; it has been retarded several days by the Prussians, who were not ready. The subject will be the affairs of Poland and Saxony.

Of the two principles involved in the question of Saxony, one, that of legitimacy, will be absolutely respected, and this is the most important to us. The other, that of equilibrium, will be less completely safe. Lord Castlereagh has not entirely relinquished his former ideas. He has still a great leaning towards the Prussians. He persuades himself that a serious effort to restrict the King of Saxony's sacrifices would drive Prussia into incalculable displeasure. He is naturally weak and irresolute; his Note of the 10th of October embarrasses him; he does not wish, as he has told me, to contradict himself too much, like M. de Metternich, who, according to him, has *no character* to sustain. As for the latter, he changes his mind without any difficulty. On the 10th of last month he considered that it was quite enough to give Prussia four hundred thousand souls out of Saxony; now he would give double that number without any scruple; on the 22nd of October he was for total destruction. The question of Saxony, in relation to the equilibrium, concerns Austria more than any other Power, but M. de Metternich treats it with carelessness and levity which always astonish me, no matter how well used to them I may be.

As for us, Sire, so that we may not contradict ourselves, and change our tone from day to day, we have only to do exactly what your Majesty has commanded us. This is the advantage of acting upon principles which do not change, and not on ideas which are constantly changing.

It is decided that the service of the 21st of January shall take place in the cathedral. The archbishop, who has been ill for some days, is better, and nothing but a serious relapse will hinder him from officiating.   I am, etc.

NOTES TO LETTER XXXIX.

1. On the 31st December, 1814, M. de Jaucourt writes: "The affairs of Spain are going as you may judge from the Marquis de Cevallos' letter. We are paying for the blunder which the princes (the King's nephews) made us perpetrate in dismissing the *chargé d'affaires*, instead of having him formally recalled, as I said and repeated over and over again. . . . The King wants to have your opinion: write to him; and also acquaint me with it if you have no objection to doing so. Prince de Laval is in a false position as regards diplomatic affairs, but in a good one personally and as a domestic ambassador. It seems to me, then, that ten days may be allowed for a decision without committing us to anything. So that to-day (the 31st) I have the honor to write to you. On the 7th you will have the letter; on the 9th you will write to me; on the 17th we shall have your answer, and if the King has not yielded to some impulse there will still be time to follow your advice or to repent of not having followed it."

2. "This morning, a fresh memorial from M. de Cevallos. He agrees that M. de Casaflores shall return to take leave; that an agreement shall be made to the effect that the State criminals on both sides, especially the men of Mina's gang and Mina himself, shall be given up. Notwithstanding the absurdity of these principles, which he tinkers up with the history of the Maccabees and a great deal of Latin, I think that we shall bring him to a compromise."—Jaucourt to Talleyrand, 25th December, 1814.

3. "Cevallos, who was for a brief space minister to Joseph Bonaparte, is driving at popular, that is to say monkish measures; and when you read his memorial you will see that it is the doing of the priests."—Jaucourt to Talleyrand, 4th January, 1815.

LETTER XL.

THE KING TO PRINCE TALLEYRAND.

No. 17.

11th January, 1814.

My Cousin,

I have received your No. 19. This letter will be short; entire satisfaction with your conduct, complete approbation of the treaty, the ratification of which will reach you by this post—that is all it contains. I am about to send off General Ricard with all possible celerity, and with the secrecy that I feel to be necessary.

I am deeply affected by the intended celebration of the service of the 21st. You will learn with similar sentiments that, on that same day, the precious remains of the King and those of the Queen will be removed to Saint Denis.

On which, etc.

12th—Morning.—I reopen my letter to tell you that General Ricard is at this moment at Toulouse, where he is in command of a division. I have despatched a courier with orders for his immediate return to Paris.

LETTER XLI.

THE KING TO PRINCE TALLEYRAND.

No. 18.

15th January, 1815.

MY COUSIN,

I have received your No. 20. In my last, believing myself more hurried than I really was, because I had not correctly calculated the time required for the ratifications, I was very laconic. Be, however, assured that my feelings on reading your No. 19 were similar to yours on receiving my despatch of the 27th December. I do not slumber, and I never will slumber, upon such interests as those which are in course of discussion at the Congress of Vienna. And yet I might feel as safe as Alexander.[1] I have indeed had something like his security; for I did not tell you to communicate a part of my letter to Lord Castlereagh, being quite sure that you would do that of yourself.

I ardently desire the realization of the hope which your letter to Count de Jaucourt affords, that Prussia may be satisfied without usurping Saxony; then there would be an end, and the glory would be ours of having cut the Gordian knot without resorting to the sword. Nevertheless, I approve of the negotiations with the Porte,[2] and I am about to hasten the departure of the Marquis de Rivière. He is not yet entirely convalescent after a severe illness, but I know his zeal.

I await without misgiving the arrival of General Pozzo di Borgo. If this were a question of a Prince not already Sovereign, I might regard his forming a small State in my neighborhood with satisfaction; but in the case of the King of Saxony, even were he to consent to the exchange, I could not lend my hand to it.

To be just towards one's self is a sacred duty; to be so towards others is no less so, and one who refused to relinquish his rights when he had nothing but alms to live upon,[3] will not be false to rights as legitimate as his own[4] now that he rules twenty-five millions of men, and has to defend the interests of Europe, as well as justice.

The question of Sweden is a very delicate one. The last treaty has placed Russia in such a position that she can reach Stockholm without much difficulty. Is it prudent to involve a kingdom in so dangerous a war, without securing for it in case of defeat indemnities, which it would be difficult even to find? Gustavus IV. has said to me more than once that he regarded his uncle as the legitimate King of Sweden, but has the unfortunate prince, in abdicating for himself, been able to abdicate for his son? Admitting this hypothesis, which would legitimize the doctrine of Bernadotte, does the existence of the latter involve any consequence which should make one hesitate to ally one's self with him? I shall read your observations on these various points with interest.

The existence of Bernadotte recalls that of Murat, which is much more dangerous. My despatch of the 27th of December dealt with Naples and Saxony: we are in very good case with respect to the latter; let us strive for the former with equal zeal and success.[5]

The Sardinian ambassador has requested an audience; Count de Jaucourt will inform you of its result.

On which, etc.

NOTES TO LETTER XLI.

1. This is an allusion to the deep sleep of Alexander before the battle of Arbela. Bossuet, in his celebrated funeral oration, had said of the great Condé: "This second Alexander had to be awakened."

2. "I have reason to believe that the Emperor of Russia will consent to include Turkey in the general guarantees which it is purposed to stipulate for all the Powers, after the settlement of the affairs which are occupying the Congress."—Talleyrand to the Department, 15th January, 1815.

3. Louis XVIII. makes an allusion here to his wandering and precarious life in Italy, Courland, Prussia, Poland, and England.

4. In 1814 he said to the Emperor Alexander, who was surprised at his resumption of the old formula, "King of France and Navarre by the grace of God"—
"Divine right is a consequence of religious dogma, and of the law of the country. Owing to that law the monarchy has been hereditary in my family for eight centuries. Without Divine right, I am nothing but an infirm old man, long proscribed, reduced to beg for shelter; but by that right the proscribed old man is King of France."

5. "They say he (Murat) is very uneasy; that he constantly says he will not go and be buried alive in an island of Elba, but talks confidently of his troops, of the public spirit of Italy, and of sixty thousand men ready to arm for independence, if Austria does not respect her pledges."—Jaucourt to Talleyrand, 15th January, 1815.

"The King appeared to be, as usual, very well satisfied with your progress, and with the success which seems probable in the case of Saxony; but he said to Monsieur (with whom I had exchanged a few words behind the King's chair, and whose answer was the question, 'Do you not think Prince Talleyrand will soon come back?'), 'But after this battle is fought, there is another to come; what about Naples?' Monsieur replied, hesitating a little: 'I fear Murat will not be so easy a matter.'

I say the same. Murat does not seem to me an easy matter. He is attacked by a mortal malady, but it is a lingering one; the best chance that can be offered to him, in my poor opinion, is that of fighting as soon as possible. If you destroy the feeling with which his people regard him in hope of their independence; if you isolate him; if you create federal States with national representation, the great Joachim Murat is no longer necessary, and he becomes ridiculous: but what is useful and necessary is never really ridiculous."—Jaucourt to Talleyrand, 20th January, 1815.

LETTER XLII.

THE KING TO PRINCE TALLEYRAND.

No. 19.

19th January, 1815.

My Cousin,

I have received your No. 21. I was not uneasy about your views on the Spanish affair, but I am very glad to find that they are in conformity with the measures which I have taken, and also that M. de Labrador does not share the insensate ideas of his Cabinet; I hope he may be able to inspire it with others more reasonable, and in accordance with its true interests.

Last week, I was very well satisfied, but now I cannot but regard the tendency of Lord Castlereagh to his former weaknesses, and the versatility of Prince Metternich, with some uneasiness. Lord Castlereagh ought to bear in mind that the path of honor is a firm adherence to what is right, or a prompt return to it if unhappily there has been any straying from it. Prince Metternich forgets that to augment the share of Prussia is to weaken Austria. As for me, I will never lend myself, as you know, to the entire spoliation of the King of Saxony. I know that he will have a certain surrender to make, but if such concessions were required from him as would reduce him to being a fourth-rate, or even a third-rate Power, I am not disposed to consent to that. I await with equal impatience the result of your conference and the opening of the great affair of Naples.

These are days of mourning and sadness. I should have wished to be present at the ceremonies which are to take place on Saturday; but I am prevented by the dread of the gout. One does not suffer less, however, in giving the orders for such ceremonies, than in witnessing them. You will thank the Archbishop of Vienna, on my behalf, for having officiated at the service.

On which, etc.

LETTER XLIII.

No. 22.

Vienna, 19th January, 1815.

SIRE,

I have received the letter of the 7th of this month, with which your Majesty has deigned to honor me, and I have derived fresh encouragement to zeal and energy from the expressions of kindness which it contains.

I have the honor to write to your Majesty to-day only because I do not wish that there should be too much interval between my letters, for I have nothing new to announce to your Majesty. We make but slow progress in our affairs, and yet we are not idle.

Bavaria has joined the triple alliance; Hanover and Holland will come after. The Grand-Duke of Darmstadt joins Bavaria with a like purpose, and promises six thousand men.

The Commissions on the affairs of Italy, Switzerland, and the statistics are in full work. My letter to the ministry, which will be laid before your Majesty, will inform you of the state of affairs in this respect, the obstacles which have to be encountered, and the reasons why everything cannot be arranged in the most desirable manner.

Austria, England, Bavaria, Holland, Hanover, and almost the whole of Germany are agreed with us upon the maintenance of the King and the Kingdom of Saxony. Saxony will therefore be maintained, although Prince Hardenberg has ventured once more to demand the whole kingdom in a plan for the reconstruction of the Prussian monarchy, which he recently sent in. M. de Metternich was to reply to this plan, and I awaited his answer before despatching my courier; but it is not yet complete. I have only seen the elements of it; these are very good. The mere inspection of the Prussian plan leads to the conclusion that what Prussia had in 1805, and which is all she is entitled to demand, may be restored to her, and one million five hundred thousand subjects be preserved to Saxony. But Prussia claims that she ought to have six hundred thousand more than in 1805, under the pretext of aggrandizement obtained by Russia and Austria.

All that concerns the principles of legitimacy has been agreed upon between Lord Castlereagh, M. de Metternich, and me. We have only to arrive at a complete understanding touching the equilibrium to be enabled to make a joint proposal. With this we are occupied daily, and again to-day I have had a conference with them on the subject. M. de Metternich was at first ready to make unlimited concessions, but I checked him in that direction by placing before him the consequences to himself of a readiness which would endanger his Monarchy, and he now warmly defends what he would previously have relinquished. I have advised him to bring some of the best-informed Austrian officers to our conferences, to give their opinions and the reasons upon which they are founded; and, to induce him to take my advice, I told him that, if he did not act upon it, I would proclaim that I had given it. He made up his mind to act on it. Prince Schwarzenburg will have a conference with Lord Stewart, and will afterwards attend with some of his officers at a conference which we are to hold the day after to-morrow. It is unfortunate that Lord Castlereagh, in addition to the remains of his former liking for Prussia, and his fear of compromising what he calls his character, by consenting to leave only a small portion of that kingdom in the hands of Prussia, after having given up the whole of Saxony by his Note of the 10th of October, has such imperfect, and I may say foolish, notions about everything relating to military topography, and even about mere continental geography, that, while it is necessary to convince him in even the smallest things, he is extremely difficult to be convinced. A story is told of an Englishman who was here in the time of Prince Kaunitz, and who talked a great deal of nonsense in his presence about the States of Germany. Prince Kaunitz exclaimed, in a tone of the utmost amazement, "It is prodigious all that these English do not know." How many times have I had occasion to make the same remark to myself in my conferences with Lord Castlereagh!

We have some reason to hope that in the arrangement of the affairs of Italy which is in preparation, the Archduchess Marie Louise will be limited to a liberal pension. I must tell your Majesty that I lay great stress on this, because the name of Bonaparte will be by that means expunged from the list of Sovereigns, now and for all future time, as the island of Elba is the property of the dweller in it for his own life only, and the son of the Archduchess cannot possess any independent State.

The preparations for the ceremony of the 21st are almost finished. So great is the general eagerness to witness the service, that it is difficult for us to answer the applications, and the church of St. Stephen, the largest in Vienna, could not hold all who wish to attend.

All the Sovereigns have been apprised of the ceremony, and all, with the exception of the Emperor[1] and Empress of Russia, whose answer has not yet been received, have made known their intention of being present.

The Empress of Austria, whose health does not permit her to attend, wished her excuses to be presented to your Majesty (I use her own words). The Archduchess Beatrix, her mother, will be present. The ladies will all be veiled; this is the mark of deepest mourning.

General Pozzo is still awaiting his instructions. He was told to hold himself in readiness, and he has been prepared for a week past; but the instructions do not arrive.

General Andréossi passed through Vienna on his return from Constantinople. He speaks us fair, and made to me a profession of faith such as I desired. He is a clever man, who has filled important posts, and might be employed with advantage.[2]

I am, etc.

NOTES TO LETTER XLIII.

1. "The Emperor Alexander only, without sending a refusal, made a simple observation. He said that nobody could doubt what were the sentiments of Europe towards the unfortunate Louis XVI., nevertheless this ceremony was a party demonstration, which, while it was very impolitic in Paris, was at Vienna a clumsy and undignified imitation."—Thiers, "Consulat et Empire," vol. xviii. p. 588.

No doubt La Harpe had reminded his royal pupil of the following passage from Tacitus: "Valerius Messalicus proposed to erect a golden statue in the temple of Mars the Avenger; Cecina Severus, to raise an altar to Vengeance. Cæsar opposed both. 'Monuments of this kind,' said he, 'were made for foreign victories. Domestic misfortunes ought to be hidden beneath a veil of mourning.'"—Burnouf's Tacitus, Book iii. p. 105.

2. "We shall receive General Andréossi as your satisfaction with him prescribes. We are your echo; but we should like to be that of your thoughts, and to divine them is not given to everybody."—Jaucourt to Talleyrand, 30th January, 1815.

CHAPTER XLIV.

No. 23.

Vienna, 21st January, 1815.

Sire,

I am to-day to have the honor of writing to your Majesty respecting the ceremony which was celebrated here this morning.

I have had a circumstantial but simple account of it drawn up, to be inserted in the *Moniteur*,[1] if your Majesty approves of it. I thought it best merely to narrate the facts, but to abstain from offering those reflections which will come naturally to the minds of all readers, and, because they are withheld from expression, will impress themselves all the more deeply.

The address of the curé of St. Anne, who is a Frenchman by birth,[2] is included in this narrative. It is not a funeral oration; it is not a sermon; it is a speech. He had only a few days in which to prepare it, to adapt it to the object of the ceremony, and to the quality of the principal personages among the spectators; it was less necessary that it should be eloquent than that it should be prudent, and those who heard it are agreed that in this respect it was all that was to be desired.

The ceremony lacked nothing, neither the pomp befitting its object, nor quality in its spectators, nor the sorrow which the event that it recalls must ever awaken. By evoking the memory of a great misfortune it affords a great lesson. Its aim was both moral and political, and personages of importance who dined with me after it had taken place have led me to believe that its aim has been attained.[3]

I cannot speak too highly of the kindness and graciousness with which the Emperor of Austria permitted and indeed prescribed every arrangement that could add to the orderliness and the dignity of the ceremony. He alone attended at the church in black; the other sovereigns wore uniform.

Count Alexis de Noailles in particular seconded my efforts; but I was admirably assisted by all.

M. Moreau, the architect who was entrusted with the preparations, has acted with equal intelligence and zeal. The music was very fine; it was composed by M. Neukomm, who conducted the performance of it, conjointly with the first Kappelmeister to the Court, M. Salieri.

I entreat your Majesty to be pleased to give those three artists, and also M. Isabey who has been very useful, a mark of your satisfaction, by sending me decorations of the Legion of Honor for them.

I also entreat your Majesty to be pleased to grant the same grace to MM. Rouen, Damour, Formont, Saint-Mars, and Sers, *attachés* to your Majesty's embassy, with whose conduct I have reason to be extremely pleased and who only, of all the *attachés* to the embassies of the Congress, have no decorations.

On Wednesday I purpose to send off a courier, by whom I shall have the honor of writing to your Majesty on the subject of the marriage. I feel all the importance and have never lost sight of that subject.

I am, etc.

P.S.—General Pozzo's departure is, it seems, fixed for Saturday, the 24th.

NOTES TO LETTER XLIV.

1. The *Moniteur* published this account, on the 30th January, 1815, under the form of correspondence from Vienna. On the 22nd the following appeared: "At the corners of the catafalque were placed four statues, representing *France sunk in grief, Europe shedding tears, Religion holding the Will of Louis XVI., and Hope raising her eyes to heaven.*"

2. The *Moniteur* gives his name, Abbé de Zaignelins, and publishes his address in full.

3. "You will hear so much, Prince, of the effect which you produce at Court, among private individuals, as well as in the royal family, that my little tribute of special praise will not be very interesting to you. It was a grand and fine idea to make a political stroke out of a ceremony quite simple and natural in appearance, and a regular affair of Congress out of a religious act. Joachim would be very glad to get rid of it with only the cost to pay, and your 'speech' will do him more harm than the Austrian army. As I am nothing if not critical, I confess, to praise you in strict conscience, that I would have changed the phrase 'sixty years of unbelief,' for if we have been unbelievers for sixty years, we can only be hypocrites to-day; and if, as you afterwards say, the innovators have brought nothing but evils and errors among us, we ought to have back again Church Lands, parliaments to try us, and Jesuits to teach us Latin."—Jaucourt to Talleyrand, 1st February, 1815.

"I wind up by once more admiring your expiatory, monarchical, European idea; the idea which has given the Congress its first result: the meeting of the Sovereigns at a solemn requiem for Louis XVI. . . . We call you the prince of diplomatists."—Jaucourt to Talleyrand, 25th January, 1815.

LETTER XLV.

No. 24.

Vienna, 25th January, 1815.

Sire,

I was present yesterday at a conference with M. de Metternich and Prince Schwarzenburg, for the purpose of deciding, according to the judgment of the Austrian military authorities, what points of Saxony may, and what points may not, be left to Prussia, without endangering the safety of Austria.

The Emperor of Austria wished this conference to take place, and desired that I should be present at it.

Two plans were proposed.

The first would leave Torgau to Saxony, with the sole condition of razing the fortifications of Dresden.

The second would give Torgau to Prussia, but razed. Dresden would also be razed.

In either case Prussia would keep Erfürth.

It was agreed that the two plans should be submitted to his Majesty the Emperor of Austria, and that a draft of a Memorandum upon that which he adopts should be made; this draft the Emperor himself will hand to Lord Castlereagh, as it is Lord Castlereagh whom it is essential to convince.

Russia has offered Austria the restoration of the district of Tarnopol, containing four hundred thousand souls. Austria renounces it on condition that a similar population shall be given to Prussia in the contiguous portion of Poland, so as to diminish by so much the sacrifices which Saxony will have to make. This will be explained in the memorandum.

I do not know which of the two plans has been adopted; but I know that Lord Castlereagh is to go to the Emperor of Austria this evening. I will send an account of what shall have taken place at that audience, by the first post.

Your Majesty will judge of the amount of confidence that is placed by the Emperor of Austria in his minister, on learning that he sent Count Sickingen to me this morning, to ask whether the report which M. de Metternich had made to him of the conference of yesterday was the truth.

The Emperor Alexander, with his liberal ideas, has made so little way here, that it has been found necessary to triple the police force in order to prevent his being insulted by the people in his daily walks.

I have the honor to send to your Majesty an article from the *Beobachter*, which I have had drawn up by M. de Gentz.[1] I subjoin the translation that he has made; it is very well done. It seems to me that the article might appear in the *Moniteur* with advantage, under the heading of "Vienna;" and that it would be well if the other journals were to copy it.[2]

I am, etc.

NOTES TO LETTER XLV.

1. This article from the *Observer* (*Beobachter*) of Vienna was reproduced by the *Moniteur* on the 2nd January, 1815. The King informs Talleyrand of this in a later letter.

2. "Our journals have a much stronger influence abroad than that which is exercised by the Press in other countries, because it is well known that ours are under the supervision and censorship of the Government."—Talleyrand to Jaucourt, from Vienna, 24th November, 1814.

"The journals think proper to give, on what authority nobody knows, a list of the persons who compose several of the Commissions formed here for the different objects that are in negotiation, and they do not name any French plenipotentiary, just as if France were excluded from affairs, whereas a French plenipotentiary, who is present at the conferences, and whose opinion, I am able to assert, carries some weight, is attached to each Commission. Then, they say that the Emperor of Austria wished to defray all the expenses of the service that was celebrated on the 21st of January; whereas he never even thought of making such an offer, and France paid, as it was fitting she should pay, the whole cost. A newspaper, which is, I believe, published under the auspices of one of the ministers, announces that I attend the receptions (*cercles*) of the Archduchess Marie Louise. Now, she never receives. I have not seen her even once, and she has certainly no desire to see me. I can understand that newspapers should be left entirely free—that they should not be meddled with in any way; that is a system which may, like any other, have advantages as well as drawbacks; but that they should be supposed to be supervised and directed, and yet be neither, is for a Government to take upon itself the blame of the untrue and uncalled-for things which they report; in fact, to render itself responsible, without any utility, for all the ill effects which they produce."—Talleyrand to Jaucourt, 7th February, 1815.

LETTER XLVI.

(PRIVATE.)

No. 24 (A).

Vienna, 25th January, 1815.

SIRE,

It seems likely that General Pozzo di Borgo will leave Vienna this week, on his return to Paris. He will probably have received orders relative to the marriage from the Emperor Alexander. I think it my duty to lay before your Majesty to-day some observations upon a matter which is so delicate, and in many respects so serious.

Your Majesty requires, and is quite right to require, that the princess, whomsoever she may be, to whom the Duc de Berry shall give his hand should enter France as a Catholic princess. Your Majesty makes, and could not dispense with making, this an absolute condition.[1] The Most Christian King and Eldest Son of the Church cannot carry concession on that point farther than Bonaparte himself was inclined to do when he asked for the hand of the Grand-Duchess Anne.

If this condition were accepted by the Emperor Alexander, and supposing that your Majesty had given your word, your Majesty would certainly not feel yourself free to retract it; but it seems that the Emperor, while he does not oppose his sister's change of religion, does not choose that it should be imputed to him, and there would be fair grounds for such an imputation if the change were a stipulation. He wishes the adoption of the Princess by Catholic Faith to be regarded as the result of a resolution of her own, arrived at when she had passed under other laws, and he therefore wishes the change to follow, instead of preceding, the marriage. He requires, then, that his sister shall proceed to France accompanied by her "chapel,"[2] but consents that the pope, who is to attend her, shall wear lay costume. The reasons which lead him to adhere to this are his own scruples—for he is deeply attached to his creed—and his fear of wounding the susceptibilities of his people on so delicate a point. By persisting in these views he will himself release your Majesty from any engagement into which you may have entered, and he will furnish the means of release if he delays his consent to the conditions which your Majesty has imposed. Now, I have no hesitation in acknowledging to your Majesty that anything which may tend to set you free in this matter seems to me most desirable.

Eight months ago, when, even amid the general joy of the actual moment, and the happy hopes which we all formed for the future, it was, nevertheless, impossible to regard that future with security untroubled by any fear, a family alliance with Russia might well appear, and did appear to myself, to offer advantages whose utility would outweigh those considerations which, in a different position of affairs, I should have placed in the first rank and regarded as decisive.

But now that the throne, so marvellously restored by Providence, has also been established by the same power; now that it is girt and guarded by the love and veneration of the people; now that the coalition is dissolved, that France has no further need to count on foreign aid, but that, on the contrary, it is from her that the other Powers expect succor, your Majesty has no longer to sacrifice any of the *convenances* which are essential to this kind of alliance to the necessities of circumstances, but may consult them only.

The Grand-Duchess Anne is considered the handsomest of the five daughters of the Emperor Paul,[3] and beauty is a most precious and desirable quality in a princess who may be called by the course of events to ascend the throne of France. No people are so tenacious as the French of being able to say of the princes who rule them—

"Le monde en les voyant reconnaîtrait ses maîtres."

The Grand-Duchess appears to have been very carefully brought up. To personal charms she adds, it is said, a good disposition. She is twenty-one years old, so that the frequently injurious effects of a too early marriage are not to be apprehended in her case. She was destined for the present reigning Duke of Saxe-Coburg, before Bonaparte asked for her hand. It was entirely Bonaparte's own doing that the marriage did not take place; for it is certain that they would not have asked better than to give her to him, if he could and would have waited. I do not know whether these two circumstances could be held to raise a sort of objection to the marriage of the princess with the Duc de Berry, but I must say, that if the marriage is to take place, I should prefer their not having existed. . . .

Its being necessary, not that the Grand-Duchess should change her religion, but that she should change it in such fashion that it would appear impossible to attribute the act to any except purely political motives, is, it strikes me, a strong objection, for such an impression would inevitably tend to foster the religious indifference among the people which is the disease of the age we live in.

As marriage binds not only those who contract it, but their families also, suitability between the latter ought to be the first consideration even in the marriages of private individuals, and with still greater reason in those of kings, or princes who may be called to occupy thrones. That the House of Bourbon should ally itself with houses which are inferior to it is a necessity of the case, since Europe does not possess a house which is its equal. I will not therefore object that the House of Holstein, although it occupy the three thrones of the North, is comparatively new among kings. But I may say that when the House of Bourbon honors another house by its alliance, it is better it should be a house which holds itself to be honored, than one which might pretend to equality by pretending that nobility and antiquity of origin can be balanced by extent of possessions. One of the four sisters of the Grand-Duchess Anne married an Austrian Archduke; the other three married petty German princes.

Is Russia, who has never been able to place any of her princesses upon a throne, to see one of them called to that of France? I venture to say that such a prospect would be good fortune too great for her, and I should not like the Duc de Berry to find himself brought by means of this kind into close relations of kindred with a crowd of princes in the lowermost ranks of sovereignty.

The chief object of Russia in marrying her princesses as she has done has been to secure pretexts and means for intervention in the affairs of Europe, to which she was almost unknown a century ago. The effects of her intervention have made the danger of her influence sufficiently evident.[1] How greatly would that influence be increased if a Russian princess were called to ascend the throne of France!

A family alliance is not, I am aware, a political alliance, and the one does not necessarily bring about the other. The projected marriage would certainly not make France favor the ambitious views and the revolutionary ideas of which the Emperor Alexander is full, and which he seeks to disguise under the specious name of liberal ideas; but how are we to prevent foreign Powers from being of a different opinion, and conceiving mistrust of us? How are we to prevent the ties between ourselves and them from being weakened in consequence, or their being deterred from forming any; and Russia from availing herself of all this for the accomplishment of her purposes?

Such, Sire, are the objections to which the marriage of the Duc de Berry with the Grand-Duchess Anne appears to me to be open. I was bound to lay them unreservedly before your Majesty, but I have not exaggerated them. Your Majesty's wisdom will judge whether they have all the weight with which I invest them.

I must add that it appears to me the greatness of the House of Bourbon would be most fittingly displayed, especially at this time, when all its branches, buffeted by the same tempest, have been simultaneously raised up again, by seeking the means of perpetuating itself in its own bosom only. I hear a young princess of Sicily, the daughter of the Prince Royal, very highly praised. Portugal, Tuscany, and Saxony offer princesses, among whom your Majesty might make a choice. I have the honor to subjoin a list of them.

If the negotiation for the marriage with the Grand-Duchess should be broken off in consequence of the impossibility of arranging the religious difficulty, or if your Majesty should think fit to relinquish it, I would entreat your Majesty to be pleased so to manage matters that the affair shall not be irrevocably decided until we have brought the others with which we are occupied here to a conclusion; for if the Emperor Alexander has shown us so little good will, notwithstanding the hope of such a marriage for his sister, that hope being so flattering to himself, what might we not expect from him if he had lost it?

I am, etc.

NOTES TO LETTER XLVI.

1. "The Duc de Berry asked me whether you spoke to me of his marriage; he let me see that he is annoyed by the papist and Roman rigidity of the King."—Talleyrand to Jaucourt, 20th October, 1814.

2. "I gave a dinner yesterday, among others to M. Butiakine, the Russian chargé d'affaires. . . . We talked about the marriage, which I suppose you discuss with the King, and of which the Duc de Berry speaks to me every day, while I, not knowing what to say, do not say a word. Marry him, however, to some one or other, for that is just now his *idée fixe*, and nothing can turn him from it. M. Butiakine spoke to me of the extreme facility with which the princess might be brought to perfect submission to the Roman Church, but said that it was indispensable to the dignity due to her rank that she should have a chapel, or the equivalent of one, *at least in her apartment.*"—Jaucourt to Talleyrand, 22nd November, 1815.

3. The Emperor Paul had six daughters: 1. Olga, died young; 2. Alexandra,

wife of the Archduke Joseph, died in 1801; 3. Helena, wife of the Duke of Mecklenburg-Strelitz, died in 1803; 4. Mary, Grand-Duchess of Saxe-Weimar, died in 1859; 5. Catharine; 6. Anne.

4. "From thenceforth (1806-1807) M. de Talleyrand felt great alarm at the importance which Russia might assume in Europe; he constantly urged that an independent Power should be set up between us and the Russians, and he was in favor, with this view, of the ardent though vague desires of the Poles. 'It is the kingdom of Poland,' he always said, 'which ought to be created; there is the real bulwark of our independence; but it must not be done by halves.'"—Mémoires de Madame de Rémusat, tom. iii. p. 90.

LETTER XLVII.

SUBJOINED TO NO. 24 (A).

Austria.

Archduchess Léopoldine, born 22nd January, 1797; Archduchess Marie Clémentine, born 1st March, 1798.[1]

Tuscany.

Archduchess Marie Louise, born 30th August, 1798.[2]

Saxony.

Princess Marie Amélie, born 17th August, 1794; Princess Maria Ferdinanda, born 27th April, 1796 (daughters of Prince Maximilian).[3]

Portugal.

Princess Maria Teresa, born 29th April, 1793 (widow of Pedro Carlos, Infante of Spain); Princess Isabella, born 9th May, 1797; Princess Maria Francisca, born 22nd April, 1800.[4]

Savoy-Carignan.

Princess Maria Elizabeth, born 19th April, 1800 (sister of the prince).[5]

Two Sicilies.

Princess Maria Caroline, born 5th March, 1798 (daughter of the hereditary Prince).[6]

There are no other unmarried Catholic princesses over fourteen and under twenty-five years of age.

NOTES TO THE ABOVE LIST.

1. Both daughters of Francis II., Emperor of Austria, and his second wife, and, consequently, sisters of the Empress Marie Louise. The Archduchess

Léopoldine married the Emperor of Brazil, Don Pedro I., and died in 1826; she was mother of Doña Maria II., Queen of Portugal, of Don Pedro II., of the Countess d'Aquila (Two Sicilies), and of the Princess de Joinville. The Archduchess Marie Clémentine was married 28th July, 1816, to the Prince of Salerno (Two Sicilies); she became a widow in 1851. Her daughter married the Duc d'Aumale.

2. Daughter of the Archduke Ferdinand (1769-1824), successively Grand-Duke of Tuscany (1790), of Salzburg (1813), and of Wurzburg (1806), and again Grand-Duke of Tuscany (1814). She did not marry, and died in 1852.

3. Both daughters of Prince Maximilian (who died in 1838), father of Augustus III. and Anthony, successively Kings of Saxony, and of a Princess of Parma, and aunts of the present King of Saxony. The first did not marry; she died in 1870. The second married, in 1821, Ferdinand, Grand-Duke of Tuscany, and died in 1865.

4. All three daughters of Juan II., King of Portugal (1816-1826). Maria Teresa, Princess of Beira, was the widow of the Infante Pedro Carlos from 1812; on the 2nd of February, 1833, she married the Infante Don Carlos, the chief of the Carlists and widower of her second sister.

Isabella was the second wife of Ferdinand VII., King of Spain, and died in 1834; she was mother of the future Condé de Montemolin and of the Infante Don Juan, and grandmother of the present Duke of Madrid.

5. The prince to whom Talleyrand alludes here was Charles Albert, father of Victor Emanuel II., and afterwards King of Sardinia. His sister Marie Elizabeth married, in 1820, Regnier, Archduke of Austria, Viceroy of the Lombardo-Venetian kingdom, and died in 1856. His daughter, the Archduchess Marie Adelaide, married Victor Emanuel II., and was mother of Humbert I., the present King of Italy; of Amadeo I., ex-King of Spain; of the Princess Clotilda Napoleon Bonaparte; and of the present Queen of Portugal, Maria Pia, wife of Dom Louis I.

6. Carolina Ferdinanda Louisa, daughter of Francis I., King of the Two Sicilies, and of an Archduchess of Austria, granddaughter of King Ferdinand I., married the Duc de Berry in 1806, became a widow in 1820. The children of the marriage were *Mademoiselle*, afterwards Duchess of Parma (1809-1864), and the Duc de Bordeaux (Comte de Chambord), the present head of the elder branch of the Bourbons.

Of the eleven princesses whom Prince Talleyrand destined for the Duc de Berry, the only one now living is the Archduchess, widow of Leopold, Prince of Salerno.

LETTER XLVIII.

THE KING TO PRINCE TALLEYRAND.

No. 20.

28th January, 1815.

My Cousin,

I have received your No 22. Long before this reaches you, you will have seen the Duke of Wellington, the selection of whom to replace Lord Castlereagh has been very agreeable to me. I saw him before his departure; I could not have been better pleased with him, and I think he has gone away not ill satisfied with me.[1] The Duke also has a *character* to sustain, that, not of a king-maker, but of a *king-restorer*, which is better.[2] Besides, he is not committed by the acts of his predecessor, for while walking in his footsteps he has, so to speak, the choice between two extremes. I do not know exactly what is the total population of Saxony. I think the King ought to consent to a reduction of fifteen hundred thousand; but if it be proposed to diminish the number still more, bear in mind what I wrote to you lately.

Count Jules de Polignac[3] arrived here on Sunday. His report, which agrees with those I had previously received from various sources, describes Italy as in a state of ferment, and the existence of Murat as very dangerous. I have reason to believe that England would enter into a compact to secure a pecuniary provision for this man on his relinquishing his pretended throne. I would gladly lend myself to a measure of the kind, provided it be agreed at the same time that, if he prove obstinate, force shall do that which negotiation has failed to effect.

The sorrowful and consoling ceremony of Saturday passed off very well. I charge you to express my feelings to the Sovereigns who took part in the solemnization at St. Stephen's, and in particular to say to the Empress of Austria how deeply I am affected by her wish to attend, and by the regret which she has been good enough to express to me on this occasion.

On which, etc.

P.S.—General Ricard has arrived, and will be at Vienna shortly after this letter.

NOTES TO LETTER XLVIII.

1. "The Duke of Wellington starts for Vienna to-morrow evening. He had a private audience of the King at half-past eleven this morning. In this audience the King was very gracious to the Duke, and even treated him, it seems to me, with some *cajolerie*. The King expressed his intentions, principles, and sentiments very strongly. The Duke of Wellington responded to the King's overtures with a respectful friendliness, but nevertheless maintained the strictest reserve. 'Fate destines you,' the King said to him, 'to bring the greatest affairs to a termination, when it does not charge you with them throughout. You know my intentions; I shall never depart from them. They are—to restore his crown and his States to the King of Saxony; to drive out Murat, and form a ministry which shall guarantee peace. This is what I want to do. For these ends Prince Talleyrand has zealously worked; he will

work still better in concert with you.'"—Jaucourt to Talleyrand, 25th January, 1815.

2. No doubt an allusion to the Earl of Warwick, called "the King-Maker," who was killed at the battle of Barnet (1471) in the Wars of the Roses.

3. Jaucourt wrote to Talleyrand on the 19th of December, 1814: "This is the history of M. de Polignac's journey. Some days ago he came to ask me whether, before going to Munich, he might not have a month's leave of absence. . . .

"I promised him that I would ask the King's pleasure. He then told me that his purpose was to go to Rome. I talked with him, and found that he knew all about the affairs of the Concordat as well as I did; it was not difficult for me to perceive that he was being sent, by whom, and with what intention. Then I came to the conclusion that the best means of regulating his conduct and fixing his ideas, was to put him in thorough relations with us."

LETTER XLIX.

No. 25.

Vienna, 1st February, 1815.

SIRE,

The audience given to Lord Castlereagh by the Emperor has had no effect, beyond making the former say that the Emperor appeared to him to be full of loyalty and candor. Otherwise, Lord Castlereagh remained unshaken in his opinion that Prussia must be great and powerful, and that a large portion of Saxony, and the fortress of Torgau in particular, should be given to her.[1] I wanted to save Torgau, and the Austrians were of the same mind at first, but they finally relinquished it, according to their usual custom. In consequence, neither one nor the other of the two plans which I have had the honor to lay before your Majesty has been adopted. A third has been formed, and according to it a population of seven hundred and eighty-two thousand Saxons is given over to Russia. This plan of the Austrians has been drafted and sent to the Prussians, who have taken it *ad referendum;* they have not yet replied to it.

We had announced from the first our consent that from four to five hundred thousand souls should be taken from Saxony. Lord Castlereagh, after having abandoned Saxony, and just because he had abandoned it, obstinately required that a million should be taken. Although I was very ill supported by the Austrians, I have succeeded in obtaining very nearly the middle term between those two numbers, and I am still astonished at my success. The Saxon Minister, who is here, had drawn up a table of those portions of the kingdom that might not be considered absolutely essential to its existence. The population of these portions amounted to seven hundred and fifty thousand souls. The new project cedes only thirty-two thousand more than that number, and of the portion ceded certain parts would revert, by exchanges, to the ducal houses of Saxony.

The Prussians are said to be little disposed to be content with what is offered to them, or else to be feigning discontent. It is not only a question of territory with them, it is also one of *amour propre*. After having demanded the whole of Saxony, and that quite recently; after having occupied it; after all the Powers with the exception of France had abandoned it to them; after having so many times declared that they would never renounce it, it must be painful to them to forego their claim to two-thirds of that kingdom. But they will not make a struggle without the co-operation of Russia, and the Emperor Alexander, who has got what he wanted in Poland, and whose interest in the matter is solely one of *amour propre*, will, according to all appearance, advise the Prussians to accept the proposals that are made to them, and there is reason to believe that they will be accepted with very few changes.

Never did the fate of a country appear to be more irrevocably fixed than that of Saxony, at the moment of our arrival here. Prussia demanded the whole of it for herself, and Russia demanded it for Prussia. Lord Castlereagh had completely abandoned it, and so had Austria, with the exception of certain frontier arrangements. Your Majesty undertook singly the defence of the King and the kingdom of Saxony; your Majesty only has sustained principles. Your Majesty had to win a triumph over passions of every kind, over the spirit of coalition which existed in all its strength, and, perhaps a more difficult task, over the *amour propre* of all the Great Powers, who had so far committed themselves by their pretensions, their declarations, and their concessions, that it appeared as though they could not retreat from the position they had assumed without disgrace. Your Majesty's noble resistance to an almost consummated injustice has gloriously vanquished all these obstacles; and not only has it achieved that triumph, but the coalition has been dissolved, and your Majesty has entered into an agreement with two of the greatest of the Powers, which will probably save Europe[2] from the dangers with which it is threatened by certain States.[3]

The kingdom of Saxony, which was a third-rate Power, will continue to hold that rank. Its population, added to that of the ducal possessions, and to that of the Houses of Reuss and Schwarzburg, which are inside the bounds of the kingdom, will form a compact body of two millions of inhabitants interposed between Prussia and Austria and between Prussia and Bavaria.

The affair of Saxony being terminated, I shall devote myself entirely to that of Naples, and I will bring to it all the energy and skill of which I am capable. England will not oppose us in this instance, but she will not serve us openly and in a decided way, because she has again committed herself in the matter, as your Majesty will see by the document which I have the honor to send herewith. Lord Castlereagh has received instructions from his Government with respect to this, given in the sense that I have just indicated.

Lord Castlereagh will remain here with the Duke of Wellington for a week only. I am convinced, by despatches received from his Court, which he has shown me, that his partiality for Prussia, and his tenacity on the Saxon question, are to be imputed to Lord Liverpool as much as to himself. Lord Bathurst tells him that he must be liberal towards Prussia, and that, after having advanced so far with respect to Saxony, the honor of the British Government would be compromised by a too retrograde step. For the rest, the treaty which he has concluded is entirely approved, and he is informed that the ratifications are to be sent out immediately.

He dwelt upon his desire to see the best understanding established between France and England. He does not delude himself to the point of believing that the result of the arrangements which shall be made here can be a peace of long duration; he only desires that war should not break out for two years to come. Then, if it must take place, he would wish France, England, and Austria to be united; and as he thinks it necessary that all should be in readiness, and that we should concert measures beforehand, he proposes to maintain a direct correspondence with me. But he looks upon a change of ministry in Austria, where the ministry is very weak, to say the least of it, as desirable.[4]

I am, generally speaking, satisfied with the disposition he has manifested.

He proposes to solicit an audience of your Majesty on his way through Paris.

I am, etc.

NOTES TO LETTER XLIX.

1. Torgau was, in fact, given to the kingdom of Prussia.
2. A secret treaty of defensive alliance, concluded at Vienna, between Austria, Great Britain, and France, against Russia and Prussia, 3rd January, 1815 (see D'Angeberg, p. 589).
3. "I am quite convinced of all that you have the goodness to tell me respecting the principles that govern the Cabinet of France and the success which will attend them. The very dangerous design of drawing back our frontiers, binding ourselves to Russia, sacrificing Saxony, and making matters up with Murat was probably a preparation for fresh adventures.

"If, as I think, you have founded peace; if you have restored Europe to a spirit of conservatism and wisdom; and if to that, Prince, you enable us to unite those principles that the Revolution laid down, and which must either remain for the welfare of nations, or bring about fresh revolutions if they be attacked, I believe your life will be the greatest and the most illustrious of your epoch."—Jaucourt to Talleyrand, 8th February, 1815.

4. "Persons well acquainted with Viennese politics have told me that everybody is tired of M. de Metternich, and want to have him replaced by M. de Stadion; that you are co-operating in this, and that the change would expedite affairs which are delayed by his indecision and frivolity."—Jaucourt to Talleyrand, 28th December, 1814.

LETTER L.

THE KING TO PRINCE TALLEYRAND.

No. 21.

Paris, 4th February, 1815.

MY COUSIN,

I have received your Nos. 23 and 24. I did not answer the first immediately, as it did not deal with official matters, but I was none the less gratified and affected by its contents. Neither St. Denis nor any of the churches of Paris, except that of St. Thomas Aquinas, where the preacher simply read out the will of the Martyr King, re-echoed to a discourse at all worthy of comparison with that which was delivered at St. Stephen's in Vienna, and I desire that you will make my compliments upon it to *the author*. I was also much pleased with the extract by M. de Gentz, and had it immediately inserted in the *Moniteur*.[1] I have given Count de Jaucourt the necessary orders on the subject of the marks of approbation which you wish to have bestowed upon the artists engaged in the ceremony of the 21st.

The cession of Erfürth to Prussia affects me little, but I should regret to see the fortifications of Dresden razed, especially if Torgau be left to the King of Prussia.² I wish the Emperor Francis had given the preference to the first plan, and had got Lord Castlereagh to adopt it; but he is no longer at Vienna. You know how pressing the Duke of Wellington has been about the abolition of the slave-trade; you will very soon be made acquainted with the report on St. Domingo, made to me on Monday at the Council by Count Beugnot.³ I confess that I begin to reconcile myself with the idea of the advantages that may ensue from the almost instantaneous relinquishment of a traffic which it seems to me very difficult to maintain beyond the epoch fixed by the treaty.

Marshal Soult has written to you on the subject of Bouillon.⁴ The matter is one of protection and not of possession, and for that reason it is important that the duchy should belong to Prince de Rohan, who besides has right on his side a hundredfold, notwithstanding the English patronage.

On which, etc.

P.S.—Your ideas on the marriage are identical with my own. I shall await the coming of General Pozzo di Borgo, and not hasten anything.⁵

NOTES TO LETTER L.

1. See the *Moniteur* of the 2nd February, 1815.

2. "The positions on the Elbe were of more importance than the extent of the soil. One was hotly contested—that of Torgau. It was a grave matter, after having given up Wittenberg, to give up Torgau, which, according to the well-known opinion of Napoleon, and one which he had himself acted upon, had become the principal fortress of the Upper Elbe. Prince Schwarzenberg and M. de Talleyrand wanted to resist, but as they were deserted by Lord Castlereagh, they were constrained to yield."—Thiers, " Histoire du Consulat et de l'Empire," tom. xviii. p. 590.

3. In 1664 France had occupied the western part of the island of St. Domingo. A terrible insurrection broke out in 1791. Spain ceded the eastern part of the island to France by the Treaty of Basle. The First Consul sent General Leclerc (his brother-in-law) to Hayti; he captured Toussaint Louverture, but died of yellow fever. The French were completely expelled in 1809, but France did not recognize the Republic of Hayti until 1825. An indemnity was then stipulated for by the French Government.

4. According to the Treaty of Paris, which replaced France within the boundaries of 1792, the canton of Bouillon, acquired in 1792, could no longer be considered as belonging to France. Admiral Philippe d'Auvergne disputed the right over Bouillon with Prince de Rohan Guéméné. A prolonged arbitration assigned it to the latter on the 1st of July, 1816. He required an indemnity from the King of the Netherlands, who incorporated the duchy with his States (see D'Arenberg, p. 1200).

5. "The letter (private) to the King has remained in his *heart*, for the Duc de Berry said to me yesterday, 'Does Prince T—— not speak to you of it?' 'Provided he speaks of it to the King, Monseigneur,' I replied, 'that is all that is necessary.' 'Tell me only whether there is a breaking-off with Russia.' 'Monseigneur, at the distance at which things are placed, no one wishes to take another step.' 'Come, come,' said he, 'write to Prince Talleyrand that a line must be taken.' "—Jaucourt to Talleyrand, 4th February, 1815.

LETTER LI.

No. 26.

Vienna, 8th February, 1815.

SIRE,

The Duke of Wellington arrived here on the evening of the 1st. At ten o'clock the next morning the Emperor of Russia went to see him, and began by saying, "Things are going on very badly in France, are they not?"[1] "By no means," replied the Duke. "The King is much loved and respected, and behaves with admirable circumspection." "You could have told me nothing," rejoined the Emperor, "which could have given me so much pleasure. And the army?" "For foreign wars, against any Power in the world," said Wellington, "the army is as good as ever it was; but in questions of internal policy it would probably be worthless." From what Prince Adam told me, these replies struck the Emperor more than he allowed to appear. They certainly influenced the decision which he was anxious to make on the affairs of Saxony, which, on the arrival of Wellington, were still in much uncertainty. They may now be considered as settled.

It is not only to the Emperor of Russia that the Duke of Wellington sounds your Majesty's praises. He repeats them in every direction, not alone in general terms, but entering into details, quoting facts, and thus adding to the great estimation in which your Majesty's character is held here. He treated the affair of St. Roch as a trifle.[2] The German newspapers had much exaggerated its importance. He owns that everything in France is not exactly as he would have it, but he adds that all will come right in time. According to him, the thing wanted above all others is a ministry. "There are," he says, "ministers, but no ministry."[3]

The conclusions that we may draw from his language are, that as the army cannot yet be relied on in questions of home policy, every care must be taken not to raise questions in which the army would have to take part, and, with regard to any remaining agitation in the public mind, we should be neither astonished nor annoyed by it. Too sudden a conversion would be suspicious. I myself gave utterance to this observation, and its justness was acknowledged by every one.

On Saturday last I gave a great dinner to the Duke of Wellington. All the members of the Congress were present. I was glad that he should be introduced to them through the medium of the French Legation.

The Austrian proposal, which I had the honor of mentioning to your Majesty in my last letter, did not satisfy the Prussians. They wanted more: especially Leipsic. The King of Prussia, in an audience he granted to Lord Castlereagh, expressed himself with much warmth, declaring that, after having had Saxony given to him, and having occupied it with his troops, it was making him play a sorry part to allow him to keep only a portion of the country; that he had conquered Leipsic, and that, after the battle, all the Allies had considered the town as belonging to him, and had congratulated him thereupon.

Lord Castlereagh, always convinced that Prussia ought to be strong, and wishing above all things to avoid war (the Duke of Wellington himself believes that England could not make war at the present moment, and that France alone is in a position to do so), maintained that in order to calm down Prussia it was necessary to give her something more.

To increase the share awarded to them, a hundred thousand souls have been taken from Holland and fifty thousand from Hanover. Fulda has been added to it. The Emperor of Russia, to do him justice, wished also to contribute to this settlement, and restored Thorn to Prussia, so that the affair may be considered as arranged, although it is not finally settled.

Saxony will be reduced to less than one million five hundred thousand souls; but, besides this population, that of the duchies of Saxony and the States of Schwarzburg and Reuss must be counted; they are enclosed within the kingdom, and, if it had been Prussia instead of Saxony, would doubtless have been acknowledged as belonging to her in fact. But if our consent had been withheld to the reduction of Saxony to less than one million five hundred thousand souls, we must have formally protested. By protesting, the principle of legitimacy,[4] which it was so important to preserve, and which we have preserved as if by a miracle, would have been compromised; we should in reality have given to Prussia two millions of subjects, which she could not have acquired without danger to Bohemia and Bavaria; and the captivity of the King, who will now be at liberty, would have been indefinitely prolonged. (I asked Prince Hardenberg to allow the King to repair to Austria, and that orders might be immediately issued to this effect. He consented, and gave me his word that it should be so. The necessary order will be despatched to-morrow to Berlin, and the King may leave at once). Although we have not succeeded in obtaining all we wanted for Saxony, she will remain a third-rate Power. If it be an evil that she has not a few hundred thousand more subjects, it is a comparatively slight one, and one which is possibly not irremediable; while if Saxony had been sacrificed in the presence of Europe unwilling or unable to save her, the evil would have been extreme and fraught with most dangerous consequences. The important thing, therefore, was to save her, and the glory of having done so belongs solely to your Majesty. There is no one who does not feel and say this; and we have obtained our object without quarrelling with anybody, and it has even been the means of giving us supporters in the Naples affair.

Lord Castlereagh, whom I told, in order to flatter him, that I had been honored by your Majesty's command to express your Majesty's desire to see him as he passed through Paris, has thereby been determined to take that route. He had at first intended to go by Holland. Lady Castlereagh hopes that she may be permitted to see the Duchess of Angoulême. They will not be able to stay more than twenty-four hours in Paris. Their intention is to start on Monday, the 13th, but not without Lord Castlereagh's having made some overtures with regard to the Naples affair that I think it would be advisable to have made by him. The Duke of Wellington is sound upon this question. I hope that we shall also have Russia and Prussia on our side. Nevertheless I foresee more than one kind of obstacle, and I will strain every nerve to overcome them.

It would complicate and spoil this affair to mix it up with that of Bernadotte, which is of a totally different character.

Bernadotte did not succeed in Sweden by conquest, but by the adoption of the reigning sovereign and the consent of the country. He is not a king, but only an heir-presumptive. He cannot be attacked without attacking the King who adopted him, a King whose legitimacy is acknowledged even by the man[5] whom he has displaced, and whom your Majesty has also recognized, having made peace directly with him. As long as the King lives, Bernadotte has only eventual rights, which relatively to Europe are the same as non-existent, and consequently any dispute concerning them is in no way the business of Europe or of the Congress. It is undoubtedly an evil, a very great evil, that that man should have been called upon to succeed to the throne of Sweden. But it is an evil which, if ever it can be remedied at all, can only be remedied by time and the events that time will bring.

War, which is desired by no one, which probably scarcely any Power is in a position to make, will most probably not take place. There will therefore be no need to ask Sweden for her alliance, nor for Sweden to ask us for a guarantee, which your Majesty would shrink from granting.

General Ricard has arrived, but I now hope that his journey will prove unnecessary.

General Pozzo's departure will not take place yet. I have even asked him to take no step to hasten it; he is of use to me as a medium of communication with the Emperor of Russia.

I hear that the King of Sweden is to go to Presburg, and to stay there until the conclusion of negotiations.

In a conference held to-day the affairs of the blacks were settled. Spain and Portugal will definitely give up the slave-trade in eight years. For these two countries eight years are a much shorter time than five years were for us, taking into consideration the enormous difference in the respective possessions, and, above all, in the progress of intelligence. We have yielded nothing, and yet the English are satisfied with us. Lord Castlereagh thanked me in the public conference for the assistance I had rendered to him. Another conference took place to-night, in which the Prussians replied to the proposals which have been made to them. The substance of their answer is that they accept. They will get neither Luxembourg nor Mayence.[6] Your Majesty's instructions were that they were not to obtain the latter; they will not have Luxembourg either.

The next few days will be employed in drawing up and signing the articles included in the protocol concerning the arrangements agreed on for Poland, Prussia, and Saxony.

I am, etc.

NOTES TO LETTER LI.

1. "During the last few days I have seen the Abbé de Montesquiou and M. d'André. Neither of them appeared to me to be satisfied with the progress

which affairs are making, or with their present position. There is a general cause for this in the divergence of opinions. The great, the very great majority of the nation wishes to be guided by a constitutional charter, *i.e.* to adopt the ideas, opinions, modes of looking and judging, which the advance of intelligence has for nearly a century gradually introduced in Europe, especially in France, but which in our country are the results of twenty-five long years of calamity and bloody experience. In opposition to this immense majority is a party feeble in point of numbers, but strong by virtue of the influence, the power, the places to be given away, and the confidence of the sovereign—the ancient nobility—which is always preaching the return to the old monarchy, to its abuses, its customs, its fundamental prejudices. This party is gradually taking possession of the important posts in the administration, and giving the inferior places to its adherents, endeavoring by these means to propagate its opinions. The daily dismissal of the men whom I call, but in the most honorable sense of the term, the men of the Revolution estranges those who have been sent away, disturbs those who have not yet been dismissed, and alarms everybody. Add to this that the majority of the new placemen are totally unversed in administration, so that their ignorance reacts upon the general progress of affairs, while their counsels influence the opinions of those over whom they are set. Here is the real evil. The struggle can have, however, no doubtful issue: it is clear that the majority will carry the day; but if the majority has power as well as firmness, it is clear that there will be a fight for it, and who can say what this may lead to? This state of affairs, and some tidings which are said to have come from Italy, and which have been spread abroad during the last few days, have revived the hopes of the Bonaparte faction. Savary, who came to see me three days ago, said to me with an air of extraordinary conviction, "*We shall see Bonaparte again,* and it will be entirely *their* fault (speaking of the Bourbons). I tried to disabuse him, to prove to him that he was wrong in entertaining the slightest hopes of the return of any member of that family, which is so justly detested by the French, and, indeed, by the whole of Europe. I saw that my efforts did not succeed in persuading him. I feel that Daru and Maret agree with him. The latter is kept accurately informed as to all that is going on by little Monnier, formerly his private secretary, whom some unknown fatality has placed at the side of M. d'André, and who is considerably trusted by him. I am assured that M. d'André is beginning to find out that his surroundings are bad, and that he says so. But why, then, does he hesitate to get rid of those who embarrass him and do him harm?

"Another cause which seems unimportant, but the effects of which are daily and keenly felt because it concerns the vanity of the nation, is the sort of humiliating position in which the Government places us with regard to foreigners. The English and Spanish newspapers are filled with gross insults to us. We are forbidden to reply: we are forbidden to insert in a French newspaper *a single word* against England or Spain. From a tragedy written and acted in 1769, this line has been suppressed—

'In all times England has been fruitful in crime.'

What happens when this tragedy is performed? The line is recited by the whole pit. We ask each other with reason if the Comte de la Châtre would dare to ask in London for the suppression of a single line of Shakespeare; and if even he did venture, whether the Government would accede to his request. All this increases the exasperation against the English, and those who came to Paris, or who still a e in Paris, must often have been aware of it. Of course, it would be much more proper if neither party insulted the other. But as we are a mark for all the most offensive things which hatred can inspire in our neighbors, let us at least be permitted to answer them.

"It is round you that all the partisans of the charter and of what I still call *liberal* ideas (although the term has been so much abused) rally. Your position at Vienna has magnified you in the eyes of the public, and your long absence has made your presence all the more eagerly desired. Believe me, there is not a shade of flattery in all this."—D'Hauterive to Talleyrand, 14th February, 1315.

2. "We are far from doing things as well and as *vigorously* as you do at Vienna. The funeral of poor Mademoiselle Raucourt was a mischievous and ridiculous misadventure. That curé of St. Roch has the misfortune of always giving trouble. The King was asked what he thought would be proper. He replied with his usual perfect good sense and judgment, 'I do not in the least object to Mademoiselle Raucourt's body being received in the church, but I will not give any orders to the clergy.' Neither the officials, nor the Ministry for Public Worship, nor the friends of Mademoiselle Raucourt warned D'André, and D'André accordingly expected the ceremony would not take place until the following day, and that he would have due notice of it. Neither Maison, nor Grundeler, nor any other authorities were informed. The body was, notwithstanding, on its way to the cemetery, when about twenty people turned it back. When it reached St. Roch, the procession was ordered to pass on by half a dozen gendarmes sent by the police. But at the Rue de l'Échelle, four or five hundred people assembled, brought it back, and, finding the principal door shut, took it in by a side door. No impiety or scandal was committed; the police officer only went to the curé. The curé had already sent to M. de l'Espinasse, who, like the curé, thought that nothing ought to be conceded to an old *grand vicaire*. The police officer easily proved the danger of this resolution, and the curé allowed them to have a priest, four acolytes, an ophicleide, and the officer put on a blue scarf, got up on a chair, and announced that they were going to sing or say (I forget which) the absolution and the *De profundis*. When the officer showed himself, the church resounded with cries of 'Vive le Roi!' The priest got over the business as quickly as possible; the funeral procession started again, and all was finished. But they say that the curé had considered Mademoiselle Raucourt a sufficiently good Catholic to accept from her the *pain bénit** last month, and a purse containing three or four hundred francs for charitable purposes."—Jaucourt to Talleyrand, 20th January, 1815.

3. "If we make haste, if at length we manage to understand the position of a ministry in a representative Government, we may gain sufficient time to allow you to come back. But we really are going on very badly, and we must do better if we do not wish to perish utterly."—Jaucourt to Talleyrand, 25th January, 1815.

4. The word "legitimacy" is, in this sense, a creation of Talleyrand himself, who meant to express by it dynastic right as opposed to the right of conquest. (See Thiers, "History of the Consulate and the Empire," tom. xviii. p. 5.)

5. Gustavus IV.

---

* Which was distributed in the Parisian churches on Sundays. TRANSLATOR.

6. Luxembourg and Mayence were federal fortresses, but the one belonged to the King of the Low Countries as Grand-Duke of Luxembourg, and the other to the duchy of Hesse-Darmstadt.

LETTER LII.

THE KING TO THE PRINCE DE TALLEYRAND.

No. 22.

11th February, 1815.

My Cousin,

I have received your despatch No. 25. Lord Castlereagh's praise of the Emperor of Austria would be flattering if spoken of a private individual, but when addressed to the sovereign who has just been manifesting extraordinary weakness, it resembles irony. As for me, I ought certainly to be satisfied, when I consider the condition of affairs four months ago, with the fate of the King of Saxony; but I hoped better things from the Emperor Francis, and I shall be uneasy until I see at least his last plan definitely adopted.

The document[1] added to your despatch is by no means reassuring for the King of Naples, in whom I take a much greater interest than in the King of Saxony; but, although it unfolds the secrets of the most shameful policy that ever was heard of, I am not discouraged, and I continue to be convinced, with a steadfast belief which I will never abandon, that in the end we shall destroy the scandal and the danger of Murat.

I am astonished that the Duke of Wellington had not already arrived at Vienna on the 1st of this month; but I fancy he cannot have long delayed, so I suppose that Lord Castlereagh will reach Paris towards the end of next week. To speak truly, I am not much edified by his behavior at the Congress; but I have too much reason to preserve the alliance which I have just formed to omit treating him so as to insure his satisfaction with the reception I shall give to him

On which, etc.

NOTE TO LETTER LII.

1. The treaty of the 11th of January, 1814, between the King of Naples and Austria, in which Austria guaranteed to Joachim the possession of his kingdom, and promised him a similar guarantee from the other allies, as well as the renunciation by Ferdinand IV. of his rights on Naples.

LETTER LIII.

No. 27.

Vienna, 15th February, 1815.

SIRE,

Lord Castlereagh starts to-day (the 18th), and although he intends to sleep every night on the road, he expects to reach Paris on the eighth day of his journey.[1] He will spend the whole of the next day there, and will set off again on the following day, so as to be in London on the 1st or 2nd of March.

The fate of the duchy of Warsaw, of Saxony, what we call here the reconstruction of the Prussian monarchy, the additions to be made to Hanover, the demarcation of the United Provinces, which are to take the name of the kingdom of the Netherlands, are points which are now entirely settled. They were the most complicated, and the only ones which might have caused war. Lord Castlereagh therefore carries with him to England the assurance that peace will be maintained.

Saxony is left with a population of one million three hundred thousand.[2] The King, to whom a courier has been sent, will, towards the end of this month, be, not at Presburg (I represented that the choice of this town would be very like an exile), but at Brünn, on the road to Vienna, where nothing will prevent his arriving as soon as he has given his consent to the cessions which the Powers have agreed upon.

The duchy of Luxembourg, with Limbourg and the adjacent territories, will be given to the Prince of Orange, as an indemnity for the old hereditary provinces which he yields to Prussia,[3] and the latter will not touch our frontier on a single point.[4] This appeared to your Majesty to be an object of the highest importance. The duchy of Luxembourg will, however remain German territory, and the fortress will remain a federal fortress.

The retrocessions Austria asks from Bavaria, and the equivalent to be granted to the latter, are the most important, and even the only important, territorial arrangements which remain to be settled in Germany.[5] The two Courts, on each side, ask for our support. The one will yield nothing without a perfect equivalent, and will not give up the things which the other covets ardently. From different motives we are almost equally interested in conciliating them both, which renders the part of arbitration very delicate. I hope, however, the difficulty will not surpass our power.

With regard to the territorial arrangements in Italy, the Commission charged with drawing up the plan proposed to restore to the Queen of Etruria Parma, Piacenza, and Guastalla, and the legations to the Holy See; and to give to the Grand-Duke of Tuscany Lucca, the State of Presidi, the sovereignty of Piombino, and the reversion of the island of Elba. The Archduchess Marie Louise was to have only a pension paid by Tuscany, and certain fiefs belonging formerly to the German Empire, and now in the possession of the Grand-Duke of Tuscany, to whom they were given by the Diet of the Empire as part of his indemnity. These fiefs, which are in Bohemia, afford a revenue of four hundred thousand florins. This scheme was presented to the Congress by our influence. It was found to possess two advantages: one that of diminishing the number of petty principalities in Italy, and the other, far more important, of keeping away the son of the Archduchess, and depriving him of all hope of reigning.

Austria let a whole month slip by without explaining herself.[6] The Emperor at last decided on restoring the duchies to the Queen of Etruria, saying that he could not with propriety take for himself or any member of his family one of the States of the House of Bourbon, with whom it was his interest and his desire to keep well. But, knowing that his daughter was anxious to have an independent establishment, he selected Lucca, and desired his minister to negotiate the affair with the Archduchess, and to this effect he gave instructions containing the arguments which the minister was to use. Prince Metternich, under the Emperor's instructions, has presented us with a counter-project, which suits us in most respects, as the Archduchess' son is not mentioned in it, and the reversion of Lucca would fall to Austria or Tuscany. Although we shall have to make several objections, I thought I perceived in my conversation with Prince Metternich that he would give way.

This counter-proposal states that the duchies should be restored to the Queen of Etruria, with the exception of Piacenza, with a circumference round the town containing a population of thirty thousand; that Lucca be given to the Archduchess for her life only, with two pensions, the one chargeable on Austria, the other on France, and that Austria should receive and hold permanently— 1st, Piacenza and the circumference above stated; 2nd, the part of Mantua on the right bank of the Po; 3rd, the Valtelline; 4th,

Lucca, after the Archduchess; and, finally, the imperial fiefs, as much in compensation for Parma and Piacenza, with its *enceinte*, as to afford material for exchange.

The proposal of charging a pension on France in compensation for things which France is never to receive, that of making Lucca revert to the Austrian Empire, and that of putting the imperial fiefs, even those enclosed in the neighboring States, at the disposal of Austria, were almost equally inadmissible, and Prince Metternich seemed pretty well aware of this. There would have been fewer objections to surrendering to Austria the part of Mantua on the right of the Po, and even Piacenza, which, from what General Ricard told me, is, from its position and in the present state of Italy, of little importance.

It is not essential to deprive Austria of the Valtelline,[1] as that territory is no longer indispensable for her communication with Lombardy. But Switzerland, to whom the Valtelline once belonged, has demanded it, and has been promised its restoration. The Emperor of Russia, as I shall have occasion further on to inform your Majesty, seems anxious to give it back.

Prince Metternich presented his counter-project, and discussed it with me before he had seen the Archuchess. His great presumption and shallowness prevented his foreseeing that he would not obtain complete success. But at the very first word the Archduchess Marie Louise showed her indisposition to content herself with Lucca, or even to care at all about that principality, where, she said, it would not be agreeable for her to reside as long as Napoleon was at Elba. She, or rather her counsellors,[8] stipulate for the right conceded to her by the treaty of the 11th of April. She does not ask to keep Parma, but she wants something equivalent, or nearly equivalent. The only way to satisfy her would be to give her the Legations, reserving the reversion to the Holy See. But the Court of Rome, which cannot reconcile itself even to the loss of Avignon,[9] would cry out loudly, and would perhaps even have recourse to employing force, which would recoil upon itself. Prince Metternich has asked me for three days in which to make up his mind for the one course or the other, and to give me his answer.

When once these difficulties are raised, the only serious objections will be in regard to the question of Naples, to which I am coming by-and-by. The arrangements relating to the free navigation of rivers are as yet barely sketched in; but the principles have been decided on, and they will secure to commerce all the advantages that European industry could ask for, and particularly it will secure to France, by the navigation of the Scheldt, all those which the possession of Belgium could give her.[10]

Finally, the question which is an object of passion, even of frenzy, for the English—the abolition of the slave-trade—has been yielded by the only two Powers who had not yet given it up.[11]

Lord Castlereagh is therefore armed against all attacks of the Opposition, and he carries with him all that is necessary to flatter public opinion.[12] But, as I have taken care to point out to him, ministers in a representative Government have not only to please the popular party; they must likewise satisfy the Government, and this "you can effect," I told him, "only by acting in concert with us, and in a new direction in the question of Naples."

I spent the last eight or ten days in exciting his interest in this question, and if I have not quite persuaded him to adopt a policy (which he does not consider himself free to do), I have brought him to desire almost as ardently as we do the expulsion of Murat, and he leaves us with the resolution of doing all he can to induce his Government to concur in it. He is embarrassed by two considerations: first, to see how to declare himself against Murat without appearing to violate the promises made to the latter[13] (this is what Lord Castlereagh calls not compromising his reputation); the other, to choose the means of execution, so as to make sure of success in case of resistance, without compromising interests or wounding prejudices, and without exciting alarm in any quarter. He promised me that on the third day after his arrival in London he would send a courier bearing the decision of his Court, and, armed with all our arguments, he hopes that the decision will be favorable. What I wish is, that without entering into discussions, all of which weaken the principal object, the Duke of Wellington may be authorized to declare that his Court recognizes Ferdinand IV. as King of the Two Sicilies. It is in this sense that I entreat your Majesty to be kind enough to speak to him in Paris. In the latter days of his stay in Vienna, Lord Castlereagh lent himself very obligingly to making the overtures I was anxious for. He spoke against Murat to the Emperor of Russia, whom he saw at the same time with the Duke of Wellington. He said to the Emperor of Austria, "Russia is your natural enemy; Prussia is devoted to Russia; the only Power you can possibly depend upon on the Continent is France: it is your interest, therefore, to keep well with the House of Bourbon, which you cannot do unless Murat is turned out."

The Emperor of Austria replied, "I feel the truth of all you say." Finally, he told Prince Metternich, on whom he and the Duke of Wellington called together, "You will have a sharp contest on the question of Naples; do not think that you can escape it. I warn you that it is a question which will be brought before the Congress. Take, therefore, measures in consequence; send troops to Italy, if necessary." Each told me separately that this declaration had thrown Prince Metternich into great dejection—these were their words— and your Majesty will understand Prince Metternich's dejection still better after reading the secret articles of his treaty with Murat, of which I have the honor of enclosing a copy.[14] That he should have guaranteed the kingdom of Naples to him under the circumstances existing at that time, is easy to conceive; but that he should have carried his humiliation so far as to allow a clause to be inserted in the treaty, stating that Murat has the generosity to renounce his rights to the kingdom of Sicily, and to guarantee that kingdom to Ferdinand IV., is a fact which seems incredible even though it be proved.[15]

Your Majesty will probably learn, not without surprise, that attachment to the principle of legitimacy enters little into the calculations of Lord Castlereagh, or even of the Duke of Wellington, with regard to Murat; it touches them very feebly; they do not even seem quite to take it in. In Murat it is the man whom they detest more than the usurper. The principles on which the English act in India prevent their having any exact ideas as to legitimacy. Nothing has made so much impression on Lord Castlereagh, who wishes above all things for peace, as my declaring to him that peace would be impossible if Murat were not driven out, for that his occupation of the throne of Naples was incompatible with the existence of the House of Bourbon.

I have also seen the Emperor of Russia. It was on Monday morning, the 13th instant. I wished to speak only of Naples to him, to remind him of the promises he made to me on this subject; but he took the opportunity of talking to me of many other things which I must report to your Majesty, whom I would ask to allow me, as I have already done in several other letters, to employ the form of dialogue for that purpose.

I began by telling the Emperor that I had long refrained from troubling him, out of respect for his occupations, and even for his pleasures; that the carnival having put an end to these, and the others being now arranged, I had asked for an audience. I added that even the Congress had only one more affair of the first importance to settle.

"You wish to speak of Naples?" "Yes, Sire." And I reminded him that he had promised his support. "But you must help me." "We have done so as far as it depended on us. Your Majesty is aware that, as we could not think of completely re-establishing the kingdom of Poland, we did not help her private arrangements when they clashed with the views of your Majesty, who must surely have forgotten that in the beginning of the Congress the English were rather ill-disposed on this question." "In the affairs of Switzerland?" "I do not known that we have ever been in opposition to your Majesty in the affairs of Switzerland. It was our plan to use every endeavor to calm excitement. I do not know to what extent we have succeeded, but that was our only aim. The Bernese were the most irritated; they had lost most and demanded most. An indemnity which they considered very insufficient had been offered to them; we induced them to put up with it.[16] All I know is that they ask the whole of the bishopric of Basle, and that they are determined not to accept less." "And what will you do for Geneva?" "Nothing, Sire." "Ah!" (in a tone of surprise and reproach). "It was not possible for us to give her anything; the King will never give up French subjects." "And can nothing be got from Sardinia?" "I am perfectly ignorant on the subject." "Why do you give the Valtelline to Austria?" "Nothing, Sire, has been decided on that subject. The Austrian affairs have been badly managed." "It is her fault," replied the Emperor; "why does she not choose skilful ministers?" "As Austria has had to make great sacrifices which must have cost her much, I should think it natural, especially in matters of such importance, to endeavor to please her." "The Valtelline was promised to be restored to Switzerland, to whom it belonged." "The Valtelline has been separated from Switzerland for the last eighteen years; it has never known anything of the government to which your Majesty would restore it. To give it back to the Grisons, to which it formerly belonged, would be to make it miserable. It seems to me that it would be best to make a separate canton of it, unless Austria obtained it." "This will be arranged. And what will you do with Prince Eugène?"[17] "Prince Eugène is a French subject, and in that character he can demand nothing. But he is the son-in-law of the King of Bavaria —he owed this to the position and influence of France at that time;

it is therefore right that France should try to obtain for him all that it would be reasonable and possible for him to obtain in consideration of this alliance. We wish, therefore, to do something for him; we wish him to receive an appanage from the House of Bavaria, and that the King's share of the territories still undisposed of may be increased for this purpose." "Why not give him a sovereignty?" "Sire, his marriage with a Princess of Bavaria is not a sufficient motive. The Prince Radziwill is brother-in-law to the King of Prussia, and he has no sovereignty." "But why not, for instance, give him Deux-Ponts? That is a small thing." "I ask your Majesty's pardon; the duchy of Deux-Ponts has always been considered as something considerable, and, besides, the territories remaining at our disposal are scarcely sufficient to fulfil the engagements already entered into." "And the marriage?" "The King has done me the honor of informing me that he still ardently desired it." "And so do I," replied the Emperor. "My mother [18] is also equally anxious for it; she speaks of it to me in the letters I have had lately." "The King," I said, "has refused several other proposals while waiting for your Majesty's answer." "I have also refused one, but I have also been refused myself. The King of Spain asked for my sister,[19] but on being told that she must have a chapel, and that this was a peremptory condition, he retracted his offer."[20] "From the conduct of the Catholic King, your Majesty may see what are the obligations of the Very Christian King." "I wanted to know what I was to think." "Sire, my last orders resemble what General Pozzo told you." "Why do you not execute the treaty of April 11th?"[21] "As I have been absent from Paris for five months, I do not know what has been done in this respect." "The treaty has not been executed; we ought to insist on its execution. Our honor is at stake; we cannot possibly draw back. The Emperor of Austria insists upon it as much as I do, and I assure you he is hurt at its not being executed." "Sire, I will report all that you have done me the honor of saying to me; but I must observe that in the unsettled state of the countries round France, and particularly of Italy, it may be dangerous to furnish the means of intrigue to persons who we think it probable may take advantage of them."[22]

At length we returned to Murat. I recapitulated briefly all the reasons of justice, morality, and propriety which ought to unite Europe against him. I distinguished his position from that of Bernadotte, which particularly affects the Emperor, and in support of my words I quoted the Royal Almanack,[23] which I had just received. He begged me to send it to him, adding, "What you tell me gives me the greatest pleasure. I feared the contrary, and Bernadotte also was very much afraid of it." The Emperor then spoke of Murat with the utmost contempt. "He is a vulgar rascal," he said, "who has betrayed us all. But," he added, "when I meddle with an affair, I like to be sure of the means of success. If Murat resists, he must be driven out. I have spoken of it," he added, "with the Duke of Wellington. He thinks that a considerable force would be wanted, and that, if it were necessary to send one, there would be great difficulties in the way." I answered that I did not ask for troops (for I knew that they would not be given to me), but a line—a single line—in the new treaty, and that France and Spain would undertake the rest. On which the Emperor replied, "You shall have my support."[94] During the whole of the conversation the Emperor was cold, but, on the whole, I was rather satisfied with him than otherwise.

Lord Castlereagh also spoke to me warmly about the treaty of the 11th of April, and I have no doubt he will mention it to your Majesty. This subject has been revived lately, and is now in every one's mouth. I ought to tell your Majesty that it is constantly recurring, and in a disagreeable way; its influence is felt in the question of the *Mont de Milan*,[25] which interests so many subjects and servants of your Majesty.

It seems to me, however, that your Majesty might get rid of all that is most embarrassing in the treaty of the 11th of April by coming to an agreement with England.

In the beginning of my sojourn here Lord Castlereagh expressed his desire that France should at once renounce the slave-trade, offering in return certain indemnities. It is generally more easy to obtain pecuniary than any other indemnities in England. At that time I thought it necessary to elude this proposition without decidedly rejecting it, reserving to ourselves the right of taking it into consideration later on. In speaking recently of Murat, and of the provision which could not be withheld from him if he submitted to the adverse decision of Europe, Lord Castlereagh did not hesitate to assure me that England would willingly undertake to assign an income to Murat out of the English funds, in case France consented to give up the slave-trade. If such an arrangement were considered practicable, I have no doubt that it would be easy to include the pensions stipulated by the treaty of the 11th of April in the payments charged upon England.

This arrangement would, in consequence of the passion of the English for the abolition of the slave-trade, have certainly the advantage of uniting England closely to our cause in the question of Naples, and of inducing her to second us in every way.

It remains to be seen whether, considering the present state of our colonies, the sacrifices France would make by renouncing the slave-trade for the four years and three months which it has yet to run would be greater than the advantages she would probably derive from the arrangement I have just suggested. I venture to ask your Majesty to have this closely examined into, so as to express your Majesty's intention on the subject to Lord Castlereagh, who will probably not fail to mention it.

I could have wished that the treaty of the 3rd of January, which, when once the Congress is over, will have no further meaning, had been postponed for a longer or shorter period, if only by common consent. Lord Castlereagh finds some difficulty in the way, as he has no confidence in Prince Metternich; but he assures me that, even after the expiration of the treaty, its spirit will survive. Above all things, he is anxious to give no umbrage to the other continental Powers, which does not prevent his desiring that a great intimacy may be established between the two Governments, and that they may continue to concur in peaceful and conservative views.[26] In one word, he left Vienna in a frame of mind which I can only praise, and in which he cannot help being confirmed by all that he will hear from your Majesty's lips.

I see that my letter is enormously long, and I fear lest your Majesty should consider it too long for what it is worth; but I had rather run the risk of being too diffuse than suppress any details which your Majesty might think necessary.

By the next courier I shall have the honor of enclosing the treaties of the coalition, which I have succeeded in procuring.[27] I would ask your Majesty, after looking through them, to give them to M. de Jaucourt, to be preserved at the Foreign Office.

General Pozzo has again been spoken to about his departure.

I am, etc.

NOTES TO LETTER LIII.

1. "Lord Castlereagh arrived last night in Paris. The King honored his Excellency to-day with a private audience."—*Moniteur Universel*, 27th February, 1815.

2. "The portion of the kingdom of Saxony which has been preserved, joined to the ducal territories, will altogether interpose a tract covered by two million inhabitants between the Prussian and Austrian monarchies."—Talleyrand to the Department, 8th February, 1815.

3. M. Himly says, in his "History of the Formation of the States of Central Europe," vol. ii. p. 509, "They wish to make Luxembourg an equivalent for the German patrimonial possessions which have been given up by the line of Nassau-Orange, and to assure their reversion to the line of Nassau-Nassau. This is why it was treated as joined to the kingdom of the Low Countries only by a personal tie, so personal that the King was authorized to transmit it to any one of his sons."

4. The events of 1815 seem to have determined the Powers on establishing an absolute contact between Prussia and France.

5. The question of the retrocession of the provinces of the Inn and Hansruck, of the duchy of Salzburg, and of Berchtolsgaden had been referred to the Congress of Vienna, which did not settle it definitely. By the treaty of Munich, on the 14th of April, 1816, Bavaria accepted the territories which were to be disposed of on the banks of the Rhine as an indemnity. She also refused to give up Berchtolsgaden, which is still in her possession (see Himly, vol. i. p. 461). The principle followed out in these territorial arrangements of Bavaria with Austria had been already mooted in Paris.

6. "The Italian affairs make no progress; they all stop in the bureau of Prince Metternich."—Letter from the French plenipotentiaries to the Department, 24th January, 1815.

7. The Valtelline (Val Tellina) is a little valley about three thousand three hundred kilomètres in extent, and containing ninety thousand inhabitants. It is divided by the Adda; its chief town, Sondrio. The Bishops of Coire gave it up to the Grisons in 1530. Spain wanted to take it to establish permanent communications between the Italian possessions and those of the House of Austria in Tyrol, but Richelieu succeeded in driving out the Spanish troops (1624). This was one of the most important acts of his glorious administration In 1814 Austria incorporated it in the Lombardo-Venetian kingdom. Since 1859 it has belonged to the kingdom of Italy.

8. The position of the Archduchess Marie Louise was long a cause of anxiety. On the 9th of August, 1814, Talleyrand wrote to Prince Metternich:

"On your last visit to Paris, my dear Prince, you told the King that you did not approve of the visit of the Archduchess Marie Louise to Aix-les-Bains.

"As soon as it appeared that these waters would be of benefit to her, the King shut his eyes to any inconveniences attending this journey, if indeed there were any to be seen. But you, my dear Prince, thought that it might give rise, not to intrigues, but to gossip. You know how they cackle at watering-places; you know how idle people are there, and all the consequences of idleness. Some thoughtless heads have even been known to compromise themselves, and it is this that we must avoid. Joseph Bonaparte, who lives not far from Aix, has committed follies which he would never have thought of in another neighborhood. All this has little importance, and the King attaches none to it, but the rumor of it reaches Paris; it is talked of in every direction, by diplomatists among the rest. People try to impute very secret and grave motives to perfectly simple and natural actions.

"I fancy, my dear Prince, that you will think it advisable, both for you and for us (the Archduchess's cure being now complete), that she should not prolong her stay at Aix. You will not, I am sure, misapprehend the motives which prompt my speaking to you in this way. . . .

"Adieu, dear Prince; preserve a little friendship for me, and believe in my very sincere attachment to you.

"PRINCE BENEVENTO."

9. The Holy See acquired the marquisate of Provence (Comtat Venaissin) in 1271 by the will of Alfonso, Count of Artois and Toulouse, and in 1348 Avignon was purchased by Pope Clement VI. from Jeanne of Anjou, Queen of Naples and Countess of Provence. During the Revolution it was occupied by the French, and the Comtat and Avignon itself were formally reunited to France. On the 19th of February, 1797, Pope Pius VI. renounced his ancient right to both (Treaty of Tolentino). The Court of Rome, in the name of that very principle of legitimacy, which Talleyrand tried to use as a factor in the affairs of Europe, redemanded Avignon.

10. "By the fifth article in the Treaty of Paris the signatory Powers contracted the engagement to consider at the future Congress the principles on which the navigation of the Rhine should be regulated in the fairest and most favorable manner for the commerce of all nations. The special Commission, charged with this part of the negotiations, has adopted a basis in agreement with the Treaty of Paris, and, among other questions of importance to French commerce, it decided that the tariffs should not be raised, and that the Powers should each receive their share of the funds produced by the *octroi* in proportion to the distance watered by the river in their respective territories. As only one bank of the river belongs to France, she will share the sum due to her with the opposite bank.

"It was not, however, on this question that we had most difficulty in gaining our point. The right which was disputed to France of sharing in the administration of the *octroi*, and of sending a French delegate to the Central Committee which will direct this administration, was the object of the most lively discussion. But the firmness and pertinacity which enabled his Majesty's embassy to succeed in still more important affairs have also assured its success on the present occasion. This is the more satisfactory, as the obstacles were more difficult to vanquish; for, besides private interests, it was necessary to overcome the ill will which some of the intervening Powers bore to France in this question."—Letter to the Department, 3rd March, 1815.

11. Spain and Portugal.

12. The conduct of the English Cabinet, and of its plenipotentiary at the Congress of Vienna, was at that time the object of the most violent attacks in both Houses of Parliament. In the sitting of the 21st of January Lord Grenville said to the Lords, "England is affording the unique spectacle of a nation which is granting subsidies not only to her allies, in support of her own interests or to attain some great object, but which grants them also to every nation to enable it to uphold against some other nation interests which that other is paid to at-

tack. England, since the Treaty of Paris and for a year after the conclusion of the peace, subsidizes every power, whether military or not, on the Continent."* And, in truth, in the supplementary Convention signed (29th May, 1814) between Great Britain and Russia, England bound herself to maintain her army on a war footing, not only as long as her own interests required it, but also as long as the negotiations were not terminated between the other Powers, so that the engagement had no limit.

The transfer of Genoa to the King of Sardinia had also raised a very ardent opposition in the House of Commons.

The English Cabinet was reminded that in September, 1806, Austria had declared that the occupation of Genoa by Bonaparte was a sufficient reason for declaring war; that in the month of May, in the same year, Russia had refused to mediate between France and England for the same reason; that at the Peace of Amiens Austria had demanded that the Ligurian Republic should be restored to the independent position it held in 1795; that finally, the Treaty of Chaumont had solemnly declared that a general treaty of peace should be negotiated, and that the rights and liberties of every nation should be established by it, and that by virtue of this treaty Lord William Bentinck had promised independence to Genoa in the proclamation he made on his entry into Italy.

It was in this House of Commons that a member of the Opposition quoted the following principle from Vatel's "Rights of Nations:" "If during a war a nation has been unduly oppressed, the first care of the victorious nation should be, not to change the ruler of that people, but to restore to the oppressed nation its ancient liberties."

13. "A general who is still almost in the service of Murat, whose wife is still at Naples, who is a clever man, and who intends to return to the King's service, unless indeed the freedom with which he answered Marshal Soult does not hang him, called upon me. He even said that Murat had asked him to do so, and he told me that Murat was determined to fight and to die sword in hand, but that he depended on the promises of Austria; that they were of ancient date and had been renewed; that the Allies, in his opinion, were wrong in never having come to an understanding with Murat, for he would have sold himself soul and body, etc., etc., but that to this day he was sure of Austria, the proof of which was that he had not seized the Roman States and set Italy in a blaze."—Jaucourt to Talleyrand, 14th February, 1815.

14. Treaty between Austria and Naples, concluded on the 11th of January, 1814. Secret Articles signed by Metternich, Campo-Chiaro, and Cariati (see D'Angeberg, p. 81, et seq.).

"Prince Metternich has all sorts of intrigues with the Queen of Naples. It is certain that he acts in concert with her."—Letter from Jaucourt to Talleyrand, 4th January, 1815.

15. Talleyrand forgets that at the time when Metternich negotiated and signed the treaty of the 11th of January, 1814, with Murat, there had not been any question between the Allies of overthrowing Napoleon and the dynasties established under the Empire. Austria would not otherwise have founded and settled this negotiation on the basis of the maintenance of Napoleon's own brother-in-law.

---

* These are not the exact words of the speech; the French of which this is a translation gives only the substance.—TRANSLATOR.

16. "The canton of Berne had formerly been so vast and so wealthy, and was so little of either at the present time, that there was both justice and prudence in compensating it. The French Empire, whose remains were used at that time to put everybody in good temper, had left unoccupied some fragments of the territory beyond the Jura. They were Porentruy and the ancient bishopric of Basle. Together they formed an indemnity which was offered at once to Berne and finally accepted."—Thiers, "History of the Consulate and the Empire," tom. xviii. p. 305.

17. The eighth article of the treaty was in these words: "Prince Eugène, Viceroy of Italy, shall be given a suitable establishment out of France."

18. Paul I., after the death of his first wife, a princess of Hesse-Darmstadt, married, on the 18th of October, 1776, the Princess Dorothea Sophia Augusta (Marie Feodorowna), a Princess of Würtemberg, who was the mother of the Emperors Alexander and Nicholas. She died on the 5th of November, 1828.

19. The Grand-Duchess Anne.

20. "*Monsieur* wishes you to tell us about the Princesses of Prussia, Saxony, and Portugal, as he wants you to arrange a marriage for him; he has reproached me for forgetting to tell you about, etc. I did not forget, but I trusted to Pozzo and to the compromise which you might arrange with Heaven."—Jaucourt to Talleyrand, 13th February, 1815.

21. At the end of the conference held in Paris on the 10th of April, 1814, between the plenipotentiaries of the Emperor Napoleon and those of the Allies, between Caulaincourt, Metternich, Castlereagh, Hardenberg, Nesselrode, Ney, and Macdonald, the same plenipotentiaries concluded the treaty of the 11th of April, called the Treaty of Fontainebleau, between the Emperor Napoleon, Austria, Prussia, and Russia. It contains the following articles:

"Art. 1. His Majesty the Emperor Napoleon renounces for himself, his successors, and descendants, as well as for all the members of his family, all right of sovereignty and dominion, as well as to the French Empire and the kingdom of Italy, as over every other country."

"Art. 3. The isle of Elba, adopted by his Majesty the Emperor Napoleon as the place of his residence, shall form, during his life, a separate principality, which shall be possessed by him, in full sovereignty and property; there shall be besides granted, in full property, to the Emperor Napoleon an annual revenue of two million francs, in rent-charge, in the great book of France, of which one million shall be in reversion for the Empress."

"Art. 4. The duchies of Parma, Placentia, and Guastalla shall be granted, in full property and sovereignty, to her Majesty the Empress Marie Louise; they shall pass to her son, and to the descendants in the right line. The Prince, her son, shall from henceforth take the title of Prince of Parma, Placentia, and Guastalla."

"Art. 6. There shall be reserved in the territories hereby renounced, to his Majesty the Emperor Napoleon, for himself and his family, domains or rent-charges in the great book of France, producing a revenue, clear of all deductions and charges, of two million five hundred thousand francs. These domains and rents shall belong in full property, to be disposed of as they shall think fit, to the princes and princesses of his family."

Most of these articles were still unexecuted when Napoleon returned from the island of Elba.—D'Angeberg, p. 148, et seq.

It was this violation of the Treaty of Paris of which the Commission of the Presidents of the Conseil d'État complained, when they were called upon for their opinion on the declaration of the 13th of March, 1815, to authorize and legitimatize Napoleon's return from Elba.

22. I must tell you that, according to him [M. d'Osmond, French ambassador at the Court of Sardinia], the distribution of the Bonaparte family all over Italy, at Trieste, Bologna, Parma, Florence, Rome, and Naples, seems inconceivable. . . ."—Jaucourt to Talleyrand, 11th February, 1815.

23. It is true that the Royal Almanack of 1815 does not mention Murat as King of Naples, but mentions Bernadotte as Prince Royal of Sweden, without omitting his wife, Mademoiselle Joséphine Clary. On his return from the island of Elba Napoleon published, in May, a supplement to the Royal Almanack of 1815, excluding the Bourbons and mentioning Murat, who had already been driven out of his kingdom, as King of Naples.

24. The Emperor of Russia had formally promised us his support. I hear, nevertheless, that his language to those who are around him is not much in harmony with this promise. Not being able, he says, to make the whole of Italy independent, he wishes that there should be a strong power in that country, under the influence neither of France nor of Austria. As this power can only be Naples, it is evident that, in order to attain this object, Naples must not belong to the House of Bourbon. He therefore intends to support Murat."
—Talleyrand to the Department, 27th February, 1815.

25. *Mont de Milan.* See note in the Appendix at the end of this volume.

26. "Lord Castlereagh seemed to me to be full of confidence in you and esteem for your character, disposed to concur in your views, and to combat the unfriendly disposition of the two nations by a durable system of peace and alliance. There seem to be the conflicting sentiments of a desire for peace and extreme vanity in the English nation with respect to the Congress."—Jaucourt to Talleyrand, 4th March, 1815.

27. The treaties of Kalisch, Reichenbach, Teplitz, and Chaumont (see D'Angeberg, vol. i.).

LETTER LIV.

THE KING TO PRINCE TALLEYRAND.

No. 23.

18th February, 1815.

MY COUSIN,

I have received your letter No. 26, and I received it with great satisfaction. I certainly should have preferred that the King of Saxony should have kept all his territories, but I did not hope it, and I consider it as a miracle that, being as little seconded as we were, we have been able to preserve for him all we have done. Another thing on which it gives me great pleasure to express my satisfaction is, that Prussia has obtained neither Luxembourg nor Mayence; such a neighbor would have been dangerous to the future peace of France. Let us, therefore, leave the sword in the scabbard; General Ricard will have taken an unnecessary journey, but one which will have proved to my allies my eagerness to set myself right with them.

The Duke of Wellington's conduct at Vienna touches me, but does not astonish me. He is an honorable man. Your reflections on his language are very just.

I expect, as you do, difficulties in the affair of Naples, but they must be conquered. Putting aside all sentiment, Murat's position seems to me to become every day more threatening.[1] That of Bernadotte is peculiar, but when once the principle has been conceded the consequences must be admitted.

Newspapers are full of the admirable conduct of the Governor of Kœnigstein (whose name escapes my memory at this moment).[2] I should like to make him a commandant of the Legion of Honor: but I wish to know, first, if the facts are true; secondly, if the King of Saxony would approve of my giving this decoration to his officer: and I ask you to obtain information on both points.

On which, etc.

NOTES TO LETTER LIV.

1. "Our anxiety respecting Rome is not without grounds, but it seems that the report that Murat was on the march to seize it was untrue. It is very possible that you may have had some share in this plot, but I have too much respect for my minister to venture a too curious glance into his—shall I dare to call it?—diplomatic game-bag?"—Jaucourt to Talleyrand, 8th February, 1815.

"You will see, from Mariotti's despatch, that on the 2nd of March Italy was perfectly tranquil. Nevertheless, the consul, who arrived this morning, assures me that the public mind is stirred up, and carries the desire for independence to the utmost. He does not believe that Murat was in league with Bonaparte in this affair. Murat was still convinced of the hidden protection of the Emperor Alexander and of the certain support of Austria; he was therefore careful not to offend those Powers. But if Bonaparte throws himself with his troops into Milan, if he raises the people, Murat will act with all his might."—Jaucourt to Talleyrand, 8th March, 1815.

2. The name of the Governor of Kœnigstein was Saares de Saar. He refused to yield up the fortress, which was the private property of the King of Saxony, to Prussia.

LETTER LV.

No. 28.

Vienna, 20th February, 1815.

Sire,

I have the honor of sending to your Majesty the papers announced in my last despatch. If they are not a complete collection of the treaties between the Allies, they are at least the most important.

They are

1. A convention in the form of a Note exchanged between Austria and Russia, on the 29th of March, 1813, called the Convention of Kalisch.

2. The treaty of peace and alliance between Russia and Prussia. This has often been called the Treaty of Kalisch, because it was negotiated and even minuted down there; but it was signed at Breslau on the 26th of February, 1813.

3. The Treaty of Reïchenbach[1] of the 27th of June in the same year, between Austria, Russia, and Prussia.

4. The Treaty of Teplitz[2] of the 9th of September between the same Powers, and the secret articles of this treaty.

5. Finally, the Treaty of Chaumont,[3] which was intended to continue the alliance against France for twenty years after the war, and which it was proposed to renew before the expiration of this term, for the purpose of perpetuating the coalition which has been dissolved by the treaty of the 3rd of January.

It may be agreeable to your Majesty to look over these different papers. In them will be found an explanation of some of the difficulties we have had to struggle against, and the reason for the embarrassment experienced by the Allies themselves, particularly by Austria, for want of having made, when it depended entirely upon her, stipulations which the most ordinary common sense would have shown her to be indispensable.

I entreat your Majesty to be kind enough to give these papers, after reading them, to M. de Jaucourt, to be kept in the archives of the Foreign Office. I have already had the honor of announcing to your Majesty that the Kings of Bavaria and Hanover had acceded to the alliance of the 3rd of January. I intended not to have sent their acts of agreement until I could have sent with them that of Holland, but the latter has not yet been forwarded, and Prince Wrède is so anxious for me to exchange the ratifications of that of Bavaria, that I have the honor of sending the enclosed at once to your Majesty. I also send duplicates of the acts of acceptance which I have signed. The last two acts are those which ought to be ratified by your Majesty.

I entreat your Majesty to transmit them to M. de Jaucourt, in order that he may, if your Majesty thinks proper, prepare the ratifications.

A courier has just arrived, bringing me the letter with which your Majesty has honored me, dated the 11th of this month. I shall await with lively impatience the one containing the result of Lord Castlereagh's conversations. I should like the article on Naples to be such as I may show to Prince Metternich. It cannot be too explicit.

I am, etc.

NOTES TO LETTER LV.

1. Prussia and Austria became reconciled at Reichenbach. On the 27th of June, 1813, the convention was signed there between Great Britain and Prussia for defining the nature and extent of the subsidies and mutual assistance they were to afford each other (D'Angeberg, p. 59).

2. The treaty was signed in the old hotel of Guillaume Rose, now occupied by the mint. By this treaty the allies decided to restrict France to her limits before the Revolution (D'Angeberg, p. 116).

3. See D'Angeberg, p. 59.

LETTER LVI.

No. 29.

Vienna, 24th February, 1815.

SIRE,

Joachim's minister here has received from his master an already executed Note, with instructions, after communicating the contents to Prince Metternich (which he has done), to address it to me.

The object of this Note is to demand an explanation of the steps I have taken against him, so he expresses himself, at the Congress, and a declaration specifying whether your Majesty considers yourself at peace with him or not.

As Joachim's minister has no doubt that this letter was written, and the order to transmit it to me given, only in consequence of the communication he himself made to Joachim while under the belief that we should not come to an understanding about Saxony and that war was imminent, he therefore thought that now that this supposition is falsified, he could no longer make use of the Note without hurting the interests of his master instead of serving them. He has therefore taken upon himself to suppress it, and it will not be sent to me.

I learnt these details from the Duke of Wellington, with whom I considered what advantages we could derive from Prince Metternich's having been made acquainted with the note.

We agreed to ask Prince Metternich to profit by it by announcing, in a declaration addressed to me as well as the Duke of Campo-Chiaro, that Austria will not allow any foreign army to pass through her territory; and to support this declaration by recalling the troops which are actually on the frontiers of Poland, and sending them to Italy.

The Duke of Wellington spoke to this effect to Prince Metternich, whom I saw afterwards, and to whom I held similar language.

The result is that this very day the Emperor of Austria has issued orders for a hundred and fifty thousand men to march into Italy, and that the declaration which I mentioned above will be placed in our hands to-morrow.

Austria's chief pretext for adjourning the question of Naples was that she was not ready, and that she feared Murat might excite a revolution in Italy.[1] This objection was not without force, and made an impression on the English and the Russians; but it will be powerless as soon as the Austrians have a considerable army in Italy. We may thank Joachim's Note for this result, which makes me think the incident very useful.

The fact of this Note not having been handed in, because it was ill-timed and opposed to the interest of the writer now that the affairs of Saxony have been arranged, proves that we may congratulate ourselves on their having been settled; and, in fact, Austria would not otherwise have been able to march a considerable force into Italy.

If I can procure a copy of the Note through Prince Metternich, I shall have the honor of sending it to your Majesty.

This being the state of affairs, does not your Majesty think that there might be some advantage in collecting, under some pretext other than the real one, a considerable force in the south of France?

According to all probability, the affairs of Switzerland will be terminated in a few days, with a single exception, that of the Valtelline, which the Powers seem to have resolved to leave in suspense—at any rate, until they have obtained the acquiescence of the cantons to the proposals which will be made; for it has been decided to offer the terms which are considered most expedient to the cantons before taking measures for enforcing them in case of a refusal.

Austria and Bavaria are in negotiation for the retrocession demanded by Austria of the countries occupied by Bavaria, and the compensation to be given to the latter. As the two Powers are far from being agreed, it has been proposed to take France and England as arbitrators. But it seems to me that by leaving the honor of this arbitration to England alone, France would be able to influence the arrangement without committing herself with regard to either of the two Powers, which it is equally her interest to conciliate.

Prince Metternich has come to ask me very mysteriously to give him a respite for the affairs of Italy until the 5th or 6th of March, by which period he supposes that I shall have received your Majesty's commands, after Lord Castlereagh's visit. Although I do not quite understand his motive for this demand, it did not seem to me possible to refuse. But, on the other hand, I should see a great objection to Austria arranging everything that concerns her, with the exception of Italy, and that the affairs of that country, which are those which most affect us, should remain exposed to chance, and ourselves to all the impediments which Austria may raise up against us. I hope, therefore, that the affairs of Bavaria may not be hurried. Therefore, although my impatience to be once more with your Majesty, after such a long absence, did not require to be increased by the *ennui* which seems to have fallen upon Vienna ever since the opening of the Congress, I find myself obliged to hurry nothing at present, to slacken even, as far as depends upon me, the progress of events, and to wait.

I annex to this letter the act of accession of Holland,[2] which has just been signed. I entreat your Majesty to be pleased, after ratifying the act of acceptance, to order it to be returned to me by M. de Jaucourt.

I am, etc.

NOTES TO LETTER LVI.

1. "In a private conversation with M. de Jaucourt, the Marquis of St. Élie—recognized here as the Chamberlain, and virtually, although not recognized in that character, *chargé d'affaires* of Murat at Paris—said to him: 'It is a great mistake to suppose that Austria can take an active part against Russia, serve the plans of France, and free Saxony, if the kingdom of Naples is not united with this project. Believe me, Austria knows for certain that Italy is on a volcano, and that nothing but the fidelity of the King of Naples to the mutual engagements which unite the two countries can allow Austria the free disposition of her forces. The duke of Campo-Chiaro has, no doubt, told all this to Prince Talleyrand; but telling and persuading are very different things, and I can once more assure you that the devotion of the King of Naples to the King of France, a devotion which the King can command, can alone be a guarantee for executing the political views of Prince Talleyrand.'"—Letter from Jaucourt to Talleyrand, 27th November, 1815.

2. Note of the plenipotentiaries of the Low Countries in reply to the Note addressed to them by the plenipotentiary of Great Britain, inviting the sovereign princes of the Low Countries to accede to the treaty of defensive alliance concluded on the 3rd of January, 1815, between Great Britain, Austria, and France. Vienna, 2nd January, 1815 (see D'Angeberg, p. 692).

LETTER LVII.

No. 30.

Vienna, 26th February, 1815.

SIRE,

I have the honor of sending to your Majesty a copy of Prince Metternich's Declaration mentioned in my last despatch, with the answer I have just written to him.

Your Majesty will see that this answer agrees entirely with the letter I wrote to Lord Castlereagh, in which I told him that we had no intention of passing through Italy in order to put down Murat.

I could have wished Austria to declare herself more explicitly against Murat. But they feared to give him a pretext for hostilities, the Austrians not being ready in Italy. Orders have been given to send troops thither.

They will have one hundred and fifty thousand men there, and another fifty thousand in reserve in Carinthia, which will be enough to keep Murat quiet or baffle his attempts. But as everything is done very slowly here, Prince Schwarzenberg asks for seven weeks to enable all his troops to reach their destination.

The Note which determined their being sent still seems to me to have been a fortunate incident.

I go to-morrow to Presburg to see Madame de Brionne,[1] who received yesterday the last sacraments, and who has sent for me. I shall return on Monday night, and public affairs, which make no progress, will not in any way suffer from these two days' absence.

It is settled that General Pozzo leaves on the 1st or 2nd of March: he will be ten days on his journey.

The Emperor of Russia is very active in the affairs of the Archduchess Marie Louise; he has made a scheme for taking away almost all the Legations from the Pope. This brings him into opposition with the principles agreed on by the plenipotentiaries of the Great Powers. His new scheme has hitherto remained in M. d'Anstett's portfolio.

I am, etc.

NOTE TO LETTER LVII.

1. M. Beugnot says of her in his Memoirs, vol. i. p. 57 (Paris, 1867), "Madame de Brionne had been one of the most beautiful women of her time. Before the Revolution she was intimate with the Abbé de Périgord, Bishop of Autun."

On the 22nd of March, the day after her death, Talleyrand wrote to M. de Jaucourt:

"Tell Madame de Vaudemont, or get some one to tell her, that Madame de Brionne died yesterday. Her sufferings were terrible during the last days. I regret her deeply. She was one of the supports of my youth; during more than fifteen years she tended me as if I had been her own child. I took the Duke of Wellington to see her; she made herself delightful to him. Good-bye. At our age sorrow and anxiety try us much."

LVIII.

NOTE SUBJOINED TO LETTER LVII. (NO. 30).

The undersigned, Minister of State and for Foreign Affairs of his Imperial and Royal Apostolic Majesty, is commanded to address the following official communication to his Highness Prince Talleyrand.

During the course of the negotiations at Vienna between the plenipotentiaries of the Powers who signed the Treaty of Paris, the undersigned has never ceased affording, in the name of his august master, the Emperor, proofs of his Imperial Majesty's desire to obtain for Italy a condition of peace and security which is directly bound up with that of Europe and his Empire.

The tension still subsisting between the Courts of France and Naples has all the more attracted the Emperor's attention, as, at the present moment, large bodies of troops are occupying the frontiers of the kingdom of Naples, and equal numbers are concentrated in the south of France.

Although far from attributing hostile intentions that might compromise the peace of Italy, and consequently that of an important portion of the Austrian monarchy, to either of these Powers, the Emperor-King has thought it well to renew the declaration that the undersigned found it necessary to make in one of the first conferences, of his Majesty's firm determination never to permit the peace of his provinces, or of those governed by princes of his house, to be troubled by the entrance of foreign troops into Italy; the Emperor being obliged to consider all views or measures contrary to this determination as directed against his interests, and consequently against himself.

The undersigned, while informing Prince Talleyrand that he is addressing a similar Declaration with the same objects to the Court of Naples, entreats his Highness to accept the assurance of his deep respect.

(Signed)   Prince Metternich

Vienna, 25th February, 1815.

LIX.

NOTE 2 ENCLOSED IN NO. 30.

The undersigned, Ambassador of his Majesty the King of France and Navarre to the Congress, and Minister and Secretary of State in the Department of Foreign Affairs, has received the declaration which his Highness Prince Metternich has done him the honor of addressing to him, dated to-day.

If circumstances should exact that, in defence of the principles constantly professed at the Congress of Vienna by the ambassador of his Most Christian Majesty relating to Naples, French troops should be obliged to advance, those troops would not march through the Austrian provinces in Italy, nor through those which are governed by the princes of the House of Austria. It has never entered into the mind of his Most Christian Majesty to undertake anything which could disturb or compromise the peace of those provinces, a peace in the maintenance and consolidation of which he takes, on the contrary, the most lively interest.

The undersigned hastens to transmit this assurance to his Highness Prince Metternich, and at the same time renews the assurance of his deep respect.

(Signed)   Prince Benevento.

Vienna, 25th February, 1815.

LETTER LX.

THE KING TO PRINCE TALLEYRAND.

No. 24.

Paris, 3rd March, 1815.

My Cousin,

I have received your Nos. 27 and 28. I did not write to you last week, first, because I was expecting Lord Castlereagh every minute, and also because I had (as is usual with me in the beginning of a fit of the gout) a good deal of fever, which is not very favorable to dictation. Lord Castlereagh arrived on Sunday evening. I saw him on Monday and Tuesday. I found him very sound in principle on the Naples question, but rather overscrupulous in his official capacity, and always very partial to the Cabinet of Vienna. After repeating to me all that, as you told me, he said to Prince Metternich, he came to certain proposals on which he was at one mind with Prince Metternich. Their substance is that the Court of Vienna asks for nothing better than to co-operate in the expulsion of Murat; "but," he said, "while yielding in the south of Italy, she expects the same compliance from us with regard to the north, and she wishes Parma, Piacenza, and Guastalla to belong to the Archduchess Marie Louise, and that the three Courts of the House of Bourbon should undertake to indemnify the Queen of Etruria."[1] I replied that the State of Parma was an hereditary succession brought into my family by the Queen Elizabeth Farnese,[2] and had nothing in common with France, Spain, and the kingdom of Naples, and that, setting aside family interests, justice alone forbade me to allow a branch of my family to be dispossessed; that, nevertheless, if Austria insisted upon the execution of the convention of the 11th of April, with regard to the Archduchess Marie Louise, I would consent to the Queen of Etruria, or rather her son, receiving Lucca and the State of Presidi in exchange, provided that the sovereignty of Parma was recognized as her property, to revert to her on the death of the Archduchess, at which time Lucca and the State of Presidi should be reunited to Tuscany. He did not seem at all averse to this arrangement, which, however, concerns Austria more than England.

I saw yesterday Baron de Vincent, who had a direct and secret mission to me. He gave me a confidential Note, of which the principal article, with regard to which, he said, his instructions were very precise and very inflexible, was the one relating to Parma that I have just mentioned to you. I answered by a counter-proposal to the same effect as my reply to Lord Castlereagh. We separated, each holding our ground, but I think it will not be difficult to arrange the affair. He said that after this first overture addressed personally to me, Prince Metternich wished the negotiations to be carried on at Vienna, but directly between you and him, without admitting any other member of the diplomatic body. As I saw no objection I promised that it should be so managed.

I will send you a copy of the documents I have mentioned, with a few notes of instructions, by the next courier.

I add a line to say that your conversation with the Emperor of Russia interested me very much, although I thought that on his side it was very vague and shallow. I am perfectly satisfied with the manner in which you answered him.

What I must not forget to tell you is that Lord Castlereagh—who pressed me very closely, 1. on the article in the treaty securing the payment of the British claims; 2. on the execution of the conventions of the 11th of April, relating to the Bonaparte family (a subject to which I shall recur in my next letters)—did not say one word about the slave-trade.

My gout is going on well, and I have reason to think this attack will not be as long as usual.

On which, etc.

P.S. I have this instant received your No. 29. I agree with you in thinking the incident of Murat's undelivered Note very favorable to us. You will find in this letter (and you will have further details in the next) the key to Prince Metternich's mysterious request.

NOTES TO LETTER LX.

1. The Queen of Etruria had an agent at Vienna, M. Goupil.
2. Parma was given by the Treaty of Aix-la-Chapelle (1748) to Don Philip, second son of Philip V. and Elizabeth Farnese, and ancestor of the Bourbons of Parma.

LETTER LXI.

No. 31.

Vienna, 3rd March, 1815.

SIRE,

The Duke of Saxe-Tetschen, who went to meet the King of Saxony at Brünn, came back here this morning. The King will stop to-day at two stages from Vienna, and will go to await at Presburg the departure of the two northern sovereigns, who would certainly be much embarrassed by his presence here, and whom he probably does not care to meet. It was thought that he would be too far off at Brünn, and there was no suitable residence to offer him between Brünn and Vienna; for which reasons Presburg was chosen, in spite of the objections I had the honor of mentioning to your Majesty in one of my preceding letters.

The Emperor of Russia talks of his departure; preparations are even being made for it. At first it was said to be fixed for the 14th of this month, then for the 17th; and now they speak of the 20th. The Emperor has promised to be at home for the Russian Easter,[1] and I think this is the only one out of his many promises that he will keep, because it would be personally inconvenient to him to break it. When he is gone the other sovereigns will not stay. The Emperor of Austria, on his side, has long meditated a visit to his Italian provinces, and he would not like to put it off later than the month of April. This desire on the part of every one to go away will expedite the conclusion of affairs.

In accordance with my promise to Prince Metternich, I allow the Italian question to sleep, until I have news of Lord Castlereagh's visit to Paris and arrival in London.

Austria and Bavaria are agreed, with one exception, that of Salzburg, of which Austria wants to have the whole, and Bavaria to keep a portion. I exhorted the two negotiators severally to try to come to an understanding, in order to give Russia and Prussia no loophole for intervention, which would be inevitable if they could not come to an agreement. I think my advice will not be without effect, and I gave it to escape the necessity of pronouncing in favor of either, which could not possibly have been done without offending the other, while it is almost equally essential for us to keep well with both.

The affairs of Switzerland are, or will soon be, ready to be carried from the Commission which has been preparing them, to the conference in which they will be settled. There is no longer any question of keeping Porentruy in reserve. It will be ceded, as we wished, with the rest of the bishopric of Basle, to the canton of Berne. The fate of the Valtelline alone will remain in suspense until the affairs of Italy are settled; even the Russians agree to this.

The philosopher La Harpe, who thinks he can never do enough harm to the Bernese, took it into his head to prevent Berne² from becoming one of the sovereign cantons, and he inspired his illustrious pupil with this mad idea. Consequently, a Russian minister went to one of the ministers of Ferdinand IV., whom he did not know, and said to him, "Try to obtain the consent of France to the exclusion of Berne from the number of sovereign cantons, and the Emperor Alexander, who is exceedingly anxious for the concession of this point, will be very favorable to you." The same minister went on the same day to Prince Metternich, to whom he said, "The Emperor Alexander has not yet made up his mind respecting Murat; he will help you to support him according your wishes, if you will contribute to excluding Berne from the number of governing cantons." Prince Metternich replied that what he asked was not feasible; I had, on my side, rejected the proposal at the very first word. The Russians have in consequence relinquished their scheme, and derived from their attempt only the shame belonging to such gross duplicity, which they probably think an instance of the most delicate and admirable diplomacy.

At the outset, when the Emperor Alexander asked for the greater part of the duchy of Warsaw,³ it was, he said, to form into a kingdom with which to console the Poles by this shadow of their old political existence, and to diminish, as much as possible, the outrage to morality caused by the partition.⁴ He afterwards abandoned this idea, but he announced that he would give a special constitution to that part of the duchy which would fall to his share, and now he hesitates even on this point. Prince Adam Czartoryski, whose penetration is far from equalling his honesty, begins to suspect that he was amused by a chimerical hope, and he complains of it. It is probable that the Emperor will escape from his difficulty with the Poles by staying only a very short time at Warsaw, and with Prince Czartoryski by taking leave of him coldly and refusing all explanations with him.

Your Majesty may judge of the regret which the Emperor will

leave behind him here by what has happened during the last few days.

In the perplexity of finding some way of passing the time now that we no longer dance, and to divert the *ennui* which consumes us all, we have recourse to all sorts of games and amusements. One that has become the fashion in several houses is to establish lotteries. Each person belonging to the society brings a prize; in this way every one contributes, and every one wins. On the day before yesterday there was a lottery of this kind at the Princess Marie Esterhazy's; she wished, and her conduct in this respect was severely criticised, to contrive that, by special management, the four chief prizes should fall to the lot of the ladies especially distinguished by the Emperor of Russia and the King of Prussia, who were both present. But this combination was upset by the young Countess Metternich,[5] the minister's daughter, who went to the basket which held the tickets, and took one out of her turn. Her ticket proved to give her the claim to the most magnificent prize, which the Emperor of Russia had himself brought. The Emperor could not conceal his annoyance, and all present were much amused by it. (Your Majesty will remember that the Emperor latterly gave up going to Prince Metternich's balls, and did not speak to him when they met in other places.)

Everything turned out ill for the Emperor that evening. A prize which had been brought by the young Princess of Aversberg, for whom the Emperor seems to have a preference, was gained by an aide-de-camp of the King of Prussia. The Emperor proposed an exchange; the aide-de-camp refused. The Emperor insisted—he even hinted that the prize was intended for him; the aide-de-camp replied that it was too precious then to be parted with. This delighted everybody, so much so that the Emperor begins to think that the parties at Vienna are no longer in such good taste as they were when he first came.

I have just received the roll of the troops which are marching towards Italy. There are one hundred and twenty battalions and eighty-four squadrons, all complete, and forming a hundred and twenty-nine thousand infantry and fifteen thousand cavalry. The generals in command are Bianchi, Radetsky, Frimont, and Jérôme Colloredo. There is besides a reserve of fifty thousand men in Carinthia, Styria, etc.

General Pozzo is expecting a last despatch from the Emperor before he goes. I am, etc.

NOTES TO LETTER LXI.

1. The Russian Easter in 1815 fell on the 30th of April.
2. This Directory, as is well known, was composed of Berne, Zurich, and Lucerne.
3. "We have been told in the most positive manner that Russia abandons none of her pretensions to Poland; she declares that the whole of Warsaw is occupied by two armies, and that she would have to be driven out of it. . . . Prussia has given up to Russia what she calls her rights upon the country, and is seeking for an indemnity in the kingdom of Saxony."—Letter from Talleyrand to Jaucourt, 29th September, 1814.
4. In 1830 Prince Talleyrand wrote from London: "The events which have taken place in Poland remind me of what, when I was still very young, I and all France felt on the occasion of the partition. It is impossible to forget the impression it made in the last century; the political honor of France was tarnished by it, and neither the Duc d'Aiguillon, Minister of Foreign Affairs, nor the Cardinal de Rohan, ambassador at Vienna, ever overcame the shame of having taken no notice of the negotiations which preceded this great act of injustice and spoliation. Later on, a most favorable occasion presented itself for restoring the kingdom of Poland; the Emperor Napoleon might have restored its independence, which was so important to the balance of power in Europe, but he would not. . . .

"In 1814 the chances of war brought us to the point of being unable to think of anything but our own existence, and we were obliged to be silent when the servitude of Poland was consummated."

5. This lady was Metternich's eldest daughter, by his marriage with Marie Eleonore de Kaunitz. Countess Marie Léopoldine was born on the 17th of January, 1797; she married Count Joseph Esterhazy in 1817. On the 2nd of April, 1811, Talleyrand wrote to Metternich: "Be so good as to present my compliments to Madame de Metternich and your divine Marie."

LETTER LXII.

ADDENDUM TO NO. 31.

Instructions addressed by the King to Prince Talleyrand.

Paris, 5th March, 1815.

Prince Talleyrand is to make every effort to hasten the conclusion of a second treaty between France, England, and Austria, in conformity with the principles adopted in the Memorandum No. 1 presented by Lord Castlereagh, and with the propositions contained in the counter-project No. 2.

The points on which it is most necessary for the prince to insist are—

1. The settlement of an early period for executing the plan agreed upon. It seems that on this point there will be no obstacle in the way.

2. The recognition of the hereditary rights of the Infante Charles Louis to the sovereignty of Parma, Piacenza, and Guastalla, while adopting for the Archduchess Marie Louise the temporary arrangements mentioned in the counter-project. It is probable that the cession of the Presidi will be the principal difficulty raised by Austria. In this case Prince Talleyrand must try to obtain for the Infante and his mother, the Queen, an equivalent, in which the possession of Lucca and its territory shall be included, under the condition of its reversion to Tuscany.

None of the other articles of the proposed treaty seem open to discussion. The reunion of the Valtelline to the Milanese was already considered as almost inevitable, and, consequently, all that can be done is to treat it as a very important concession on the part of France. With regard to the Austrian acceptances,[1] Prince Talleyrand is authorized to pledge himself to the extent of twenty millions, the amount defined in the offers which England may make with regard to the same object, and on the advances in kind which may be agreed upon.

Prince Talleyrand will treat directly with Prince Metternich and the Duke of Wellington on all these points, not admitting any member of the French Legation to join in the negotiations, and he will carefully set aside every proposal differing from the bases already established in the project and counter-project, by which bases he is to be guided, as well as by the present instructions.

(Signed)   Louis.

NOTE TO LETTER LXII.

1. "The Austrian funds are falling rapidly. According to the opinion of business men, they cannot fail to go on falling day by day. The last quotation was three hundred. To illustrate the state of the public funds in Austria, a man who in 1811 (when by a royal decree paper suffered a reduction of four-fifths) had fifteen hundred francs, saw them diminished to three hundred; and nowadays those three hundred francs would not be equivalent to a hundred francs. Therefore the public has lost since that period fourteen-fifteenths of its revenue, or 93 to 94 per cent."—La Tour du Pin to the Department, 30th January, 1815.

LETTER LXIII.

THE KING TO PRINCE TALLEYRAND.

No. 25.

7th March, 1815.

My Cousin,

I have received your No. 30. I think that Prince Metternich's declaration, which would not satisfy me under any other circumstances, is explained by what I told you the other day, and by the papers I annex. The instructions show you my wishes so clearly that it would be superfluous to add anything to them here.

I intended to-day to have once more gone over with you the convention of the 11th of April last. Bonaparte saves me the trouble. Before you receive this letter you will no doubt have heard of his audacious enterprise.[1] I took at once the measures which I judged most calculated to make him repent of it, and I am confident of their success.[2] This morning I received the ambassadors,[3] and addressing them altogether, I asked them to tell their Courts that they had found me not in the least uneasy in consequence of the news I had received, and firmly persuaded that the tranquillity of Europe would no more be disturbed by it than I was myself.

My gout has made considerable progress for the better since the other day.

On which, etc.

NOTES TO LETTER LXIII.

1. The *Moniteur* of March 8th announced the landing of Napoleon at St. Juan on March 1st.

2. "I proposed to the King: 1st. To send off a courier as soon as the news arrived; he wished to delay. 2nd. To address a circular to the ambassadors and ministers. I send you a copy; it has been sent with the *Moniteur*. 3rd. I proposed to the King to inform you of his intention to proclaim Bonaparte *out of the pale of the International Code of Europe*, and to instruct you to propose this to the Congress. Yesterday evening he told me of his letter to you of this morning; I took the liberty of asking him if he had spoken of my proposal to you. We were alone, and he said, 'No, but I desire you to mention it to him. The consequence of this measure would be to obtain the consent of those sovereigns who are not at the Congress.

"We gained an immense victory by persuading the King to convoke the Chambers. I believe that even if events should prove favorable to us and against Bonaparte, there might be enormous difficulties in the way of the Government. The proclamation and coronation will cause constitutional monarchy to be adopted into the heart and language of the whole nation. The Chancellor, M. de Blacas (who at first had favored it), and especially the *Marshal*, were against us; we declared that we should consider the public safety endangered without this measure. The King made up his mind to it.

"An address to the King will be proposed to-morrow to the Peers and Chamber of Deputies. The session will open naturally and simply.

"Marshal Soult lost (I think on purpose) twenty-four hours in sending Marshal St. Cyr. The latter left his château in an hour, and two hours after his arrival in Paris was on his way to Lyons. He will find, and this is what Soult wanted, all preparations made, and the generals already stirring at Lyons. I cannot help thinking that the object was to give a personal success to *Monsieur*, and to give it to him with the assistance of a few persons, without any constitutional aid; but our firmness has baffled these petty and very dangerous calculations."—Jaucourt to Talleyrand, 8th March, 1815.

8. The ambassadors and *chargés d'affaires* accredited to the court of Louis XVIII. were:

> Baron Vincent (Austria).
> Mr. Crawford (United States).
> Baron Woltersdorf (Denmark).
> Count Peralada (Spain).
> The Duke of Wellington (England).
> Baron Ompteda (Hanover).
> General de Fagel (Low Countries).
> Marquis Marialva (Portugal).
> Count Goltz (Prussia).
> General Count Pozzo di Borgo (Russia).
> Marquis Alfieri Sostigno (Sardinia).
> M. de Signeul (Sweden).
> Count Zeppelin (Würtemberg).

LETTER LXIV.

No. 32.

Vienna, 7th March, 1815.

SIRE,

I believe that your Majesty must know already, or will have heard before the arrival of this letter, that Bonaparte has left Elba, but in any case I hasten to inform your Majesty. I learned it first from a note of Prince Metternich,[1] to whom I replied that I saw, from the date, that Bonaparte's escape was connected with Murat's asking Austria to permit his troops to pass through her provinces. The Duke of Wellington showed me afterwards a despatch from Lord Burghersh, of which I have the honor of enclosing a translation, as well as of an extract from a letter of the vice-consul of Ancona,[2] also communicated to me by the Duke of Wellington.

It was at nine o'clock in the evening of the 26th that Bonaparte embarked from Porto Ferrajo. He took with him about twelve hundred men, ten pieces of cannon, of which six were field-pieces, some horses, and provisions for five or six days. The English, whose duty it was to watch his movements, were guilty of a negligence which they will find it difficult to excuse.[3] The direction he has taken—that of the north—seems to indicate that he is directing his steps towards Genoa or the south of France. I cannot believe that he would dare to make any attempt upon our southern provinces. He could not venture to do this unless he had confederates there, which we can hardly suppose possible. It is, however, equally necessary to take precautions in that quarter, and to send thither chosen and perfectly safe troops. For the rest, any attempt of his on France would be the act of a brigand, and it is thus that he ought to be treated, and every measure lawful against brigands ought to be employed against him.

It seems to me much more likely that he will choose the north of Italy as his field of operations. The Duke of Wellington tells me that there are at Genoa two thousand English and three thousand Italian troops, who fought in Spain, and who have entered the service of the King of Sardinia. He has no doubt but that these troops, which he says are excellent, will do their duty. The King of Sardinia is at this moment at Genoa, and must have his guards with him. There are also three English frigates in the harbor. If, therefore, Bonaparte made a descent upon Genoa with his twelve hundred men, he would fail. But it is to be feared that he will cross over the mountains towards Parma and Lombardy, and that his presence may be the signal for an insurrection which has been long prepared, to which the bad conduct of Austria and the false policy of her Cabinet have been only too favorable—an insurrection which, if supported by the troops of Murat, with whom Bonaparte is probably in league, will set all Italy in a blaze. Both Prince Schwarzenberg and Prince Metternich have told me that if Bonaparte appeared in the north of Italy, they would be greatly embarrassed, because they are not yet ready for him. Last night express messengers were sent to all the corps intended for Italy, with orders to hurry their departure; but, however much haste they make, they will take a full month to reach their destination, and in a month much may take place. It seems that Prince Schwarzenberg will be ordered to repair himself to Italy.

In any case your Majesty will certainly think it necessary to assemble sufficient forces in the south, to be ready to act according to circumstances.

The consequences of this event cannot yet be foreseen, but they may be fortunate if we know how to turn them to account. I will do all in my power to keep people here from going to sleep, and to induce the Congress to depose Bonaparte from a rank which, by an inconceivable weakness, he has been suffered to preserve, and to render him at length incapable of preparing fresh disasters in Europe.

We have been deliberating on the manner of acquainting the King of Saxony with the cessions which the Powers have decided on his making to Prussia, and for which his consent is necessary. We have determined to extract from the general protocol the articles containing the cessions, and to make them into a private protocol, which, to show greater respect, will be delivered to the King by the Duke of Wellington, Prince Metternich, and myself. We shall all three go to Presburg for this purpose on the day after to-morrow. Any resistance on the part of the King of Saxony would be useless for him and very annoying for every one else, especially at a time when it is imperative to unite all minds and all opinions against the attempts of the man of Elba. We shall do, therefore, all that is requisite for inducing the King of Saxony to submit with a good grace to what this juncture renders necessary.

We have come to an agreement on the affairs of Switzerland. The Russians, forced to give up the idea of excluding Berne from the number of directing cantons, have asked that it may be at any rate advised to modify its constitution by introducing partially the representative principle. All the Powers joined in this demand, which is in harmony with modern ideas, and France was not able to refuse, as the letters of MM. de Watteville and de Mullinen showed that this refusal would entail no serious difficulties on Berne; and the Bernese envoy, M. de Zerleder, is of the same opinion.

I am, etc.

NOTES TO LETTER LXIV.

1. "When the ministers came to me they were still ignorant of the event. Talleyrand entered first. I made him read the despatch I had received from Genoa. He did not change countenance, and we held the following laconic conversation:

"*Talleyrand.* Do you know whither Napoleon is going?

"*I.* The report says nothing.

"*Talleyrand.* He will land somewhere on the coast of Italy, and throw himself into Switzerland.

"*1* He will go straight to Par's."—Memoirs of Metternich, vol. i. p. 206.
2. M. Dumorey.
3. In the sitting of the House of Commons of the 7th of April the English minister said—

"We have been asked why Bonaparte was not watched more closely in the island of Elba.

"The reason was that Bonaparte was not there in the character of a prisoner. That island was assigned to him as a sovereignty." (See Hansard.)

Article 3 of the Treaty of Paris of the 11th of April, 1814, was in these words:
"The island of Elba, adopted by his Majesty Napoleon I. as his place of residence, shall form, during his life, a separate principality, which shall be possessed by him in full sovereignty and property." (See d'Angeberg, p. 148.)

Article 17 of the treaty ran thus:
"The Emperor shall be allowed to take with him and retain as his guard four hundred men, volunteers, as well officers as sub-officers and soldiers."—From the *Annual Register* for 1814.

LETTER LXV.

No. 32 (A).

Vienna, 7th March, 1815.

SIRE,

General Ricard is returning to Paris, in consequence of the orders he has received from the Minister of War, in case his presence here should no longer necessary. His journey hither has not attained the object for which it was undertaken, and this cannot be a subject for any regret; but it has been useful in many other respects. General Ricard has been presented to the sovereigns; he has seen the principal ministers at the Congress; many questions have been asked him, and his answers, and in general his language and his behavior, have given a just and favorable idea of the situation of France, and particularly of the army. I beg your Majesty to express your satisfaction to him on this subject.

I am, etc.

LETTER LXVI.

No. 33.

Vienna, 12th March, 1815.

SIRE,

I have received the letter with which your Majesty has honored me, dated the 3rd of this month. I am waiting for the one which your Majesty is pleased to announce to me, as well as for the instructions relating to the affairs of Parma, to open this matter to Prince Metternich, who has already asked me if I were not yet ready to treat it. The mystery with which he tries to surround it, the overtures which he made, unknown to me, to your Majesty, his wish to settle it with me alone, are in consequence of his being as well aware as any one else of the objections to be made to his scheme. By agreeing to it your Majesty will certainly be making a sacrifice, and one which, in my opinion, may not be without serious consequences. I own, however, that I shall not think it too great if Austria, in return, co-operates loyally with us against Murat, and if Prince Metternich is faithful to his offers and promises.

The Duke of Wellington, Prince Metternich, and I started for Presburg on Wednesday evening, and arrived there at 4 a.m. At noon the King of Saxony received us all three, took the protocol Prince Metternich presented, and handed it without opening it to his Minister, who was present, telling us that he would take cognizance of its contents; and drawing nearer to us, he addressed us in very polite terms, but very coldly. At one o'clock we had the honor of dining with him and the Queen. In the evening he received us each separately—Prince Metternich at four, me at five, and the Duke of Wellington at six. He expressed his gratitude to your Majesty several times over. On the next day we all three had a very long conference with his minister, Count Einsiedel, who does not understand French well, and who speaks it even worse. In this conversation we exhausted all the means which ought to induce the King to make the concessions agreed upon by the Powers in favor of Prussia. The King and his ministers brought forward nothing but objections. They seemed to nourish a hope that the terms which have been agreed upon were still open to negotiation. As this hope was renewed in the Note addressed to us by the King's minister on Saturday, we thought it necessary to destroy it by a positive declaration in the answer we gave him just as we were leaving Presburg. I have the honor of annexing copies of these two documents.[1]

When we delivered our account of our mission at the conference of the five Powers, the Russians demanded that the part of Saxony which has been accorded to them might at once pass from under martial law to ordinary civil rule, and that the other portion might for the present remain under martial law.

9*

This demand, which it would be difficult to refuse, will probably decide[1] the consent of the King of Saxony, who, according to the information which we have obtained, wishes to consent, but at the same time wants to appear in the eyes of his people to have yielded to extreme and invincible necessity.

When we were at Presburg the news reached us that Bonaparte, repulsed by the guns from Antibes, which he had summoned to surrender, had landed in the Bay of St. Juan; these are the last tidings we have received of him. It was supposed that he had no confederates either at Marseilles or Toulon, as he did not present himself there, nor at Antibes, which has repulsed him. These reflections seem reassuring. But the Powers have nevertheless thought it right to set on foot preparations enabling them to offer assistance to your Majesty, if it should be necessary. The English, Prussian, and Austrian troops in the neighborhood of the Rhine have been ordered to concentrate and to hold themselves in readiness. The Emperor of Russia has ordered the Russian troops which had returned to the Vistula, and to draw near to the Elde and the Oder.

So long as no one knew whither Bonaparte was going, or what were his intentions, no declaration against him could be made. We tried to get one adopted as soon as we knew. The draft has been prepared by the French Legation and communicated to the Duke of Wellington and Prince Metternich. It will be read to-morrow in the committee of the eight signatory Powers of the Treaty of Paris, and it will probably undergo some alterations. When it has been adopted, I shall have the honor of transmitting it to your Majesty by a courier, who will leave a copy with the Prefect of Strasbourg, whom I shall ask to have it printed and distributed in his and the neighboring department. I shall do the same with Metz and Châlons. I shall desire M. de Saint-Marsan to take similar means for distributing it in Nice, Savoy, and Dauphiny.

The Emperor of Russia, who, on the whole, has behaved very well at this juncture, is sending off General Pozzo,[3] and will entrust him with a letter for your Majesty, to whom he offers his whole army. It would be sad if France were obliged to accept this offer, which must not be positively refused, but which your Majesty will assuredly not think of accepting except in an extreme case, and one which I hope will not occur.

I have no doubt that your Majesty has ordered troops to be sent to the south. If I ventured to offer an opinion as to the general whom it would be most advisable to set over them, I should mention Marshal Macdonald, as a man of honor, who can be trusted, and who possesses the confidence of the army; and likewise, because, as he signed the treaty of the 11th of April on Bonaparte's side, his example will have all the more weight when he marches against him.

I have seen a list of the generals appointed to command the thirty thousand men whom your Majesty has ordered to be assembled between Lyons and Chambéry. The names of several of them are unknown to me; but there are some among them in whom I can have no confidence, among others General Maurice Matthieu, who, I believe, was the devoted servant of Joseph Bonaparte.

The presence of the latter in the Pays de Vaud cannot fail to be dangerous at the present moment. I shall try to induce Russia, England, and Austria, who have influence over that canton, to ask that he may be sent away.[4]

The Emperor of Russia, to do him justice, has already, without prompting, ordered the new cantons[5] to be written to in the way that we wish. I have mentioned this to M. Auguste de Talleyrand,[6] and advised him to come to an understanding with the Russian *chargé d'affaires*, Baron Krüdener.

This in other respects very disagreeable event of Bonaparte's appearance in France will have at least one advantage, that it will hasten the conclusion of affairs. It has doubled the diligence and the zeal of every one. The committee for drawing up the treaty will set to work actively. The end of our stay here may therefore be several weeks nearer.[7]

I am, etc.

NOTES TO LETTER LXVI.

1. See D'Angeberg, p. 908, 909.

2. The King of Saxony did not give his adhesion to the treaty until the 20th of May, 1815. From the date of the provisional establishment of a Russian administration he refused the subsidy which had previously been assigned to him.

3. "We want General Pozzo. Send him to us; he may be of use to us, and I think that M. Butiakine is very anxious to have him."—Jaucourt to Talleyrand, 8th March, 1815.

4. "I had the honor yesterday of writing to you that I had asked Prince Metternich and Count Nesselrode to take measures for obliging Joseph Bonaparte to leave the Pays de Vaud, and to keep at a distance from the French frontier. They hastened to take these steps, and Austrian and Russian officers have already been sent to Switzerland for this purpose, and have even been de-

sired to take Joseph Bonaparte to Grätz as soon as the canton of Vaud shall have complied with this request."—Talleyrand to the Department, 4th March, 1815.

A letter from Jaucourt to Talleyrand, dated the 18th of October, 1814, says, "M. Dessoles has shown the King a letter from Joseph Bonaparte, who submits, if the order is peremptory, to going away, but only for a time and without selling his property. An answer to this effect was approved by the King and despatched by Dessolles."

5. The new Swiss cantons in 1814 were the Valais, Neufchâtel, and Geneva.

6. M. de Jaucourt writes of him on the 8th of December, 1814: "Old as I am, I still love danger; but I have a sovereign contempt for worry; all fidgety people are intolerable to me. I hope I shall not offend you by saying that Count Auguste de Talleyrand is one."

7. "MY DEAR HENRY,

"Things here are in such a state that I think we shall finish them towards the end of the month, although there are several matters which have not yet been settled. The King of Saxony has not yet accepted the arrangement by which a large portion of his dominions will be given to Russia, but I think that he will accede to it. The subjects under discussion between Austria and Bavaria have not yet been arranged, but we have the materials for settling them, and the end is approaching. The Italian question has not yet been attacked. I do not think, however, that it presents any very great difficulties. I wish you could have been here last night and have seen Labrador conferring with the plenipotentiaries. He is a perfect representative of Spain, and the portrait you drew of him was excellent.

"You must have heard of Bonaparte's escape from Elba and landing in France, near Antibes. We are going to issue here a proclamation, of which I will send you a copy if I can get one before I close my letter. If we find that the King of France is not able to make an end of him alone, we shall set in motion all the armies of Europe. Every one is very zealous and profuse in offers; and I think that even if Bonaparte should succeed in re-establishing himself in France, the forces directed against him, as well as the influence of opinion, would be so considerable that we should certainly succeed in overthrowing him. "I am, dear Henry,

"Yours most affectionately,

"Vienna, 12th March, 1815. "WELLINGTON."

This letter is addressed to the Marquis of Wellesley, British Minister at Madrid. (N.B.—I have not had the opportunity of collating the above with the original English.—TRANSLATOR.)

LETTER LXVII.

No. 34.

Vienna, 14th March, 1815.

SIRE,

I have just left the conference, in which the declaration[1] which I had the honor of mentioning in my letter of yesterday to your Majesty has been signed. It was settled this morning in the conference of the five Powers; we carried it this evening to that of the eight Powers by whom it was adopted. I hasten to forward it to your Majesty; I send copies of it at the same time to the Prefects of Strasburg, Besançon, Lyons, Nancy, Metz, and Châlons-sur-Marne, requesting them to have it printed and distributed in their respective departments and sent to the neighboring Prefects.

I am sure that your Majesty will think it advisable to order its publication in every part of the kingdom. M. de Saint-Marsan, to whom I have given a copy, will send it to Genoa and Nice.

It seems to me that this proclamation leaves nothing to be desired in respect of strength, and I hope that it will in no respect fail in the effect it is intended to produce, in France as well as in the rest of Europe, where it will be circulated in every direction. One of Bonaparte's sisters (Pauline Borghese) has been arrested at Lucca, on her way from Elba to Italy. Jérôme, who was at Trieste, will be conveyed to Grätz, as well as Joseph, as soon as the Pays de Vaud has acceded to the request which I have instructed M. de Talleyrand to address to that canton in conjunction with the ministers of Austria and Russia.

Some Russian and Austrian officers are carrying the demand to the canton of Vaud, and are desired to escort Joseph Bonaparte to Grätz.

Orders have been issued for the occupation of the island of Elba in the name of the Allies.

All therefore is working towards the same object with a concert and unanimity which I think hitherto unexampled among nations.

I have obtained information respecting the generals appointed to command the troops stationed between Chambéry and Lyons. Generals Sémélé and Dijon, and especially General Marchand, were represented to me as worthy of absolute confidence. I have seen no one who knew General Roussel d'Harbel.

I am, etc.

P.S.—I think there ought to be a very clear line to break the declaration from the protocol which follows it, at the end of which all the signatures should be appended as they are in the enclosed copy.

NOTE TO LETTER LXVII.

1. **The declaration of the 13th of March, 1815, issued by the signatory Powers of the Treaty of Paris, assembled at the Congress of Vienna, relating to Napo-**

leon's escape from the island of Elba. It is printed in the *Moniteur Universel* of the 13th of April, 1815 (see D'Angeberg, p. 912).

"I send to the King, my dear friend, the declaration I mentioned to you yesterday. It is very strong; there has never been a document of so much power and importance signed by all the sovereigns of Europe. It must be printed just as I send it, with all the signatures. It had to be cast in the form of an extract from a protocol in order to enable us to sign it. Take care that no change is made in printing it. Put a break between the declaration and the extract from the protocol, to which the signatures are appended. I am sending this document to Nice, to Strasburg, to Besançon, and to Metz, and I ask the Prefects to print and distribute it.

"Adieu. I do not think that we could have done better here."—Talleyrand to Jaucourt, 14th March, 1815.

LETTER LXVIII.

No. 35.

Vienna, 14th March, 1815.

SIRE,

The courier I am sending off to-day carries with him to Switzerland, to M. de Talleyrand, orders to take, in concert with the ministers of Austria and Russia, the steps which I had the honor of mentioning to your Majesty yesterday, for the purpose of removing Joseph Bonaparte from the frontiers of France.

He will be longer on the way than the couriers we send straight to Paris. I should not, however, have liked to despatch him without a letter to your Majesty, although I have no news to communicate, the courier bearing the instructions which your Majesty has done me the honor of announcing in the letter of the 3rd having not yet arrived.

I hope that these instructions will not be, as Prince Metternich flatters himself, such as to postpone the decision as to the fate of Murat to a distant period. We cannot and ought not to believe in Prince Metternich's promises. I had rather a warm discussion with him to-day on the subject. My opinion is that if the Murat question is put off, it will be lost for us, and in that case public opinion, which is now all in our favor, will go against us.

I have procured, and in the next letter which I shall have the honor of writing to your Majesty I will enclose, a paper drawn up by this same Prince Metternich, which will enable your Majesty to understand in what position with respect to the other Powers the French envoys to the Congress found themselves on their arrival at

Vienna, and to see how different is the position which we now occupy.

I annex one of the declarations[1] printed at Vienna and distributed throughout Germany.

I am, etc.

NOTE TO LETTER LXVIII.

1. Here is this furious declaration:

" ADDRESS TO THE NATIONS.

"The object of Bonaparte's reign will in future be the happiness of the Jacobins. He is satisfied with the present limits of France, and wishes to live in peace with the rest of Europe.

"His guarantees for this are—

"1. The grape-shot with which he destroyed the Parisian sections.
"2. His poisoning the hospitals in Egypt.
"3. The assassination of Pichegru.
"4. The murder of the Duc d'Enghien.
"5. His oaths to the French Republic.
"6. His repeated attacks on the sovereigns of Europe.
"7. The pillage of the churches in Russia and Spain.
"8. His escape from the island of Elba.
"9. The organization of three thousand battalions of National Guards in the place of the conscription.
"10. The violation of all the treaties he has signed, including that of Fontainebleau.
"11. The abolition of all duties interfering with the practice of drunkenness.

"He also promises to issue, immediately after the Assemblies of May, if they should be favorable to him, an edict against perjury, drawn up by Regnaud de Saint-Jean d'Angely, and countersigned by Ney."

LETTER LXIX.

No. 36.

Vienna, 14th March, 1815.

SIRE,

My letter No. 35 will not reach your Majesty until after the one I now have the honor of writing, because the courier who has charge of it has gone round by Zurich.

Although Bonaparte has only a handful of men with him, I thought it would be a good thing to deprive him especially of those who, not being French, and finding themselves at a distance from their own country, would have a double reason for devotion to him. I have therefore requested that the Polish troops in his service should be recalled by their Government.[1] My suggestion was received with alacrity. The order for their return was minuted in conjunction with me, and executed on the spot. The courier I send is taking it with him, and I have the honor of enclosing a copy. I beg your Majesty to have the kindness to give the necessary orders for providing these troops with the route they will require for their journey. The Emperor of Russia and Prince Czartoryski have shown much good will in this little affair.[2]

A Prussian courier, who preceded by twelve hours the one sent to me on the 8th, brought news which has been confirmed by all my letters from Paris. This news, which was circulated without delay, excited general rejoicing. Every one praises the wisdom of your Majesty's measures; every one is persuaded that Bonaparte will not be able to escape punishment, and is glad of it.

M. de Jaucourt speaks of the good effect which a declaration on the part of the Congress would produce.[3] He even speaks on behalf of your Majesty, who by this time knows that his wishes have been anticipated. I sent some printed declarations to be distributed on the frontiers of Switzerland by yesterday's courier. I have the honor to-day of sending some copies to your Majesty. The date of Vienna and the official Austrian type seem to me calculated to produce a good effect.

The principles of legitimacy, which had to be drawn from beneath the ruins under which the overthrow of so many ancient and the establishment of so many new dynasties had, as it were, buried them, which were accepted so coldly by some and rejected by others when we first produced them, have at last become appreciated. Your firmness in supporting them has not been without its effect. The whole honor of it belongs to your Majesty, and the unanimity with which the Powers have pronounced against Bonaparte's last attempt is entirely due to it.

I have often had the honor of informing your Majesty that in the beginning the Allies had made every arrangement for making us simply spectators at the Congress; but I thought their agreement to this effect was only verbal, and I had no idea that they had put it in writing. The two protocols[4] which I have the honor of forwarding to your Majesty prove the contrary, and they also show how little resemblance our present position has to that which they intended us to assume. These two protocols are copied from the originals, which I have actually held in my hand. Certainly the distance is enormous between the wishes of the Powers on the 22nd of September and the declaration which they have just made.

I shall have the honor of replying by one of the next couriers respecting the orders which your Majesty has been pleased to give me with regard to the Italian affairs.

I received them only this evening.

I am, etc.

NOTES TO LETTER LXIX.

1. In the official account of Napoleon's return, inserted in the *Moniteur Universel* of the 25th of March. 1815, it is said that the Emperor left Elba with a hundred Polish light horse, etc.

2. "I have received your despatches of the morning of the 14th. Continue to send us information by every possible opportunity. We have no doubt as to the energy or the loyalty of the nation. Set Lafitte at rest. The delay in paying him was occasioned only by the delay in General Pozzo's return. I am sure that, if you were obliged to quit Paris, he would be able to furnish you with the necessary funds out of our balance in his hands.

"Here the strongest possible measures continue to be taken. If France does not make an end of Bonaparte, Europe will bring him to justice. Never has Europe been more unanimous, and all the Powers at the Congress vie with each other in zeal and energy. I advise you to follow the lead of the diplomatic corps, and, as far as possible, to follow the King. Adieu; I wish you courage and resignation."—Nesselrode to M. Butiakine, Vienna, 22d March, 1815.

3. This is what M. de Jaucourt wrote to Prince Talleyrand on the 14th of March:

"Our position grows more and more critical. Monsieur goes off again to-day. He came from Lyons, where Macdonald behaved with noble fidelity but very bad success; he harangued three thousand men who were at Lyons; he collected the officers. The officers, instead of yielding to duty, declared that they had no influence over their troops; they recriminated by talking of the faults committed with regard to the army, the injustice, the humiliation, etc.; they spoke of the men chosen to surround the princes, etc. Macdonald, however, drew them up behind the bridge of La Guillotière; as soon as they caught sight of the first hussars of Bonaparte they overset the Marshal, joined the hussars, and *fraternized*, as they call it. The Marshal escaped, was followed for six leagues, accomplished eleven in three hours, and rejoined Monsieur at Moulins. Monsieur is to set off for Châlons with him; Dupont is on the way, but will arrive late with the rear-guard. The garrisons in the north are sound. There may be, perhaps, some firmness in the troops under Marshal Ney; those of the Duc de Trévise behaved well at La Fère. We make too much of this small success. I do not believe in the steadiness of the Royal Guard, nor in the good will of the National Guard; I believe only in the firmness of the King. The Bonapartists are doing all they can to induce him to leave. This would be taking a step which would suppose the existence of some views, calculations, or at least plans; God has not permitted this miracle as the result of our royal or ministerial councils.

"The tears came to my eyes at the Council yesterday, when I saw the King, his brother, his nephew, and all his ministers deliberate for three hours on the *arrests* to be made. There is to be a battle, *i.e.* an assemblage of troops, at 1 know not what distance from Paris. The Duc de Berry is to join them. The servants at Fontainebleau are preparing the castle for Bonaparte. M. de Blacas said to me, 'This will, you know, give us a great many places to distribute.' I replied, 'You may promise them to a hundred people, you will not be compromised.' I still think that Bonaparte will give the slip to the Duc de Berry and will reach Paris without a battle. He will steal a march and arrive in Paris, unless the presence of the King, as is very probable, embarrasses him. He dares not use violence; he cannot frighten him. If the King decides on remaining, at the risk of being taken to Valençay, Bonaparte will probably considerably tarnish his unheard-of success. I shall not close my letter until I have seen M. de Blacas.

"The courier came from Lyons through Burgundy; at Mâcon he found all the people in a ferment, crying, 'Long live Bonaparte!' and he was obliged to take off his badge to pass. It cost him some buttons stamped with the fleur-de-lys from his coat.

"When I went out I left my vote in writing for M. de Bourrienne, whom it is proposed to make Prefect of Police.

"I proposed, with the consent of the Abbé de Montesquieu, to write thus to Oudinot: 'If the Old Guard swears fidelity, to offer the rank of officers to all the grenadiers, of nobility to all the officers, and to seize the Post horses for transport. If the guard accept they will keep their word; but the choice must be left to them, for no one is really gained over unless his heart is in it.'

"Monsieur will not go away again; he expects wonders from the review he is going to hold to-morrow of the Imperial Guard. . . . It seems to me that the Congress is making up its mind to issue a declaration. The King must be able to say that as long as he is master here foreigners shall not come in, but that if Bonaparte should by any possibility become master, this calamity would be caused by him alone, and the consequences would fall upon his head, etc.

"It seems to me that this would make the King popular, and excite animosity against Bonaparte.

4. A separate protocol of a conference held on the 22d of September, 1814, by the plenipotentiaries of Austria, Great Britain, France, and Russia, on the form and order of the discussion at the Congress at Vienna (see D'Angeberg, p. 245).

The second protocol mentioned by Talleyrand, and which he annexes to his letter, does not appear in any of the collections of the archives of the Congress of Vienna.

LXIX. (A).

COPY OF THE ORDERS GIVEN TO COLONEL JEZAMANOWSKI, OR, IN HIS ABSENCE, TO THE OFFICER IN HIS PLACE.

By virtue of the commands of his Imperial Highness the Grand-Duke Constantine, Commander-in-chief of the Polish troops in the grand-duchy of Warsaw, I transmit to you, sir, the present orders, in receiving which you will be kind enough, without entering into any discussion with any other person, to repair to Warsaw with the Polish troop which you brought from the island of Elba, and to receive on your arrival the further orders of the general of division, Count Vincent Krasinski. You will communicate a copy of this order to the general under whose command you may happen to be, informing him that his Imperial Highness has desired you, on pain of a most serious personal responsibility, to fulfil this order literally and immediately on its reception.

The annexed orders of the French Government authorize you to demand a route of road from the Government of the country nearest to the spot which you now occupy. With regard to the pay of your troop, as well as any arrears that may be due, you will apply in writing to Colonel Jankowski in Paris, transmitting to him at the same time the nominal lists and all the ordinary and necessary proofs for this purpose.

You will also send a report to M. Tolinski, the chief of the staff of his Imperial Highness the Grand-Duke Constantine, to tell him on what day you commence your march, the stages which will have been appointed for you, and the condition of your detachment.

(Signed)   KRUKOWIECKI,
Brigadier-General.

LXX.

APPENDIX TO NO. 36.

Protocol drawn up and signed on the 22nd of September, 1814.

The Ministers of Austria, Russia, England, and Prussia have met together to deliberate on the modes of procedure to be adopted at the Congress of Vienna, in order to bring it to a fortunate and speedy conclusion.

They have taken into consideration the stipulations of the Treaty of Paris relating to the Congress.

These stipulations are contained in—

1. Article 32 of the public treaty in the following words:

"Within a period of two months all the Powers who have been engaged on either side in the present war, shall send plenipotentiaries to Vienna in order to regulate in a general congress the arrangements necessary for completing the disposition of the present treaty."

2. In the first secret article, as follows:

"The arrangements to be made respecting the territories to which his Most Christian Majesty relinquishes his claim by Article 3 of the public treaty, and the deliberations which it is hoped will result in the establishment of a real and durable balance of power in Europe, will be regulated at the Congress on the basis settled by the Allied Powers in council, and in accordance with the general arrangements contained in the following articles," etc.

The above-mentioned Article 32 evidently reserves, to all the Powers named in it, the privilege of watching over their own interests at the Congress.

The first secret article gives to the Allied Powers the initiative in every discussion, inasmuch as they have the right to lay down as a basis the arrangements settled by themselves.

Taking into consideration that it would be impossible for so many Ministers as will be assembled at the Congress to settle the subjects for deliberation, and draw up a scheme of arrangement, the Ministers have agreed in the opinion that the course prescribed on the following points would be the most favorable to the true interests of the intervening Powers, and that it alone would bring the negotiations to a speedy and fortunate conclusion.

1. In this course, the subject for discussion may be divided into two parts:

The former relating to the great European interests comprised in the mutual relations of the Powers, the territorial divisions, the demarcation of boundaries, and the disposal of the countries occupied and administered provisionally by the Allied Powers.

The latter relating to the formation of the federative league of the German States.

2. That the preliminary work in both cases shall be confided to two commissions, composed in the following manner:

Austria, Russia, England, Prussia, France, and Spain, charged with the preliminaries relating to the European question.

The Commissioners of Austria, Prussia, Bavaria, Hanover, and Würtemberg to be charged with those relating to the organization of Germany.

3. In accordance with the separate and secret Article 1 of the Treaty of Paris, the four Cabinets are to draw up a plan fixing the

territorial arrangements consequent on the principles announced in the Treaty of Paris and recognized by France. This plan to be communicated to France and Spain.

4. The six Powers will then communicate with the other Powers and ask them to make known their opinions and wishes.

5. As soon as the French plenipotentiary arrives, the present plan shall be communicated to France and to Spain, and not until that time shall the method and the steps requisite for executing the arrangements indicated in the present protocol be definitively settled, in conjunction with their plenipotentiaries.

6. As soon as the bases of the Germanic federation are settled, the internal details of the federal compact of Germany shall be referred to a session of the German Diet.

Approved by Metternich, Nesselrode, Castlereagh, Hardenberg, Humboldt.[1]

NOTE.

1. This is the protocol which does not appear in the catalogue, although it is a very complete one, of Télot, nor is it reproduced in Count d'Angeberg's work on the Congress of Vienna.

LXXI.

APPENDIX TO NO. 36.

Separate Protocol of the Conference of the 22nd of September, 1814.[1]

A discussion arose on the Memorandum to be sent to the plenipotentiaries of France and Spain as to the forms to be observed at the Congress. The ministers present at the conference adopted it, after making a few changes.

At the same time they observed, on reading this instrument, that it was entirely for the sake of not annoying or giving umbrage to the French Court that they had abstained from fully developing the third article, which speaks of the initiative to be taken by the four Cabinets. For this reason, and with this object in view, it seemed to them to be doubly necessary to settle between themselves, and very accurately, the difference between the deliberations of the four and of the six Powers, and they have decided as follows:

1. That the four Powers only should decide on the distribution of the *provinces*[2] which the late war and the Peace of Paris have placed at their disposal, but that the other two Powers should be admitted afterwards to give their opinions, and make, if they please, objections which shall be afterwards discussed with them.

2. That, in order not to swerve from this rule, the plenipotentiaries of the four Powers shall not confer with the two others on this subject, until they have *entirely terminated, and are perfectly agreed on*, each of the three points relating to the territorial distribution of the duchy of Warsaw, of Germany, and of Italy.

3. That, in order to give themselves ample time for these preliminary discussions, these four plenipotentiaries shall meanwhile, and from the opening of the Congress, try to occupy themselves and the other two plenipotentiaries with other questions, in which the whole six Powers are fully entitled to take leading parts during the discussions.

These three principles have been defined during the conference as follows:

The disposal of the conquered provinces belongs naturally to the Powers to whose efforts their conquest was due. This principle was fixed by the Treaty of Paris itself, and the French Court already consented to it from the first, for the secret article of the Treaty of Paris asserts in the most precise terms:

"That the distribution of the territories shall be settled at the Congress in accordance with the principles laid down by the Allied Powers themselves."

The words *settled* and *laid down by themselves* clearly express that there is no suggestion here of simple proposals, or of discussions in which France would take part. It is not stated either where or how these principles are to be settled, and it would be an entirely unjust and arbitrary interpretation if it were contended that the clause meant only the contents of *treaties already existing*[3] between the Allies.

But as France has adopted a legitimate Government, the four Allied Powers do not wish to banish either her or Spain from any discussion on the distribution of territories in which these two Powers may have a particular interest, or even which may concern the general interests of Europe, as they would have done had the peace been concluded with Napoleon.

Therefore of the three courses open to them on this question—[4]

1. To be admitted from the first with perfectly equal influence in the deliberation;
2. To be admitted only when the other parties are already of one mind;
3. To agree beforehand to all that the others decide;

The second is evidently the one which France has a right to claim, but with which she ought to be satisfied.

Any other course would be fraught with extreme inconvenience. If France be not admitted until the other four Powers are already agreed among themselves, she will still make all the objections which she thinks advisable for her own safety, and for promoting the general interests of Europe, but she will not make any other objections. If she be present at the first discussion, she will take sides for and against every question, whether her interests be involved in it or not; she will favor or oppose this or that prince, according to her particular views, and the petty German princes will be encouraged by this to begin again all the manœuvres, intrigues, and plots which had so great a share in causing the misfortunes of late years. This is why it is of the greatest importance not to admit the French plenipotentiaries to take part in any discussion until the *subject in question* has been entirely settled.[5]

Approved by Metternich, Hardenberg, Humboldt, Nesselrode.

NOTES TO ABOVE PROTOCOL.

1. See D'Angeberg, p. 249.
2. Martens writes "Powers," which is unintelligible.
3. Martens gives here an erroneous text "of the already existing treaty."
4. Martens, and afterwards D'Angeberg, gives here another text:

"*a*. Not to be admitted at all;
"*b*. Not to be admitted until all the other Powers are agreed;
"*c*. To assent beforehand to all that the others may conclude;
"The second is evidently the alternative which France has a right to claim, but with which she ought to be satisfied."

Talleyrand's text is evidently preferable.

5. It is impossible to explain how it is that this instrument is found in Martens, and that the preceding one, *drawn up to be seen by France*, is not there.

At the head of this instrument Martens writes:

"France with the limits which were assigned to her," by M. Kératry, 2nd edit. 1824, Paris, p. 184–187. Perhaps Kératry was acquainted only with this second instrument, and Martens took it for his book.

LETTER LXXII.

No. 37.

Vienna, 16th March, 1815.

Sire,

Finding myself obliged to send again to-day a courier to Paris with the order recalling the Poles who are with Bonaparte, which was omitted by mistake in last night's packet, I take advantage of this opportunity to have the honor of telling your Majesty how much I wish to be kept as fully and accurately informed as possible of all that is going on in France, and how necessary it is that I should be so.[1]

However well disposed the sovereigns, and even the people, may be at Vienna, it would be a miracle if there were not here evil-minded men ready to spread alarming intelligence, and a great many credulous people ready to receive and promulgate it. Therefore it is very important that your Majesty's Legation may be always in a position to correct it.

The news of Bonaparte's arrival in France made the funds fall here. The declaration of the Congress has made them rise again. I hope that it will produce a similar effect in France. This morning's news will perhaps make them fall again.

The Genevese Government has written to the Federal Government at Zurich that they heard this morning that a regiment sent to oppose Bonaparte had joined his standard; that he entered Grenoble at eight o'clock on the evening of the 7th, and that the town was illuminated. The Government therefore asked for aid, in case Geneva should be threatened by any attempt of Bonaparte.

The King of Würtemberg has sent this news by express to the Emperor Alexander; all his people were repeating it this morning. I give what are at any rate probable excuses for denying it; but they are not enough to destroy an impression which is produced, I think, by the apprehensions of the Genevese.

I am, etc.

NOTE TO LETTER LXXII.

1. On the same day Talleyrand wrote to Jaucourt: "I send you a courier again to-day, my dear Jaucourt, to set you a good example; and I must tell you that it is of the greatest importance that I should be informed of the smallest details relating to Bonaparte. Bad news is flying abroad; it ought to be contradicted, and that I cannot do unless I have direct information. So do not

lose a minute in sending me all the news you hear. Remember this: that the very Europe which has been brought to making the declaration I sent you, is intensely jealous of France, of the King, of the House of Bourbon. These sentiments show themselves whenever the news is unfavorable. This morning three expresses from Geneva came to the Emperor of Russia and to Austria, to announce that Bonaparte was at Grenoble, and that a regiment had deserted our colors to join his. I saw one of these letters addressed to the Emperor of Russia. For Heaven's sake, send me some news. We have no reason to fear; our cause is safe; but news must be met by news. When the foreign couriers leave Paris for this place, give them a line for me; I cannot be too well informed. I am writing to M. Buisson to make him responsible. As the Chambers are to meet, all must be set in order, and I must do at once what I intended to do only on my return. I beg of you to see to this. If you act with the Constitution and with the Constitution alone, you are strong. I am sorry not to be with you, but I must finish my work here."

On the same day he wrote to the Duchess of Courland:

"I am setting a good example in the matter of couriers, for I am sending another off to-day. Try to persuade Jaucourt to send me one every day. It is too trying to be in a large town abounding in false news and to have nothing direct or trustworthy to tell people.

"If not every day, at least they might write to me whenever anything happens. Everything is of importance; I would rather be written to every day. Adieu, dear friend."

On the same day, 16th March, he wrote to M. de Laval:

"Yesterday, the 15th, I had at last a courier. Of all the ministers at Vienna I was the last to receive letters. This caused me two very disagreeable days. The news is good, so I console myself. I think that this last dreadful attempt of Bonaparte's will not last long."

LETTER LXXIII.

No. 38.

Vienna, 17th March, 1815.

Sire,

I have the honor of sending to your Majesty a letter which I received this morning from Murat's minister here; I send it in the original, in order to avoid delay, and also because I do not want it here.

The Duke of Campo-Chiaro made a similar communication to the Duke of Wellington, and afterwards to the Court of Vienna, it having been already communicated to the Austrian minister at Naples. This proceeding, in addition to the news received here to-day, and the language held by the plenipotentiaries of the Great Powers, makes me foresee that if Bonaparte should advance on Paris, and if the Powers assemble their forces on our frontiers, it

10

will be almost impossible, not only to obtain a declaration from the Congress against Murat and in favor of Ferdinand IV., but even to persuade Austria, and perhaps England, to enter into any actual and substantial engagement against him. I must therefore ask your Majesty to be kind enough to give me precise orders on this subject. We must think of ourselves before thinking of others.

The news received to-day came to Prince Metternich and by way of Milan. It announces the defection of two regiments, the entry of Bonaparte into Grenoble, and his departure from Grenoble for Lyons on the evening of the 8th; and it adds that the disposition of the provinces he has passed through is very unfavorable to us.

This news seemed of sufficient importance to warrant a conference between the Legations of Austria, Russia, England, Prussia, and France, at which the following questions were proposed and discussed:

1. What shall be the policy of the Allied Powers in case Bonaparte should succeed in re-establishing himself in Paris?
2. What are the military resources actually at their disposal?
3. What measures shall be proposed?

The declaration issued by the Congress has already proclaimed their policy. They will adhere to that.

A military committee has been appointed to deliberate on the other two questions. It is composed of Schwarzenberg, Wellington, Wolkonski (Russian), Knesebeck (Prussian). The committee will meet to-night. The Emperor of Russia wishes to be present. If I learn to-night the result of their deliberations, I shall not wait till to-morrow to send another courier to your Majesty.

M. Anatole de Montesquieu's[1] visit here, ostensibly in order to see his mother, having been suspected by the Austrians to have a totally different object, and not to have been without some political motive, I have advised him to return immediately to France.

I am inclined to think that in a few days the Emperor of Austria will take under his care and lodge in his palace Bonaparte's son, lest the boy should be carried away; it has even been suspected that this was the object of M. Anatole's visit. The language held by his mother, which was reported by the Austrian police charged with watching her, afforded some grounds for this belief.

.I am, etc.

NOTE TO LETTER LXXIII.

1. M. de Montesquieu-Fezenzac was detained at Vienna, and on the 5th of June his mother was still asking for a passport for her son, and entreated M. de Talleyrand to obtain for him, before his departure, the passport for which he had been wishing and waiting so long, together with all the necessary safeguards for enabling him to reach the French frontier.

LETTER LXXIV.

No. 39.

Vienna, 19th March, 1815.

SIRE,

The Duke of Wellington despatches a courier to-day to London, who, if possible, will pass through Paris. I take this opportunity of informing your Majesty that in the military conference held on the day before yesterday, at which the Emperor of Russia was present, it was decreed that Bonaparte, with whom the Allied Powers will never treat, must be stopped by prompt and enormous efforts. They have therefore decided on renewing the Treaty of Chaumont, of which I have had the honor of sending a copy to your Majesty. But it is to be directed only against Bonaparte, and not against France, who, on the contrary, will be one of the consenting parties. Sardinia, Bavaria, Würtemberg, and Baden will likewise accede to it, as well as Holland and Hanover.

The Sublime Porte will be invited, not to take part in the war, but to refuse admittance to French rebels, as well as to their ships.

Proposals are also to be made to Switzerland. The actual state of affairs allows of no neutrality, the man who is forcing all Europe to arm being no better than a brigand.[1]

I have received from Austria a Declaration[2] relating to the Valtelline, to Bormio, and to Chiavenna. This Declaration states that those places must be included in the arrangements to be made respecting Italy, and used for purposes of compensation.

I am, etc.

P.S.—The courier who left Paris on the 11th has arrived without any obstacle.

NOTES TO LETTER LXXIV.

1. "These arrangements will, therefore, set all Europe at war, no longer with France, but, on the contrary, to save France from Bonaparte and his

adherents. Therefore, when the object for which this war has been set on foot has been attained, there will be no treaty required, because the French nation is at peace with every other. The treaty of the 30th of May is still valid, and will continue to regulate our relations with foreign Powers."— Talleyrand to Jaucourt, 19th March, 1815.

M. Henri Martin (vol. iv. p. 150) says that "Bonaparte sent a message to Murat, desiring him to inform Austria that he would soon be in Paris, and that he accepted the treaty of 1814." M. Martin adds, "If he was sincere, his return had not even the excuse of an attempt to restore to France the frontiers of which his conduct had deprived her."

2. See D'Angeberg, p. 1933.

LETTER LXXV.

No. 40.

Vienna, 19th March, 1815.

SIRE,

No news has reached us to-day. I have the honor of writing to your Majesty at 6 p.m.

The affairs of Switzerland were finished this morning. The deputation which was at Vienna is to carry the Declaration[1] agreed upon by the Allied Powers and signed by them. I am sending a copy to M. Auguste de Talleyrand. The Swiss plenipotentiaries think that it will satisfy no party completely, but that it will not much offend any one. It is generally believed, therefore, that the stipulations it contains will be adopted.

The next news that we receive here will probably decide Wellington's departure. His courier ought properly to arrive on the 21st; he will make up his mind on the 22nd.

An excellent spirit reigns here. We think of nothing but Bonaparte. All the acts of the Congress will be directed against him.[2]

I am, etc.

NOTES TO LETTER LXXV.

1. Declaration of the Powers assembled at Vienna on the subject of Switzerland. Annex No. 11 of the act of the Congress of Vienna. (See D'Angeberg, p. 934; Thiers, " History of the Consulate and the Empire," vol. xviii. p. 604.)

2. " You are doubtless already aware that Bonaparte has appointed M. de Caulaincourt Minister for Foreign Affairs; he has also nominated Carnot Minister of the Interior. The appointment of M. de Caulaincourt will, I think, necessitate on your part some steps which of course you have already considered. As for me, I am good for nothing; do not give me any mission—I will not have any. All that will have to be done outside of the Congress, if indeed the Congress lives, will be a certain amount of intrigue, and already there are signs of

emigration which are odious to me. You have round you men who are a hundred times more capable than I am.

"Durand has made me such noble frank proposals that, if I mentioned no one else, I should feel obliged to speak of him. Reinhardt is at Brussels; he will retire to his country house between Bonn and Cologne. He has, in accordance with my wish, carried off the seals of the ministry, as well as some important documents; he will send them by a safe opportunity. He writes to me in the bitterness of his heart, 'My family is safe, and I did not see Bonaparte enter Paris. This must be enough for me.'

"He believes that Bonaparte will leave the nation to the National Guard, even if they should come to blows; and march with his soldiers (who in reality are his only nation) to the banks of the Rhine, where, thanks to the dilatoriness of the Congress, he may find some adherents, as well as in Belgium. I myself thought that he would like to be attacked in order to unite all parties in a common hatred against the foreigner; but perhaps it is true that the reannexation of Belgium and of the frontier of the Rhine are objects of almost equal interest to the nation; and a success, if the rapidity of his advance should give him one, will have a prodigious effect.

"The precautions taken in the country are an evidence of uneasiness. No newspapers; they are all stopped. Passports are not given or *visé* without extreme difficulties. Trade is beginning to complain. Do you not think that M. Zeppelin will stay at Paris? I have written as strongly as I could to tell them to send you at least a duplicate of the whole correspondence. It is important that you should know all that is going on in the diplomatic corps. I have given passports to them all; but I have some idea that M. de Zeppelin and M. de Waltersdorf will remain, perhaps even M. de Fagel, the latter to watch: the pretence of waiting for orders would be already a concession. You will, however, have means for obtaining information. At this juncture we shall derive great advantage from the spirit which dictated the appointments of our ambassadors. I think that the Prince de Laval, who had asked for his passport, will stay at his post, or even would return to it. He will be more in the way of corresponding with you than many others as long as Italy remains quiet. They will have, of course, the sense to think of their five or six thousand exiles, whom they must not throw into the arms of Bonaparte, but who are very much embittered.

"We are expecting the Duke of Wellington. Nothing less than his presence can assure the English, who are all moving away.

"The great Biacas has drawn out his travelling equipage; he has not achieved wonders, he has made only a great middle-class fortune. Louis leaves all his, amounting to thirty-five millions; it is distressing, for this would have been enough to advance upon the Rhine. The *bonhomme* has already taxed cotton and increased the severity of the custom-house: people will kiss the tyrant's hand and pay.

"Adieu. My misgivings were not premature when I sent you my sad conjectures; well I am not any happier.

"The King's philosophy points to Hartwell, and the activity of the princes just suffices to make them listen to every suggestion and follow their own inclinations blindly. Perhaps you will write the epitaph of this madman; this will be a fine thing, but then France will be ruined.

"D'André is at Brussels, where he is playing his own little game with Fouché.

"Good-bye. I hope you will be able to keep enough to be only poor. The position is honorable, but I am not fond of poverty. Bresson has thought of the sum which is not included in the budget, and is no doubt awaiting your orders; it is reduced to eighty thousand francs. I dare say that he will be able to keep the disposal of it. As for me, dear friend, I have fifty thousand francs, and yet not a sou, if, as is reported, the hero of Elba seizes the property of the Provisional Government and banishes its members."—Jaucourt to Talleyrand, Ostend, 27th March, 1815.

LETTER LXXVI.

No. 41.

Vienna, 19th March, p.m., 1815.

Sire,

I have the honor of forwarding to your Majesty a letter which I have just received from the Russian minister. It seems to leave nothing to be desired on the subject it relates to. The sentiments it expresses are excellent, and in accordance with the language the Emperor holds at present. He has throughout shown the very best spirit.

It is proposed to have two armies in the field and two in reserve.

The line of operations of the one will extend from the sea to the Main; it will be composed of English, Dutch, and Hanoverians, with the North German contingents and Prussians. All to be under the command of the Duke of Wellington.

The second will have its line of operations between the Main and the Mediterranean, and will be commanded by Prince Schwarzenberg. This army will consist of Austrians, Piedmontese, Swiss, and South German contingents.

The commander-in-chief for the Italian army has not yet been named.

Of the two armies in reserve, the one will be called the Army in reserve of the North, and commanded by Marshal Blücher.

The other, commanded by General Barclay de Tolly, will be the Army in reserve of the South.[1]

All this is only what is proposed, but it seems to suit Austria and England. We shall shortly have some definite information as to the strength of each of these armies.

I am, etc.

NOTE TO LETTER LXXVI.

1. A letter from Vienna inserted in the *Moniteur* of the 21st of April, 1815, said, "Lord Wellington will operate in the Low Countries, Field-Marshal Blücher between the Rhine and the Moselle, and Field-Marshal Schwarzenberg on the frontiers of Switzerland."

LETTER LXXVII.

No. 42.

Vienna, 20th March, 1815.

SIRE,

The Emperor Francis has just ordered Madame de Montesquieu to deliver up to him the boy who is under her care. Her language at the present juncture has been so opposed to the decisions taken by Austria and the other Powers, that the Emperor would not any longer allow his grandchild to remain with her. She will to-morrow receive orders to return to France. The boy will be established at Vienna, in the palace. It will be impossible, therefore, to carry him away. Several circumstances induced the belief that this would have been attempted.[1]

I am, etc.

NOTE TO LETTER LXXVII.

1. The day when Talleyrand wrote this letter about the King of Rome was the one chosen by Napoleon for his entry into Paris, as being his son's birthday.

LETTER LXXVIII.

No. 43.

Vienna, 23rd March, 1815.

SIRE,

The Duc de Rohan-Montbazon arrived on the night before last and brought me your Majesty's letters. All the measures had been already taken when he arrived, and he found the declaration of the 13th of this month posted up in the Rhenish provinces. By this time it must be circulated all over France. I hope that its effect may be to deprive traitors of confidence and to give courage to the loyal.

The forces which Austria, Russia, England, Prussia, Bavaria, Holland, Germany, and Sardinia will bring into the field, will form, including the garrisons, a total of more than seven hundred thousand men, ready to act whenever they are required. The Prussians have already eighty thousand men on the Rhine; the English, Dutch, and Hanoverians, an equal number. Two hundred and fifty thousand Russians will arrive there at the end of April, with five hundred and ninety pieces of ordnance. I think that, instead of three, there will be four armies in the field, one of which will be under the command of Marshal Blücher.

The Allied Powers themselves earnestly wish that it may not be necessary to employ any portion of these forces, and that France may be able to do without their help. But a request from your Majesty will bring them at once into the field. The newspapers we have received to-day from Paris, and which reach to the 14th inclusive,[1] give me hopes that your Majesty will not be obliged to leave Paris.[2] If the contrary should be the case, what appears to us here as most desirable would be that your Majesty should retire, if it were absolutely necessary, to some strong place in the north,[3] on the fidelity of which you could perfectly rely; that the two Chambers and the portion of the army which remains faithful, and to which some of the National Guard might be added, should follow your Majesty thither. The most important of all things to avoid is to allow your Majesty to appear isolated, which might have the effect of dividing your Majesty's cause from that of the nation, whereas they are in reality one and the same.[4]

The Duke of Wellington wishes he were already in Belgium at the head of the troops he is to command, so as to be ready whatever may happen, and this makes him very anxious to despatch the affairs which have still to be terminated.

Some objections have been started here to the departure of Madame de Montesquieu, and to-day there was a talk of sending her to Linz.

Your Majesty will no doubt be sorry to hear that Madame de Brionne died yesterday. She was eighty-one years of age.

I am, etc.

NOTES TO LETTER LXXVIII.

1. "The newspapers, my dear Jaucourt, give a good impression—I am speaking of those of the 12th, 13th, and 14th, which are full of the regimental addresses; and I advise you to arrange with the Foreign Ministers to send off, one or other of you, every day, a courier to Vienna."—Talleyrand to Jaucourt, 23rd March, 1815.

2. "To confess the truth, the King's part would have been a splendid one if he had remained in Paris. The King announced this resolution at first; he changed his mind twice. It is a great pity. I shall never believe that the town of Paris would have allowed him to be murdered by that man. The troops would have fired on us. However, it is all over. It is absolutely necessary to reconstruct a nucleus, to gain over the commander of a fortified post and keep a footing on the sacred soil. For if the King returns in the rear of a foreign army, he will give famous opportunities to all the machinations of the Jacobins

and of Bonaparte, who make common cause at present."—From Ghent, Jaucourt to Talleyrand, 4th April, 1815.

3. "I believe I told you what passed on the day of the King's departure. In the first place, M. de Blacas did not own to it except very ambiguously, begging at the same time that it might be kept secret. I found myself in the King's way as he left his apartment. He whispered to me, 'Tell my ministers that I am going to Lille, and that I wish them to assemble here. Tell the ambassadors that I shall be charmed to see them at Lille, but that they are perfectly free, if they prefer it, to return to their respective Courts.'"—Jaucourt to Talleyrand, 2nd April, 1815.

4. On the 19th of April Talleyrand writes to Jaucourt: "We cannot understand here why so many people have been sent away. It seems to me that it would have been very useful if a nucleus of Frenchmen of all opinions and conditions had surrounded the King. . . .

"Marshal the Duke of Ragusa's wish not to remain inactive is, no doubt, as natural as it is praiseworthy; but, in my opinion, it is not with the aid of foreigners that it becomes him and the other generals who surround the King to give proofs of their devotion.

"The Swiss, although they have long been friendly to France and well affected to our royal family, are, nevertheless, not French. The thing to be desired is that the King should raise an army of Frenchmen, under the orders of his officers, of which the nucleus, it seems to me, might be formed at once, and which, beyond doubt, would be easily recruited, and would become numerous as soon as, by means of the King's armies entering our territory, the country they occupy will be freed from the influence of Bonaparte. The return of the King to his kingdom at the head of a national army would exercise, both in the provinces which are faithful to him, as well as in those which have not yet returned to their allegiance, a very different and more powerful influence than that which he would produce by entering only at the back of foreign armies.

"As for you, Count, it is necessary that you should remain with the King. You must be with him in order to lay before him the correspondences of his ministers at foreign Courts, to transmit his orders and instructions to them, and to give them intelligence. It is very essential that, in circumstances like the present, he should receive frequent information on all that is going on. I beg of you to write to them as often as possible."—Talleyrand to Jaucourt, 10th April, 1815.

LETTER LXXIX.

No. 44.

Vienna, 23rd March, 1815.

SIRE,

This letter will be taken to your Majesty by a Prussian courier who starts to-day.

I have just seen a letter written entirely by the hand of Bonaparte, and addressed to the Archduchess Marie Louise. It is dated the 11th of March from Lyons, and announces that he will reach Paris about the 21st. This letter, which is entrusted to General

Songeon, who betrayed your Majesty, was carried by an officer of the 7th Hussars, called Nyon, to M. de Bubna, who sent it on hither. It is written for two purposes: first, to make his army and his followers believe that he is in relations with Austria; and, secondly, to persuade Austria that he has an immense following in France. To this letter were added a number of proclamations,[1] all horrible. He talks of a former letter which has not arrived.

At Lyons his army was composed of the 14th Hussars, and the 23rd, 24th, 5th, 7th, and 11th of the line. Each of these regiments consists of only one thousand men, and, added to those he had already, bring his army up to from nine to ten thousand men at the utmost. (His date is the 11th.)[2]

It was reported that he was marching towards Charolais, where the feeling in general is said to be unfavorable to us. He was still at Lyons on the 13th.

Here there is complete unanimity. Your Majesty may rely upon this. I will answer for it.

To accelerate matters the Emperor of Russia proposes to draw up the stipulations relating to Poland as a special treaty between Russia, Austria, and Prussia. This was settled at this morning's conference. This private agreement will be inserted in the general treaty.

The sovereign prince of the Low Countries will take the title of King of the Netherlands. It will be announced to-morrow, and acceded to on the same day.

We are now going to tackle the question of Italy, in which we have gained considerable ground against Murat.

I have obtained the recall of Herr von Schraut, the Austrian minister in Switzerland, who has been holding very objectionable language. It seems that his health has a great deal to do with his misdemeanors.

I am sending to France M. de la Tour du Pin, who is, at present, of no use to me here. My object is to place him with Marshal Masséna, to encourage the Marshal to take possession in your Majesty's name of all that Bonaparte has temporarily seized; to let him know that he has no possible cause for fearing the disposition of the Allied Powers, and to offer him all the external succors which your Majesty thinks he can require. I shall take no steps in this matter until I have received a formal order from your Majesty.

I am, etc.

NOTES TO LETTER LXXIX.

1. This allusion is to Napoleon's two proclamations, one to his soldiers, the other to the French people from the Gulf of St. Juan, 1st March, 1815.

2. "When the King left Paris his effective force, all included, amounted to one hundred and fifty thousand men. To increase it Bonaparte recalled all who were on leave. One hundred and six thousand of these have returned. He also recalled all who had retired, and the opinion of the military bureaux is that this recall will bring in one hundred and fifty thousand men; but the country between Bordeaux and Marseilles will yield few or none at all, so that the best calculators estimate that the utmost this measure would afford would be one hundred thousand men, but these would be seasoned troops. On the whole, therefore, the army at his disposal on the 20th of March would amount to two hundred and fifty thousand men; of which fifty thousand must be subtracted for the depôts and those in hospital, so that his army will consist of not less than two hundred thousand efficient troops between the 20th and 25th of March.

"The cavalry of this army amounted, when the King left, to twenty-one thousand. Marshal Macdonald, who furnished these details to me, estimates that, in spite of the paucity of saddle horses, it may be carried to thirty thousand. These are naturally included in the two hundred thousand efficient troops.

"The King left behind twelve thousand pieces of ordnance of all calibres; so Bonaparte may have as large an artillery force as he wishes. He will have plenty of draught horses; he will take one or two from every commune according to its strength, and he will pay for them by reducing his requisitions, by which means he will not exhaust his funds. He will take the peasants' carts to supply his want of ammunition wagons.

"I do not attach much value to the two million two hundred and fifty thousand National Guards that he is forming into battalions in every department. The Marshal thinks, however, that he will be able with the battalions of grenadiers and chasseurs to furnish the garrisons of his fortresses, which he will hold by throwing into them the depôts, with officers of the line to command them.

"Bonaparte, when I left, had three hundred thousand muskets, without including the arms of the hundred and fifty thousand men of his army. He can therefore only arm four hundred and fifty thousand men. He has powder and projectiles enough for his summer campaign."—Ghent, Beurnonville to Talleyrand, 26th April, 1815.

LETTER LXXX

No. 45.

Vienna, 26th March, 1815.

SIRE,

The Emperor Alexander having yesterday desired me to go to see him, this morning, at 11 o'clock, I went to the Palace. He has never been so civil to me since I reached Vienna. "We must," he said, "banish all recriminations, and consider frankly what may be useful in the present state of affairs, not in order to seek out what has led to it, but to find a remedy." He talked to me abundantly, and with enthusiasm, of his affection for your Majesty. If necessary, he is ready to spend his last soldier and his last shilling in your Majesty's service. He even spoke like a valiant soldier who does not fear the risk of life or limb. He would sacrifice his life rather than abandon a cause in which he feels that his honor is engaged. On my side, I professed the utmost trust in him; and indeed I have for some time let him know that I entertained this confidence, through the medium of those who are most with him, and with whom I am intimate. If the assistance of foreign Powers becomes indispensable, it will be good for us that the Emperor, who can have no ambitious project at our expense, should play the chief part.

He often repeated to me: "Tell the King that this is not the time for clemency; he is defending the interests of Europe." He several times praised your Majesty for having resolved on not quitting Paris.

The forces to be employed, and of which he had the return, make up a total of eight hundred and sixty thousand men.

The Treaty of Chaumont, the stipulations of which are renewed, gives six hundred thousand, and this without counting the Army of Italy, which amounts to a hundred and fifty thousand, besides the Russian and Prussian reserves.

The Prussians have already on the Rhine seventy thousand infantry, seven thousand cavalry, and five thousand artillery. They are preparing in addition a hundred and fifty-nine thousand infantry, nineteen thousand cavalry, and six thousand artillery.

The Russians begin to understand that they cannot repose a full confidence in Austria until she has absolutely declared herself against Murat. I found the Emperor very well disposed on this subject. We meet this evening to sign the treaty of co-operation. I proposed yesterday to insert in it the following article: "The present treaty, having no other end in view but to support France, or any other country which may be invaded, against the enterprises of Bonaparte and his adherents, his Most Christian Majesty shall be specially invited to accede hereunto; and, in the event of his Majesty's requiring the forces stipulated in the second article, to make known what assistance circumstances will allow him to bring forward in furtherance of the objects of the present treaty." Although this article has not been definitively adopted, I have every reason to believe that it will be.

I am, etc.

LETTER LXXXI.

No. 46.

Vienna, 29th March, 1815.

SIRE,

I need not express to your Majesty my feelings on learning the disasters which have followed each other with such incredible rapidity. Your Majesty may estimate my sorrow by remembering my attachment to your person, which is as well known as my zeal and devotion. All my energies shall be always consecrated to your Majesty's service. I say so once for all; I shall not repeat this.

The treaty of co-operation was signed on the evening of the 25th; it was officially notified to me on the 27th. I have the honor of enclosing to your Majesty a copy of this treaty,[1] as well as copies of the Note communicated to me at the same time by the plenipotentiaries, and of my reply.[2]

As soon as this important affair was concluded, the Duke of Wellington would no longer put off joining his army; he left Vienna this morning at six o'clock.

We are redoubling our efforts to bring the affairs of the Congress to a termination. In my opinion, it will end in April. More than ever I think it important that its last act should be one of solemn significance, for it will prove to the whole world that the Powers are of one mind, and steadfastly determined on maintaining the conditions which Bonaparte's attempt is calculated to overturn.

As your Majesty may be embarrassed at this moment for defraying the expenses of the French Chancellerie, of the mission to the Congress, and of the couriers and other messengers for obtaining information, I have made arrangements with England to meet them. Your Majesty need not, therefore, be troubled with this subject.[3]

I am very anxious for news, and to hear of your Majesty's arrival. I trust that your Majesty has taken with you all the letters I had the honor of addressing to your Majesty, and that you have ordered M. de Jaucourt to carry with him every paper relating to the Congress.[4] I think that there must be some things in my letters which would displease the Powers who now are favorable to us, but who may often have been severely commented upon during the last six months.

I am keeping with me two[5] trustworthy couriers to communicate with the place chosen as a retreat by your Majesty. They will never attempt to enter France except by the frontiers which your Majesty considers safe.

I am, etc.

NOTES TO LETTER LXXXI.

1. Treaty of the Quadruple Alliance, concluded at Vienna on the 25th of March, 1815, between Great Britain, Austria, Prussia, and Russia (see D'Angeberg, p. 971).

2. A Note of Prince Talleyrand's of the 27th March gives the adhesion of France to the treaty of the 25th March (D'Angeberg, p. 984).

3. "I suppose that M. de Blacas has made you acquainted with his pecuniary situation. If he speaks truly it is very indifferent. He has the crown diamonds and four millions. I hear from other quarters—not from him—that he has, besides, all that remains out of the extra six millions which may have been squeezed out of the taxes for the works at Versailles."—Ghent, Jaucourt to Talleyrand, 10th April, 1815.

"I recommend you to take the King's orders with regard to his ministers at foreign Courts who are neither able nor willing to return to France: they must receive a salary. We can do nothing here in this respect, because our payments have been suspended since the date of the 20th of March, the day of Bonaparte's entry into Paris. I have arranged for ourselves at Vienna with the English Legation, which, after receiving the assent of its Government, will advance us enough for our daily expenses."—Talleyrand to Jaucourt, 19th April, 1815.

4 Reinhardt writes to M. de Talleyrand from Brussels, 28th March, 1815:

"I did not take with me, Prince, any important papers. At midnight M. de Jaucourt came to the office to send off couriers to Vienna, and he signed the circular letters giving to the foreign envoys the choice of either joining the King at Lille or returning straight to their respective Governments.

"M. de Jaucourt, knowing that I was resolved not to remain, wrote an order to M. d'Hauterive authorizing him to sign in the interim; but, as I was the first in rank, I was obliged to have a reason to enable me to leave. He gave me the commission of carrying the seals of the office.

"As for the papers, not one of the Department took any away. Not one of the subordinates was willing to follow without an express order from the King. It would have been more dangerous to carry them away than to hide or burn them, as M de Bresson ordered with regard to those under his charge which might have compromised people. . . .

"Nevertheless, I am sorry that I did not take away the treaties of the 3rd of January. I cannot remember that there were any others in the Chancellerie which might lead to serious consequences."

"Reinhardt was to have joined us with some of the materials of his office. He broke the seal, and started probably on the same day as I did, which was the day after the King's departure. All I did was to burn your letters and to leave word that Mariotti's should be burnt. . . . I should have done better if I had removed those documents; but, besides that I was very much hurried, the chiefs of the Department were in bed, and I do not know if they would have been willing to allow me."—Jaucourt to Talleyrand, 27th March, 1815.

5. "I strongly suspect that your courier, who I am told was Augustin, did not take much pains to go straight to M. de Caulaincourt."—Ghent, Jaucourt to Talleyrand, 4th April, 1815.

LETTER LXXXII.

No. 47.

Vienna, 30th March, 1815.

SIRE,

General Pozzo is setting out to join your Majesty; I cannot let him go without a letter from me.

All the Powers are perfectly agreed as to the destruction of Bonaparte; they consider it a matter of personal interest.

The Emperor of Russia holds the very best language; he is setting all his troops in movement, and thinks this question of such importance that he ought to spend in it his last soldier and his last shilling. He will himself march with the army. I hope the diplomatic corps has followed your Majesty. I am expecting news of your Majesty's movements with extreme impatience.

I am, etc.

LETTER XXXIII.

No. 48.

Vienna, 3rd April, 1815.

SIRE,

As Lord Clancarty is sending a courier to London who will pass through Belgium, I seize the opportunity for acquainting your Majesty with the present state of affairs here.

A few days ago, we heard that Murat had entered the Papal States, and that the Pope had been obliged to quit Rome. This event has at last opened the eyes of Austria, and made an end of all her hesitations. We are now very nearly of one mind with regard to the Italian question, which will very soon be definitively settled. All that will then remain for us to do will be to collect all the articles already agreed upon, and form them into the act which is to terminate the Congress; for I am more than ever anxious that there should be such an act.

Your Majesty's embassy here has not lost position; it enjoys as much respect and exercises as much influence as if your Majesty were still in Paris and the royal authority unimpaired throughout the kingdom. I can assure your Majesty that this position will not be altered.

I have received no direct news since your Majesty's departure from Paris;[1] I am awaiting it with extreme impatience. I venture to add that it is of the highest importance that I should be kept informed of your Majesty's movements and intentions.

I am, etc.

P.S.—I much wish that your Majesty would bestow on me a detailed list of the persons who followed the Court, and those who are expected. Proper names are very useful. Was the Archbishop of Rheims able to follow your Majesty?

I have heard nothing from M. de Jaucourt. Your Majesty will allow me to put this letter into his envelope.

M. de Vincent arrived here this morning. The Austrian Government will probably receive through the Secretary of the Austrian Legation, M. Lefébvre, a letter from Bonaparte or the Duke of Vicenza; but this communication will receive no answer and produce no effect.

My letter No. 45, which has come back to me, will show your Majesty how many have miscarried.

NOTE TO LETTER LXXXIII.

1. On the night of the 19th-20th March, 1815.

LETTER LXXXIV.

No. 49.

Vienna, 5th April, 1815.

Sire,

The events which have taken place in France have in no respect altered the position of your Majesty's ministers at the Congress, where the affairs which concern the future arrangements of Europe continue to be discussed in the same way as they were before. I have reason to hope that all that remains to be settled will be arranged in conformity with the wishes which your Majesty has expressed to me.

In several letters which I have had the honor of writing, and which have perhaps not reached your Majesty, I said that it appeared very important to all who are here, as well as to myself, that your Majesty should not quit French territory, or, at any rate, if this were impossible, that you should remain as near to it as practicable. If I were to venture to give an opinion, which is also that of the ministers of all the Powers, I should say that a residence in a town as near the sea as Ostend can only produce a hurtful effect on public opinion, because it may give the impression that your Majesty is disposed to quit the Continent and to put the sea between yourself and your kingdom. The residence which, under the present circumstances, seems, if the state of affairs will allow of it, the most suitable for your Majesty, would be Liège; it is thought that the disposition of the army would make that town safe.

We are now occupied here in settling a second declaration of the Congress, which will confirm all the arrangements announced by the Powers in that of the 13th of March. It will be an answer to all Bonaparte's [1] proclamations since he has become the master of Paris, and I cannot help thinking that it will produce a great effect wherever it is published; it is especially calculated to affect the public mind in France.

The only letter I have received since your Majesty quitted Paris is the one with which you condescended to honor me, dated the 26th of March.[2] I have received none from M. de Blacas nor from M. de Jaucourt, and I must inform your Majesty that this neglect is extremely painful to me and hurtful to our affairs here.

I am, etc.

P.S.—I enclose a letter which I sent by a courier, and which has come back to me, as well as one which the same courier was taking to M. de Jaucourt.

NOTES TO LETTER LXXXIV.

1. "You will have seen an answer from M. Bignon to the Declaration of the Powers in which there is some of Bonaparte's own work. He takes care to suppress the document, and afterwards choosing some isolated passages, he answers and distributes in every direction his reply to an unknown document. Lally is charged with answering it, and he will do so admirably, but the diffi-

culty is how to make his answer known to the French public."—Ghent, Jaucourt to Talleyrand, 9th April, 1815.

2 This letter is wanting in the manuscripts of the Department for Foreign Affairs. It will be found after Letter C.

LETTER LXXXV.

THE KING TO PRINCE TALLEYRAND.

No. 1 from Ghent.

Ghent, 9th April, 1815.

My Cousin,

I have received your No. 46 by the hand of Prince V. de R———.[1] Your expressions of attachment are always very agreeable to me, and in such a painful moment they are, of course, more welcome than ever; but I had no need of them to give me an absolute trust in your fidelity.

The treaty of the 25th of March, the sequel and complement of the declaration of the 13th, being directed solely against Bonaparte, I do not hesitate in desiring you to accede to it in my name. If you require an authorization *ad hoc*, you shall have it immediately; but in the meanwhile I authorize you in these words to act as if you had received one.

The weight that I am able to put into the balance is nineteen-twentieths of the French nation, of whose sentiments neither I nor the Powers can entertain any doubt. But this powerful engine cannot be set in motion without external succors; the Allied armies must therefore enter France, and the sooner the better. Each instant of delay deprives me of strength, because it is in the nature of intense excitement to be always on the point of declining: and, on the other hand, delay gives strength to the enemy, because it gives him time to assemble his forces, and, by means which he knows only too well how to employ, to turn in his favor those who at present ask nothing better than to arm in my cause.

The Duke of Wellington, whom I saw yesterday, and whose zeal in my service I cannot possibly overpraise, has despatched a courier to ask permission to act without waiting until all the other armies are assembled. I need not tell you to support this request earnestly. If they wait until all the forces are assembled, it will be impossible for the troops to effect anything before the 1st of June. I have no doubt as to our ultimate success, but Bonaparte would then be crushed only under the ruins of France,[2] while immediate action will still more certainly insure his destruction and save our country. This may not be the object of other nations, but it must be ours.

The Duke of Wellington tells me that the counter-proposal which I sent to you on the 7th of March has been adopted. I am very glad of it. I am also much pleased with the arrangements you have made regarding the Chancellerie, the couriers, etc. It relieves my finances, which are very slender at present.[3]

I have brought with me all the letters and documents you have sent me since you reached Vienna, and I ordered M. de Jaucourt to do likewise.

Your courage has not been shaken by these events; of this I was convinced beforehand. You see that mine is not so either.

On which, etc.

NOTES TO LETTER LXXXV.

1. Prince Victor de Rohan.
2. "I would bet ten to one that Bonaparte will fall, but I should not like to bet that the Bourbons will succeed, still less that they will remain. Nothing is so easy as to destroy and lay waste France, and to bring about a revolution in her Government; nothing is so difficult as to maintain her—to replace her as she was on the day after the royal Council.

"Great God! what a long way have we travelled since that day!

"To express it in one word, the road led straight to the island of Elba."—Ghent, Jaucourt to Talleyrand, 10th April, 1815.

3. In a letter to Talleyrand, dated 24th April, 1815. M. de Jaucourt says—

"I own that the confusion of orders, the shame of the flight, our impotency in consequence of our not having a penny, the quiet imbecility with which M. de Blacas replies, 'I am very sorry, but I could not make the King unpopular,' as if the twenty-five millions which ought to have been taken out three days earlier might not have been replaced a week later. . . . I could fill ten pages with this subject, and I say all this renders indispensable some measure which will banish M. de Blacas from the ranks of politicians."

LETTER LXXXVI.

No. 50.

Vienna, 13th April, 1815.

Sire,

Since Bonaparte is now master of Paris, the Allied Powers have thought that it might be advisable to renew, by a second Declaration, the proclamation of the sentiments expressed in the Declaration of the 13th of March. There is every reason to believe that, with the exception of a few individuals, all who in France belong to any party or opinion desire the same thing—the fall of Bonaparte. We wish to make use of this unanimous desire to effect his destruction. When once this object is accomplished, the private opinions of each individual party will find themselves without support, without power, without means of action, and will no longer offer any obstacle.[1]

The Declaration, therefore, was calculated to persuade every member of every party to compass the fall of Bonaparte. Although of one mind as to the substance, they could not agree as to the form, and for the present its publication is adjourned. They even think of substituting for a declaration of the Congress an identical proclamation, to be issued by all the generals commanding the Allied troops on their entrance on French territory; and I am not indisposed to adopt this idea, which seems to me to possess many recommendations.

All that I hear from France proves that Bonaparte is in great difficulties. The emissaries he has sent here also lead me to believe this.[2]

One of them, M. de Montrond, has reached Vienna, with the assistance of the Abbé Altieri, an *attaché* of the Austrian Legation in Paris. He had no despatches or ostensible mission, and he was more probably sent by the party which favors Bonaparte than by Bonaparte himself. This is what I am inclined to think. He had messages for M. de Nesselrode, Prince Metternich, and me. He was to ascertain whether the foreign Powers were determined on not recognizing Bonaparte, and on making war against him. He had also a letter for Prince Eugène. What he was desired to ask me was if I really could make up my mind to excite a war against France. "Read the Declaration," I replied; "it does not contain a single word with which I do not agree. The question, too, is not of a war against France, but of a war against the man of Elba." He asked Prince Metternich if the Austrian Government had entirely lost sight of the views it entertained in March, 1814. "The Regency? We do not wish for it," replied Prince Metternich. Lastly, he tried to find out from Prince Nesselrode what were the intentions of the Emperor Alexander. "The destruction of Bonaparte and his followers," was the reply; and so the matter ended.

Pains were taken to acquaint M. de Montrond with the strength of the forces which are to be immediately employed, as well as with the treaty of last March. He returned to Paris with this information and these replies, which will probably give considerable matter for reflection to those who are now attached to Bonaparte's fortunes.

His second emissary was Count Flahault. When he reached Stuttgart, the King of Würtemberg had him arrested and taken back to the frontier. He had despatches for the Emperor of Austria, the Emperor Alexander, the Empress Marie Louise, and for your Majesty's Legation at Vienna (these were, we supposed, the despatches being marked private, letters for annulling the powers of your Majesty's Embassy at Vienna). The Allied Powers continue very favorable. I can assure your Majesty that it is an enterprise of extreme difficulty to drive so many people to the same goal. I labor unceasingly to keep them all from straying out of the right path.[3]

The territorial arrangements for Southern Germany were settled yesterday. A few days more, and I hope that the Congress will have finished all its business.

I shall have the honor of sending you by the next English courier, who will start on Saturday, the 15th, the declaration of war on the part of Austria against Murat.[4] It is very badly expressed. This affair will, I hope, be soon terminated, and to your satisfaction.

I am, etc.

P.S.—M. Fauche-Borel is the bearer of this letter.

NOTES TO LETTER LXXXVI.

1. "The measures taken ever since he reached Paris by the Government of Bonaparte, the men he has chosen for ministers, the direction in which every means is tried to force public opinion, prove Bonaparte to be under the influence of all that are left in France of the old Revolutionary parties, and that it is from them alone that he derives all his power of action within the country. It is nevertheless notorious that none of these parties, or of the men of whom they are composed, really like Bonaparte, because they are perfectly aware that if he succeeds in consolidating his authority, he will deprive them (as he did when for the first time he seized the reigns of government), of the share of power he is obliged to leave to them, now that he requires their support. It is, therefore, evident that they have joined him only because they could find no other means of escaping from a state of things in which all participation in public business was withheld from them and they even thought they had reason to fear for their own safety.

"But it does not seem to me doubtful that they would be the first to overthrow Bonaparte if the Government which they expected to succeed him would offer guarantees on which they could perfectly depend, which would not only deliver them from all anxiety, but might also satisfy their ambition. The Allied Powers agree in this opinion, and this is why they wish that the King, in a proclamation to precede the meeting of the electoral colleges which Bonaparte has summoned to Paris, should endeavor to rally all parties to his standard by assuring to every one without distinction all the advantages of the constitutional system. The Allied Powers consider that a royal declaration couched in these terms would be a powerful auxiliary to the forces they are about to bring into the field. Several of the Powers would also wish that the King, imputing the blunders which may have been committed to his former ministers, should form a new ministry just as if he were in France, and that its composition should offer the requisite guarantees to each party. I am writing to the King on this subject by the Comte de Noailles, who also takes this letter to you. As I know that the ministers who are to be sent by the Allied Powers to his Majesty will mention the subject to him, I should wish that his Majesty might forestall their arguments by a resolution in accordance with the views which I have had the honor of expounding to you; and I beg you to do everything in your power to persuade the King to take this course."—Talleyrand to Jaucourt, 22nd April, 1815.

2. Here is what Napoleon says of this mission in his Memoirs:

"Montrond's mission had several objects: to gain over Talleyrand; to carry letters to the Empress and bring back answers; to furnish Talleyrand with an opportunity for writing to France, and for seizing the threads of the plots which he had woven there.

"All these objects were accomplished." 9th May, 1815.

"Saint-Léon reached Vienna yesterday, my dear Prince. He is a friendly envoy sent by M. de Mollien, and has come partly on business of my own. His instructions were to make me uneasy about a great law-suit which is to be instituted against me in the National Court of Justice. Montrond had failed with his measure of sequestration; something more was wanted. Here it is!

"In other respects Saint-Léon is a good and fine fellow, but about as fit for politics as Dupont de Nemours, who also would have certainly been sent to me, if he had not already started for America. Always yours."—Talleyrand to Metternich.

3. "I am convinced that you are, and that you think yourself, the real diplomatic Cabinet of France, and that the whole diplomacy of Europe is assembled at Vienna."—Ghent, Jaucourt to Talleyrand, 4th April, 1815.

4. Declaration of the Court of Vienna on the conduct of the King of Naples, 12th April, 1815 (see D'Angeberg, p. 1065).

APPENDIX TO NO. 50 (LETTER LXXXVI).

Proposed Declaration laid before the Conference of the Eight Powers assembled at Vienna by the French Plenipotentiaries, on the 11th of April, 1815, and annexed to the Despatch of the 13th of April.

DECLARATION.

The European Powers had flattered themselves that they had secured a lasting peace to the world by the treaties of the 11th of April and 30th of May, 1814.

France was the first to profit by it; all her direct interests had been consulted, while those of the other nations remained liable to the future decisions of the Congress. Her ancient limits, far from being restricted, were extended. A monstrous despotism had been replaced by liberal institutions. Her colonies were restored to her, the seas once more opened to her. There was no longer any obstacle to the development of all the germs of prosperity within her frontiers. The evils of which she had been the instrument were no longer laid to her charge; there was a full and complete reconciliation between her and the rest of Europe. While she was enjoying at home all the blessings of a paternal Government under her legitimate monarch, she drew new strength from the confidence she inspired abroad. Invited to the Congress, she exercised in it a full share of the influence appertaining to one of the principal members of the great European family. The man who to-day is loudly proclaiming that for fifteen years he has been meditating the subjection of the whole world,[1] and who, in the execution of his impious design, was willing to sacrifice the lives of two millions of Frenchmen, carrying everywhere sword and flame, and working incessantly for its attainments of violence and fraud; this man, unanimously rejected by the nation which had entrusted her happiness to him, and whose life even had had to be protected against the just indignation of this nation;[2] this man, whose character and actions have been blasted by the unanimous testimony of the authorities he had himself established,[3] by the declarations of the generals, and recently even by the proclamations of those[4] whom he has succeeded in seducing;—this man, who not only was deposed, but himself abdicated his authority, and subsequently renounced it for himself and his family, by a solemn treaty with the Powers of Europe, who therefore alone could set him free, has returned to seize once more that sceptre, in the hope of again satisfying his unparalleled passion for tyranny at the expense of France and of Europe.

Europe neither can nor ought to suffer this; she is arming, not against France, but as much for the welfare of France as for her own security. She acknowledges no other enemy than Napoleon Bonaparte, and all who fight in his cause.

When, on the 1st of April, 1814, the Powers declared[5] that they would not treat for peace with him, every nation, the French among the first, applauded this resolution.

When first they heard of his appearance in the south of France in the month of March last, they declared that they would give him neither peace nor rest.

Now that he has made himself master of Paris, and has succeeded in once more seizing the reins of power, they renew this declaration in the most solemn manner.

No blow will be aimed at the independence of the French nation.

The treaty of the 30th of May and the political and territorial arrangements settled at the Congress will continue to regulate the relations between France and the rest of Europe.

If Europe should find herself driven into this new and unexpected war, she is determined that neither Napoleon Bonaparte nor his family shall profit by his criminal attempt; that this obstacle to the peace of the world shall be removed; and that France shall guarantee security to the rest of the world and to herself by her institutions. When this end has been accomplished, then, and not till then, will the Powers lay down their arms.

NOTES TO THE APPENDIX.

1. Napoleon, it is true, said in his proclamation that he had wished to rule over Europe; but he added, "We must (now) forget that we have been chief among nations."

2. This allusion is to the threatening attitude of the South in 1814 towards the Emperor when on his way to the island of Elba.

3. The Senate, which proclaimed his deposition in a Declaration much resembling the above.

4. Of Ney, among others.

5. Prior to the abdication at Fontainebleau, 6th April, 1814.

LETTER LXXXVII.

No. 51.

Vienna, 15th April, 1815.

SIRE,

I have delivered the three letters which your Majesty desired M. de Jaucourt to send to me. I venture to mention that it seemed to me, from some questions whose object was to discover whether your Majesty was pleased with the Declaration, that the Emperors had expected to find some expressions of satisfaction in these letters.[1] Nevertheless, I perceive, both in their words and in their actions, nothing but proofs of the perfect concord at present established among them, and which I will do my utmost to keep up to the end. M. Pozzo must have told your Majesty what trouble it was, in circumstances which were much less complicated, to reconcile interests which were determined to think themselves incompatible.

The Russian troops reached Bohemia four days sooner than they were expected. It would not be surprising if, although they come from the Vistula, they reached the Rhine before, or at least as soon as, the Austrian troops.

There are such conflicting opinions here on the strength and position of the army under the Duke of Wellington's orders, that I should be very glad if your Majesty would have the kindness to desire M. de Jaucourt to give me precise information on this subject, and especially as to the period when it may be expected to enter France.[2]

Marshal Wrède leaves us in two days. He will stay at Munich four days, and thence repair to his command. The troops under his orders, as well as the Prussian troops, are extremely eager.[3]

The Austrians have received news from Italy, dated the 7th of April, with which, on the whole, they are satisfied. But they are very easily satisfied. Their motive for satisfaction is that Murat's troops, after having tried without success to carry the bridge of Occhiobello,[4] were forced to retire, and his whole army is between Modena, Ferrara, and the coast. General Frimont hoped to be in a position to give battle towards the 12th.

I have the honor of transmitting to your Majesty the Declaration against Murat, which has been officially communicated to me by Prince Metternich.

I am, etc.

NOTES TO LETTER LXXXVII.

1. **Talleyrand** wrote to Jaucourt on the same subject on the 19th of April, 1815, from Vienna:

"I have delivered the King's letters which you enclosed; they make me more and more sorry that M. Reinhardt is not with the King. They did not give much satisfaction. The sovereigns expected to find in them some gratitude for the Declaration they have published, and they let me see their disappointment. However, what I tell you about this is a mere observation; it is intended only to induce you to carry all matters connected with our department with a high hand, for M. de Blacas seems to know very little about them. We cannot understand here why so many people have been sent away; it seems to me that it would have been very useful to collect a nucleus of Frenchmen of all opinions, and from all parts of the country, round the King."

M. de Jaucourt answers from Ghent, 23d April:

"I not only wrote at once to Reinhardt, but I made use of the people who were passing through Frankfort, where he is watched by the police, to tell him to come hither. I think I may be certain that among the motives which may postpone his return, there is none personal to me. He has some friendship for me, and he is aware of my great esteem for him. His presence would be all the more useful to us because, without reference to his former opinions, he would at the present time be most anxious to represent the King as the preserver of liberty guaranteed by the Constitution. All who have not forgotten the state of France agree in this, but here, unfortunately, they are not the majority."

2 "The Allies, although they are the King's allies, are at the best only generous enemies to France, and what is their generosity? You have seen the Russian proclamations—they are furious. The Duke of Wellington has written about them to the King of Prussia. You may be sure that Bonaparte will post them up, and will treat us to some of his own performances to the same tune." —Ghent, Jaucourt to Talleyrand 10th April, 1815.

3. "All that I hear of the behavior of the Prussians disturbs me, not only on account of the mischief and excesses of all kinds of which they are guilty, but because there may be more analogy than is convenient between the spirit which animates them and that which inspires those who at present rule over France."—Ghent, Talleyrand to Jaucourt, 23d April, 1815.

"My policy reduces itself to points on which I am certain . . . to give the King the most popular aspect which can be attributed to a sovereign who follows in the wake of *hostile* armies. To his person is attached the integrity of France; to his cause is attached the generosity of the Allies; to him, finally, is attached the Treaty of Vienna. All kinds of promises should be held out to the soldiers who rally round the King, and these promises should be kept. Paris must be spared—it will count on this beforehand; the same language should be held which you and your friends have always held, and wished others to hold. Do not forget, dear friend, that the mortal enemies of Bonaparte are the friends of liberty; that they are detested by him; and that, through our folly, he has found an entrance among those who voted for his death. You know that Bonaparte has granted the liberty of the Press. . . .

"The devil himself could not persuade M. de Blacas to let me have the newspapers, which are rigorously suppressed here."—Ghent, Jaucourt to Talleyrand, 2nd April, 1815.

4. The *Moniteur* of the 30th April said—

"Vienna, 15th April.

"On the 8th King Joachim commanded in person several very sharp attacks against the bridge of Occhiobello. He failed in each attempt, and in the evening the enemy was forced to retreat, after suffering considerable loss."

LXXXVIII.

APPENDIX TO NO. 51 (LETTER LXXXVII.)

Declaration against Murat.

The Minister of State and for Foreign Affairs of the Emperor of Austria has submitted to his Imperial Majesty the Declaration that the plenipotentiaries of Naples did him the honor of forwarding to him on the 8th of this month. He is ordered to make the following reply:

The treaty of alliance between Austria and the Court of Naples had hardly been concluded when it was impossible to help remarking, from the prolonged inaction of the Neapolitan army, as well as from many undeniable proofs which fell into the hands of the allied armies, that the King, far from uniting with them in promoting the common objects which the Powers were endeavoring to attain in the war of 1813-14, had principally regulated his behavior according to the issue of the event.

The Emperor, nevertheless, remained faithful to the treaty of alliance of the 11th of January, 1814. Unwilling to attach importance to the motives which might have led to the negotiation, or to the circumstances connected with the King's accession, his Imperial Majesty put aside all considerations save those involved in the terms of the treaty. His Imperial Majesty immediately endeavored to establish friendly relations between his allies and the Court of Naples. The reasons which prevented the development of these relations into formal alliances are so well known by the Neapolitan Cabinet that the undersigned does not think it necessary to repeat them. The more the King has thought fit to choose a different course from that pursued by Austria from the beginning of the alliance, the less right has he to impute to the Cabinet of Austria disasters to his own Government which were the necessary result of this divergence.

The Emperor has never ceased to represent to the King the consequences which would ensue from his prolonged occupation of the Marches at a juncture when a sound policy pointed out to the King the duty of limiting his pretensions to the preservation of his kingdom, to the exclusion of all ideas of conquest—a juncture in which the same policy laid upon him the honorable duty of assisting the

Governments in Italy to secure the peace of the peninsula, instead of keeping up a ferment in the minds of the people by continually reinforcing armies out of all proportion to the resources of his territories, and still more by massing these armies on points which, in consequence of the geographical position of the Austrian possessions, were protected against all attacks from the Powers which were unfavorable to the Court of Naples, and therefore could be considered only as offensive positions against Austria and all the other sovereigns in Italy.

Although the general affairs of the Empire at this moment claimed his Imperial Majesty's whole attention, he omitted no effort to bring the King back to a position more in accordance with the King's real interests. He left no proof of confidence and no means of persuasion untried until the period when, the Neapolitan armaments assuming an attitude of direct aggression, the Emperor was forced, in February last, to take a step which was provoked by the demands of the Neapolitan Cabinet—demands which proved only too plainly the King's objects, as to which there can remain no uncertainty since his late manifestation to the Papal Court, and the recent development of his plans.

The undersigned received orders to hand, on the 25th of February, to the plenipotentiary of Naples and to the plenipotentiary of France an explicit Declaration that the Emperor would not, in any case, allow foreign troops a passage through his territory. The Declaration addressed to France was communicated to the Neapolitan plenipotentiary. If these simultaneous Declarations differ in terms, the reason is easily given. It was Naples which had raised this question; it was she who had placed herself in an attitude of aggression.

The Emperor considers it due both to the safety of his States and to his general relations with Europe to make these declarations. It is due to his dignity to maintain them. His Majesty would have rejected any demand on the part of France to send armies through Italy; he would have considered any reiterated attempt of the kind, after the Declaration of the 25th of February, as a declaration of war.

The Emperor is forced, in like manner, to consider the irruption of Neapolitan troops on the frontier, and their encampment in the Marches, as a rupture of the alliance, and a measure directed against Austria. His Majesty looks upon the entrance of the Neapolitan troops into the Legations, and their hostilities against the Imperial troops, as a positive declaration of war, whatever may be the color which the Cabinet of Naples may seek to give to these transactions.

The undersigned has therefore orders to recall the Imperial Legation at once from Naples, and at the same time to give passports to the Neapolitan ambassadors at Vienna.

(Signed)   Prince Metternich.
Vienna, 10th April, 1815.

LETTER LXXXIX.

THE KING TO PRINCE TALLEYRAND.

No. 2 from Ghent.

Ghent, 21st April, 1815.

My Cousin,

I have received your No. 49, including No. 38. Very soon after you despatched it, you must have received news of me, and I hope that since that time you have continued to do so; but the want of the means I had at my disposal in Paris must necessarily make our correspondence unpunctual.

I am anxious to receive the Declaration you speak of, which was, your letter gives me reason for hoping, in part your work. Chevalier Stuart has just told me that it was signed on the 11th. I, on my side, am writing the proclamation which I shall issue when I set foot in France.[1] I will send it to you as soon as it has been corrected and read, before it is approved by the Duke of Wellington and General Pozzo di Borgo. If the allied sovereigns are still at Vienna when it reaches you, I hope that you will gain their suffrages in its favor. I do not wish, however, that it may find them still there; celerity is the thing wanted above all others in our operations. All the reports from the interior are excellent, but we must not allow time to the enemy.

On which, etc.

NOTE TO LETTER LXXXIX.

1. "I have the honor of sending you several copies of a newspaper which we are bringing out under the name of the *Journal Universel.* You will recognize in it M. Lally's pen. . . . A manifesto drawn up by him will appear in two days; it will precede the King's proclamation when he enters the French territory. . . . It was read yesterday at the royal Council. This Council con-

sists of the Duc de Blacas, the Duc de Feltre, myself, Lally, and Chateaubriand. It was read to-day to General Pozzo, who was much pleased with it, and will take it to-morrow to the Duke of Wellington."—Ghent, Jaucourt to Talleyrand, 23rd April, 1815.

LETTER XC.

THE KING TO PRINCE TALLEYRAND.

No 3 from Ghent.

22nd April, 1815.

My Cousin,

I was just about to reply to your No. 49, enclosing No. 38, when I received No. 50, enclosing No. 44. You, no doubt, influenced the Declaration of the sovereigns; I hope that if there is still time you will influence that of the generals', which will be a very important document. If it is to produce all the desired effect, it is necessary that, in conformity with the Declaration of the 13th of March and Article 3 of the treaty of the 20th, Europe should declare herself the ally of the King and the French nation against the invasion of Napoleon Bonaparte;[1] the friend of all who declare themselves on the side of the former, and the enemy of all who arm in favor of the latter; which excludes at the same time all ideas of conquest and all middle courses, of which even the possibility must not be entertained.

On my side I am engaged in drawing up the Declaration or Proclamation which I shall issue when I return to France. I will send it to you as soon as it is finished, but I hope sincerely that it will not find you any longer at Vienna. Your No. 46 announces the speedy termination of the Congress. You must, of course, sign the final treaty in my name, but I am most anxious to have you with me,[2] especially under the present circumstances.

You have heard of the unfortunate issue of my nephew's courageous attempt;[3] you know that my niece herself was not able to save Bordeaux. The public mind is not, however, demoralized in France; all reports are unanimous on this point; the great thing is to act promptly, and this is entirely the Duke of Wellington's desire and opinion.

I shall make only one observation on your letter No. 38. It is that it is right to preserve the Duc de Campo-Chiaro's letters, as a proof of the utter perfidy of his master.[4]

On which, etc.

NOTES TO LETTER XC.

1. "If you succeed in maintaining this salutary resolution to make war against the individual only, and not against the nation, to support the royal cause conjointly with that of liberty, against usurpation, including in the term every species of oppression, you will, my dear friend, have performed, conscientiously and honorably, the finest exploit of which civilized nations are capable."—Ghent, Jaucourt to Talleyrand, 9th April, 1815.

2. "Every one tells me that the divine Blacas only enjoys a *vacant favor.* This favor would be given to one who, like you, would add personal authority to skilfulness. Of those here, some are foolish, and others, like Marmont, are ill at ease; others again, like myself, are men whose principles and habits are distasteful, although their persons and even their characters are liked."—Jaucourt to Talleyrand, 10th April, 1815.

"You must come, I assure you. You may take any place you like at present. The ministry will be composed by your advice. If this ministry be strong, the old habits, predilections, and prejudices of Monsieur will give way to it; again, it must be so strong that its resignation shall be dreaded."—Jaucourt to Talleyrand, 28th April, 1815.

On the 28th of April Chateaubriand writes to Talleyrand:

"Since the last letter which I had the honor of sending you from Brussels by the Duc de Richelieu, things have somewhat changed for me: the King has called me to his Council, but without a title; he has charged me with reporting to him the state of our internal policy. But, Prince, one must have an internal policy—we are waiting for you to give us one once more. Your presence here is absolutely necessary. Come before we commit any new blunders. You must put yourself at our head; we must form a ministry of which you will be the guide and support.

"You are aware, Prince, of my devotion to you. I should be too happy if I could contribute a little with you to the restoration of France, which for a second time needs your services.

"I told you that we should be lost if we did not remove Bonaparte from Elba. Well, Prince, we shall be lost if you do not come to remove the King from Ghent. Come, come; nothing on earth is more important."

3. The Duc d'Angoulême was taken prisoner and carried to the Spanish frontier by the partisans of Napoleon.

4. This is the letter enclosed by Prince Talleyrand:

"Monseigneur,

"A courier despatched from Rome by the Chevalier Cuvilli on the 4th, has brought the news of Bonaparte's escape from the island of Elba to Naples on the morning of the 5th; it says that he left Elba on the 26th for Fréjus, having been invited to France by a party in his favor.

"The King immediately assembled his Council, and called to it all the heads of administration and counsellors of State to announce this event to them. Far from wishing to consult them, he declared that, whatever might happen in the future, his resolution was taken to remain faithful to his engagement with his ally in the interests of peace and order in Europe; that he saw no other security for his States than that which was based on loyalty and honor. He repeated these sentiments himself to the Austrian minister, and sent a courier to me at Vienna to announce his intentions. This courier reached me on the 15th, at 4 P.M.

"As I think it right to show respect for the eminent talents and high character of your Highness, who, while fulfilling zealously the duties of your position, would certainly dislike to fall into mistakes or disguise facts through false information, I have the honor of making this confidential communication, relying upon your Highness's unvarying kindness, irrespective of our relative positions.

"I venture to point out to your Highness that when the King found himself threatened by France, and did not know whether this escape was an act of madness or the result of an agreement with another party—a question which was unwisely mooted—the part taken by the King was entirely that of the present Government in France. May the justice which is not one of the least remarkable attributes of the magnanimous sovereign now on the throne, induce him to sacrifice the object of restoring tranquillity to Europe (who, after all, is only reaping the fruit of her own acts) to other considerations."—The Duc de Campo-Chiaro.

LETTER XCI.

No. 52.

Vienna, 23rd April, 1815.

SIRE,

Something has occurred here of such a painful nature that I should like to be able to conceal it from your Majesty, but it is of great importance that it should be known in the present state of affairs, with which it is intimately linked; and, besides, it would be sure to come to the ears of your Majesty by some other means, unaccompanied by the considerations which will correct and balance its effect.

For some time I have had occasion to observe that the Emperor of Russia's opposition to your Majesty's wishes was not always caused by any design he entertained himself, but in some cases because he thought himself slighted—1. That your Majesty did not offer him the blue ribbon,[1] which was given to the Prince Regent; 2. Because of the rejection of his pressing intervention in favor of the Duke of Vicenza, in whom he takes a lively interest,[2] and who has been excluded from the Chamber of Peers;[3] 3. On account of the firmness with which your Majesty, in the question of the marriage, refused to yield to his wishes on the religious question; 4. Because the constitutional Charter differed in many respects from the views he announced on the subject in Paris,[4] and which his liberal ideas caused him to consider as very useful and important.

I knew that he had long been complaining of these things in his intimate circle, but this seemed to me of little importance. Now, however, I have reason to think that these ideas influence his opinion regarding the situation of France and that of your Majesty.

From the news we receive from France, and the information brought thence by individuals, it seems that on your Majesty's side is to be found the whole body of the nation, and on the other side two parties: the first, that of the army, which is entirely devoted to Bonaparte, those who are well disposed being subjugated or drawn away by the majority; the second party, formed out of the remnants of the old revolutionary faction. The second joined the first only because the former had the start and obliged the latter to follow. They agree only on one point—the desire of change; but they desire it for different motives and to accomplish different ends. The army, tired of quiet, wanted a chief who would give it once more all those chances of danger, fortune, and fame to which it had been accustomed for twenty-two years.[5] Bonaparte was eminently the man. The chiefs of the second party know him and detest him. They are aware of his insatiable love of domination; they know that civil liberty has no more cruel enemy. They know very well that where a rebel army has unseated the supreme government only a faint reflection of civil power can subsist; that without a civil government they can have no existence, and that passive obedience will be their lot as well as that of every one else. They have no illusions as to Bonaparte's motive in conciliating them: they know that his union with them is on his part a forced union; that the chains by means of which they will try to restrain him, and which at this moment he is willing to bear, will endure only so long as he is not strong enough to break them, and that if he obtains a succession of victories, he will acquire that power. They do not conceal from themselves that what the army has done once, it may do a second and a third time, and that in such a state of things there will be no safety either for the master or his slaves. Disabused of their old chimeras, they no longer dream of a republic. The titles and fortunes they have acquired bind them to the monarchy. They were not opposed to the legitimate dynasty, but they could not endure a Government under which, excluded from any share in active employment, they found themselves deprived of all political existence and threatened with still greater losses in the future.[6] Their aversion for this state of things is so great, that they would have been willing to escape from it at any price, and rather

21*

than return to it they would throw themselves into all the horrors and hazards of revolution.

Bonaparte's first object is to nationalize the war in which he will have to engage. The first object of the Powers is to prevent him. He feels that he cannot attain it by persuasion, and that to strike fear is his only chance of success. But his army, which he must draw to the frontiers, and which will be engaged with foreign armies, is not a sufficient instrument for him. He must have others, and he can find them only in the party to which he formerly belonged, on the ruins of which he raised himself, which he has long oppressed, and whose support he is now seeking. The Powers think that if pains were taken to calm the fears of this party, it might be induced to abandon a man whom it does not like; that Bonaparte would thus lose his chief resource, and the one which would render his resistance the most protracted and dangerous. A memorandum has been drawn up of a Declaration to this effect. When it was proposed only to declare that Europe was not arming against France, but for France, that Europe recognized no other enemy but Bonaparte and his followers; that she would grant neither peace nor truce to him; and that she would not lay down her arms until she had overthrown him, all opinions were unanimous. But when there was a question of saying in the Declaration that the ultimate aim of the war was to restore the legitimate dynasty, opinions were divided. "If you do not allude to this re-establishment," said some, "those who armed within the country and were induced by the Declaration of the 13th to take up arms in the King's cause, will think themselves abandoned. You will deprive yourselves of a certain support to obtain one which is uncertain; if you only announce your intention to overthrow the usurper, and leave it to be supposed that when once he has fallen France may do as she pleases, you will deliver her over to Jacobinism, and to factions that are even more dangerous to the welfare of Europe than Bonaparte himself."

Others say that "the re-establishment of the legitimate dynasty is an object with regard to which there ought to be no doubt as to the intentions of the Allied Powers. The Declaration of the 13th of March sufficiently asserts this. If you insist upon it again too positively, you will miss your aim, which is to detach Bonaparte from those who can only be reconciled by concessions which the Powers may hint at, but which the King alone can promise or bestow."

Affairs were in this stage when the Emperor Alexander sent for

Lord Clancarty, who, since the departure of Lord Castlereagh and the Duke of Wellington, is at the head of the British embassy.

Their conversation was in part reported to me by Lord Clancarty, but in much greater detail by Lord Stewart and Prince Metternich. The task of reporting it to your Majesty is one of extreme difficulty, all the more that in several instances I find myself divided between my sense of respect for the person and my devotion to the cause of your Majesty; I fear that what I yield to the one may appear to be wanting to the other. But your Majesty,[8] whose interest it is to be aware of the sentiments of the most powerful of his allies, would acquire a very erroneous impression of them if I left out the reasons he advanced, or even the reproaches by means of which he pretended to justify them. The importance of this consideration alone induces me to report them.

The Emperor asked Lord Clancarty, in the first place, why he did not approve of the proposed Declaration, and what objection he had to make. "It is," replied Lord Clancarty, "that the Declaration does not, in my opinion, say all that it ought to say. It is not enough to overthrow Bonaparte; we must not open the door to the Jacobins, who would suit us still less than Bonaparte himself."

"The Jacobins," retorted the Emperor, "are formidable only when allied to Bonaparte,[9] and this is why we must try to separate them from him. When once he has fallen, they will not be the party to succeed to his inheritance. The first object is to overthrow him, and in this we are all of one mind. As for me, I shall devote all my strength to effect this, and shall take no rest till it is done. For the remainder, I am willing to postpone any declaration or proclamation to the time when our troops shall be nearer France. This, indeed, is what I should prefer. But the overthrow of Bonaparte is not the only point on which we must come to an understanding. In an enterprise of the magnitude of that on which we are engaged, we must from the very beginning keep our end in view. The overthrow of Bonaparte is only half our work; there will still be the security of Europe to provide for. She can never be tranquil as long as France is not quiet, and France will only be quiet under a Government which is generally popular."

"France," said Lord Clancarty, "was happy under the King; the hopes of the whole nation are centred in him."

"Yes," replied the Emperor, "of that part of the nation which has never been anything but passive, which has for twenty-six years submitted to every sort of revolution, which only murmurs, but interferes with none. But the remainder, which appears like the whole nation because it alone comes forward, it alone acts, it alone governs—will this party submit voluntarily and be faithful to a Government it has just betrayed? Will you force such a Government upon this party against its will? For the sake of so doing will you set on foot a war of extermination to which there might be no end? And are you sure that you will succeed?" "I feel," replied Lord Clancarty, "that duty ends where impossibility begins. But until impossibility is proved, I hold that the duty of the Powers is to support the legitimate sovereign, and not to allow it even to be a question of abandoning him."[10]

"Our first duties," replied the Emperor, "are towards Europe and towards ourselves. Even if it were easy to re-establish the King's Government—as long as there was no certainty of its future stability, what would be the effect of re-establishing it but to prepare fresh misfortunes for France and for Europe? If what has once happened should happen again, should we be as united as we are to-day? should we have nearly a million men under arms? should we be ready when danger broke out? and what probability is there, should the same elements of disorder subsist, that the King's Government would be more stable than it has been now? For the rest, whatever may be our opinion on this subject—the re-establishment of the King, which we all, and I more than any other, desire—may meet with insurmountable obstacles; as this is not an impossible case we are bound to provide for it, and to settle beforehand what ought to be done. Last year a regency[11] might have been established; but the Archduchess Marie Louise, to whom I have spoken, will not at any price return to France. Her son is to have an establishment in Austria, and this is all that she wishes for him. I have ascertained that Austria, on her side, no longer thinks of a regency or wishes for it. Last year it seemed a means likely to conciliate conflicting interests; but the situation is no longer the same. It is a thing, therefore, which we must not any longer take into consideration. The only way to conciliate all parties is to choose the Duke of Orleans. He is a Frenchman; he is a Bourbon; he is the husband of a Bourbon; he has sons; he has served in his youth in the Constitutional cause; he has worn the tricolor cockade, which I often said, when I was in Paris, ought never to have been left off.[12] He would unite all parties. Do you not think so, my lord; and what would be the opinion of

England?" "I do not know," replied Lord Clancarty, "what would be the opinion of my Government on a proposal which would be as new to it as the idea is to me; as for my own private opinion, I do not hesitate to say that it seems to me extremely dangerous to abandon the principle of legitimacy in order to take up any sort of usurpation. But your Majesty would certainly wish me to communicate to my Government all that I have had the honor of hearing."

The Emperor told him to write, and after repeating how essential it was to make sure of the aim one has in view from the beginning of such an important enterprise, he retired.

Lord Clancarty accordingly did write, but laid great stress on the reasons which should attach England to your Majesty's cause. Prince Metternich, to whom Lord Stewart and Lord Clancarty repeated this conversation, thought that the question raised by the Emperor was at least ill-timed; that it would not do for the Powers to lose themselves in hypotheses which might never occur, but that they ought to wait until each question presented itself, and treat each singly. He desired the Austrian ambassador in London to speak in these terms.

The Emperor Alexander, who does not take in very clearly the principle of legitimacy, has, without waiting for the opinion of the English Cabinet, inserted in the *Frankfort Gazette* an article which I have before me, and which says that the Powers only want to overthrow Bonaparte, but that they in no way pretend to interfere with the interior administration of France, or even to impose any Government upon the country, which will then be free to choose the one she prefers.

But so far he is alone in his opinion. Even Prussia, which is in the habit of agreeing with all he wants, is well disposed towards your Majesty, and has even expressed a wish that your Majesty should issue a Proclamation, and that this Proclamation should precede the assembly of the electoral colleges in Paris, which has been summoned by Bonaparte. This desire is also that of the majority of the Powers. It is thought of the utmost importance that your Majesty should rally all parties to yourself by assuring them, without distinction, all the benefits of a constitutional Government. The Powers would consider a Proclamation of this kind issued by your Majesty as a powerful auxiliary to the forces they are bringing into the field. Several of them also wish that your Majesty, making your ministers responsible for the faults which may have been committed, would constitute a new ministry, just as if you were in France, the members of which would offer the requisite guarantees to all parties.[13] I have been asked to write this to your Majesty. I have even been told that this desire will be expressed in the suggestions to be made by the ambassadors whom the Powers are about to send to your Majesty, and I should therefore like them to be anticipated by your Majesty.

To all that the Emperor of Russia said to Lord Clancarty I ought to add what has reached me of his language by channels which I have ever reason to think trustworthy.

He has, on several occasions, repeated that when he was in Paris a few months ago, all that he saw and heard made him fear that the Government would not be able to maintain itself. It seemed to him to be difficult for the sentiments and opinions of the princes[14] to be sufficiently in harmony with the opinions and habits of a generation which had been born during their absence, and which on several points had neither the opinions nor the habits of its fathers.

The Emperor, who is fond of generalizing, frequently says that it is impossible to govern in opposition to the ideas of the time. He says that his fears increased when he saw that your Majesty was calling into the ministry and into the royal councils men who were, no doubt, very estimable, but who almost all had spent the period of the Revolution away from France or in retirement, and consequently neither knew France nor were known by her, and were totally wanting in that political experience which even genius cannot make up for. He thinks that they have done great harm to the royal cause, and although he thinks that similar evils will be avoided in future by your Majesty's choosing other advisers, I must add that he remarks that the one of your ministers who excites the most animadversion from all parties is, more than any other, in your Majesty's confidence.[15] He even went so far as to say that the greater part of the mischief proceeds from the power which your Majesty has given to the princes who surround your person, or has suffered them to take;[16] that their unpopularity seems to him to be an irremediable evil; that if your Majesty had been personally unpopular the effect would have been much less disastrous, because discontent against the reigning monarch is tempered and softened by hope in his successor, while if it falls upon the successor that hope cannot exist.

The Emperor often repeats in ordinary conversation that he is quite willing to believe that your Majesty would, if alone, be welcome to France, and be loved and respected there, but that as it is impossible to separate your Majesty from your surroundings,[17] he fears that your throne will never be firmly established.

I have the satisfaction of seeing that all the Powers are sincerely interested in your Majesty; even the Emperor of Russia's language is due more to ill humor and to his philosophical ideas, than to any profound calculation. I wish I could add that this interest extends to Monsieur, and to their Royal Highnesses the Dukes of Angoulême and Berry, but when once power is exclusively concentrated in the hands of your Majesty and of responsible ministers, who will enjoy at the same time your Majesty's confidence and that of the nation, the exaggerated impressions produced both within and without the country by past errors and inadvertencies, will be gradually effaced.

The Baron de Talleyrand has arrived here with the letter with which your Majesty has honored me, dated April 10th.

I am continually stimulating activity here, and urging the importance of haste. But the Duke of Wellington, in a letter subsequent to the one your Majesty did me the honor to mention, writes that, in consequence of the bad news from the south, he feels the necessity of postponing operations until the Powers are able to attack on all points and with larger forces. Now, the distances are so enormous that, with all the good-will in the world, it is impossible for the Austrians to assemble a hundred thousand men on the Rhine until the end of May.

Your Majesty will be glad to hear that the Austrian troops in Italy have obtained victories which promise still more important ones. Prince Leopold[18] will leave in a few days to join the Austrian army. The Viennese newspapers have at last left off writing "King Joachim;" they say simply "Murat."

M. de Blombelles, formerly Portuguese Minister, now a canon at Glogau, and father of the Blombelles who was in Paris, would like to re-enter the diplomatic service in any capacity, from that of ambassador to that of *chargé d'affaires*. He thinks that he might be useful as *chargé d'affaires* at Munich, and he thinks that he could live there on a salary of eight thousand francs.

I am taking advantage of M. de Noailles' kindness to transmit this despatch, which he will have the honor of delivering to your Majesty.

He has been very useful here in many ways, and I think that there is no one who could give your Majesty better information on the military and political condition of all the Cabinets whose assistance is now so urgently needed by us. I entreat your Majesty to confide to him all the orders you desire to transmit to me. He ought to return hither before the end of the Congress; and the affairs of Germany and Italy, which must be terminated, advance so slowly that he will arrive in good time to affix his signature.

I am, etc.

NOTES TO LETTER XCI.

1. The Order of the Holy Ghost, instituted by Henry III. The cross was suspended by a blue watered silk ribbon.

2. "On his arrival at St. Petersburg M. de Caulaincourt at first was greatly embarrassed. The murder of the Duc d'Enghien had left a stain on his forehead. The Empress-Mother would not receive him. . . . The Czar received him kindly, and gradually took a liking to him, which in the end grew into a real friendship."—Memoirs of Madame de Rémusat, tom. iii. p. 273.

3. The Duc de Vicenza gave in his adhesion to the acts of the Senate and the Constitution of the 6th of April, on the 16th of April.

4. On the 1st of April, 1814, the Emperor Alexander declared, in the name of the Allied Powers, that he would recognize and guarantee the Constitution which France would adopt. Talleyrand, who during all that time inspired Alexander, thought that he was re-establishing a legitimate monarchy with the aid of the nation, the King, and the laws. Being always in favor of a constitutional monarchy, he demanded at this time a Constitution, a Declaration of Rights, a Charter by which the King himself should be bound—not a Charter *wrung from the King*, but one that was to be drawn up and voted beforehand. And, in fact, it was only on the 6th of April, after the vote of the Constitution, that Louis Stanislas Xavier, *brother of the late King* (Louis XVII. is obviously and purposely omitted), yielded to the wish of the French nation: "He shall be proclaimed *King of the French* as soon as he has sworn fidelity to the new Constitution." As yet there was no mention of the "kingdom of Navarre" or the "grace of God."

Here is what M. Henri Martin says with great wisdom of this Constitution:

"The public neither liked nor esteemed the Senate, which was natural enough after the behavior of the latter under the Empire; and saw nothing in this Constitution but the principles of hereditary right and pensions to the senators. Political interest, which had been stifled by the Empire, was not yet thoroughly awake, and the people did not understand that to turn the Senate into ridicule was to play into the hands of the Émigrés; it was not understood that the Senate, however unworthy, was at this time defending the principles and the rights of the nation. It was not, however, the admirers of the Empire; it was the old opposition, the men of the Revolution—such as Lanjuinais, Lambrecht, Garat, Grégoire—who sustained the leading part in the debate."—Martin's "History of France," tom. iv. p. 96.

It was the arrival of the Comte d'Artois which destroyed the work attempted by the constitutionalists, and drove the Restoration into the road which led successively to Ghent and Goritz.

We shall see that after the Hundred Days, M. Durbach, in the sitting of the

Chamber of Deputies of the 29th of June, 1815, accused Louis XVIII. of having despised the constitutional throne offered to him by the nation.

5. "M. de Chateaubriand is astonished that there are no records; Madame de Staël is always of the opinion of the malcontents; Benjamin (Constant) scatters praises, but praise dies in a grimace on his lips. This is what our Paris is like now. France wants peace, but the army wants Belgium."—Jaucourt to Talleyrand, 20th January, 1815.

6. "Your old diplomatic phalanx is much neglected; its members all trust to you, and believe that the present system has set them on one side. I assure you that an ancient name, when it is borne by a man of your ability, will always preserve its value, but the time for fools of quality is passed."—Jaucourt to Talleyrand, 1815.

7. "Patriotism decided Carnot upon accepting the post of Minister of the Interior. The year before, he assisted Napoleon in defending the country. He did still more in 1815; he abjured all his past career by entering the Imperial Government. He was convinced that every nerve must be strained in the defence of France, and no other consideration could move him."—H. Martin, tom. iv. p. 137.

8. "We ought to have accurate information as to all that is going on. This evening I put M. d'André, who is at Brussels, at the King's service; but the proper means are not taken to obtain information, and we are reduced to reports which are falsified. . . . The devil himself could not persuade M. de Blacas to give me the newspapers, which are rigorously excluded here!"—Ghent, Jaucourt to Talleyrand, 2nd April, 1815.

9. "The measures taken by Bonaparte's Government ever since he reached Paris, the men who compose his ministry, the manner in which every possible means is taken to force public opinion, prove that Bonaparte is under the influence of all that are left of the old revolutionary parties in France, and that it is from them alone that he derives all his power of action in the country. Nevertheless, it is notorious that not one of these parties, or of the men of whom they are composed, really likes Bonaparte, because they know perfectly well that if he succeeds in consolidating his authority, he will soon tear from them, as he did when he for the first time seized the reins of government, the share of power which he is obliged to give them now that he is in need of their support. It is, therefore, evident that they joined him only because they saw no other way of escaping from a system in which they were deprived of all share in politics, and in which they thought they had ever reason to fear for their personal security. But I do not doubt but that they would be among the first to overthrow Bonaparte if the Government which is to succeed him would offer them guarantees on which they could perfectly rely, which would not only deliver them from all anxiety, but would hold out baits to their ambition. All the Powers agree in thinking this, and they consequently wish that the King should endeavor, by means of a proclamation to precede the assembling of the electoral colleges whom Bonaparte has summoned to Paris, to rally all parties round his standard by promising to them all, without distinction, every advantage attached to a constitutional Government. The Powers would consider a royal proclamation in this sense as a powerful auxiliary to the forces they are about to employ. Many of them also wish that the King, making his ministers responsible for all the blunders which have been committed, would appoint a new ministry, just as if he were in France, composed of men whose nomination would afford sufficient guarantees to every party. I am writing to the

King by the Count de Noailles, who will take this letter on the same manner to you. As I know the ministers who will be sent to the King by foreign Courts will also speak of it to him, I should wish his Majesty to anticipate by a resolution in accordance with the suggestion I have just had the honor of proposing to you, all that they may say to him, and I beg of you to do all in your power to persuade the King to adopt this resolution. . . .

"I told you that Murat had failed in his attempts to cross the Po; he has since been repulsed from its banks and pursued. In the last place he was turned out of Bologna, and General Bianchi obtained a decisive victory over him. The affairs in Italy are going on well."—Talleyrand to Jaucourt, 22nd April, 1815.

10. "The Chevalier Charles Stuart (ambassador from Great Britain to the King Louis XVIII.) called on me yesterday evening. . . .

"He insisted on the objections to acting entirely on foreign ground and of assuming (this was his expression) an *attitude of emigration*. . . . We declare that we are making war on Bonaparte; we declare that we are not making it on the French nation; therefore, when once Bonaparte has fallen, we shall have no other *common cause* for war. Bonaparte retorts to our declaration that he is the choice of the nation; that to make war on him is really to make war on France, and above all to make war for the sake of replacing Louis XVIII. on the throne and inflicting him for the second time on the nation. In order to restrict himself to the prescribed limits, Lord Castlereagh was obliged to speak as he did, and his speech announces the only principles that we can publicly avow. Nevertheless our wishes as well as our endeavors are in favor of the King; we desire his success—we do not doubt it; but we cannot escape from the conditions of the treaty and the declaration of the Powers."—Jaucourt to Talleyrand, 25th April, 1815.

In the sitting of the House of Commons of the 26th of April, Lord Castlereagh communicated the Memorandum relating to the treaty of the 25th of March, and positively denied all intention of imposing a definitive Government in France.

Lord Liverpool made a similar announcement on the 27th, in the House of Lords, and asserted that England had not promised to re-establish the House of Bourbon.

11. The allied sovereigns had thought of it for a short time in 1814. It is well known that Napoleon, when he started on the campaign in France, himself gave the regency to Marie Louise, with King Joseph as lieutenant-general.

12. "The Bourbons end with the King and make a new beginning with the Duke of Orleans. This is true; but the King is neither aware nor willing to believe in all that ought to be done to justify his re-establishment—the apprehensions of the purchasers of forfeited estates, the strain put upon the Concordat, etc. There must be pamphlets, articles in the newspapers, and publicity. The King has been received from the hands of foreigners. If he is to be accepted as a condition of peace, he will never be re-established. Do you think that Bonaparte was re-established by the love of his soldiers? No, he was elected. The 'grace of God,' 'the 19th year of his reign'—all this shocks and disgusts. If he is determined to owe nothing to us, he will get nothing. Look at the tricks of Napoleon! with his usual Machiavellism he is going to give us an Assembly in May."—Ostend, Jaucourt to Talleyrand, 27th May, 1815.

"Lally and M. de Chateaubriand cry you mercy, and are writing or rewriting to you; for they have all written to you. The Court party, which draws nearer and nearer to the King, whispers that you must be Prime Minister; Monsieur's followers say the same thing, especially lately, when we hear the Duke of Orleans' name on all sides. M. de Chateaubriand, who was consulted on this point, proposed to send for the duke and make him generalissimo of our armies; this is rather romantic. It would be, no doubt, perfectly safe, as regards the heart and the sense of duty characteristic of this prince, to put ourselves to such an extent in his hands; but he is so popular with the army that it would be perhaps giving him a too easy and too dangerous power of distinguishing himself.''—Ghent, Jaucourt to Talleyrand, 6th May, 1815.

13. "All that you tell me, my dear Prince, on the necessity of a Cabinet is very true, very right, very urgent, very impossible. I do not know what your fortunate and honorable return, your superiority, and your wish to establish a ministerial system similar to that of England, might effect; but just now, what we must try for is, instead of a patched-up union which gives only an appearance of unanimity, to have a free opposition which will give opportunities for a criticism which will oblige all parties to be careful and to do their best. The responsibility of Ministers will be effected by eager debate in the Chambers, by petitions and denunciations, and not at all by a strict law which no one will have the courage to propose in the Cabinet or the wisdom to pass in the Chambers."—Jaucourt to Talleyrand, 25th February, 1815.

14. Count d'Artois and the Dukes of Angoulême and Berry. "The travels of the young princes and princesses are unpopular. Great expense, a great many complaints, many prejudices—this is what they will spend and bring back. Louis (the Minister of Finance) must take care."—Jaucourt to Talleyrand, 5th February, 1815.

15. "The King will write to you through the Duc de Blacas, for it is he who writes for the King, and when he came to visit me he had already your letter to the King in his pocket. I was alone with the King, as you may suppose, when I delivered the letter. . . . You may judge, therefore, of what the King said to Blacas. Perhaps he thought that if he wrote a few lines to you with his own hand you would answer them; and you know that unless you put a separate sheet in your letter, the King would be very much embarrassed to avoid giving it all to Blacas.

"Every one who comes from France cries out on Blacas as if he were a ravening wolf."—Ghent, Jaucourt to Talleyrand, 2nd May, 1815.

16. "In this circumstance, as in every other, we feel the fatal effect of the influence of the princes, who are always patronizing, always at work, always interfering, and often ordering."—Jaucourt to Talleyrand, 2nd May, 1815.

"The King received a list from the Duc de Feltre; he said that he would think it over at his leisure. Every time that the King thinks at his leisure, Monsieur thinks with him. I know that it has been said at Monsieur's that it was necessary that Monsieur should have at least one person devoted to him, who would tell him all that passed in the Cabinet and in the King's Council when he was not present. My dear friend, if you do not arrive, invulnerable and armed at all points, they will circumvent you, and the King's cause will be lost."—Jaucourt to Talleyrand, 11th May, 1815.

17. "All irritation turns to the benefit of Jacobinism, but while everything is done to irritate, it is all done unwittingly. There are twenty people who worry, who are in the way, who are ubiquitous, and who wish to be a body, a power in the State."—Jaucourt to Talleyrand, 28th February, 1815

18. Leopold Jean Joseph, Prince of Salerno.

LETTER XCII.

No. 53.

Vienna, 1st May, 1815.

SIRE,

Baron de Vincent starts to-day to join your Majesty, and he is kind enough to take charge of the letters I have the honor of writing.

Murat, when he commenced hostilities, counted on a rising of the Italian populations, but his expectations have been completely deceived; in this belief he advanced to the banks of the Po, where the first engagement took place. Since then he has had nothing but defeats. He is retreating in all haste towards the kingdom of Naples, in fear lest he should be cut off by an Austrian force which is in Tuscany. The last engagement of which we have received any official intelligence, occurred at Cesena, where he recrossed the Ronco and suffered considerable losses. His army, already much diminished by the prisoners that have been taken, to the number of seven thousand, diminishes every day through desertion. There is every reason to hope that this war will soon be over. The advantage of replacing King Ferdinand IV. on his throne will not be the only one that we shall derive from the fall of Murat. By setting free the troops employed against him, and by removing all uneasiness as to the maintenance of peace in Italy, it will greatly facilitate operations against Bonaparte. It will also produce an immense effect in France, by showing to everybody that no Power in Europe will endure these new dynasties founded on violence and injustice, and that all Europe is determined to overthrow them.[1] These are the fruits of our efforts in supporting the principle of legitimacy.

This principle is now explicitly recognized.[2] A treaty has just been signed by Prince Metternich and the Commander Ruffo, King Ferdinand IV.'s minister at Vienna. This treaty stipulates the subvention to be furnished by Sicily in the war against Murat. Instead of the twenty millions which your Majesty intended to give for this war, King Ferdinand, I am told, promises twenty-five millions. My next despatches will inform your Majesty as to the stipulations of the treaty, which I have not yet been able to see.

Prince Leopold of the Two Sicilies leaves on the 4th of this month for the Austrian head-quarters.

Although the affairs of Parma are not yet terminated, the Emperor of Austria has published an edict, in which he assumes in his daughter's name the definitive administration of the three duchies.[3] Your Majesty will perceive by this that the arrangements the Congress was to decide upon are executed before they are discussed, which is very objectionable, but which we are not powerful enough to prevent.

The Austrian and Russian troops are marching forward. The head-quarters of Prince Schwarzenberg is at Heilbrunn, in Würtemberg, and the Prince himself left yesterday for that place. He will pass through Bohemia, where he will stay for only a few days.

The arrangements with Bavaria, which I had announced to your Majesty as finished, but which were not signed, have, after having occasioned new discussions, at last been agreed on. Their settlement, however, could be only eventual. They will not be definitively arranged until after the war, because they must be subordinate to the negotiations with the Courts of Baden and Darmstadt, which are to make cessions to Bavaria, for which they are to be indemnified on the left bank of the Rhine; and these Courts do not care to receive concessions of which the chances of war, should they be unpropitious, might deprive them.

The Danish minister, General Waltersdorf, is to start on the day after to-morrow on his mission to your Majesty. He, as well as Baron de Vincent, is accredited as an envoy to the Duke of Wellington. I am, etc.

NOTES TO LETTER XCII.

1. "The King sent for me before the Council; he rose and said, 'I am sending the Count de Noailles off at once; it is absolutely necessary that Prince Talleyrand should come. I am writing this to him; I tell him that I want him very much, I wish to see him. You know that he writes to me on a great many points which he will discuss when he comes.'

"At the Council was read a royal proclamation, proposed by Pozzo, looked over by M. de Pradel, revised, altered, and settled by the King. There is one very ingenious passage in it; it is that the King sets forth, as an act of his own co-operation in the treaty, the engagement taken by the Powers not to interfere in the Government to be established in France after the fall of Bonaparte."
—Jaucourt to Talleyrand, 6th May, 1815.

2. See D'Angeberg, p. 1156.

3. Parma, Piacenza, and Guastalla.

LETTER XCIII.

THE KING TO PRINCE TALLEYRAND.

No 4 from Ghent.

5th May, 1815.

My Cousin,

I received your No. 52 by M. de Noailles. I add to this despatch the proclamation which I am about to publish, and which, I flatter myself, will be as much approved by the sovereigns as it has been by the ministers who are with me here. But this subject, however important, is not the most important of all. There is another point in your despatch which, ever since I received it, has been, and continues to be, the subject of my most serious reflections; in order to come to a final decision, I need wise counsels, and it is impossible to give them by letter. I told you to join me as soon as you had signed the final act of the Congress in my name; but I now feel more impatient to see you. Therefore, unless this signature is likely to detain you for only two or three days at the utmost, start without waiting for it. It is of very little consequence which of my plenipotentiaries signs the treaty, but it is of great consequence that I should have you at my side.[1]

On which, etc.

NOTE TO LETTER XCIII.

1. "Come to us. When you come you will be able to do as you like; but if once measures have been taken in contradiction to your views and projects, it is you who will be obliged to make concessions, arrangements, and take half measures. Your Cabinet must be very strong, very national, thoroughly in accordance with public opinion."—Jaucourt to Talleyrand, 30th April, 1815.

"You cannot judge from where you are of the need of your presence here. The Court is acquiring a likeness to Coblenz, which will drive away, first me, and then all who are loyal to France and the King, and who repudiate the idea of emigration. Come with a Cabinet already settled, or even without a Cabinet, but speak in the name of a Cabinet. . . . You are surrounded at present with an aureole of glory from the Congress; you possess the omnipotence of an extraordinary political career; you will arrive in the name of all the sovereigns, with a caduceus in your hand. But if you allow the Congress to terminate before you come, after every one has discussed, examined, pulled to pieces, and conjectured, and set on foot all the petty intrigues that fools understand so well, you will not have half your influence. . . .

"Chevalier Stuart is so convinced of the necessity for your arrival that he said to me, 'You may be certain that if he does not come, it is because he prefers an agreeable and comfortable position to any other.'"—Jaucourt to Talleyrand, 2nd May, 1815.

"Pozzo says that you can be useful, necessary, the saviour of the King and his cause, only by coming here; that you have terminated the affairs of the Congress with glory; that the departure of the sovereigns from Vienna will not allow you to remain there; that their position is becoming warlike, and is no longer in harmony with yours.

"The Court party, which is becoming more and more identified with the King, whispers that you must be Prime Minister; Monsieur's people say the same thing, especially lately, when the name of the Duke of Orleans has been heard on all sides; M. de Blacas makes loud protestations of disinterestedness; and as for the Chancellor Dambray, he does not know what to be at."—Jaucourt to Talleyrand, 6th May, 1815.

LETTER XCIV.

No. 54.

Vienna, 5th May, 1815.

SIRE,

A former Chamberlain of Bonaparte's, M. de Stassart, who, having accompanied the Archduchess Marie Louise hither, became a Chamberlain of the Emperor Francis, and some time ago had returned to Paris, has lately been sent thence, bearing a letter from Bonaparte for the Emperor, and one from M. de Caulaincourt for Prince Metternich. Protected by his title of Chamberlain, he got as far as Munich; but he was arrested there, and the letters in his charge have been sent hither. Both these letters urge, from different motives, the return of the Archduchess and her son. The turn taken by Bonaparte and his ministers is one of moderation and affection. The letters remained sealed till the moment of the conference; they were opened in the presence of the ministers of the Allied Powers. It was decided that they should remain unanswered. Opinion was unanimous. Your Majesty may see, therefore, that every attempt, of whatever kind, on the part of Bonaparte to enter into relations with foreign Powers, is repulsed and remains fruitless.

The English ministers, to whom I applied for obtaining the pecuniary supplies needed by your Majesty's mission to the Congress, and who had acceded willingly to my request, have received letters from their Government, authorizing them to advance no more than a hundred thousand francs at six months' date.[1]

Our credit on the Bank of France, which was far from being exhausted, has been suspended from the 21st of March. This arrangement debits us with the expenses incurred, and which ought to have been paid on the 1st of April. The members of the embassy have received no payments from Paris since January.

The most reduced expenditure for the months of April and May, without including arrears, will consume a good part of the sum which was promised to us by the English Government, and the rest will only take us on to the beginning of August. Your Majesty will consider what arrangements it will be possible to make at that period.

I am, etc.

NOTE TO LETTER XCIV.

1. "M. de Blacas has only four million five hundred thousand francs here; the eight millions which he hoped to pass in bills of exchange have been stopped at Perregaux' and refused in England."—Jaucourt to Talleyrand, 26th April, 1815.

LETTER XCV.

No. 55.

Vienna, 14th May, 1815.

Sire,

The Count de Noailles has just arrived, and has delivered to me the letter with which your Majesty has honored me, dated the 5th of May. His arrival is followed so closely by the departure of the courier of whom I have to take advantage, that I can only have the honor of writing a very short letter to your Majesty.

My anxiety to find myself at your Majesty's side would make me start to-morrow, if affairs were sufficiently advanced to render only my signature necessary, or if the termination of the Congress were still in the distance. But the Italian questions are not yet settled, although they soon will be. The delay in settling these is detaining M. de Saint-Marson and the Commander Ruffo here for a few days longer, although the departure of the latter is very urgent, and the former has been summoned to Turin, where he occupies the post of Minister of War.

Besides these reasons, the sovereigns will soon leave Vienna, and as in a coalition every step is liable to a thousand misinterpretations, I could not leave before their departure without more inconvenience than advantage accruing to your Majesty's affairs; and at any rate the difference, taking into consideration the preparations I see are being made, will be of only forty-eight hours, more or less. Indeed,

I do not think that it is possible, in our position, to leave at a time when every one needs urging forward.[1]

I have had rather a long conversation with the Emperor Alexander, which I shall have the honor of reporting to your Majesty. I must only say now that his language was very favorable—that he spoke very earnestly and properly of our affairs. His opinion is that, for the present, a passive attitude is the one suitable to your Majesty, and to those who are about you. He is particularly anxious to make it clear that every step taken by any one Power with a view to the common good, or entailing a danger common to all, should be undertaken in concert with all the others. This was the chief object of the mission to the different armies; and he hopes that this rule will be adopted by your Majesty.

I am, etc.

NOTE TO LETTER XCV.

1. "I will join the King as soon as the Congress is over. But it seems to me that, as it will last only a week or a fortnight longer, it would be inconsistent in me, and extremely hurtful in every respect to the interests of the King, if I were to withdraw. Nothing, in my opinion, is more important to the King, under present circumstances, than the conclusion of an act in which the whole of Europe takes part; and it is of the greatest possible interest to the whole of Europe, and nothing is more calculated to make an impression on the mind of every nation, and on that of his Majesty's subjects, than seeing this act signed by his ambassador just as if the King were enjoying his full and legitimate authority without any obstacle or opposition. Besides this, it does not seem to me that there is any difficulty in the King's present position. His part is to be entirely passive, for he ought not to appear to take any active share in the aggression which is preparing against his kingdom while under the yoke of Bonaparte. It will not become an active one until after the allied troops have entered France, and his Majesty will have to interfere in order to prevent with all his might the violence and vexations which are unfortunately inseparable from war, and to diminish as much as possible the evils by which it is always accompanied. But the King must give no loophole for thinking that it is for his sake, in defence of his interests, that this war is undertaken. It would render him hateful. And, in fact, it is certain that the foreign Powers are making this war much less for his sake, than because they think their peace and safety compromised as long as the power of France is in the hands of Bonaparte. It seems, then, advisable that the royal princes should not join the army, and that even the French troops who surround the King should not be employed aggressively, but should be set only to occupy the recovered provinces, to maintain order and to protect life and property in them, and at most to repulse the attacks of Bonaparte's partisans.

"As for the proposals from Paris, I think that for the present we must content ourselves with listening to them and waiting."—Talleyrand to Jaucourt, 13th May, 1815.

LETTER XCVI.

No. 56.

Vienna, 17th May, 1815.

Sire,

In place of the second declaration which was proposed, and which I had the honor of mentioning several times to your Majesty, it has been arranged to substitute a report which will answer the same object. This report will be published to-morrow in the *Gazette de Vienne*,[1] and afterwards in the different newspapers of Germany and other countries; it has likewise been printed by the press of the Austrian Chancellerie. I have the honor of sending several copies to your Majesty.

Your Majesty will see that this report fully confirms the disposition manifested by the Powers in the Declaration of the 13th of March—that it refutes the sophistries of Bonaparte and exposes his impostures. But it will, above all, strike your Majesty that Europe does not profess to be making war for the sake of or by the demand of your Majesty. Europe makes war for her own sake; her own interests depend upon it; her safety demands it. Not only is this the only true aspect of the war, but, furthermore, it is believed by everybody to be the only one suitable to your Majesty. It is the only one which will not place your Majesty in a false position with your own subjects, for nothing could contribute so much to their alienation as a wrong opinion on the cause of the war. They must never attribute the evils which war is about to bring on them to your Majesty.

I am, etc.

P.S.—In obedience to your Majesty's commands, I have written to the Legations of the sovereigns and archdukes who are here to ask for my dismissal.

I send to M. de Jaucourt some letters from M. de la Tour de Pin, which may interest your Majesty. M. d'Osmond's letter, in which they are enclosed, gives some details on the late proceedings in Italy.

NOTE TO LETTER XCVI.

1. For this report of the 13th of May, see Martens, New Series, vol. ii. No. 263

LETTER XCVII.

No. 57.

Vienna, 23rd May, 1815.

SIRE,

In my farewell audience I received from all the sovereigns proofs of the most friendly sentiments towards your Majesty. These audiences were not merely formal; they were much longer than those which are usually granted in similar circumstances. I shall have the honor of reporting what passed to your Majesty. Although all was not finished, my anxiety to be with your Majesty had determined me on starting to-morrow, but Prince Metternich and M. de Nesselrode, as well as the Chancellor Hardenberg, urged me to sign the protocols which contain the arrangements settled by the Congress, together with all the principal members. I thought I ought to accede to their wish, as my departure will be postponed by it only for two days. These protocols will contain the definitive text, with the exception of some slight modifications which will concern only the modes of expressing the articles composing the instrument settled by the Congress. A Commission, to consist of a plenipotentiary from each Power, will be left here, to put the articles in proper order and separate those that refer to particular interests from those that concern the general interest. I shall leave M. de Dalberg here to represent France in this Commission. This work will not take more than eight or ten days, if the delegates will work a little faster than their chiefs have done.

I have the honor of enclosing to your Majesty two letters from the Duc d'Angoulême. I have had the honor of writing one to him which is probably lost. Some day we shall perhaps see it in the French newspapers.[1]

I have sent to Lord Castlereagh by to-day's courier a letter from the Duchesse d'Angoulême. In order that your Majesty may have a complete collection of my voluminous correspondence, I have the honor of enclosing copies of the letters which I expect have not reached their destination.

If no unforeseen obstacle arise, I shall be at Ghent, at your Majesty's disposal, on Sunday, the 4th.[2]

I am, etc.

NOTES TO LETTER XCVII.

1. The *Moniteur Universel* had published the letters addressed to the Duc d'Angoulême which were found at the Tuileries on the return of Napoleon.

2. "Your Highness left us on Sunday, the 11th of the month. It was not until that day that the great act of the Congress, enriched at the last moment by a dozen additional articles, was definitely settled."—Gentz to Talleyrand, 16th June, 1815.

LETTER XCVIII.

No. 58.

Vienna, 27th May, 1815.

SIRE,

I can now tell your Majesty all the fears I have experienced during the last week. The question was raised whether the circumstances which oblige us to leave some points unsettled ought not to determine us to put off the signature of the act to some future time.[1] A rather powerful intrigue was on foot for this purpose. The object was to call in question points which were already decided, and to come to no resolution on others which were still undecided. There was nothing more essential to your Majesty's interests than for your name to be placed in an act which was to proclaim the union of all the Powers. I was therefore bound to strain every nerve to attain this object. I was very well seconded by the English and Austrian ministers. The signature will take place to-morrow or the day after.

I have the honor of sending your Majesty a Declaration addressed by the Swiss Diet to the ministers accredited to it, and a convention signed between those ministers and the ministers of Switzerland. Your Majesty will see that, although Switzerland seems in this Declaration to wish to preserve her neutrality, her intention, which is clearly expressed in the convention, is nevertheless to do all that can be expected of her in the cause of Europe. Urgent necessity, of which the generals of the coalition must judge, will authorize the passage of the allied troops through the Swiss territories. In all the letters received here yesterday by the different foreign ministers, Baron Auguste de Talleyrand's endeavors for attaining this salutary end have been highly praised.

Both from a moral and a military point of view, the conduct of Switzerland is considered by the Allied Powers to have been highly useful.

I shall not again have the honor of writing to your Majesty from Vienna; I am just starting, and shall myself lay the assurances of my respect and devotion at the feet of your Majesty.

I carry no documents with me. I am, etc.

NOTE TO LETTER XCVIII.

1. "I am alarmed by a proposal which is said, my dear Prince, to be yours. It is reported that there is to be no signature. Before taking an irrevocable decision, let me tell you that it is of the highest importance for the cause of the King, for the opinion that will be held in France as to her position in relation to the Allied Powers, for the opinion which will be formed in France of the union between the Powers, for the dignity of the Congress—that something shou d be signed. When once articles have been settled and signed, one may leave the final arrangement to the plenipotentiaries of the different Courts. But if the protocols are not signed it will be thought that there are hesitations, and the moral force of the coalition will be considerably diminished. Adieu, dear Prince. Always yours, Talleyrand."—To Prince Metternich.

XCIX.[1]

CONGRESS OF VIENNA.

May, 1815.

The Powers who had made common cause with France in the war terminated by the treaty of the 30th of May, 1814, had agreed on such arrangements for the negotiations of the Congress as would have reduced France to playing an entirely passive part.

The majority had pretensions to which they were well aware that France must be opposed. They wished to neutralize her opposition, and for this reason they tried to attach suspicion to her motives. She was supposed to have ambitious projects; she was accused of wanting to recover the left bank of the Rhine and Belgium. It was reported that her ambassadors were furnished with double instructions; that they professed great disinterestedness; that they talked of nothing but justice and principle, but that their object was to sow discord between the *Allies*. Austria, Russia, England, and Prussia continued to call themselves by this name. The spirits of the coalition had survived the peace, and seemed even to have acquired new strength.

The French embassy, against which public opinion had been raised by these means, found itself completely isolated. It was almost a crime to have anything to do with it. No one dared to visit its members; the ministers of some petty Courts were reprimanded and threatened for having done so. One of the sovereigns at Vienna asked a member of the Portuguese embassy if he ever saw

Talleyrand. "Sometimes," was the reply. "And I also," said the king, "should like to see him, but I dare not."

This state of things continued for two months and a half. The ministers of the four Powers negotiated with each other, exchanged Notes which they concealed from France, and held conferences at which her representatives were not present.

Russia wanted to have the whole, or nearly the whole, of the duchy of Warsaw; to give it special institutions, and to make it a sort of phantom of Poland. This would be, said Russia, a sort of expiation for the partition of that kingdom; it would pave the way for the civilization of all the old Polish provinces and for their future independence.

Prussia supported these views of Russia, and wanted nothing for herself in Poland, being well aware that as, in agreement with the treaty of alliance, her power was to be restored to what it had been in 1805, it would become necessary to compensate her for the Polish subjects she had lost by giving her German subjects.

She asked, and Russia asked for her, the whole of Saxony. Lord Castlereagh, in a Note of the 10th of October, and Prince Metternich, in a Note of the 22nd, consented: the former, on condition that Prussia, whom he wished to make extremely powerful, should stipulate for her ancient rights over the duchy of Warsaw, and should take Saxony, not as a compensation, but by way of an increase of power; the latter, with the sole reservation of the arrangements to be made as to the military frontiers of the two States.

The fate of Saxony, therefore, seemed to have been irrevocably fixed in the month of October, yet the French ambassador was still ignorant of this transaction in December. A plan had been conceived of uniting Austria, Prussia, and Holland, including the Netherlands, the States of Germany, and even the Swiss Confederation, in a close and perpetual league. The chief object was to isolate France in Europe—to surround her with States in which it would be impossible for her to find one ally. The way had already been prepared for the execution of this plan, by obliging Spain to promise that the ancient family compact should never be renewed under any circumstances.

But as at the same time they wanted this league to serve as a barrier against Russia, it was necessary to detach Prussia from Russia, which they could not effect, and to obtain from Russia the voluntary or involuntary renunciation of her designs on the duchy of Warsaw. Every means of persuasion was employed without effect; and as for force, both England and Austria were well aware that they were not sufficiently strong to act against Russia and Prussia combined.

In this state of affairs France ought naturally to have encouraged the resistance of Russia, by showing her perfect indifference to the solution of a question discussed without her concurrence, and by offering at the same time her assistance to the other Powers. But as the Powers could not have accepted this offer without renouncing their favorite idea of isolating France, it only raised their apprehensions, and caused assistance from such a quarter to be regarded as a remedy worse than the disease. They were alarmed at the idea of seeing a French army reappear, even as an auxiliary or an ally, in the countries which the French had so often overrun as conquerors. These apprehensions were increased and fed by many publications which appeared in Paris. Nevertheless the French embassy succeeded in allaying them by patience, moderation, and good sense.

A treaty of alliance between France, Austria, and England was concluded on the 3rd of January, to which the Low Countries, Bavaria, and Hanover acceded. The coalition was thenceforward entirely dissolved, and France had no longer to fear being imprisoned in the iron circle which the Powers were preparing to draw round her.

This alone would have been much, even if France had derived no further advantage from her presence at the Congress. But this treaty caused a complete change in the position of the French embassy: on all sides advances were eagerly made to us. Those who had formerly repelled us now sought for our advice or support, and France found herself in the possession of the part which either Russia or England might have played, the former if she had been disinterested, the latter if she had cared, but which both these Powers allowed to escape them. In fact, the English Parliament made this a matter of reproach to Lord Castlereagh.

Had Austria been less timid, and Lord Castlereagh less anxious to preserve peace, the treaty of the 3rd of January might have led to the re-establishment of Poland and the preservation of the whole of the kingdom of Saxony. As it is, Russia has been obliged to relinquish the half of her claims upon the duchy of Warsaw, and Saxony has been as it were dragged from the grave, not, it is true, unscathed, but nevertheless with a territory equal to that of the kingdom of Hanover or Würtemberg, and this she certainly owes to France.

The French ambassador was instructed to use his utmost endeavors—

1. That Prussia should not be placed in contact with France. The frontiers of the two countries will nowhere touch.

2. That Prussia should not acquire Luxemburg and Mayence. She will have neither; both will be federal fortresses.

3. That her influence in Germany should not become exclusive, nor too predominant. This, indeed, was the principal object intended to be accomplished by the federal organization, which, however, there was no time to carry into effect.

4. That the organization of Switzerland should remain as it was; and it remains so.

5. That the independence of Switzerland should be secured; and it is secured.

6. That in all future European wars Switzerland should enjoy permanent neutrality, which is as essential to French as to Swiss interests. This neutrality has been guaranteed.

There was reason to fear that when, as is likely soon to happen, the reigning branch of the House of Savoy becomes extinct, Austria might take advantage of the marriage of one of the Archdukes with the eldest daughter of the present king, and claim the inheritance of the House of Savoy for the Archduke. The French ambassador was instructed to take care that the rights of the Carignan branch were recognized and respected; and they have been.

The foregoing were doubtless the most important points for France in the then situation of Europe and of France herself. To obtain them all her efforts were therefore directed, and at first she had small hope of succeeding. Yet when the event happened, which brought about the present war, the French embassy had obtained them all.

As Austria, in the person of her sovereign, or of the princes of his house, must always possess almost the whole of Upper, and part of the centre of Italy, French interests indisputably require that Austrian influence should not, either directly or indirectly, be predominant over the whole of Italy. It was the duty, therefore, of the French embassy, in the interests of France, and without respect of persons, to endeavor to re-establish in Italy an influence which, in the state of affairs in Europe at that time, might be backed by external support, and serve as a balance to the influence of Austria. The conduct of the King of Naples has contributed more towards accomplishing this object than any wishes of the House of Bourbon, for by his ill-timed aggression he has destroyed his excellent chance of preserving his throne. The approach of hostilities, which obliges the sovereigns to leave Vienna, prevents the construction of the political organization of Germany; the foundations of it only will therefore be laid, and the work will be subsequently finished at a Diet.

NOTE.

1. This paper is entirely in conformity with No. 9 of tom. cccviii., "France and the States of Europe," entitled, "Memorandum on the Conduct of the French Embassy at the Congress of Vienna," drawn up by M. de la Besnardière, *attaché* of the embassy.

LETTER C.

REPORT PRESENTED TO THE KING DURING HIS JOURNEY FROM GHENT TO PARIS.[1]

June, 1815.

SIRE,

In April, 1814, France was occupied by three hundred thousand foreign troops, to be followed, if necessary, by five hundred thousand more. She had only a handful of soldiers left in the country: they indeed had performed prodigies of valor, but were thoroughly exhausted. She had large forces abroad, but these, being dispersed and without communications, could no longer be of any use to France, nor even assist each other. A portion of these forces was shut up in distant fortresses, which they might hold for a longer or shorter time, but which must necessarily yield to a blockade. Two hundred thousand French soldiers were prisoners of war. In this state of affairs it was absolutely necessary to put an end to hostilities by an armistice, which was declared on the 22nd of April.

This armistice was not only necessary; it was good policy. It was essential that the fear inspired by the strength of the Allies should be followed by confidence; but to effect this it was necessary to give the Allies confidence in the good intentions of France

This armistice deprived France of no present or future advantage, nor of anything that she could have the least hope of keeping. Those who maintain that more favorable conditions of peace might have been obtained if the surrender of the fortresses had been put off until after the conclusion of peace, either do not know or forget that no armistice could possibly have been obtained without the surrender of the fortresses, and that any effort to prolong their occupation would have excited the suspicion of the Allies, and thereby have changed their favorable disposition towards us.

As it was, the disposition of the Allies towards France was all that could be wished; in fact, much better than we had any right to expect. They were welcomed as liberators, and were constrained to justify the praises lavished on their generosity by showing themselves generous. It was all-important to take advantage of this enthusiasm when it was at its height, without allowing it time to calm down. It was not enough merely to have caused a cessation of hostilities; it was necessary that French territory should be evacuated and the interests of France thoroughly settled, leaving no uncertainty as to her future, in order that your Majesty might at once assume your proper position. The signature of peace, therefore, had to be hastened, in order to obtain it on the best terms and with all the possible advantages to be derived from it.

By the treaty of the 30th of May France lost only what she had conquered, and not even all that she had conquered, during the struggle to which it put an end. She was deprived of nothing that was essential to her safety, and she lost only the power of domineering, which had not conduced either to her happiness or to her prosperity, and which was incompatible with the advantages of a durable peace.[2]

In order to come to a right judgment concerning the peace of 1814, we must consider the impression which it made upon the allied nations. At St. Petersburg the Emperor Alexander, and at Berlin the King of Prussia, were received, not merely with coldness, but even with dissatisfaction and murmurs, because the treaty of the 30th of May did not fulfil the expectations of their respective subjects. France having everywhere raised immense war contributions, it was now expected that she would in her turn be treated in the same way; instead of which no demand was made upon her. She retained possession of all the objects of art which she had acquired by conquest, all her monuments and public buildings were respected, and it must be owned that she was treated with a consideration of which history presents no example under similar circumstances.[3]

While all the immediate interests of France were settled, those of the other Powers were left subject to the decisions of a future Congress. France was invited to this Congress, but her plenipotentiaries found on their arrival that the passions and prejudices which should have been extinguished and destroyed by the treaty of the 30th of May, had again been roused after its conclusion, perhaps even in consequence of the incomplete satisfaction given by its provisions to the Powers.

They therefore continued to describe themselves as "allies," just as if the war had still been going on. Their plenipotentiaries having been the first to arrive at Vienna, came to an understanding in writing that the intervention of France in the business of the Congress should be merely formal. The French Legation suspected this from the very first, but could not obtain absolute certainty of the existence of these protocols till four months afterwards.

The substance of two of these protocols, dated the 22nd of September, 1814,[4] and which have been laid before your Majesty, is as follows:

"That the Allied Powers should take the initiative in all the subjects to be discussed" (Austria, Russia, England, and Prussia were alone meant by the term 'Allied Powers'), because these four Powers were those most closely united with one another, both by international treaties and by common object.

"That they alone should come to terms with each other as to the distribution of the provinces to be disposed of; but that France and Spain should be permitted to pronounce their opinions and advance their objections, which should then be discussed in common.

"That the plenipotentiaries of the four Powers should not enter into deliberation with those of the two others on any point relative to the territorial distribution of the duchy of Warsaw, of Germany, and of Italy, until after they had arrived at a unanimous conclusion among themselves with regard to each of these three questions."

It was intended, therefore, that France should play a purely passive part in the Congress; she was to be simply a spectator of what was going on, and to take no active part. She continued to be the object of the mistrust and animosity engendered by the remembrance of the repeated invasions and the still recent calamities which she had inflicted upon Europe. She was still feared, her strength was still formidable, and it was thought that security could be obtained only by setting the whole of Europe in array against her; in fact, it was the coalition over again.

Your Majesty will allow me to take pleasure in the recollection that I always maintained, and endeavored to persuade the most eminent officers in your Majesty's service, that it was in the interest of France and of their own reputations at the present juncture voluntarily to renounce the idea of recovering possession of Belgium and of the left bank of the Rhine. I was of opinion that unless this patriotic sacrifice was made, there could be no peace between France and Europe. And we have seen that, even after France had lost these provinces, so great was her strength that the whole of Europe was kept in a state of alarm and obliged to maintain a hostile attitude.[5] So great is your Majesty's power, that even now, when Europe has attained to the maximum of strength and France is reduced to the minimum, Europe has still misgivings as to the success of the contest in which she is embarked.[6]

My opinion coincided with your Majesty's feeling on this subject; unhappily most of your Majesty's principal servants, many highly respected writers, together with the army and the majority of the nation, did not share in these moderate views, without which any durable peace, or even the semblance of peace, was impossible, and the ambitious disposition, which was not without reason regarded as inherent in the French character, increased and justified the alarm inspired by our strength.[7]

This is why the newspapers were full either of insinuations or of open charges against France and her plenipotentiaries. We were isolated, and hardly a soul dared to associate with us; even the few ministers who did not share in this universal prejudice avoided us, in order not to be compromised in the eyes of others. Their intentions were carefully concealed from us. Meetings were held without our knowledge, and as soon as the sittings of the Congress began, a committee was formed to regulate the federal organization of Germany, each member of which was bound by a solemn promise not to communicate anything that passed to us.

Although your Majesty's Government was not actuated by the motives attributed to them, although they wanted nothing, and were determined to ask for nothing, nevertheless the questions to be brought before the Congress concerned them most materially. Although French interests might differ from the temporary interests of some of the Powers, they were fortunately in accordance with the interests of the majority, and even with the permanent interests of all.

Bonaparte destroyed so many reigning houses, and incorporated in his empire so much territory, and so many distinct populations, that when France ceased to be the enemy of Europe, and retired within the limits to which she would henceforward have to keep in order to remain on terms of peace and amity with other nations, vast countries without any government were found throughout Europe. The States whom he had despoiled without utterly destroying them, could not recover all their lost provinces, because portions of these had passed under the dominion of sovereigns with whom they had themselves entered into alliance. As it was necessary to find a government for the territories vacated by France, it was decided that they should be distributed, by way of indemnity, among the States which had suffered from Bonaparte's depredations.[8]

These allotments of population and territory, repugnant and degrading as they are to humanity, were indispensable, in consequence of the violent usurpations of a Government which employed its strength only in destruction, and thereby necessitated this work of reconstruction out of the fragments which were left.[9]

Saxony was conquered, the kingdom of Naples remained still in the possession of a usurper; the fate of these two States had to be decided.

It was laid down in the Treaty of Paris that the distribution of territories should be such as to establish in Europe a real and permanent balance of power.[10]

Every one of the Powers allowed that it was right to comply with this principle, but the private views of some blinded them as to the means of accomplishing this object.

On the other hand, the balance of power would be established to no purpose if the Congress did not adopt, as one of the foundations of the future tranquillity of Europe, those principles which alone can secure internal tranquillity in individual States, and at the same time protect them from being subject in their mutual relations to the influence of force only.

It was your Majesty's wish, on your return to France, to bring back with you the purest political morality as the rule of your Government. Your Majesty felt that it was necessary that a similar desire should be shared by other Cabinets, and that it should appear in the relations of States with each other. Your Majesty commanded us to use all your royal influence and to devote all our efforts towards causing political morality to be held in honor by assembled Europe. Your Majesty wished that the Restoration should be general.[11]

To this, however, there were many obstacles. The effects of the Revolution were not confined to France. Military conquests extended them to other countries by stirring up the passions of men and producing a general disregard of authority. In Holland and in many parts of Italy the people were accustomed frequently to see revolutionary government take the place of legitimate rule. While Bonaparte reigned in France, a people might be deprived of their independence, not by conquest only, but kings were deposed, governments were abolished, and whole nations effaced by a simple decree.

Habit and fear might make this state of things endurable, though doubtless, if it had lasted, the ruin of all civilized society must have followed, and some of the Powers, to whose interests the situation seemed for the moment to be favorable, were not ashamed to take Bonaparte for their model.

We exposed all the dangers of this misconception. We proved that the very existence of all Governments was most seriously imperilled by a system which made their preservation depend upon a party in the State or on the chances of war. Lastly, we showed that the principle of legitimacy must be held sacred in the interest of the people themselves, because legitimate Governments can alone be strong and durable, whereas illegitimate Governments, relying upon force only, fall to pieces the moment that support fails them, and then the people are delivered over to a succession of revolutions of which no one can foresee the end.

It took much time and trouble to get a hearing for these principles: they were too strict for the policy of some of the Courts; they were contrary to the system adopted by the English in India, and probably inconvenient for Russia, who had certainly ignored them in several important and recent transactions;[12] and before we succeeded in obtaining their recognition the Allied Powers had already made arrangements directly at variance with them.

Prussia demanded the whole of Saxony, and Russia supported her demand; England, in the official correspondence on the subject, not only gave her unreserved consent, but even tried to prove that the step was fair and expedient; Austria also gave in her official adhesion, reserving only some slight rectifications of frontier. Thus was Saxony completely sacrificed by the private arrangements made between Austria, Russia, England, and Prussia, from which France was excluded.

Before long, however, the French minister's language, reasonable, thoughtful, and consistent, and without the least trace of any ambitious designs, began to make an impression. He felt that trust in him was renewed;[13] it was perceived that he was arguing not more in the interest of France than in that of Europe in general, and of each individual State; and the dangers which he pointed out became apparent. Austria was the first to wish to retrace the steps which had been taken with respect to the Saxon question; she declared, in a Note delivered to Prince Hardenberg on the 10th of December, 1814, that she would not permit that kingdom to be destroyed.

This was the first advantage gained by following in the line traced by your Majesty.[14]

I reproach myself for having so often complained, in the letters which I have had the honor of writing to your Majesty, of the difficulties we experienced and the slowness of our progress. But I now bless this slowness; for if things had proceeded more rapidly, before March the Congress would have come to an end, the sovereigns have returned to their capitals, and the armies have marched home; and then how many difficulties we should have had to overcome![15]

Prince Metternich having officially communicated to me his Note of the 10th of December, I was able to explain the views taken by France, and I addressed to him and to Lord Castlereagh a full profession of political faith. I declared that your Majesty asked for nothing for France, and no more than simple justice for any one; that your Majesty desired above all that revolutions should come to an end, and that these doctrines should be banished in future from the political relations of States, in order that Governments might be enabled to prevent outbreaks, or, when threatened or attacked by revolutionary movements, to put an effectual stop to them.

The mistrust previously felt for us was completely dispelled by these declarations, and quite the opposite feeling soon took its place. Nothing now was done without our co-operation; we were not only consulted, but our approbation was solicited. An entire change came over public opinion; and those whose fears and suspicions had formerly led them to avoid us now came forward in crowds.

It was more difficult for England than for Austria to set aside the engagement taken to hand over the whole of the kingdom of Saxony to Prussia. The English instructions on this subject were more explicit than the Austrian. England had not, like Austria, made the gift of Saxony depend upon the possibility of finding other means for indemnifying Prussia for the losses sustained since 1806 by the cession of other territories equally suitable. Moreover, the position of ministers in England is such that they dare not, at the risk of losing what the English call reputation,[16] leave the road which they have once taken, and in deciding upon what road to take, their policy must always be guided by what is likely to be the opinion of Parliament. Notwithstanding this, the English Legation was induced to break its promise to Prussia, to change its plan of action, to desire the preservation of the kingdom of Saxony, to support France, and at last even to join France and Austria in a treaty of alliance. This treaty was signed on the 3rd of January.[17] It was remarkable as being the first indication of a reconciliation between Powers who, by their many interests in common, were bound, sooner or later, to stand by one another. Bavaria, Hanover, and the Low Countries acceded to this treaty; and then only was the coalition, which in spite of the peace was still in existence, really dissolved.

From this time the majority of the Powers adopted our principles, and it was clear that the others would not long continue to oppose them; it remained, therefore, only to apply them.

Prussia, deprived of the support of Austria and England, though still backed by Russia, found herself compelled to confine her claims to a portion only of Saxony; and thus that kingdom, which seemed irrevocably doomed to destruction, and whose sentence had been pronounced, was saved from ruin.

Bonaparte, after having seized the kingdom of Naples by force of arms, treated the country as his private property, and gave it, in violation of all national independence, as he might have given a landed estate, to one of his generals in recompense for his services. Acquiescence in such a title to a throne would have been no less gross a violation of the principle of legitimacy than Bonaparte's original act. Preparations, the success of which was certain, were therefore made for deposing Murat, when he accomplished his fall by his own aggression. Seven weeks have hardly elapsed since his rash attempt, and already the reign of the usurper is over, and Ferdinand IV. has regained his throne. In this important matter the English ministry courageously and thoroughly supported the conduct of France, in spite of the indiscreet and ill-timed clamor of the opposition, and in spite of the ill-advised intrigues of English travellers throughout Italy.

France is also to be congratulated upon the turn taken by almost all the other negotiations at the Congress.

The king of Sardinia having no heir male of the reigning branch of his family, there was reason to fear that Austria might attempt to have one of the Archdukes, who was married to one of the King's daughters, declared his successor; this would have placed all Upper Italy in the hands of Austria or of Austrian princes. It was settled that the right of the Carignan branch to succeed to the dominions of the King of Sardinia should be recognized. These dominions, augmented by the territory of Genoa, have become the inheritance of a family devoted to France. They will therefore form a counterpoise to Austrian influence in Italy, and serve to maintain a just balance of power in that country.

The whole of the duchy of Warsaw could not be kept out of the hands of Russia, but half of it was restored to its former possessors.[18]

Prussia required neither Luxemburg nor Mayence, and on no side did her frontiers touch those of France; along the whole line the kingdom of the Netherlands was interposed, a kingdom whose natural tendencies, especially since her accession of territory, are favorable to France.

The blessing of perpetual neutrality was secured to Switzerland, which is almost as advantageous to France, whose frontier on that side is vulnerable, as to Switzerland herself. In spite, however, of this neutrality, the Swiss have joined Europe against Bonaparte. They will enjoy the neutrality they desired, and which is now secured to them forever, in all future wars between other nations. But the Swiss themselves felt that they had no right to claim neutrality in a war which is directed against a man, not against a nation—a war which has been forced upon Europe for self-preservation, and which concerns Switzerland as much as any other country; they were therefore willing to aid the cause of Europe as far as their position, organization, and resources will permit them to do so.[19]

By the Treaty of Paris France undertook, by a given date, to abolish the slave-trade. This might have been considered a sacrifice and a concession on her part, if the other maritime Powers, who did not share in the humane sentiments which dictated this measure, had not also adopted it.

Spain and Portugal, the two other Powers who were engaged in the slave-trade, undertook, like France, to abolish it. They asked, it is true, for rather longer delay, but their demand seems not unreasonable, looking to the requirements of their colonies, and remembering that in these rather backward countries public opinion had to be prepared for the measure.

The navigation of the Rhine and the Scheldt was placed under fixed rules equally applicable to all nations.

These rules were to prevent the riverain States from placing any obstacles of their own contrivance in the way of navigation, and from exacting any dues beyond those to which their own subjects were liable. These arrangements and the facilities which they afford to commerce will restore to France much of the benefit which she derived from the possession of Belgium and the left bank of the Rhine.[20]

All the most important points, then, were settled satisfactorily for France, perhaps even more satisfactorily than could have been expected. In the minor details also her peculiar interests were cared for as much as those of the other nations.

From the time that the Powers, putting prejudice aside, recognized that, if things were to be established on a firm basis, each State must see its way clearly to securing all the advantages which it has a right to claim, earnest efforts were made to satisfy every one as far as that could be done without prejudice to the interests of others. But it was a gigantic undertaking. The ravages of twenty years of confusion had to be repaired, opposing interests to be reconciled by equitable arrangements, necessary losses to be made up for by superior advantages in another direction; the idea even of perfect political institutions, and of a perfect balance of power, had to be made subservient to the establishment of a lasting peace.[21]

The chief obstacles were overcome, the most knotty points resolved, and every exertion was made to leave nothing unsettled. Germany was to receive a federal Constitution as the result of the deliberations of the Congress; and this would have put a stop to the evident tendency there was to form a southern and a northern confederacy. The Powers intended, by equitable and judicious arrangements, to erect an effectual barrier in Italy against the frequent recurrence of the revolutions which for ages have been the scourge of that country. Measures of general utility were taken in hand, by which it was hoped that the mutual interests of the various countries would be secured, their points of contact and their industrial and commercial relations multiplied, and all profitable means of communication brought to perfection, or facilitated according to the principles of liberal policy.

We flattered ourselves that the Congress would crown its work by establishing, in lieu of temporary alliances, the results of the needs and calculations of the moment, that permanent system of general and reciprocal guarantee and international adjustment which we had taught all the Powers to appreciate. Lord Castlereagh drew up an excellent article to this effect. The Ottoman Empire was included in this grand scheme for mutual protection, and it was probably owing to the information derived from England and France that the Porte decided upon rejecting all the overtures made to it by Bonaparte. By these means order would have been established in Europe, and placed under the constant protection of all parties interested in its preservation, who, by wisely concerted measures and by loyally united efforts, would have stifled at its birth any attempt at disturbance.

The progress of revolution would then have been checked, and the Government might have turned all their attention to home administration and the substantial improvements much needed and longed for by the people, and in carrying out the many salutary schemes which have unfortunately been suspended by the dangers and convulsions of recent years. The restoration of your Majesty's Government, all whose interests, principles, and wishes are directed to the preservation of peace, alone made it possible to establish the tranquillity and future prosperity of Europe upon a solid foundation. To complete this great work it was necessary that your Majesty should retain possession of your throne. It has been interrupted by the terrible catastrophe which has for some time separated your Majesty from your people. All care for the prosperity of nations has had to be abandoned in order to save them from dangers which threatened their very existence. Many intended measures have had to be postponed to a more favorable opportunity, and many others have been passed hurriedly and without the mature reflection of undivided attention.

The Congress was, therefore, obliged to leave its task unfinished, and there was some talk of postponing its signature until the work could be completed.

Several of the Cabinets took this view, perhaps with the secret intention of taking advantage of coming events. I regarded the adjournment as a great misfortune for your Majesty, not so much on account of the uncertainty which it would cause as to the intentions of the Powers, as because of the effect which the treaty would have upon public opinion in France; the treaty being a measure in which the most important interests of Europe are involved, and in which your Majesty, in spite of actual circumstances, appears as one of the principal parties. It was my duty, therefore, to do my utmost to obtain its signature, and I esteem myself most fortunate in having succeeded.

A great nation like the French could not be satisfied unless the same respect and friendly feeling which your Majesty's Government has a right to expect from foreign Courts, but which had for the moment been extinguished by the terror inspired by the French name, were extended to your Majesty's subjects."² I have now the pleasure of informing your Majesty that since the month of December, 1814, every Frenchman whom business of any sort has brought to Vienna has been treated with special consideration, and it is not too much to say that on the 7th of March, 1815, the day on which the arrival of Bonaparte in France became known, the fact of being a Frenchman was regarded as a claim to general good will. I well know what great importance your Majesty attached to this reconciliation, and I am glad to be able to inform you that your Majesty's wishes in this respect have been completely fulfilled.

I beg to make known to your Majesty how greatly the ambassadors, my colleagues, the Duc de Dalberg, the Count de la Tour du Pin, and the Count de Noailles, together with M. de la Besnadière, Counsellor of State, who accompanied me to Vienna, have contributed to the success of the negotiations. They have rendered great service, not only by their work upon the different Commissions to which they were appointed, but still more by their conduct in society, by their language, and by the favorable opinion which they inspired, both of themselves and of the Government which they represent. Their enlightened co-operation alone enabled me to overcome the many obstacles, to extinguish the ill feeling, and to remove the bad impressions with which I had to deal—enabled me, in a word, to restore to your Majesty's Government the influence which is justly its due in the councils of Europe.

It was by determining to uphold the principle of legitimacy that we obtained this important result. The presence of the sovereigns who were at Vienna, and of all the members of the Congress, at the expiatory ceremony of the 21st of January, was a striking homage paid to this principle.

But at the very moment of its triumph at the Congress, it was attacked in France.

The truth of that which I am about to tell your Majesty is more distinctly perceived from afar than on the spot, in Paris.[23] Outside France, because there are fewer objects to distract the attention, and because a mass of intelligence arrives all at once free from the accessories which are apt on the spot to give a false coloring to facts, an observer from a distance is the best judge of all that is going on; notwithstanding this, however, I should hesitate to trust to my own observation only. Having long occupied a diplomatic post abroad, my duty to your Majesty requires that I should follow the rule laid down by the Foreign Office for all its agents employed in foreign countries. It is their duty to make a report of the opinion held in the countries to which they are accredited, of the various acts of the French Government, and of the impression which these acts produce upon enlightened and observant men.

A man can accommodate himself to any settled state of things, even to one opposed to his convictions, because under it there are no fears for the future; but he cannot accustom himself to a state of things varying from day to day, because each day gives birth to fresh fears, and we cannot tell what the end will be. The partisans of the Revolution had made up their minds to put up with the first acts of your Majesty's Government, but they were alarmed by that which was done a fortnight, a month, or six months afterwards. This is why they were resigned to the expulsion of members from the Senate,[24] but would not endure the expulsions made from the Institute, though these latter were of much less importance.[25]

The changes which your Majesty has seen fit to make in the Court of Cassation ought to have been made eight months earlier.[26]

The principle of legitimacy was also imperilled, and most seriously imperilled, by the foolish conduct of the defenders of legitimate power, who did not distinguish between the source of power and its exercise, and believed, or acted as if they believed, that legitimate power must necessarily be absolute and unquestioned.[27]

However legitimate a power may be, its exercise nevertheless must vary according to the objects to which it is applied, and according to time and place. Now, the spirit of the present age in great civilized States demands that supreme authority shall not be exercised except with the concurrence of representatives chosen by the people subject to it.

To fight against this doctrine was fighting against public opinion, and many persons occupying positions near the throne caused great injury to the Government by giving utterance to sentiments opposed to this feeling.[28] The virtues and good faith with which your Majesty is credited constitute your strength; some recent acts have tended to diminish this. Such are the forced interpretations and subtleties by means of which some of the provisions of the constitutional Charter appeared to be evaded, and especially the decrees upsetting institutions duly authorized by law.

Men began to doubt the good faith of the Government, and to suspect that it regarded the Charter only as a temporary measure extorted by the difficulties of the time and one that it intended to let fall in abeyance if the watchfulness of Parliament allowed it to do so. Reaction was feared, and this fear was increased by some of the appointments made. The selection of M. de Bruges,[29] for example, to the post of Grand Chancellor of the Legion of Honor, however great his personal merits may be, has displeased every one in France, and has, if your Majesty will allow me to say it, astonished all Europe.

General anxiety rallied to the ranks of the partisans of revolution all those who, without sharing in their errors, were attached to constitutional principles and also those who had an interest in upholding, I will not say the doctrines of the Revolution, but the results of those doctrines.

To these causes, much more than to any real attachment for his person, Bonaparte was indebted for any partisans outside the army, and even for many of those in the army, because, having risen by the Revolution, he was bound by every conceivable tie to the men who had been its leaders.[30]

It cannot be denied that, great as may be the advantages of legitimacy, it may nevertheless lead to abuses. This is felt strongly, because during the twenty years immediately preceding the Revolution the tendency of all political writing was to expose and exaggerate these abuses. Few persons know how to appreciate the advantages of legitimacy, because they are all in the future; but everybody is at once struck by its abuses, because they may occur at any moment and show themselves upon every occasion. Has any one during the last twenty years reflected enough to perceive that none but a legitimate Government can be stable? A Government that offers to every ambitious man the chance of upsetting it and placing another in its stead, lives a threatened life, and bears within itself a fermenting spirit of revolution, ready at any moment to break out. The notion unhappily prevails that legitimacy affords a sovereign too much facility for setting himself above all laws, by securing him in the possession of the throne, however ill he may govern.

With this turn of mind now manifesting itself among all nations, and in these times, when everything, and especially politics, is discussed, examined, and analyzed, people are apt to ask what is legitimacy, whence it proceeds, and in what it consists.[31]

In the time when religious feelings were all-powerful and deeply engraved in the hearts and minds of men, it was possible to believe that the sovereign power was an emanation from the Divinity. It was possible to believe that those families who were raised to the throne by Heaven's favor, and long kept there by its will, reigned over men by divine right. But in these days, in which there remains scarcely a trace of these feelings, and in which the bond of religion, if not broken, at any rate is much loosened, men will no longer allow the claim of legitimacy to this origin.

In the present time the general opinion, one that it would be vain to attempt to weaken, is that Governments exist only for the sake of the people; a necessary corollary to this opinion is that legitimate power is the form of government best calculated to secure the prosperity and tranquillity of the people. From this it follows that authority, to be legitimate, must have existed for a long succession of years; and accordingly, we see that legitimate power, from the fact that it is fortified by memories of the past, by the affection which men naturally feel for the family of their chief, and having on its side possession, which in itself confers a title in the case of private ownership, is the form of government least likely to expose the people to the perilous chances of revolution, and is, therefore, the form to which they are bound in their best interests to submit. On the other hand, if the conviction obtains that the abuses to which this power is liable constitute an evil overweighing the advantages which it offers, legitimacy must be looked upon as a delusion and a snare.

How then are we to inspire nations with confidence in legitimate authority, which alone can insure it respect and stability? We have only, but this is indispensable, so to constitute it as to remove all fear lest its power should be abused.

It is just as much in the interest of the sovereign as in that of his subjects that it should be so constituted, for absolute power would be in these times as heavy a burden upon him who wields it, as upon those who have to submit to it.

Before the Revolution, authority in France was restricted by ancient institutions; it was tempered by the action of the great bodies of the magistracy, the clergy, and the nobility, who were necessary elements in its composition and the instruments of its power. Now that these institutions, these instruments have been destroyed, others must be found to supply their place; and these others must be such as not merely are not repugnant to public opinion—they must be the objects of its choice.

Formerly the secular power could derive support from the authority of religion; it can no longer do this, because religious indifference has penetrated all classes and become universal. A Government, therefore, must now rely only upon public opinion for support, and to obtain that it must march with the times.

It will obtain it if people see that the Government, while fully able to promote their prosperity, is powerless for harm. But to insure this, they must be certain that it cannot act arbitrarily. It is not enough that they should believe in its wish to do good, because they might be afraid that this wish might change, or that the wrong means might be employed to obtain a desirable end; it is not enough that confidence should be founded upon the virtues and good qualities of the sovereign, which, like him, are perishable; it must be founded on the strength of national institutions, which are everlasting. Moreover, even the institutions most calculated to secure national prosperity would inspire no confidence, unless they were established under the form of government, which the spirit of the age looks upon as the only form adapted to obtain that object.

Guarantees are wanted; they are wanted equally for the sake of the sovereign and for that of the subjects. These guarantees would not be believed in—

Unless personal liberty be protected by law against all infringement;

Unless the liberty of the press be fully secured, and law confine itself to punishing its offences;[32]

Unless the judges be irremovable in order to secure their independence;[33]

Unless the administration, or any public body other than the courts of law, be debarred from exercising jurisdiction in any case;

Unless all the ministers, jointly and severally, be responsible for the exercise of the power entrusted to them;[34]

Unless only responsible persons be admitted to the councils of the sovereign;[35]

And, finally, unless the law be the expression of the united will of the *three separate states of the realm.*

With old and populous countries, in which new wants have developed intelligence, and intelligence has added force to the passions, it is necessary that the executive should be strong in proportion, and experience shows that the strength of authority is increased by dividing it.

These opinions are no longer peculiar to any one country; they are shared by almost all. Accordingly, we see that the cry for Constitutions is universal; everywhere the establishment of a Constitution adapted to the more or less advanced state of society has become a necessity, and everywhere preparations for this purpose are in progress. The Congress, in giving Genoa to Sardinia,[36] Lucca to the Infanta Maria Louisa of Spain, on restoring Naples to Ferdinand IV. and the Legations to the Pope, expressly stipulated, on behalf of these countries, that the form of government which appeared requisite or most suitable to their actual state should be introduced. Every sovereign and every minister I have seen is frightened at the consequences which the system of government adopted by Ferdinand VII. must produce in Spain, and bitterly regrets that Europe allowed him to recover his throne except upon the condition of his granting to his subjects institutions in harmony with the spirit of the age.[37] I have even heard sovereigns deplore as a personal misfortune that their subjects were not sufficiently advanced to be ripe for institutions implying a high degree of civilization.

I have gathered these opinions from the deliberations of assembled Europe. I found all the sovereigns with whom I conversed, together with their ministers, imbued with them. They are expressed in all the letters written by the ambassadors of Austria and Russia to London, and also in those of Lord Castlereagh. I was therefore bound to submit them to your Majesty in this report; and I was the more bound because in the farewell audiences granted me by the sovereigns, they all commissioned me to inform your Majesty, that they are firmly convinced that France will never be tranquil, unless your Majesty unreservedly adopts these opinions, and takes them for your sole guide in government. They said that the whole past must be forgotten in France,[38] and that without restriction; the least exception would be dangerous; and that there would be no assurance of safety for the sovereign, unless it were one in which all parties could share, and that such assurance would not be considered satisfactory, unless it were judged so to be by all classes of society. They said that your Majesty must arrive at a complete system, in which every component part illustrates and makes manifest the honesty of the whole, in order to enable the public at once to see clearly the aims and objects of the Government, and then every one will understand and be free from anxiety as to his own position.[39]

They added that although it may at first seem that no one is interested so much as your Majesty in the preservation of tranquillity in France, yet in reality they are just as much interested in it themselves, inasmuch as the present critical situation of France compromises the existence of all Europe, and because it would be difficult, after they had once returned home, to renew the efforts which they have made this year.

The sovereigns, after reading your Majesty's last proclamation to your subjects, told me that they remarked with regret one phrase in it, by which your Majesty seems to imply, though with much caution, that you submitted to accept their assistance, whence it might be inferred that if your Majesty had declined it, the peace might have been unbroken. They are afraid lest this should injure your Majesty's cause in France by giving your Majesty the appearance of having been imposed upon her by them. They think that, in order to disabuse your subjects of so unfortunate an idea, your Majesty and those about you should remain quiet. This will be difficult, for your Majesty will have to restrain and even suppress the zeal of your servants. In their opinion your Majesty should appear to be grieved by what is going on, rather than to take part in it; your Majesty, either in your own person or in that of your adherents, should intervene between the allied sovereigns and your subjects, to diminish as much as possible the evil effect of war, and to make the minds of the Allies easy respecting the fidelity of the fortresses which may be surrendered, and which, I presume, will, according to the arrangements to be made between your Majesty's ministers and the Duke of Wellington, be confided to persons selected by you. Lastly, that in order that your Majesty may clearly appear to be not only not making war, but not even instigating it, they think it would be best that neither your Majesty nor any of the royal princes should accompany the allied armies. Never were politics handled with so much delicacy.[40]

If any part of France should succeed, thanks to the events which are about to happen, in shaking off Bonaparte's yoke, I think that your Majesty could not do better than proceed to the spot immediately, accompanied by your ministers, and then and there summon the Chambers and resume the government of the kingdom, just as if the whole country had returned to its allegiance.[41] The projected advance upon Lyons, which I was very anxious to have carred out on account of the excellent effect which it would produce upon the southern provinces, would have been very favorable to the execution of this plan.

The intelligence that so great a number of commissioners have been appointed to the army has produced a bad impression.[42] I think that all your Majesty's measures should be taken in concert with the Allies, and subject to their approbation. This act of deference should go far towards placing clearly before their eyes the object of the war, of which, I am bound to say, the different Cabinets do not take exactly the same view. England certainly wishes earnestly for your Majesty's restoration, without any ulterior objects;[43] Austria also wishes for it, though less eagerly; but I am not at all sure that Russia is not inclined to enter into other entanglements, or that Prussia would not make her own aggrandizement her chief object.

Could not your Majesty, at the moment when the foreign armies are about to enter France, issue a second proclamation to your subjects, carefully soothing the self-esteem of the nation, who, not without reason, resist having even what they desire imposed upon them by foreigners? This proclamation, after dealing first with the erroneous opinion which Bonaparte is trying to spread concerning the cause and the object of the present war, might go on to say that the foreign Powers have not embarked in this war for the sake of your Majesty's interests, knowing, as they do, that France needs only to be delivered from oppression, but for the sake of their own safety; that the Powers would not have made war unless they had been persuaded that Europe would continue to be threatened with the greatest calamities, while the man who for so long has loaded her with misfortunes remained master of France; that the return of this man to France is the only cause of the war, and is its chief and immediate aim to wrest from him the power which he has seized; that, in order as far as possible to soften the rigors of war, to ward off its disasters, and stop its ravages, your Majesty, surrounded by Frenchmen, takes the place of intermediary between the foreign sovereigns and your people, with the hope that the consideration due to your Majesty may be extended to your dominions; that this, and this only, will be the position occupied by your Majesty during the war, and that you have forbidden the princes of your house to accompany the foreign armies or to take any share in hostilities. Passing next to the measures to be taken within France, your Majesty should make known your readiness to enter into any engagements, which may be deemed necessary. And as the best pledge for the security of good government lies in the selection of those who have to administer it, your Majesty should announce that your present ministry is provisional only, and that you are prepared, on arriving in France, to make any changes that may be desirable in order to secure the services of a ministry, whose appointment shall be a guarantee to all parties and all opinions, and one that shall relieve all anxiety

Lastly, it would be useful if in this same proclamation your Majesty alluded to the national domains,[44] dealing with this question in a more absolute, decided, and encouraging spirit than that of the constitutional Charter, the provisions of which have not succeeded in calming the minds of those who have become possessed of these domains It is most essential just now to remove all cause, or any pretext even, for anxiety on this head, because the present feeling has already stopped the sale of the forest lands, which we want as much as possible to encourage, as the produce is more than ever needed.

It is the general opinion, in which I share, that it is desirable, I may say necessary, that your Majesty's address to your people should be framed in the spirit of the foregoing suggestions,[45] and, above all, that it should contain the most entirely satisfactory pledges in the matter of constitutional government. If, as I venture to hope, your Majesty shares this opinion, you will probably see fit to charge some of your confidential advisers with the duty of preparing a draft of the proclamation for submission to your Majesty.

I have given your Majesty a full and correct report of the results of the negotiations of the Congress, and of the impression produced in Vienna by the state of affairs in France. There remain only a few trifling matters of detail.

During my stay in Vienna a great mass of papers accumulated on my hands. As most of these do not contain matter of sufficient interest to be wanted again for reference, and as your Majesty has copies of all that are important, it was needless for me to bring them all away. I have, therefore, burnt the greater portion of these papers, and left the remainder in Vienna in safe hands.

I have now completed my long task, one that from the nature of the things which I had to submit to your Majesty has sometimes been a very painful task, and it affords me great pleasure to be able to conclude it by bringing to your Majesty's notice the zeal and devotion above all praise unceasingly shown during the sitting of the Congress by your Majesty's ambassadors and ministers at the various Courts to which they were accredited. The same causes which led me to encounter so much opposition made their position difficult from the very beginning; these difficulties were subsequently much increased in consequence of the painful events which have succeeded each other since the beginning of March. They have regarded these difficulties, however, only as an additional opportunity for proving their attachment towards your Majesty. In addition to this, several of them have for some time past found themselves in great pecuniary embarrassment. They did their best to live in a manner becoming the dignity of the several positions in which your Majesty's confidence had placed them. I trust that some provision has been made for improving their present condition; some of them are in really distressed circumstances.

NOTES TO LETTER C.

1. "At Roye a consultation was held. M. de Talleyrand had two old worn-out horses harnessed to his carriage and proceeded to the King. His equipage occupied the whole space from the inn in which the minister was staying to the King's door. He alighted from his carriage with a Memorandum, which he read to us, and discussed the course to be taken on our arival."—Chateaubriand, Mémoires d'Outre Tombe, tom. vi. p. 388.

2. In his celebrated Memorandum of the 25th of November, 1792, M. Talleyrand said, describing the foreign policy which the Republic ought to follow:

"We no longer need—as we were advised some years ago by eminent statesmen—to adopt the policy of restoring France to the rank assigned to her by her extraordinary extension, and to the leadership in all respects due to her among the continental Powers.

"We know now what all these grand ideas of rank, leadership, and preponderance are worth. We know what to think of the political stage upon which the turbulence and incapacity of European Cabinets have struggled so long and so ostentatiously, at the expense of their people's interests. We have at last learnt that the only real profitable and reasonable leadership—that which alone becomes free and enlightened men—consists in being master at home, and in never entertaining the ridiculous pretension of being other people's master. We have at last learnt—rather late, perhaps—that for States, as for individuals, the real way to get rich is, not by conquering and invading foreign countries, but by improving your own. We have learnt that all increase of territory all the gains of force or cunning, long associated by time-honored prejudices with the idea of rank, leadership, national coherence, and superiority among the nations of the world, are but the cruel mockery of political folly and false estimates of strength, increasing the expense and complications of government and diminishing the well-being and safety of the governed, for the sake of the transient advantage or vanity of those in power.

"The reign of illusions is, then, over in France. In her maturity she will not be seduced by the grand political considerations which so long and so deplorably led astray and prolonged her childhood. Circumstances, which no human sagacity could foresee, have placed her in a position without example in the history of nations.

"By her courage, her perseverance, and her intelligence she has marked out for herself a new career, and, having ascertained the object to be aimed at, she will know how to obtain it."

3. It is well known that the events of 1815 were followed by a second Treaty of Paris (in November), which made a great change in the situation described by Talleyrand. Henri Martin, speaking of M. de Talleyrand's behavior when the Louvre was pillaged by the Allies under the second Restoration, says—

"The Great Powers, who were less interested in the question, might probably have been brought by negotiation to consent to the retention by France of part, at least, of the art treasures. But Talleyrand, knowing that he could not long remain Minister of Foreign Affairs, affected a prudery most unusual in him, and refused to run the chance of incurring unpopularity by compromising the matter in any way. The King had the same feeling on the subject. There was no attempt at negotiation, and consequently the Allies, unchecked and acting on their own authority, pillaged the Louvre."

4. See D'Angeberg, p. 249.

5. See D'Angeberg. The Memorandums of M. de Gagern, M. de Humboldt, M. de Capo d'Istria, the Prince of Hardenberg, and Prince Metternich, presented in August, 1815.

M. de Gagern endeavors to prove in his minute, which is extremely violent, that, even after the cession of Alsace, France would still be "the strongest and in all respects the preponderating Power."

6. "Remember this: this same Europe which has been persuaded to make the Declaration which I have sent you, is full of jealousy against France. . . . Whenever bad news arrives this feeling becomes manifest."—Talleyrand to Jaucourt, 10th March, 1815.

. There is still a good deal of the war spirit abroad. But no one except the

Bourbon family takes the slightest interest in the King of Saxony, and not a single soldier could be raised to fight for him in all France. The frontier of the Rhine in Belgium, or even the fortress of Luxemburg alone, would call out recruits fast enough; but depend upon it, there is no inclination towards the disinterested policy of taking up arms for the integrity of Saxony and the balance of power in Europe as it was in 1792."—Jaucourt to Talleyrand, 9th May, 1814.

8. According to the instructions given to the French plenipotentiaries at the Congress of Vienna, the vacant countries were divided into two classes. 1st. Countries assigned by the treaty of the 30th May: to the King of Sardinia, Savoy, the Department of Nice, and part of the State of Genoa; to Austria, Illyria, and Italy from the Po to the Ticino; to Holland, Belgium, and the frontier of the Meuse; to Prussia, the country comprised between the Meuse, France, and the Rhine. 2d. Countries not disposed of by the said treaty, viz.: the rest of the State of Genoa, part of Italy, Lucca, Piombino, the Ionian Islands, the old grand-duchy of Berg, East Friesland, Prussian Westphalia, Erfurt, and Dantzic, and also the island of Elba, of which Napoleon I. was only the temporary sovereign.

9. "On the evening of the 4th of April, 1814, Napoleon had a long conversation with Caulaincourt, upon whom it made an indelible impression. . . . He strove to persuade the solitary hearer who was to report his words to the world at large, and he strove perhaps to persuade himself that he had acted only in the interests of France; he repeated the expression which had once before escaped him, and repeated it with true and deep anguish: 'Ah! to leave France so small after having received her so great!'"—Henri Martin, "Histoire de France," tom. iv p. 93.

10. The following is the definition of the balance of power in Europe given in one of the instructions relative to the Congress of Vienna:

"It is a combination of the mutual rights and interests of the Powers, by means of which Europe aims at securing the following objects: 1st. That no single Power, nor any union of Powers, shall have the mastery in Europe. 2nd. That no Power or union of Powers shall be at liberty to infringe the actual possession and recognized rights of any other Power 3rd. That it shall no longer be necessary, in order to maintain the established state of affairs, to live in a state of imminent or actual war, and that the proposed combination shall secure the peace and repose of Europe against the efforts of a disturber, by diminishing his chances of success."

11. See D'Angeberg, p. 540.

"The part of the French ministers in the Congress of Vienna was really the simplest and noblest of all. All that concerned France having been settled by the Treaty of Paris, they had no demands to make for themselves, and were therefore at liberty to watch the conduct of others, to defend the weak against the strong, to confine each Power within its just boundaries, and to labor sincerely for the re-establishment of the political balance. And I must do them the justice to say that they pursued this course, and refrained from making any proposal or submitting any plan tending, either directly or indirectly, to produce the slightest change in the stipulations of the Treaty of Paris, to the smallest extension of their frontiers, or towards any claim whatever incompatible with the rights of neighboring nations or with general tranquillity In spite of all the lies that are going about the world, in spite of the plans, of the attempts, and of all the intrigues which inveterate hatred of

France has falsely and often ridiculously ascribed to her ministers, veracious history will have to bear witness to their honorable conduct; and I, who was a spectator of all that happened, and who am, therefore, more competent than any one else to write the history of these transactions—I wish to be the first to do them justice."—Metternich to Talleyrand.

12. In his letter to Metternich, M. de Talleyrand reminds the prince that the partition of Poland was "the prelude, partly perhaps the cause, and to some extent the excuse, for the commotions of which Europe has been the victim."

Enough notice has not been taken of the fact that M. de Talleyrand succeeded in having the partition of Poland condemned by the very Powers who consummated it.

"It was certainly a grand moral lesson to see the Powers who destroyed Poland join those who had allowed her destruction in denouncing this great crime."—Viel-Castel, "Histoire de la Restauration," tom. ii. p. 222.

13. "The King alone, among all the sovereigns, appeared at the Congress as the defender of principles. His policy, that of putting aside all selfish aims, is beginning to be universally appreciated, and has given a peculiarly noble aspect to the cause which we are pleading; this, and the frankness we have exhibited in all the discussions, make it impossible to doubt our generosity and disinterestedness, and tend more and more every day to banish the suspicions of ambition and treachery, which have been nourished against France Accordingly, we are now as much courted as we were formerly shunned."—Talleyrand to the Marquis de Bonnay 18th November, 1814.

14. See D'Angeberg, "Instructions for Prince Talleyrand at the Congress of Vienna, September, 1814."

15. These words of Talleyrand remind one of what Madame de Staël said of the Hundred Days: "If Napoleon triumphs, adieu to liberty; if he succumbs to Europe, adieu to national independence."

16. In the original "character."

17. "M. de Talleyrand did one great thing at Vienna. By the treaty of alliance, which he negotiated between France, England, and Austria, of the 3rd of January, 1815, he put an end to the coalition formed against us in 1813, and Europe was divided into two parties, greatly to the advantage of France: but the events of the 20th of March destroyed his work; the European coalition was again formed, directed against Napoleon and against France, who made herself, or allowed herself to be made, the tool of Napoleon."—"Mémoires de Guizot," tom. L p. 100.

Unfortunately, while the skilful negotiations of M. de Talleyrand at Vienna were obtaining these results, the mismanagement of affairs at home by the Restoration Government precipitated the crisis which destroyed his work. M. de Jaucourt wrote to him, under date of the 24th of November, 1814·

"If all that you do not do was managed as well as all that you do, it would be too great luck. I am devoured by zeal for the house of the Sovereign, and I therefore entreat you to consider carefully our administrative, financial, and constitutional position; above all, do give us a ministry. Bring your penetrating and judicious mind to bear upon the future. Without you we should be in a bad way."

18. "One of M. de Talleyrand's favorite ideas, and one that always appeared to me sound and reasonable was that it should be the aim of French policy to deliver Poland from a foreign yoke, and to make it a barrier to Russia as a counterpoise to Austria. He was constantly urging this with all the influence

in his power.' I have often heard him say that the peace of Europe depended upon Poland."—Mémoires de Madame de Rémusat, tom. iii. p. 53.

19. In this passage the casuistry of the former Bishop of Autun peeps out. A neutrality ceases to be real as soon as it is violated; it must be owned that after getting out of the Congress of Vienna, under the pretext of what he called high principle, all that could be advantageous to France and agreeable to Louis XVIII., M. de Talleyrand was very much inclined to barter it away whenever the cause he was upholding seemed to require it.

20. All must allow the justice of M. de Talleyrand's views on freedom of carriage; many circumstances show that he foresaw the extraordinary development which increased facility of communication would bring to trade. It should likewise be remembered that his first, as well as his last, act of diplomacy was to endeavor to establish commercial relations with England.

21. The *Moniteur Universel* of the 27th of July, 1815, contains the following passage concerning the results of the Congress of Vienna:

"From what grievous calamities a loyal and strong confederation, such as we now see, would have saved Europe and France. Those, however, who caused the evil have no right to accuse its victims. . . . And so the ancient edifice so well described by Voltaire as the European Republic crumbled away in the presence of a new power—a power that for the sake of its brand-new theories, and for the sake of one man and his usurping dynasty, insisted upon changing and modifying everything so that everything might be moulded in its new and strange forms. The European edifice had now to be reconstructed, and this was the task set before the Congress. Let us adopt the enlightened and just idea of the author of 'The Age of Louis XIV.,' and, without sharing the respectable opinions of the great Sully and of the good Abbé de Saint-Pierre, let us consider Europe, in its entirety and in the general system of its fundamental relations, as a society, a family, a republic of princes and nations. From this point of view we perceive that there is, in the midst of so many apparently conflicting and opposing interests, a fixed and indisputable principle capable of solving more than one political problem."

22. "The company of amateurs, which is to perform in a private theatre before the sovereigns, plays only the works of Racine and Molière. This exclusive use of the French language is naturally a scandal in the eyes of some of the Germans, who wanted German to be the language of the Congress."—*Moniteur Universel* of 30th June. 1814, correspondence from Vienna.

23. "You are perfectly right, one can take an accurate view only of that which is seen as a whole. It is as difficult to place yourself at the right distance for observation when you are in the midst of commotion and disturbance, as it is to bring them near and judge them fairly when you are far away."—Jaucourt to Talleyrand, 4th February, 1815.

24. Fifty-three senators were expelled from the Senate by Louis XVIII.; among them were Cambacérès, Chaptat, Curée. Cardinal Fesch, Fouché, François de Neufchâteau, Garat, Grégoire, Lambrecht, Roger Ducos, Rœderer, Sieyès, etc.

25. The following were expelled from the Institute: Cambacérès, Carnot, Guyton de Morveau, Monge, Merlin de Douai, Sieyès, Lakanal, Grégoire, David, Rœderer, Garat, and Cardinal Maury. Their places were taken by Monseigneur de Bausset, Bishop of Alais; MM. de Bonald, de Lally Tollendal, the Ducs de Richelieu and de Lévis, the Count de Choiseul-Gouffier, Ferrand, Letronne, Raoul Rochette, and Quatremère de Quincy.

On the 28th of February, 1815, Jaucourt wrote to Talleyrand:

"The Chancellor also is devoted to the King, and his robe is to him the emblem of monarchy restored. At the meeting of the Council yesterday I had a word with him and M. Ferrand. Upon the latter asking, 'Why this word Institute, a word of revolutionary creation, and invented only twenty-five years ago?' and Dambray saying that if *the ballot balls* were brought back they would pounce upon them and snatch them from each other, I said, 'Well said; yours is a grand saying—an admirable, useful, wise, conservative saying!'"

On the 4th of March he writes:

"The King expels the voters from the Institute, but preserves the name of Institute; amalgamates the academies of painting, suppressing the fourth class; restores the name of Academy to the three classes, with their former rank, and fills up vacancies."

26. On the 21st of November, 1814, the Abbé de Montesquieu presented a Bill which aimed at assimilating the proceedings of the Court of Cassation to those of the *Conseil des parties* of 1789, making the Supreme Court a department of the *King's* Council, with the Chancellor of France as president, not only of the Court of Cassation, but of each of the separate Departments. The Chamber of Requests was not to be required to assign any reasons for its judgments. The King was to have power to make orders in Council without consulting the Legislature.

The intention also was announced of calling for the resignation of those members of the Court whose services it was thought for any reason desirable to dispense with.

The opinion of the public, which was strongly adverse to the measures contemplated, found able expression in the speeches of MM. de Flaugergues and Dumolard in the Chamber of Deputies. The Bill, however, was carried, but in so modified a form that the Government did not think it advisable to send it up to the Chamber of Peers. The work of weeding out, however, was carried on by the order of the 17th of February, 1815. The illustrious Procureur-General Merlin de Douai, who voted for the death of Louis XVI., was dismissed, and also the Chief President Muraire. The place of the latter was taken by M. de Sèze, who defended Louis XVI.

27. "Méhée's pamphlet (the acts and proceedings of his Majesty's ministers in violation of the Constitution denounced to the King) has done harm enough, but its refutation in the *Journal des Debats* for yesterday, the 29th, will do still more. Do read that number. You would hardly believe, till you have read it, that people could take such pains to excite hatred. Those who are always talking and preaching about forgetting the past, about concord, peace, and the unity of Frenchmen, are daily lighting up the torch of discord, provoking civil war, and doing their best to divide France into two hostile camps."—D'Hauterive to Talleyrand, 30th September, 1814.

28. In a letter to Talleyrand, dated the 23rd of October, 1814, after praising Monsieur and the Duc d'Angoulême, Beugnot goes on to say—

"The Duc de Berry has lost popularity, both in society and in the army. The Prince has lately shown himself severe and sometimes hard. This must be an affectation on his part; for by nature he is only surly, and, like all surly people, has an excellent heart."

"It cannot be denied that M. de Blacas is believed to have had a great deal to do with recent events. The Duc de Richelieu says that this report is perfectly true with respect to home matters, and I can answer for its truth with respect to foreign affairs. Do all you can to prevent its appearing that the King is acting under his influence. You may be perfectly sure that the bare idea of his being subject to this influence will be enough to produce a most unfavorable impression. Of all those around the King you alone have stuck to him with unswerving fidelity, consequently you alone can be of any real service to him."—Talleyrand to Jaucourt, 9th April, 1815.

"The outcry against M. de Blacas is so great that the King is the only person whose ears it has not reached. The Duc de Gramont, and the whole house of Damas, and all the commanders of the army; the Duke of Ragusa, who is about to retire; the Council, Lally, Chateaubriand, Beurnonville, . . . all refuse to transact business with him, and declare that the feeling of the French nation towards him is similar to that of the Spaniards towards the Prince of Peace. . . . Monsieur said to me, 'We must allow nothing which can in any way countenance the ridiculous idea of the sovereignty of the people.' "—Jaucourt to Talleyrand, 28th April, 1815.

29. "A mischievous decree has been passed affecting the Legion of Honor, and one equally mischievous, which I mentioned to you before, affecting the University—this is what they have done. What they have not done is, to adopt a common aim, conscientious sincerity, and a firm and consistent proceeding. To-morrow, Sunday, the King will receive M. de Sèze; he has refused to receive the Chancellor of the Legion of Honor afterwards. It is a pleasure to him to touch the blue ribbon with his royal hands; this is very natural; but the hearts of thirty-seven thousand members of the Legion would have been touched if with his French hands he had thrown the grand ribbon of the Legion round the neck of M. de Bruges, or still more if it had been round the neck of some one else I could mention."—Jaucourt to Talleyrand, 18th February, 1815.

This is the same M. de Bruges concerning whom, when it was proposed to appoint him Prefect of Police, Louis XVIII. observed, "Oh no; he is not Parisian enough."

30. Napoleon, when he received Lanjuinais, President of the Chamber of Representatives, asked him if he were Bonapartist or Bourbonist. "I am a patriot," answered Lanjuinais. "Your cause is now the cause of the Revolution. Upon the condition that you reign as a constitutional monarch, I will give you my loyal support."—See Henri Martin, tom. iv. p. 151.

31. Here we see that there are two kinds of legitimacy: one that of Louis XIV., which by a singular anachronism, and with a fatal misappreciation of modern ideas, the advisers of Louis XVIII. sought to revive; the other that of M. de Talleyrand and of the constitutional royalists, whose political doctrines are to be found in the new Bill for establishing a Constitution presented to the Senate by the Prince de Benevento on the 6th of April, 1814. By this Bill the principal conquests made by the Revolution, the liberty of the press, liberty of worship, etc., etc., were guaranteed; and by Clause 2 Louis Stanislas Xavier was freely called to the throne under the title of King of the French. There was no talk at that time of divine right or of a charter to be granted.

32. Louis XVIII. sometimes recognized the services of the press. In a letter dated 21st January, 1815, Jaucourt writes to Talleyrand: "The King has said a good thing. He asked to look at a paper called *The Yellow Dwarf*. The Duc d'Angoulême said, 'Does your Majesty, then, read *The Yellow Dwarf?* It is said to be a very bad paper.' 'I do,' said the King. 'In the first place, it amuses me; and in the next, it tells me what you would not tell me.' We ex-

pect you to do the same, and even more, on your arrival, for they do not tell him much."

33. "There has been some talk of reducing the salaries of the judges and other officers of the courts of justice, with a view to facilitate the granting of retiring pensions and to enlarge the field of choice. The Abbé de Montesquieu suddenly woke up to find this mean and unbecoming. Louis, to whom everything is a matter of calculation, approved of it. The idea, however, has been relinquished; it certainly would have been both stingy and unbecoming."—Jaucourt to Talleyrand, September, 1814.

"The Chancellor, who indulges in such flowery phrases in the preamble of his ordinance of the Court of Cassation, and compares Justice to Zephyr and the rosy-fingered goddess. . . ."—Jaucourt to Talleyrand, 18th February, 1815.

"In giving his assent to the principle of the irremovability of the judges, the King reserved to himself the liberty of declining to confirm the appointments of those already in office, and the right, consequently, of revising the list of the whole bench. It followed that the judges of all ranks were kept anxiously waiting to have their fate decided, and so remained in a state of dependence, which was likely to prove very injurious to the suitors, particularly to those among them who had become the owners of national property. The Chambers, before rising, demanded that an end should be put to this state of uncertainty, and accordingly the Government began the much-dreaded weeding-out operation in the Court of Cassation in January, 1815."—Thiers, " Histoire du Consulat et de l'Empire," tom. xix. p. 9.

34. "The last sitting on Sunday was rather curious. The Duke of Dalmatia's touchiness on the subject of the royal prerogative reminds one of the short existence and long meditations of Nicholas I. M. Ferrand, who has all the caution of an old member, of a Jansenist, and of a saint into the bargain, gave us a long discourse, the opening of which was not bad. He began by justifying some rather thoughtless acts of ministers on the ground of their good intentions and their unanimity; he admitted Dupont's weakness, but at the same time sang his praises in a way that greatly disconcerted the Marshal. He then proceeded to attack the Jesuits with all the enthusiasm of youth. Lastly, he dealt unsparingly with the question of the sale of ecclesiastical property. We ended by joining in a hearty laugh. He, poor man, wrote only to discharge his conscience, and having done this, added nothing to these fine opinions. After him the Chancellor gave us some of his prose. All this is bad; it reminds me of a consultation of physicians, with the respect always shown to the opinion of the family doctor. But, after all, our ideas are ripening; we are advancing towards the supply of a want hardly recognized as yet—the want of system and of common action in Government, the want of a ruling will to direct the efforts of each department towards the attainment of one and the same end. However, if we make haste to understand the position of a ministry under constitutional government, we shall perhaps gain time enough to give you time to arrive. But the truth is, we are in a bad way, and if we do not soon get better we shall come altogether to grief. Your Congress will give us strength. We look to you and the King for support, though, at the same time, I am much inclined to think, that it would be much better if the King let you on your return name a ministry, and made a thorough clearance of the present Government. We love the King and we serve him loyally, but he can only escape censure himself by making us take the blame and incur the contempt. I do not know

whether any one else has ever spoken to you to the same effect, but on the re-assembling of Parliament I will remind you of the letter of the 25th of January.

"All that you say, my dear Prince, about the necessity of selecting a Cabinet Council out of the members of the ministry, is very true, very just, and very important, but quite impossible. When you return, bringing with you success and honor, your high position and your determination to establish among us a ministry after the English fashion may perhaps effect something; but, at the present moment, what we want in the place of this veneer of union, with its mere outward semblance of concord, is a candid opposition, which would have the merit of forcing by its criticism every one to be careful and to do their best. Ministerial responsibility will be carried by agitation in Parliament, by petitions, and by threats, and not by any carefully deliberated measure; this the ministry would neither have the courage to propose, nor Parliament the wisdom to pass."—Jaucourt to Talleyrand, 21st February, 1815.

"The Chancellor has been at work upon the regulations for the sittings of the committee and the composition of the Council. Here are the results. They are to meet as often as there is occasion. Any matters affecting the ministers or things in general are to be brought before the committee. No measure which has to pass the Council shall be introduced there without having previously been discussed by the committee. The ministers are to communicate freely with one another. The deliberations are to be binding upon the ministers and to be secret."—Jaucourt to Talleyrand, 1st February, 1815.

"The Chancellor thinks his rules will settle all difficulties; he is like Maître Jacques, and succeeds about as well as he did in promoting general harmony."—Jaucourt to Talleyrand, 4th February, 1815.

35. M. de Chateaubriand to Talleyrand:

"Ghent, 6th March, 1815.

"MY PRINCE,

"The Count de Noailles will tell you how much your presence is wanted here: so much so, indeed, that before M. de Noailles arrived I was on the point of despatching a courier to you. I will enter into no details, for you will learn all our misfortunes from the bearer. I will only say that I handed in yesterday the Memorandum which I was asked to draw up. I propose two things in this Memorandum: to appoint the Duke of Orleans commander of the army, and to appoint you, Prince, the head of a *responsible* ministry. I propose that this ministry should be chosen by you, and composed of men of European reputation, whose names alone would be a guarantee for the approval of all parties. The details of my plan are contained in a dozen clauses. I know the objections there are to the appointment of a paramount chief, or generalissimo of the army; but great diseases require heroic remedies. The time for half-measures is past; we have to save a crown, and that is worth some risk. The second proposal in my plan is too natural not to be adopted. But if you do not arrive soon, to choose your men and give your orders, I am afraid that much will be left undone. Come then quickly, Prince, and believe that I am,

"With the utmost devotion and respect,
"Your Highness's most grateful and
"Obedient humble servant,
(Signed) "LE VICOMTE DE CHATEAUBRIAND.

"P.S.—I had the honor of writing to you previously, to inform you that the King called me to his Council and commanded me to make him a report of the state of home affairs. This should give me some right to expect the post of Home Minister; but my claims are, of course, subject to the interests of the King and the country, as well as to your views and plans."

The royal princes were in the habit of attending the ministerial councils. In a letter dated the 4th of January, Jaucourt gives an account of a council held to discuss the dismissal of M. de Casaflores, and adds:

"There was much discussion. Monsieur was for moderate measures; M. de Berry, as usual, like a runaway horse; the Duc d'Angoulême judicious."

36. "On delivering to the King the conditions for the restoration of Genoa to Piedmont, I took the liberty of calling forth his opinion of the Constitution thereby given by respectfully praising our own. He read it with care and reflection, and then said, 'I perceive a great fault in it: there is no provision for re-election; this interval of four years must lead to mischief.' I reminded him of the sad and terrible consequences of the resolution to this effect passed by our first Assembly, and for a few moments we exchanged observations together (if I may be allowed thus to associate myself with the King) concerning national interests, the support given by the Chambers to the royal authority; in short, concerning the theory of national representation—observations which have convinced me that the philosophical philanthropy of the 'hero of the north' is far beneath the wisdom and elevation of mind of Louis XVIII."—Jaucourt to Talleyrand, 18th December, 1814.

37. The following extract of a letter from Jaucourt to Talleyrand, dated the 7th December. 1814, gives an idea of the state of Spain at that time: "General Alava has been set at liberty; he owes this to the fear of a rising. Numerous arrests follow one after another; whole families are led off to the Inquisition; the persecution of the liberals continues. The greatest merit is no protection."

38. "Speaking of the *Journal de l'Europe* reminds me of what I want to say to you about the *Journal de Gand*. It is generally disapproved of. It is often abusive, which is always useless and frequently injurious. You ought to tell the editor that he must have self-control enough never to appear reactionary, and this requires more self-control than many people are aware of."—Talleyrand to Jaucourt, dated Vienna, 17th May, 1815.

39. "The abbé only said in the course of the evening, before he went to bed, 'They forced me to dismiss an excellent prefect from Rennes. The one whom I shall put in his place will not be so good. Good gracious! do they suppose that I am not going to take any steps to stop the agitation in Brittany? However, I had to give way.' It is a fact that the abbé has adopted quite a new system. He now regrets having dismissed the prefects, and declares that the new prefects are not equal to the old ones; he actually defends the men now in office, and that to such an extent as quite to offend the princes; and, instead of falling in with this pretended system of restoration *alias* change, he is now all for the Constitution, stability, and even goes so far as to think that the *status quo* of the middle class, the new nobility, and of men accustomed to work should be permanently maintained *in the disposal of appointments*, and, in a word, generally throughout France."—Jaucourt to Talleyrand, January, 1815.

"My dear Count,

"I have received Nos. 3 and 4 of your *Journal Universel* (printed at Ghent). I beg you to remark to its editors that all the articles require to be written with much more pains and reflection, both in matter and style. I am now applying this observation particularly to the word 'nationaliser,' which is used in an unfavorable sense only. The Emperor of Russia, whom you ought to wish to please, continually makes use of this word both in talking and writing, and only yesterday his attendants showed great annoyance at the attempt to attach a bad meaning to an expression which he is constantly using. A paper written under the shadow of the throne needs to be written with much more care than the best papers published in Paris. Impress upon the editor that in the present state of affairs tact is talent. For example, all France will have noticed the following passage in No. 2: 'Nature, policy, and justice suggested, nay, commanded severity.' This phrase will cause anxiety in Paris, whereas you ought to do your utmost to reassure every one; you cannot take too much pains to inspire confidence, because bad consciences, of which there are so many in France, require to be reassured. *Good consciences need no management.* Tell Lally to expend all his indignation in indulgence. Indignation gives more opprtunity for eloquence, but indulgence is more favorable to wit, and as he is possessed of both, a hint will be sufficient for him.

"M. de Blacas is quite wrong in thinking that it is any excuse for letters that have given offence to say that they were written in the same spirit as those written from Hartwell. He is evidently quite ignorant that everything which recalls the recollection of the exile should be avoided. Its memories may be pleasing to a few useless people, but they do positive harm with all who are worth anything either in or out of France."—Talleyrand to Jaucourt, 6th May, 1815.

40. Metternich wrote as follows to Talleyrand, dated 24th June, 1815: "Remain steadfast to your idea. Make the King enter France; it does not matter whether he goes east, west, north, or south, provided he is at home, surrounded by Frenchmen, and far from foreign bayonets and foreign aid. By keeping your eye upon Bonaparte's plans you will clearly perceive that the emigration is the chief weapon which he intends to make use of. The moment the King is at home and in the midst of his subjects he ceases to be an *émigré.* The King must govern, and the royal army must operate at a distance from the allied armies. As soon as the King has formed a rallying-point in France, we will send him all the French deserters who come to us."— "Mémoires de Metternich," tom. ii. p. 520.

41. "The King had a superb part if he had stayed in Paris. . . . The King announced that he was resolved to stay, but most unfortunately changed his mind twice. I will never believe that the city of Paris would have let him perish by the hand of that man (Bonaparte), nor that the troops would have fired upon us. Anyhow it is done. We must now do all we can to form a rallying-point, to gain over the commander of one of the fortresses, and get a footing upon the sacred soil. For if the King arrives in the wake of foreign soldiers, he will be playing the game of the Jacobins and Bonaparte, who are making common cause together. It seems to us here that, for the moment, writings and proclamations would have little or no effect; we ought to be in France, and to have obtained a victory over a *corps d'armée* of Bonaparte. Then, as the armies advance, the French commanders attached to each army corps should order the *Conseils Généraux* of the Department to assemble; these latter should designate one or more members of their body to undertake the duties of commander or con-

troller of requisitions and of the commissariat, and to issue proclamations. We have D'André and D'Anglès already here, and to wield the pen we have MM. de Lally, Chateaubriand, who demands the title of minister of the King as payment for his first article, Lacretelle the younger, and Bertin de Vaux. You see we shall have quite a galaxy of literary talent."—Jaucourt to Talleyrand, dated Ghent, 4th April, 1815.

42. "M. de Vincent, or, failing him, M. Pozzo, has been instructed to protest against the appointment of royal commissioners to our armies."—Metternich to Talleyrand, 24th June, 1815.

43. On the 25th of April, 1815, his Britannic Majesty's ambassador handed the annexed despatch to M. de Jaucourt:

"The undersigned, upon occasion of the exchange about to be made in the name of his Court of the ratifications of the treaty concluded on the 25th of March last, is charged to declare by the present Note that the eighth article of the said treaty, by which his Most Christian Majesty is invited to accede to it under certain conditions, is to be considered as demanding from the high contracting parties, according to a principle of mutual security, a united effort against the power of Napoleon Bonaparte, conformably with Article 3 of the treaty, but is not to be regarded as laying his Britannic Majesty under any obligation to continue the war with a view to imposing any particular form of government upon France. The Prince Regent holds himself bound to make this declaration, in spite of his great desire to see his Most Christian Majesty re-established upon his throne. The Ambassador Extraordinary of his Britannic Majesty has been instructed by his Court to make this confidential communication to the ministers of his Most Christian Majesty.

"The undersigned gives his most earnest assurance that this proceeding is not taken in consequence of any unfavorable feeling towards a cause upon which the peace of Europe must depend, but is the result of the firm conviction of his sovereign that, after the British nation has spontaneously used its utmost endeavors to promote his Most Christian Majesty's interests, any positive engagement to that effect would give rise to injurious disputes, calculated to embarrass the proceedings of the Government for the advancement of this object.

  (Signed)   "CHARLES STUART."

44. It should be remembered that it was at the suggestion of M. de Talleyrand, then Bishop of Autun, that the ecclesiastical domains were declared national property. These domains were then sold, and it was upon them that the assignats were secured.

"What is still more serious is that two priests have refused the last sacraments to two dying men who were owners of property belonging to *Émigrés:* one of them persisted in his refusal till the man died, and we know where he will go to; the other consented at last, but so near the last moment that, after the priest had called the bystanders to witness the restitution, the patient died before the viaticum could be administered, and his soul had to start on its journey without due preparation."—Jaucourt to Talleyrand, 11th February, 1815.

"The Marshal (Soult), Beugnot, and I sat up together till one o'clock, after dinner was over. I attacked the Marshal in these terms. I said, 'Seeing that chance has brought together four ministers, who would all be disgraced if the King ruled without observing the Charter, it seems a good occasion to discuss the state of public opinion.' The Marshal was obliged to answer, but he was so disconcerted that he foolishly told us how he had declared to a certain General Travaut, a brave man and a good officer, that he would not employ him until he had restored all the property belonging to *Émigrés* acquired by him. Poor General Travaut has two hundred and fifty thousand francs' worth of this property, which constitute all his fortune. . . . Come as soon as you can; believe me, you are much wanted. I promise you that you shall have the Marshal for your spaniel. You will easily master him. He is a man who thinks himself superior to his patron, who does not know how to get out of the family clique by whose means he has risen; he fears and hates the Abbé, and is a man of desponding views, with no decided opinions—one who yields to obstacles and stumbles over difficulties; a military club orator, vain, coarse, shrewd, and supple, and, in the words of the old adage, 'Animal capax rapax omnium beneficiorum' (one who gets all he can and keeps all he gets)."—Extract from same letter.

The following is an extract from a letter from Paris, addressed to M. de Talleyrand, and dated the 18th of October, 1814:

"One question that greatly disturbs men's minds is that of the national domains. The law on this subject seems clear and decided, but public opinion is not. Thence arise the exaggerated expectations of some and the chimerical fears of others. Six days ago, three houses belonging to *Émigrés* in the Rue Nivienne were put up to auction. I was present. There was not a single offer, though they are the three best houses in the whole street. A report was spread in the room during the bidding that the former proprietor wanted eighty thousand francs *as the price of his patrimonial interest in them*. The fact is true; I have verified it."

45. See in the *Moniteur Universel* of the 7th of July, 1815, the proclamation of Louis XVIII., dated at Cambrai and countersigned by M. de Talleyrand, who had the chief hand in its composition. There are whole passages in it word for word with this Memorandum.

THE KING TO PRINCE TALLEYRAND.

Ostend, 26th March, 1815.

MY COUSIN,

I take advantage of an English messenger, who will probably reach Vienna before the letters of the Comte de Blacas and the Comte de Jaucourt. The desertion of the whole army left me no choice as to the steps I should take. As my life is supposed to be necessary to France, it was my duty to provide for my safety, which might have been endangered if I had stayed some hours longer at Lille. Bonaparte has the army on his side; I have the hearts of all the people on mine. I saw unequivocal proof of this all along my route. The Powers, therefore, cannot be uncertain what is the wish of France now. This is the text of what I want said; I trust to you to enlarge upon it. I cannot sufficiently praise the conduct of Marshals Macdonald and Mortier. The former has behaved everywhere as well as he did at Lyons; and the latter, who had received by telegraph orders to arrest me, saw me safe out of Lille, and on my way as far as Menin.

Upon which, my cousin, I pray God to have you in His safe and holy keeping.

   (Signed)   Louis.

APPENDIX.

Letter III. Note 10.

EXTRACT from M. d'Hauterive's letter to M. de Talleyrand, 18th October, 1814:
"It is difficult to form an idea of the disorder and irregularity that pervade the administration. Each day brings us fresh proofs of them. If uniformity of principle and action existed, we should not find the deputies creating a distinction in the mind of the nation between the King and his ministers. It is most unfortunate! The malcontents are coming forward, talking, acting with more audacity than ever. Even the most sensible people are led by this to apprehend disturbance. I have already written to you that trade is troubled; manufactures are paralyzed; landowners are overburthened with taxes which are exacted with barbarous rigor even in those districts where the Allies have left nothing but poverty. The excise duties and the tobacco monopoly are carried out as they were under Bonaparte, and with even greater severity. With all these grounds of displeasure against them, the administration lacks nerve and personal qualities. To all this has just been added what I call the fever of humiliation, with which people are bent on innoculating France. They are sure of touching a responsive chord when they tell us everywhere that we ought to avenge our injuries and wash out our disgrace in the blood of our enemies; that the English are everything, and can do everything in France; that England is hemming us in on the north with considerable forces, so that they may afterwards dictate laws to us; that Wellington governs at Paris; that we must shake off this ignominious yoke, etc.

"I beg you to pay *serious* attention to this observation, which perhaps escapes many people. Believe me that in this respect the *evil is great.* It is not that the Government does not possess the means of contesting this point of honor, which is at all events false under the present circumstances; it has all the journals and all the pamphleteers at its disposal. To get us out of the very unpleasant position in which we are, we need a man at the head of the administration who should enjoy the confidence and friendship of the King, and to whom he would reveal his mind unreservedly. But it would be necessary that this man should know France, should be of one party only, *that of the French of* 1814, and should be thoroughly convinced that the way to advance is not to go backward.

"Unfortunately this man exists only in two persons [M. de Blacas and M. de Talleyrand]; you know them. Since your departure you have grown prodigiously in public estimation. The numerous blunders that are made here contribute to that aggrandizement. I have been well pleased to hear important persons say frankly that there was no means of safety except in holding by you, because that meant holding by the King and the Constitution. A rumor, true or false, which has circulated here among all classes, has been very favorable to you. It is generally said (and I assure you that I seriously believe it) that it is only to you personally that France owes her admission to the Congress; that Austria made some difficulties, but that you handed in a Note equally remarkable for the ability and the bold character which it displays."

Letter IV. Note 9.

"You already know the principles which the King has laid down as the rule of his ambassadors' conduct at the Congress. It was natural to think that all the Powers, animated by the same feelings, would have co-operated in the maintenance of those principles, since they had taken up arms to defend them. There is therefore cause for astonishment at finding them now disposed to follow the principles against which they had contended. Some are induced to do this from motives of ambition; others are influenced respectively by jealousy and distrust of the power of France, and from a desire to increase the strength of those whose position may bring their interests into opposition with those of France; and, lastly, some through timidity or indecision. The King, at the same time that he is resolved not to recognize the fact that conquest alone gives sovereignty, and not to participate in the violation of the principles of public law, is desirous to give facility to everything which does not attack those principles. This is what you have to say on all occasions, but always speaking with moderation of the opposition directed against principles."—Circular to the political and consular agents, 29th October, 1814.

Letter V. Note 2.

The King of Saxony wrote to Louis XVIII. on the 19th of September, 1814:

"Friedrichsfeld, 19th September, 1814.

"MY BROTHER,

"The approach of the opening of the Congress of Vienna induces me to address your Majesty anew, in order to commend my interests to you, and to ask your support for my prompt reinstatement in my rights. I cannot imagine that I can have to fear being deprived of the possession of them, or that the Allied Powers or any Court of Europe could approve of a measure which would closely resemble the system that they have just struck down. Nevertheless, the reports that I shall be threatened with that dispossession gain such ground, and are so public, that I feel it due to myself and to the contracting Powers of the last treaty of peace to declare beforehand and against all attempts, that if such an idea could exist I never will consent to surrender the States which I have inherited from my ancestors, nor to accept any compensation whatsoever, no equivalent being capable of indemnifying me for their loss, and for separation from a people whom I love, and who have given me multiplied proofs of attachment and fidelity. But I repeat, the noble and lofty way of thinking of the Powers assembled at the Congress, and that of your Majesty in particular, reassure me in this respect, and is a pledge to me of the fulfilment of my desires.

"I beg you, my brother, to receive the renewed expression of the sincere friendship and high consideration with which I am,

"My brother,

"Your Majesty's good brother,

(Signed) "FREDERICK AUGUSTUS."

APPENDIX.

Letter VI. Note 3.

THE MONT DE MILAN.

"The Emperor Napoleon I., when he instituted hereditary rights, reserved to himself the resources of an extraordinary fund, destined, by a Senatus-Consultus of 1810, to remunerate great civil and military services. This department possessed scrip of the *Mont de Milan*, on which were charged the endowments that were to be the recompense of services rendered in the campaigns of Ulm, Austerlitz, Jena, and Friedland. The rights of the persons entitled to these endowments had been guaranteed by a clause of the Treaty of Fontainebleau; but Austria, after having paid in 1818 the arrears due in 1814, refused to continue the payment. The Government of the Restoration, having failed in every attempt to induce Austria to pay, was desirous of doing what they could for the endowed persons with the amount of the extraordinary fund that remained. The law of the 26th of July, 1821, substituted for the reversible endowments from male to male in order of primogeniture, reversible pensions for the widow and children of the first titulary only, in equal portions, with reversion in favor of the last survivor, being either the widow or child. These pensions are divided into six classes, and the figure was fixed: for the four first, at one thousand francs; for the fifth, at five hundred francs; and for the sixth, at two hundred and fifty francs.

"In 1861, after the War of Italy, Austria and Sardinia, upon the demand of France, placed at her disposal a sum of 12,500,000 francs, of which 6,250,000 francs was assigned to the former holders of endowments on the *Mont de Milan*. This sum was employed in the creation of *rentes*, which have been distributed proportionably to the titularies of the *Mont de Milan*, or those holding their rights, according to the rule of transmission fixed by the deed of endowment or by the decrees; the figure of the new registry never being below two hundred francs. The *rente* registered in their name, independently of the pension fixed in virtue of the law of 1821, returns to the Treasury in the case provided for by the constitutive deed."—Summary of the Report of the Commission nominated by the decree of the 22nd of May, 1851.

Letter XVIII. Note 2.

The following letter, from Talleyrand to Metternich, dated 6th March, 1811, indicates the nature of the former personal relations between the two statesmen:

"I should have much liked to answer your letter sooner, my dear Count, but I have passed nearly three weeks in my room, ill enough. I began by being rather too ill. The terrible words 'malignant fever' were pronounced over me, but all that has calmed down. When one has been seriously ill, one comes back to life in a state of purity which leaves one very ignorant of the affairs of this world. I really do not know what is going on. My common sense tells me that the sovereigns who have you for their adviser are fortunate. But you cannot be everywhere, or at Paris, where you would surely have tried to console the Duc de Bassano for the report of the Swedish Minister of Foreign

Affairs, which I have just read, and Madame Junot for her husband's departure. Each has his or her troubles, and you have remedies for all.

"When you turn your eyes towards France, and you think of those who care for you and your glory, I am inclined to believe that you will recall the friend of Marie [de Metternich]. He will always be as you have known, and liked him a little: and he would welcome renewed opportunities of telling you this, and proving that he regards you with friendship, esteem, and consideration.

Letter XX. Note 3.

The Minister of War writes to Talleyrand, 9th November, 1814:

"Our regiments are, in fact, very well organized, and our only difficulty has been to select the best among various officers. We have granted a great many furloughs, and we are below our formation on the peace footing; but I beg you to believe that I should be in a position to show you at this moment very fine *corps d'armée* on all our frontiers. Fifty thousand men upon the Rhine, fifty thousand on the north, twenty thousand on the Alps—such are our available forces at present. It is a matter of course that fortresses and the interior should be suitably guarded besides, and that we are very little inclined to adopt the foolish tactics of stripping the inside of the country to make a great effect outside. On the first day of January, the available forces will be augmented by sixty thousand men, and if it were necessary they could be increased by one hundred thousand more in March. I judge by the statements sent to me by the Prefects that there are more than two hundred thousand men in the interior belonging to the colors, and intended to raise the active army to a high degree of force all at once, or to augment it successively and in detail during several years of peace. It is this reserve, so precious because it is composed of men already drilled, which renders a law for recruiting unnecessary just now. I do not speak of the artillery, for to do so would be vanity on my part. That arm is finer than ever. We have some new inventions . . . a new musket, new powder, very superior to the old, a more serviceable cuirass; these are three discoveries which do honor to our artillery, and which have excited the curiosity of our neighbors."

Letter XXII. Note 2.

Fouché wrote to Talleyrand on the 25th of September, 1814, from the Château de Ferrières, as follows:

"A person who is going to Vienna as *chargé d'affaires* for the Marshals of France offers me his services in the matter of my dotations.

"Your Highness has given me assurances in this respect, on which I rely; I place my interests entirely in your hands.

"I presented myself twice at your Highness's house before your departure, but I had not the good fortune to find you and make my adieux. I should have wished to speak to you of the interior of France and of Paris, and especially of the Frenchmen who were in the first instance excluded from places, and will soon be forced to quit France. Garat has already passed through Bayonne, some days ago, but there are men who are not so timid, and who will remain in their country to defend themselves. Carnot is printing the memoir with which you are no doubt acquainted, as more than one copy is in circulation.

"Your Highness may rely on my information of the position of affairs and the real state of feeling : the King will find no peace or safety except in his moderation. Those who advised him to have the *Mécontents* and the *Quotidienne* [newspapers] published, journals filled with the grossest invectives, have consulted their own blind passions rather than the true interests of the King.

"If I were not kept in France by my property, I should be in London with my children; there will shortly be no tranquillity here for anybody. The Government is easy because everything seems to be making progress, but an unforeseen event may change all. I hope the continuity of your eminent services procures you at least repose.

"I will not speak to your Highness of the affairs of Naples; I know the interest which you take in them. I am writing upon them to Prince Metternich, to whom I have to write about a conversation he has had with M. Baudus on the subject of myself, and entering with him into some details respecting France and Europe.

"The Belgians who are in Paris are giving vent to their displeasure at the handing over of their country to the rule of Holland without consulting them. It seems to me that, since everything is being undone, it would be more fitting to restore Belgium to Austria, under which country Belgium was so prosperous. Besides, that would be to do homage to a century of possession, with only twenty years of interruption.

"I beg your Highness sometimes to remember a man who is and always will be attached to you."

At the same time D'Hauterive wrote to Talleyrand: "All parties seem to combine in the chorus, 'This cannot la t.'"

Jaucourt wrote to Talleyrand on the 18th of October, 1814:

"The alarm has been great among those around the King; restless Marshal Marmont gives himself infinite trouble to find out causes for apprehension.

"The petty police denounces the great, and the great has courage and boldness enough to arrest the petty.

"The King meets everything with his wisdom, his discretion, and his calmness: it is a crime to put all these royal qualities to the proof."

Jaucourt wrote on the 29th of November, 1814:

"Marshal Marmont, through restlessness, over-zeal, or I know not what motive, took fright at the idea of the King's going to the play at the Odéon, and imparted to the King the warnings he had received. He requested the King to send for General Maison and General Dessoles, which was done; but the King said to them very quietly, 'Gentlemen, your business is to guard me; mine is to go and amuse myself at the play.'"

Letter XXII. Note 5.

The following description of a Ridotto is given by the *Moniteur Universel* in its Vienna correspondence:

"The grand Ridotto of the 2nd of December afforded a unique spectacle of magnificence and rich attire. It took place in three large halls connected by galleries and staircases, and forming so spacious an enclosure that from ten to twelve thousand persons could move about without inconvenience. The decorations were of the most elegant description. The passage which led from the apartments of the palace to the hall of the Ridotto was magnificently lighte !

and adorned with flowers and shrubs, as was the small hall, which looked like a garden in fairyland. We passed through an avenue of orange trees into the great hall, from whence, beyond the great staircase, we could see the immense space which forms the riding school of the Court. This building, which is a masterpiece of architecture, had been converted into a dancing room ; the pure white hangings were relieved with white and silver most tastefully mingled, and from five to six thousand wax candles shed a marvellous brilliancy over the scene.

"The movement of so many personages in full dress, and the strains of an orchestra of one hundred musicians, lent this splendid fête animation which it is impossible to describe. At 10 o'clock their Majesties and the other august personages entered the hall to the sound of trumpets and cymbals. Their Majesties the Emperor of Russia and the Empress of Austria headed the procession. Then came their Majesties the Emperor of Austria and the Empress of Russia; his Majesty the King of Denmark, with her Imperial Highness the Archduchess Beatrix; their Majesties the King of Prus ia and the Queen of Bavaria; his Majesty the King of Bavaria, with her Imperial Highness the Grand-Duchess of Oldenburg, etc. After having walked several times through the three halls, the sovereigns took their places on a daïs in the riding school, and witnessed the performance of a ballet by children wearing masks. After the ballet their Majesties walked about separately in the hall until after midnight. The fête lasted until morning."

The *Moniteur* of the 7th of December publishes the following from a Vienna correspondent: "At the Carrousel yesterday, the quadrille was led off by the Countess de Périgord, niece of Prince Talleyrand, dancing with Count Trautmannsdorf. The quadrilles were composed of the greatest personages of the Court and of Germany.

Letter XXV. Note 3.

On the 10th of November, 1814, Jaucourt wrote to Talleyrand:

"I am assured that Monsieur has a great deal to do with the selection that has been made. Perhaps one day he who now congratulates himself *on the influence which his presence exercises* will regret to see him there. As for me, I believe in his capacity, and in his perfect indifference to what form a Government may take provided it gives him the exercise of a great authority; with all this he has, it is evident. the means of exerting influence."

On the 10th of December, 1814, D'Hauterive wrote:

"As we have no navy, and probably shall not have one for a long time, the selection of Beugnot has done neither good nor harm. People laughed, and that has been all about it. The sailors complain a little, but there are so few of them !"

THE END.

www.ingramcontent.com/pod-product-compliance
Lightning Source LLC
Chambersburg PA
CBHW030728230426
43667CB00007B/639